Upgrading & Troubleshooting Your

Mac

About the Author

Gene Steinberg is an accomplished author with a number of Mac books to his credit. He is a contributing writer for *MacHome,* a columnist for the *Arizona Republic's* Arizona Central Computing page, and a regularly featured guest on Craig Crossman's *Computer American* radio show. In addition, he and his teenaged son, Grayson, have developed a new science fiction adventure series, *Attack of the Rockoids.*

About the Technical Reviewer

John Rizzo is the author of several books about Macs, as well as a computer magazine columnist, consultant, and founder of the macwindows.com Web site. He was an editor at *MacUser* magazine and a columnist for *MacWeek* magazine.

Upgrading & Troubleshooting Your

Mac

Gene Steinberg

Osborne **McGraw-Hill**

Berkeley   New York   St. Louis   San Francisco
Auckland   Bogotá   Hamburg   London
Madrid   Mexico City   Milan   Montreal   New Delhi
Panama City   Paris   São Paulo
Singapore   Sydney   Tokyo   Toronto

Osborne/**McGraw-Hill**
2600 Tenth Street
Berkeley, California 94710
U.S.A.

For information on translations or book distributors outside the U.S.A., or to arrange
bulk purchase discounts for sales promotions, premiums, or fund-raisers, please contact
Osborne/**McGraw-Hill** at the above address.

Upgrading & Troubleshooting Your Mac

234567890 AGM AGM 019876543210

Book P/N 0-07-212325-7   and   CD P/N 0-07-212326-5
parts of
ISBN 0-07-212327-3

Publisher: Brandon A. Nordin
Associate Publisher and Editor-in-Chief: Scott Rogers
Acquisitions Editor: Jane Brownlow
Project Editor: Jody McKenzie
Acquisitions Coordinator: Tara Davis
Technical Editor: John Rizzo
Copy Editor: Lunaea Hougland
Proofreader: Stefany Otis
Indexer: Jack Lewis
Computer Designers: Jani Beckwith and Gary Corrigan
Illustrators: Beth Young and Brian Wells
Series Design: Mickey Galicia
Cover Design: Dodie Shoemaker

This book was composed with Corel VENTURA™ Publisher.

Attack of the Rockoids © 1999 Gene Steinberg and Grayson Steinberg. Excerpts used with permission.

Mac® and PowerBook® are trademarks of Apple Computer, Inc., registered in the United States and other countries.
iBook™ and iMac™ are trademarks of Apple Computer, Inc.

Screen reproductions in this book were created using SnapzPro from Ambrosia Software, Inc. and edited in Graphic Converter
from Lemke Software and Adobe Photoshop from Adobe Systems, Inc.

Photos for front cover, back cover, spine, and internal design courtesy of Apple Computer, Inc., and the following: iBook photo,
Hunter Freeman, photographer; iMac photo, Mark Laita, photographer; G4 tower photo, Davies + Starr, photography; PowerBook
G3 photo, Peter Belanger, photographer.

Information has been obtained by Osborne/**McGraw-Hill** from sources believed to be reliable. However, because of the
possibility of human or mechanical error by our sources, Osborne/**McGraw-Hill**, or others, Osborne/**McGraw-Hill** does not
guarantee the accuracy, adequacy, or completeness of any information and is not responsible for any errors or omissions or the
results obtained from use of such information.

Dedication

To my family,
who made it possible
for me to realize the impossible dream.

Contents at a Glance

Contents

Acknowledgments

Pouring 15 years of Macintosh experience into a book was an extraordinary undertaking, and making it seem sensible to Mac users of all levels of expertise was equally challenging.

I could never have done the job were it not for a group of very special people who provided advice, information, tips, tricks, and, in some respects, a look at Apple's future possibilities, so I could make this book as accurate and up-to-date as possible.

First and foremost, I want to give special thanks to my friend and agent, Lew Grimes, who has always been there with sage advice to help me get over the rough spots and to make this all happen.

Certainly Apple's corporate communications team has helped greatly in supplying information and, in some cases, review hardware for me to examine, review, and report about. Chief among these folks are Rhona Hamilton, Matt Hutchison, Keri Walker, and Nathalie Welch. I'd also like to give praise to Apple's Jonathan Ive and his industrial design wizards for developing the great look of Apple's newest computers, such as the iBook, the iMac, and the Power Mac G4 series.

I'd like to single out my friend, Pieter Paulson, long-time Mac/Windows systems wizard, who provided a huge amount of information for the chapters on cross-platform issues and Mac networking.

As I was wrapping up this book, Apple unleashed a major upgrade to their iMac product line. So special praise also goes to Jerod Havel, hardware manager at CompUSA's store in Scottsdale, Arizona, for letting me literally tear apart some of their newly delivered Apple products, so I could discover all the intricacies and changes, and report on them accurately.

A book of this sort wouldn't be a reality were it not for Osborne's superbly talented editing team, consisting of Jane Brownlow, Tara Davis, and Jody McKenzie, and freelance copyeditor Lunaea Hougland and proofreader Stefany Otis. Thanks also goes to Osborne's production team, Gary Corrigan and Jani Beckwith. And I must thank long-term Mac writer, John Rizzo, proprietor of the macwindows.com Web site, for his careful, deliberate technical editing.

Most of all, I must give my sincere thanks to my little nuclear family: my brilliant son (and sometimes co-author), Grayson, and my beautiful wife and business partner, Barbara, for tolerating the long hours I spent glued to my computer keyboard to finish this book on schedule.

Introduction

All right, I admit it, I'm a computer consultant. It wasn't always that way, however. In fact, I trained originally as a radio broadcaster. I also had a hand in writing news stories, commercials, and even a little science fiction from time to time. But things change.

When personal computers first came out, I worked for someone who had the silly idea of putting me in charge of all those strange devices. Heaven knows why. Perhaps because I had a penchant for fiddling with things and trying to fix them. I also had this annoying tendency of being somewhat of a perfectionist. They say it's a characteristic of Virgos, though I had never given much seriousness to horoscopes and other means of predicting one's individual characteristics.

Now, I must confess, those first personal computers I worked on weren't Apple products. They were, in fact, PC clones, used primarily to convert documents for a typesetting system (yes, rather dull). This was in the days before PC clones actually had to be reasonably compatible with regular software, so all they could do was run that translation program and the higher-cost versions of a few popular programs the manufacturer deigned to sell.

I won't go into the hoops and flips I had to face whenever it was necessary to upgrade the computer's operating system software or add some extra hardware. This book isn't that long, and I would prefer to forget the late hours and sleepless nights fretting over one issue or another.

Then 1984 came. Big Brother was nowhere in sight, despite what George Orwell suggested in a certain novel, but I discovered the Apple Macintosh and a new method of personal computing. Gone were many of the hassles and headaches that afflicted computers on the other computing platform. And that graphical user interface was simply a revelation compared to the clumsy command line instructions I had to feed that other computer to get it to do the simplest tasks.

But things weren't quite perfect in the Macintosh universe either.

As I tell my friends, computers aren't nearly as reliable as, say, your toaster oven. For one thing, they aren't dedicated to performing a single task or a set of related tasks. They are supposed to be able to run any of thousands of software products and a large number of hardware devices as well, with only a minimum of fuss and bother.

All those products are designed by multitudes of designers and programmers, and there is plenty of room for mistakes or oversights. In fact, soon after I first hooked up my Apple Macintosh, it froze, putting up a little rectangular screen telling me that it was sorry that a system error had occurred. There was also a Restart button that I was to click to set things right.

Now, on that first occasion, clicking on the Restart button did absolutely nothing. I discovered something called a reset switch that forced my Mac to restart.

Not wishing to just take things in stride, I decided that I wanted to learn as much as I possibly could about that strangely shaped little computer. I first pored over the instruction manuals, then went to the local bookstore to see if there was any other information I could use. Of course, there wasn't very much available in those days. The Mac was a brave new world in terms of personal computing, and the nooks and crannies hadn't been completely explored yet.

However, I was impressed enough to tell my employers that they were using computers of the wrong platform and they had to change. Well, they listened to me. If anything, they paid just a little too much attention. They decided that I'd be responsible for ordering the new equipment and managing the systems.

Over time, they even had the crazy idea to farm me out to other companies who needed help setting up and maintaining their Mac systems. And when that company one day decided to give it all up and close their doors, I soon found myself working as a Mac consultant.

It's been fun discovering new things about these little computing devices, and, I have to admit it, aggravating too, especially when problems cropped up that just didn't seem amenable to the usual troubleshooting processes.

Through the years, I have made house calls for dozens and dozens of people, ranging from business users to retirees who discovered the Internet as a neat way to keep active and stay in regular touch with family and friends.

I also became a "helper" for the Arizona Macintosh users group. I receive phone calls day and night from harried folks who wonder why their computers freeze up, why they can't surf the Internet, why they can't print a document, and so on and so forth.

Taking all those experiences, through all those years, and putting it together in a reasonably coherent form takes me to the present day. And to this book.

Upgrading & Troubleshooting Your Mac is rather unique as computer books go, because it's not just a collection of third-party instructional information on how to do things with your Mac or how to fix things up. This book is the result of a lot of reading and a lot of research, but also the practical result of my hands-on experience in the Mac computing universe.

Over the years, I've learned lots of new, unexpected things—things that shouldn't always work, but do. I discovered how to apply all this toward solving the growing complexities and pitfalls in the Mac computing world.

Yes, some day, personal computers will be just as reliable as your toaster oven. But not yet—far from it.

While most Mac users work day in and day out with few problems to hurt the workflow, problems do happen. Macs freeze more than they should, programs don't quite work as you expect, and all in all, there are hair-pulling experiences from time to time.

And as the computer gets, well, a little older (and that can seem to take only a few months the way products get updated these days), you may wonder whether it's time to retire it and get something new. Or perhaps there's some way to upgrade the computer to extend its working life.

This book addresses both these concerns.

How This Book Is Set Up

This book isn't intended to be an encyclopedia or a reference work. Instead, it's a hands-on manual with a double focus.

First, I'll show you the best ways to install new hardware and software. You'll learn about the problems you might encounter along the way, how to avoid them, and what to do if they show up anyway.

Second, I'll discuss the topic of upgrading. If you'd like your Mac to run faster, or you want to add more RAM or a piece of hardware that expands its capabilities (such as high-speed networking or adding a second display), you'll learn the best way to set up the new equipment and how to set things right if something unexpected occurs. And you'll read some guidelines as to whether it's worth doing an upgrade in the first place.

Here's what you'll find in this book:

■ Lots of background information so you know why something works, and, more importantly, why things may sometimes go wrong

■ Step-by-step descriptions of installation and troubleshooting processes

■ Pointers, tricks, and guidelines to help you handle routine installations and complex setups with ease, and to help you diagnose both common and very obscure problems

■ Notes, Tips, and Cautions that give you extra bits of information and warn
   you when to be careful

■ Case History sidebars, which are actual stories, my own or about my
   clients (names omitted to protect the innocent), showing how a problem
   was discovered and how it was solved. Some of the problems are fairly
   common, ones you are apt to encounter at one time or another. Others are,
   well, strange, one-of-a-kind situations that were difficult to solve. Either
   way, I hope you'll be able to take something away from the experience in
   case you encounter a similar problem.

Tracking a Moving Target

When it comes to Apple Computer, predicting the future is impossible. Even as
this book was written, Apple was busy rolling out new models and a major new
operating system software release. Every time this happens, the way you do things
is apt to change, not to mention the fact that potential new difficulties may arise,
especially when you try to mix the old and the new in your computing
environment. However, it also means that this book includes information about
Apple's Power Macintosh G4, the iBook, the iMac DV series, and Mac OS 9.

I hope you like the approach, and I hope it helps you have a better, more
productive (even more fun-filled) Mac computing experience.

Please don't hesitate to send me your cards and letters, both compliments and
brickbats. And I truly welcome your suggestions on things I might add to future
editions of this book.

It's been a nice ride, and I look forward to the future of personal computing.
I think some exciting things are going to be happening in the years to come, lots
more exciting than any of us (even those of us who dabble in science fiction)
can predict.

Gene Steinberg
Scottsdale, Arizona
Email: gene@starshiplair.com
http://www.starshiplair.com
http://www.rockoids.com

Chapter 1

Solving Mac Hookup Problems

The experience ought to be fun. You've just bought a new Mac (or PowerBook, iMac, or iBook), and now you're anxious to take it out of the box and put it through its paces. If you're in a work environment, it's important from a business standpoint to get your new Mac workstation into production as soon as possible, with as little downtime as possible (and make your investment a productive one).

This chapter focuses on the basic steps to consider when deploying your new computers, whether for home use or for your business.

Initial Installation: The First Day

If your new Mac is your first, read on. The Macintosh computing experience is quite unlike the one you encounter when you use that other platform.

For one thing, there's the great ease of setup and use. You can literally plug it in, turn it on, and begin computing without further ado. This is especially true if you've bought a model from one of Apple's consumer product lines, such as the iMac or iBook. With those models, you don't even have to install any application software to begin, since so much of it is provided, already on your hard drive and ready to roll.

But as with any new installation, especially if it goes into a complicated setup where existing computers are already in place, you'll want to handle each step of the installation with care. While Macs are as close to true plug-and-play as a personal computer can get, there are pitfalls to consider.

The watchword for the first day is to test, test, and test some more. It's never a good idea to put a brand new computer smack into a production situation where a potential problem can mean lost time and lost money.

The next few sections of this chapter will focus on tips to help make the transition as easy as possible.

Adding a New Mac to a Home or Home Office

In this setup, it's quite likely that you are starting from scratch. This could be your first Mac or a replacement for one you've had quite a while. In either case, you'll want to consider the following guidelines for your particular situation.

Your First Macintosh

This is your first foray into the Mac operating system, so be sure to follow each step of the setup process slowly and carefully. All new Macs (or iMacs or iBooks) come with a very simple, basic set of installation instructions to refer to first. On the other hand, the instructions are so basic that you may find yourself having more questions than you'd expect even after you have it all plugged in and turned on.

If you're adding printers, scanners, extra drives, and other products, you are apt to find little help at all, unless you pour through a number of separate manuals.

And that, in a nutshell, is one of the reasons why I've written this book: to guide you through the pitfalls of installing a new system and upgrading your old one. Either way, if you run into troubles of any sort, you'll want to read the relevant chapters in this book, so you can resolve the issues as quickly as possible.

As a new Mac user, it's not just a matter of turning on the computer and getting to work. Personal computers are not that simple—at least not yet. So I've assembled some tips that you'll want to consider as you set everything up:

■ **Learn your Mac fundamentals.**   This book isn't designed to be a basic how-to or tutorial. It's focused on upgrading, preventive maintenance, and troubleshooting. I'm assuming you've had some experience with your Mac. But you don't have to feel alone in the world. When you first turn on your Mac, you'll find an attractive desktop and a little item on the menu bar labeled Help where you can definitely find ways to get started. For most Macs (especially the consumer line), there's a Macintosh Tutorial there. You should try it out, as it'll guide you through the basic steps of learning how to use the mouse and how to handle the various elements of personal computing, such as folders, program windows, and Open and Save dialogs. These are the subjects that are apt to be confusing, even for those with a lot of experience on Macs. It's worth the 30 minutes or so that it takes to cover these fundamentals. That's how I first learned to use a Mac all those years ago.

CAUTION   *I cannot overemphasize how important it is to learn your Mac basics if you're new to the platform or computing in general. It's not unlike learning musical scales to master an instrument. You'll find your computing experience more enjoyable and more productive, and it'll be easier to cope with problems once they arise.*

■ **Test each part of your system separately.**   Once you get your Mac up and running, try out all the regular functions, such as keyboard and mouse performance. Don't hesitate to take note of where things just don't seem right. You may be able to use some control panel setting to fix the problem, but for now, just be aware that it exists.

Initial Installation:
The First Day

NOTE   *One example of a setting you'd probably want to fix right away is the speed of your mouse cursor. Apple's default setting is usually too slow. Just open the Mouse Control Panel and move the slider to the right to make it seem faster; in fact, when you do it, your perception of your Mac's performance is apt to rise in proportion.*

■ **Shut down your Mac before adding a new accessory.**   Yes, the new generation of FireWire and USB peripherals for the Mac are advertised as being "hot-pluggable," meaning you don't have to shut down your Mac to put them in and out of service. But, otherwise, you need to shut down. Also, when you first install a new component, no doubt there is driver software involved on an installation disk of some sort. You'll need to install the driver, and restart, at the very least, before you hook up your new device. That way, it'll be ready to run as soon as it's connected.

■ **Don't panic if it doesn't work.**   More often than not, a little troubleshooting will fix the problem. You may have installed something incorrectly, or perhaps you're just not following the proper setup instructions. Throughout this book, you'll find chapters that cover virtually every aspect of Mac use, and you should find the answers you seek.

■ **Choose the Internet Service Provider (ISP) that's best for you.** All new Macs are advertised as offering easy Internet access. You can use Apple's Internet Setup Assistant to get a new account, or use the AOL or EarthLink software already provided. You are not forced to use what is there already. If you had an Internet account on another computer (even from the Windows platform), you should be able to set up your new Mac to work with that account in just a few minutes, if you have the proper setup information. The provider's technical support people can probably walk you through the steps in less than 10 minutes in most cases.

Replacement or Additional Macintosh

If you already have a Mac that's been set up, the second one should be easy. You have already confronted the basics of setup and installation of a computing system.

Depending on whether you are planning to replace an older Mac or just add one to an existing installation, the following basic tips will help you make sure your new computer is set up properly:

■ **Use file sharing if you can.** This is a quick way to transfer document files from your old Mac to your new one. If it's not convenient to network, consider placing them on a backup drive, but remember, your new Mac may not support SCSI drives that worked fine on an older model.

NOTE *If your old Mac has LocalTalk and no Ethernet capability, you'll have to consider getting a hardware module, a LocalTalk-to-Ethernet adapter, to allow you to connect the two computers. I'll cover more about network issues and solutions in Chapter 17.*

■ **Don't copy the System Folder from another Mac.** The one on your new Mac is the one designed specifically to work on that model. If your other Macs have a newer version, it doesn't matter. You are best advised to do a fresh installation from a Mac OS CD (and be sure it is really later than the one that came on your new Mac). Various Macs need different sets of system files, and the newer models have software ROM called, of course, Mac OS ROM. If the Mac doesn't have the correct files, you will not be able to start it up. The system installer is designed to figure out what goes where depending on what kind of Mac you have.

NOTE *You will, however, want to consider copying your Internet and network preferences to your new Mac. This will save you the bother of having to redo all those settings.*

■ **Reinstall your applications.** Microsoft's clever "drag-and-drop" installation, which is part of their Office and Internet programs, is the exception. You can copy the program folders direct to your hard drive without running a special installer. Then, when you launch one of these Microsoft applications for the first time, a "First Run" installer will handle the files that need to be placed in the System Folder. For other programs,

Initial Installation:
The First Day

just install from scratch. If you have a special set of preference files (which are most often installed in the Preferences folder inside the System Folder) that reflect your personal taste, and you don't want to have to recreate them from scratch, you may try to copy them over.

CAUTION   *If you are upgrading from a 680x0 Mac, it is absolutely essential to reinstall your software or get the new PowerPC version of a program (the PowerPC family includes, of course, the G3 and G4). Otherwise, you'll be using older, slower software that won't take advantage of the great performance potential of your new computer.*

■ **Check for new versions.**   If you are replacing a Mac that's several years old, check with the software publishers to see if you need an update to run on a newer Mac. There's no blanket answer to this. I have run programs several years old, ones that will never be updated, without trouble. But by the same token, other programs will crash right at launch if you attempt to run them.

CAUTION   *If you have a large collection of fonts, you may be tempted to simply copy from your older Mac's Fonts folder to the new one when you use file sharing. Unfortunately, you cannot copy active (in use) files this way. You'll have to make a disk copy first or duplicate the fonts in another location on your old Mac's drive and copy from there.*

■ **Consider ways to share Internet access.**   If you need to access the Internet from more than a single Mac, consider looking into ways to share your connection among additional Macs. The possibilities include such programs as Vicomsoft's SurfDoubler and SurfDoubler Plus, or Sustainable Softworks' IPNetRouter. There are also Ethernet hubs that serve the purpose of sharing a modem connection. You may also want to explore one of the so-called "broadband" Internet connection services, such as cable modems or DSL. Any of these setups can allow you to use a single account to deliver access to the Internet even in a home (or home office) with two or three Macs. It's also possible to use a regular Internet email program and exchange messages with each other. This may be helpful if computers are in different rooms. At least you can confine your shouting to strictly family-related matters (that is just meant as a joke, of course).

TIP

In addition to the options mentioned here, all of the newest Apple computers support the AirPort wireless networking system. The AirPort Base Station has its own 56K modem, which lets you share your Internet connection with any AirPort equipped Mac.

NOTE

Please don't forget that AOL can give you up to seven mailboxes (screen names) per account, but you can only access one of them at a time on a single account. Sharing access is therefore out of the question, unless you order up a second account.

Adding a New Mac to Your Office

Are you switching over to the Mac platform, installing your first computer, or just adding to an existing Mac network? Whatever the situation, you can prepare for the arrival of your new computer so that it fits into your new environment with as little fuss as possible.

Adding a New Mac to an Existing Mac Network

If your office is already using Macs, adding another to your network ought to be a fairly easy process, although there are some things you'll want to prepare for:

- **Software licenses**   If you intend to have your new Mac serve as an extra workstation, you may need to buy an extra software license for your programs. You don't necessarily have to buy a whole new copy at the retail price; some publishers will sell you a license at a reduced price (with a larger reduction going for multiple user packs). Fonts are usually licensed on the basis of output devices (printers, imagesetters, and so on), and you generally will not have to buy another license to install fonts on an extra computer (only for extra printers).

NOTE

I don't want to overemphasize this, but many programs, even basic utility packages (such as StuffIt Deluxe from Aladdin Systems), do network checks for additional users and won't launch if another copy of the program with the same serial number is found.

- **Networking**   If your new Mac is to be part of an Ethernet network, you'll want to make sure your hub can accommodate the extra connection. Some Ethernet hubs have an "uplink" port, which lets you daisy-chain additional

Initial Installation:
The First Day

hubs as needs expand. If you're using Apple's AirPort wireless networking, you'll want to make sure your new Mac is equipped with this option. As this book was written, the iBook, second generation iMac, and AGP-port versions of the Power Macintosh G4 were ready for AirPort cards, and the PowerBook line was expected to follow suit as upgraded models appeared.

■ **Serial printers**   Apple's Printer Share software lets you share an Apple StyleWriter personal printer on a network, by setting up your Mac as a print server. This may be fine and dandy for a setup with two or three Macs, but if you want to generate a reasonable volume of work and have the utmost flexibility, consider getting an inkjet printer with a LocalTalk or Ethernet networking card or a regular network laser printer. I cover the subject of printers in Chapter 8.

TIP   *Users of Epson inkjet printers can also get a "print sharing" capability from a shareware program called, naturally, EpsonShare. You can download a copy from http://www.ses.fr/epsonshare/softUS.htm.*

■ **Internet access**   In the normal scheme of things, each Mac will have its own modem (in fact, most new Apple computers these days come with a built-in modem, standard issue), but in your office, that modem may not be suitable. One reason is that a modem can bypass a corporate network firewall (although in a small office this is rarely an issue). You may want to designate one or two computers to handle your Internet or email chores. If you want to set up an office email system, consider buying an office email program, such as CE Software's QuickMail. These programs work for both your interoffice and Internet email requirements.

Another option is to use a cable modem or DSL if available. You'll be able to share your Internet access across your network, since such services use an Ethernet hub. Once you've done that, any email program ought to do the trick. You can then use Eudora, Microsoft Internet Explorer, or Netscape Communicator and enjoy both Internet and intranet (within your office) communications. Another convenient option is a modem-sharing hub. Such products include an Ethernet hub and the ability to share one or two modems across your network. One product I've used, the MacSense Palm Router Elite, can be run with nothing more than a regular Web browser. For a larger office, you may want to look into Netopia's line of modems and routers. Netopia's R2121 Dual Analog Router, for example, has two 56K modems built in, and you can share connections among up to 15 users.

NOTE   *If you're using AOL, you can install a copy on each of your computers (Macs or PCs), but you cannot share access to a single account at the same time, regardless of how many mailboxes (screen names) you have.*

SOFTWARE UPDATES   If your new Mac is a lot newer than the ones you've had before, you may need to look for some software updates. While many older programs will work just fine with the newest Macs, including iBooks, iMacs, and Power Macintosh G4s, other programs may need to be updated. This is something you'll want to check in advance before you install software on the new computer.

Adding a Replacement Mac to an Existing Mac Network

That old computer is about to be retired, and a new Mac is to replace it. If you have a spare spot on your network, you can use Apple's file sharing feature to copy files from the old computer to the new one. But there are a few things you need to check first:

■ **Don't copy your System Folder.**   The System Folder installed on your new Mac is the one designed specifically to work on that computer. Even if you have a newer system version on the other Mac, it's best to do a normal installation from Apple's system disks to make sure that the proper files are installed. Different Macs may require different files. An example of this is the fact that new models have a software ROM (a file called Mac OS ROM in your System Folder); without it, they won't boot. But such files aren't installed on older models.

NOTE   *The exception to this rule is your Internet and network preferences. When you copy these settings, you'll ease the process of setting up your new computer.*

■ **Consider reinstalling application software.**   Except for the latest versions of Microsoft's Office and Internet software, which use easy drag-and-drop installations, many programs put various and sundry files in your System Folder. There is really no easy way to know which files are needed and which aren't. The best approach is to install the programs from scratch. That will ensure that the correct files are placed in their proper locations. You can, of course, consider copying over program preference files if you have a set of complex ways in which you customize software.

CAUTION   *If you are upgrading from a 680x0 Mac, it is absolutely essential to reinstall your software or get the new PowerPC version of a program. Otherwise, you'll be using older, slower software that won't take advantage of the great performance potential of your new computer.*

NOTE   *Some program installers are gracious enough to leave an "Installer Log" file on your hard drive. If you find one of these, you'll want to consult it to see what was changed or installed and where it was placed.*

■ **Check for updates.**   If you are replacing a Mac that's several years old, check with the software publishers to see if you need an update to run on a newer Mac. There's no blanket answer to this. I have run programs several years old, ones that will never be updated, without trouble. But by the same token, other programs will crash right at launch if you attempt to run them.

What to Do If Your New Mac Doesn't Work

There's nothing worse than switching on your computer and finding out that it just doesn't work. I cannot recall a single instance in my personal experience where I've had a Mac that turned up dead on arrival, but I know it happens sometimes. If the worst should happen, your best approach would be to first recheck your setup to make sure everything is plugged in properly and that the power strip, if you use one, is on.

Here are some suggestions to follow before you seek outside help:

■ **Recheck all connections.**   It follows that you not only have to plug it in, but also be sure that the AC outlet is operational. In a home environment particularly, some AC sockets are linked to a light switch. When you turn off the light, the power goes off too. With a power strip, check for an on/off switch of some sort. Make sure all connections are tight (check this before you turn the power strip on).

■ **Install driver software for peripherals.**   Inkjet printers, removable drives, scanners, and so on require special software to run. While Apple incorporates some of these programs as standard issue (such as Iomega's Jaz and Zip drive software) and includes drivers for some USB devices, many products won't work unless you run the manufacturer's installation first.

TIP

Apple's USB system features are clever enough to recognize when the software you need for a USB device isn't there. If you restart with the software missing, you'll see an onscreen message about it after your Mac has booted, and it will offer to search for a driver for you. Since most third-party manufacturers don't support the "search" feature, take the warning as a request to install the needed software, and cancel the search prompt.

■ **Test each item, one at a time.**   If you daisy-chain a set of peripherals, such as SCSI devices, the failure of one item to work can likely cause problems for the other items on the chain. You may even crash at startup. The best approach is to check your new Mac first, all by itself (with keyboard, mouse, and monitor as necessary), and when you're sure it is all right, power down and hook up the extras.

■ **Swap/replace cables.**   Somtimes all it takes is a bad cable, and your new computer system won't run properly. If you have a spare set (or extras used for a different product), don't hesitate to try them out to see if the cables themselves are the source of your problems.

■ **Check the rest of this book for advice.**   I have devoted separate chapters to each element of your Mac system, from RAM upgrades to the installation of new modems, drives, scanners, printers, and other peripherals. If you are adding a number of new products, you'll want to consult each of these chapters for advice on how to handle the setups to avoid potential pitfalls.

If all else fails, you should contact your dealer and insist on an immediate replacement, if possible. While most dealers will simply want to fix a product that's dead on arrival, it is usually worth arguing for another unit, even if the one you have is partly functional.

If Your Dealer Doesn't Cooperate

Apple Computer has a new product warranty that entitles you to a year's free service—onsite for desktop models. Laptops can actually be shipped direct to Apple for service; they'll even supply the shipping box and pay the shipping charges (but you have to arrange for service first with their customer service department).

What to Do If Your New
Mac Doesn't Work

NOTE

While your dealer can handle repairs, you do not have to use them if you would rather have Apple arrange for service. On the other hand, if you have full confidence in your dealer, and their technicians are certified by Apple, go ahead and let them do the job. More often than not, the repair is just a matter of simply swapping one part for another.

Don't hesitate to ask Apple for assistance to resolve your problem. Apple has more stringent requirements for dealers than used to be the case, and, even if you have to go up the corporate ladder, you will usually find a sympathetic ear and a reasonable resolution to your problem.

NOTE

This is beyond the scope of this book, but Apple does have some extended warranty policies for some models, such as the PowerBook 190 and 5300 series, a few Performas, and some AppleVision monitors. So if you buy a used or reconditioned Mac or Apple peripheral that has developed a clear hardware problem, ask Apple customer service if they know of such a repair or replacement program.

Summing Up

Most new Mac installations go quickly with little fuss or bother. And where troubles crop up, more than likely you will be able to overcome any installation problem with setting up your Mac.

But if you run into a system software problem, you'll want to read Chapter 2 and learn how to cope with the hassles that sometimes arise from something in your System Folder.

Chapter 2

How to Cope with System Software Hassles

Every single second that you use your Mac, you are using a single set of software, the Mac OS. Like your car's tires, it gets more wear and tear than anything else you use on your Mac, except for the hard drive. As a result, any problem with the system software can easily take down your Mac for the count.

Of course, it's not terribly convenient to reinstall your system software every single day, nor should you have to. Most system problems can be dealt with simply by following some basic troubleshooting.

In this chapter, you'll learn about common problems with your Mac and what they signify. You'll also discover the best ways to reinstall your system software should the need arise.

How to Handle System Crashes

There are going to be arguments back and forth among proponents on both sides of the computing aisle about whether Macs are as reliable as they could be. Both Mac and Windows computers can crash on occasion. There is no way to avoid this, and the condition will continue until you install Mac OS X, which may have arrived by the time you read this book. Well, at least it'll reduce crashing problems (or at least reduce their severity). When system crashes are no longer part and parcel of the personal computing process, the day of the true computer appliance will have arrived.

Chapter 18, which is devoted to the topic of adding things to your System Folder, also covers diagnosing system-related conflicts. This chapter will cover a few basics and then refer you to other chapters for more information.

- ■ **Frequent crashes aren't normal.**   I'm not contradicting myself here. It's normal for your Mac to crash occasionally, but when it happens ten times a day, something is most definitely wrong. Most times it's the software that's involved, and you'll want to follow the steps in Chapter 18 to deal with them.

- ■ **It's rarely the hardware.**   Macs are very reliable. There are millions of older Macs in regular use every single day in production situations, and they keep on purring. That's true even for such compact Macs as the Mac Plus. Except for hard drives, removable devices, and similar products, which are subject to mechanical wear and tear, you should expect your Mac to last for many years, way beyond the time when you'll no longer need to use it.

■ **Repair or replace?** Of course, electronics aren't always perfect. Should your Mac's logic board or power supply fail, it may be time to consider whether you're really better off getting a new Mac. If you're on a budget, and if you can locate used or refurbished parts, you may actually be able to stretch the life of that old computer for quite a long time. But if the repair bills add up, the time may have arrived to visit your Apple dealer (or check a catalog or Web site) and see what's being offered.

■ **Don't forget computer viruses.** Most system crashes on Macs aren't caused by computer viruses. They are generally related to software or system conflicts of one sort or another. However, that doesn't mean you shouldn't check for the possibility of computer viruses. Any time you share files with another user, or even browse the Internet regularly and receive files, there is always a slight risk of infection. Please read Chapter 12 for more information on this subject.

What Those Error Messages Really Mean

Wouldn't it be nice if Apple could just put up a message that says, "Sorry, your Mac crashed because the person who programmed your word processor left out a line of code because he was late for dinner"? That and similar routine mistakes are what often cause programs to quit and your Mac to freeze.

But since programs are getting larger and larger, with millions of lines of code, the possibility of error has risen dramatically. Worse, there are so many thousands of possible combinations of Mac hardware and software that it's just too easy for conflicts to occur.

Unfortunately, it's not terribly easy to know why your Mac is behaving badly. The system error messages you see on the screen—when you see them—frequently don't give you the information you need to find out what's wrong. They seem designed more for programmers than for folks like you and me who just want to use our Macs with as little fuss as possible.

While the messages may seem meaningless, they can sometimes point you in the general direction of where a problem might lie. Table 2-1 lists common Mac OS errors and what they signify, along with a general idea of where a solution may be found. I have made no attempt to be complete here; these are just some of the errors you're apt to encounter at some point in your Mac computing experience.

CAUTION *Use this table with extra care. As often as the error message may be correct, a system error may be misleading and send you off in the wrong direction in search of a solution.*

What Those Error Messages Really Mean

Error Number	Definition	Causes/Common Solutions
ID 1	Bus Error	A memory-related error. Try giving the program more RAM, or get a RAM upgrade.
ID 2	Address Error	Incorrect memory address. Check for system extension conflict or corrupted program preferences.
ID 3	Illegal Instruction	A possible programming error. Check for an application or system extension conflict.
ID 4	Zero Divide Error	This is a programming error, a remnant of a routine step in the error checking process. Check for an application or system extension conflict.
ID 5	Range Check Error	Another programming error; the number isn't within the range required for the program. Check for an application or system extension conflict.
ID 6	Overflow Error	More programming problems; a number used for calculation is too big for the space set aside in the program. Check for an application or system extension conflict.
ID 7	Privilege Violation	This is strictly a programming issue; nothing to be concerned about (one hopes) with a released product.
ID 8	Trace Mode Error	This is an indication that your Mac has apparently stumbled into a programming mode.
ID 9	Line 1010 Trap Error	Similar to ID 3; an instruction your Mac's CPU doesn't understand. Possibly due to application or system extension conflict.
ID 10	Line 1111 Trap Error	Similar to ID 9 and 3. A possible application or system extension conflict.
ID 11	Hardware Exception Error	This is a generic system error, which appears only on Power Macs, running Mac OS versions earlier than 7.6. It's pretty much the same as a Type 1 error, a general system or application conflict.
ID 12	Unimplemented Core Routine	Similar to ID 4; a relic of a programming error. Possibly due to an application or system extension conflict.
ID 13	Uninstalled Interrupt	This message indicates that your Mac cannot communicate with a peripheral device, such as a disk drive.

TABLE 2-1   System Errors and Their Definitions

Error Number	Definition	Causes/Common Solutions
ID 15	Segment Loader Error	You don't see this on PowerPC Macs. The error dates back to the era of 680x0 Macs, and indicates that part of the program didn't properly load into memory.
ID 17	Missing Package	This indicates that a specific component of your system software is missing. The best solution is a clean reinstallation of your system software, explained later.
ID 27	Ditto	Ditto
ID 30	Ditto	Ditto
ID 31	Ditto	Ditto
ID 25	Memory Full Error	Either your Mac doesn't have enough memory to run a program or perform a function, or there's a software conflict that's memory related.
ID 26	Bad Program Launch	The program you attempted to launch isn't running properly. Consider reinstalling the application, or, at the very least, delete its preferences file.
ID 20	Stack Ran into Heap	A memory error, similar to ID 25.
-34	Disk Is Full	Clear out disk space or copy file to another drive.
-37	Bad File Name	File appears to be corrupted. Use a backup, if you have one.
-39	Logical End of File	The file is corrupted and needs to be replaced. This is also a common error when a preferences file goes bad.
-60	Bad Master Directory Block	This is a disk directory error. Run Disk First Aid or a commercial hard drive diagnostic/repair program to fix.
-64	Drive Not Installed	Cannot read drive or disk. Check drive directory, update device driver or check SCSI chain.
-65	Ditto	Ditto
-66	Font Substitution Occurred	This is a font error, possibly indicating the font you tried to use is missing or damaged. Reinstall the font and try again.
-127	Internal File System Error	This indicates your Mac may have serious disk directory damage (or a SCSI chain problem). Check the SCSI chain and run Disk First Aid or a commercial hard drive diagnostic/repair program to fix.

TABLE 2-1   System Errors and Their Definitions *(continued)*

What Those Error Messages Really Mean

Case History

One Line Too Many

There is no greater frustration than encountering a software conflict that the software's publisher cannot reproduce. You become almost paranoid. You feel that perhaps you are being singled out.

This happened to me when I was using a component of a now-discontinued utility program: a simple control panel that put up a little menu bar icon displaying hard disk activity. Every time I ran that program, my Mac would crash.

I dutifully contacted the publisher's technical support people and went into endless details of my particular setup, and they took me through various stages of disabling and enabling system extensions. Even with the basic set of Apple system extensions and their lone component of the program, the crashes occurred. Technical support couldn't duplicate it.

Finally they did the impossible (and I've never heard of a similar case). They are located in the Pacific Northwest, and I'm in the Southwest. They had one of their lead programmers pack up a PowerBook containing a copy of the program's source code (the software's heart and soul) and travel direct to my home office to see what was happening.

He arrived, set up his PowerBook, and launched his software compiling program. Before his eyes, I continued to duplicate the problem. He watched it in action, then rummaged through the long lines of arcane text that formed the source of the program that was crashing my Mac.

Finally he stumbled upon a single line of computer code, a few words that made no sense to anyone but a software engineer. He muttered something about the code not actually doing anything in particular, but he thought that perhaps, in a rare situation, it might just create an "endless loop" that would cause a crash. How it got there, he wouldn't guess, as the original programmer (no longer connected with the company) may have put it there to access a function that was removed from the final version.

So he removed it, then recompiled the program. He copied the finished control panel to a floppy, and I then installed it. I restarted and crossed my fingers. The crashes stopped, for good. In days, the fixed version was ready and was incorporated into the next version of the program.

So simple, yet so complex. Imagine how difficult it is to locate an errant line of computer language in a huge word processing program that is causing a one-in-a-million system crash? My respect for the hurdles software engineers face in giving us reasonably reliable software went way up as a result of this episode.

Is It the Hardware or Software?

This is the $64 million question, and one you wonder about when your Mac crashes over and over again and no amount of system diagnostics will set it right.

There are a few sure indications, however, of a hardware-related problem. Other problems may seem hardware-related, but are really due to other causes.

Here's a listing of typical problems:

- **Weird tones appear at startup.**   This usually indicates defective or improperly installed RAM. Try reseating or removing the RAM upgrade and see if the problem disappears (of course, you've got to leave your original RAM module where it is). If the problem doesn't vanish, contact your dealer or Apple Computer for further assistance. We'll cover the subject of RAM upgrades in more detail in Chapter 4.

- **Screen remains dark and Mac refuses to start.**   On some of the early Power Macs, this is a symptom of a dead PRAM battery. The battery, costing from $10 to $20, is readily available from your Apple dealer. You may also find an equivalent at a specialty battery dealer or even a Radio Shack store. If your Mac has a graphic card in a PCI expansion slot, shut it down, open your Mac's case and make sure the card is properly seated. If not, reseat the card carefully. This condition was an occasional problem on some Power Computing Mac OS clones. If these two solutions don't apply, have your Mac or monitor checked for a power supply or logic board problem.

CAUTION   *Before you touch anything inside your Mac, you should shut down the entire system (including monitor, external drives, and so on) and touch the power supply to ground yourself. Some manufacturers are nice enough to include wrist straps (to tap static electricity). That way you won't cause a "spike" that can fry your Mac's delicate electronics.*

- **The picture distorts or there is a color shift.**   Restart your Mac. If the problem doesn't disappear, check your monitor adjustments. If the problem continues, contact your dealer for assistance. Some Apple Computer monitors, from the AppleVision series, are known to be troublesome. Call Apple Computer's customer service people for assistance. You'll learn more about Mac displays in Chapter 10.

- **Date reverts to 1956 or network settings change after a cold start.** If you power up your Mac and find the system date, network, or other settings have changed, it's time to replace the PRAM battery. These little lithium batteries store these settings. For more information, refer to the earlier section on why your Mac may refuse to start.

■ **Front bezel separates on PowerBook 190/5300 series.** This problem is covered by an extended warranty from Apple. Contact your dealer or Apple customer service to arrange for service.

■ **PowerBook or iBook battery doesn't recharge.** Your battery is generally good for a year or two of regular service. If you cannot get it to charge properly, you may want to recheck the AC adapter (they have been known to fail on earlier PowerBook models), or try another battery if you have one. You can buy a battery for most recent PowerBooks from your Apple dealer. If the battery still won't recharge, consult your PowerBook's documentation about resetting the Power Manager, which can impact such problems. Chapter 5 has much more information on this subject.

Extended Warranties: Are They Worth It?

As you prepare to leave the store with your new purchase, the salesperson tells you there's one more option: an extended warranty. You can add a year or two—or more—to Apple's standard one-year product warranty. Is this worth it?

In practice, such policies are little different from a regular insurance policy. A third-party carrier (or Apple Computer if it's an AppleCare policy) will cover repairs (perhaps with a small deductible) if your system develops a hardware problem.

The question is: Do you really need this insurance? If the policy is really cheap and you are far from a friendly neighborhood dealer or Macintosh user group, you might find this a convenient safeguard. But most electronic components will tend to fail early in their life cycle, well within your new product warranty. You should look at extended warranties with skepticism. They are a big source of profit for the dealers, and the possibility you'll actually need one is not terribly large.

NOTE

If there is any exception to this rule, perhaps it would be an Apple laptop, be it PowerBook or iBook. These models are subject to more wear and tear than the usually stationary desktop models, and an economical policy may well be worth your consideration. The LCD display, for example, can be especially expensive to replace if it fails.

There are occasional articles in *Consumer Reports* magazine on the subject, and you may want to consult them for additional insights.

The Right Way to Do a System Upgrade

The vision of the one-click installation has been part and parcel of the Mac computing experience from the very first. In those days, your entire System Folder fit on a single 400K floppy disk (well, at least at the very beginning).

Today, your System Folder consists of hundreds of files, and the contents can easily fill more than 300MB of storage space, even with the minimum of extras. There are so many possible combinations of Macs and required system components, there's no way to just guess what works.

The most efficient way to do a system upgrade is to run Apple's Mac OS installer. Trying to drag a completed System Folder from another Mac to yours will almost always run into trouble, unless they are identical in make and model.

The Two Types of System Installations

There are two types of Mac OS installations. Which you choose depends on whether you've had problems with your current system software, or whether you're upgrading to an all-new version.

- **Upgrade installation**   This is the standard option available when you double-click the Mac OS installer. The components of your System Folder will be updated with the newer versions from Apple Computer, and your System file will be updated as well. If any untouched files are damaged, they will still be present. In addition, if your System file is damaged, the update may only make matters worse.

- **Clean installation**   No, you don't have to reinstall all of your software to do a clean system installation (although you might have to consider this as a last resort to deal with serious system problems). The actual process will create a brand new System Folder. Your existing System Folder will be deactivated and renamed Previous System Folder. Nothing from your older System Folder is transferred. That means you'll have to reinstall or drag over your third-party extensions, control panels, fonts, and preferences.

What's Right for You

Unless you are in a real hurry, or you're just reinstalling your system software to add or remove a component, it's best to start from scratch. And that means a clean installation.

The advantage is that no components that may be damaged from your existing System Folder are carried through, and, if you're upgrading to a new system version, you'll be assured of as reliable an upgrade as possible.

The sad side effect, however, is that you have to go through a process of merging non-Apple components from your existing System Folder. This can be confusing and perhaps time-consuming, but if you follow the suggestions in the next section, you'll be able to keep the process as painless as possible.

If you really want to try to automate the process, consider trying out Conflict Catcher (described in the section entitled "Clean System Merging: The Easy Way," later in this chapter), which does a lot of the work for you. A demo copy is included on this book's CD.

The Steps to a Clean Installation

Once you're ready to proceed, first create an Apple System Profiler report of your original System Folder. You'll need it later on. Get your system CD and follow these steps:

> **NOTE** *The steps described here apply to Mac OS 9, but should apply in equal fashion to any Mac OS 8 version, with the exception of system updates (which require a regular system installation beforehand).*

1. Go to the Apple menu, and launch Apple System Profiler, bringing up the screen shown in Figure 2-1.

2. Choose New from the File menu to choose your report options (see Figure 2-2).

3. Since you are only concerned with the contents of your System Profile, check only the boxes at right, and uncheck the ones at left. Then click OK to begin the process, which will bring up a progress screen as shown in Figure 2-3.

4. Once your report is generated, choose Print from the File menu to get a hard copy of the report.

> **NOTE** *If you don't have a printer at hand, you can simply save the profile report, but it'll take a lot more time to compare the contents back and forth when you're ready to merge System Folders.*

5. Now you're ready for the main event. Insert the new system CD in your Mac's CD-ROM drive.

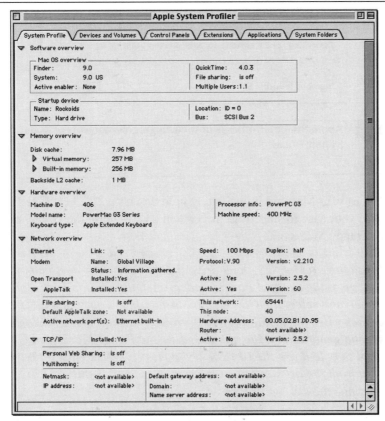

FIGURE 2-1   Discover the ins and outs of your Mac's configuration from this screen

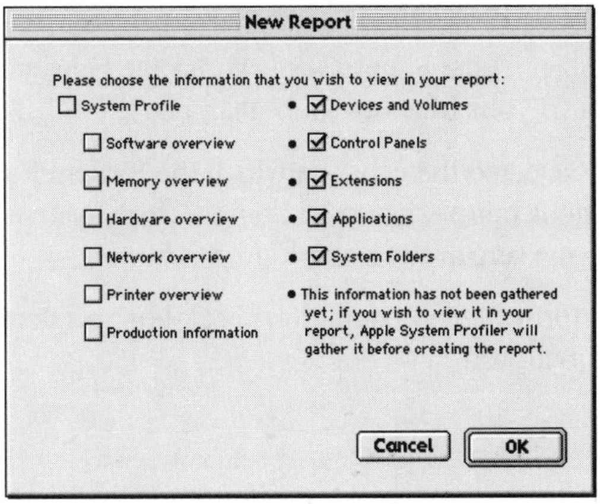

FIGURE 2-2   Check only the options shown at the right

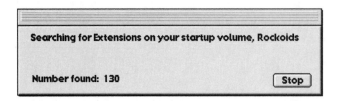

Searching for Extensions on your startup volume, Rockoids

Number found: 130   [Stop]

| FIGURE 2-3 | Apple System Profiler is now cataloging the contents of your Mac's System Folder |

6. Restart your Mac and immediately hold down the "C" key, which will force your Mac to start from the system CD. Release the key when you see the Happy Mac icon.

NOTE *If you have a Mac OS clone or your Mac refuses to start from the system CD, go to the Control Panels folder, open the Startup Disk Control Panel, and select the CD as your startup disk. You'll just have to change it back when the installation is through. For the "Slot Loading" or second generation iMac, the iBook, or the Power Macintosh G4, you need to hold down the OPTION key at startup. Then click on the CD's icon from the list you see on the screen, and click the right arrow to continue the startup process.*

7. After your Mac has started, locate and double-click on the Mac OS Install icon, which brings up a screen similar to the one shown in Figure 2-4. Click Continue to proceed.

8. On the next screen (see Figure 2-5), choose the Destination Disk from the pop-up menu (if your Mac has more than one drive).

9. Once you've selected the drive on which the System Folder is to be placed, click the Options button, if you're doing a clean system installation. This will bring up the screen shown in Figure 2-6.

10. Click the Perform Clean Installation check box to select that option, then click the OK button.

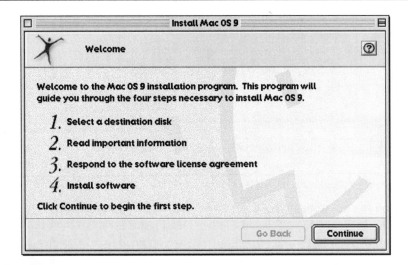

FIGURE 2-4 Begin your clean installation from this screen

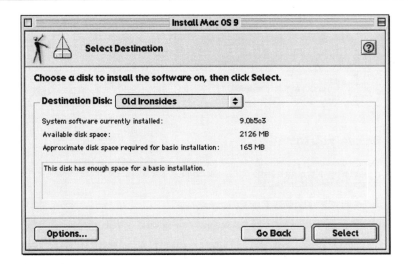

FIGURE 2-5   Pick a disk for your system software installation

The Right Way to Do
a System Upgrade

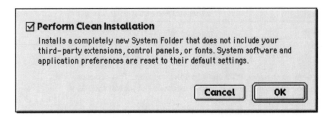

FIGURE 2-6   Choose the Perform Clean Installation option here

11. On the next screen, you'll see an Important Information message, which is actually your Mac OS Read Me file (see Figure 2-7). Go over this to make sure there aren't some last-minute steps you need to take to ensure a seamless system software upgrade. When you're finished reading the document (you can also save or print it), click Continue to move on to the next step. If you don't print the Read Me file at this point, no problem. It'll be copied to your hard drive during the normal system installation.

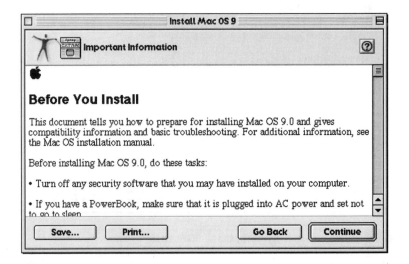

FIGURE 2-7   Consult this file for last-minute tips and cautions about your Mac OS installation

> **NOTE** *If you find something in the Important Information file that prevents you from doing your system installation right away, choose Quit from the File menu to end the process. You can always go back to it later.*

12. On the next screen, you can opt to go right on to the system installation, or you can make a few more choices. If you wish to continue with the standard installation process, click Start. You'll see a progress bar and an estimate of how long the system installation will take. Expect it to last from five to twenty-five minutes, depending on the kind of Mac you have.

> **NOTE** *At the very start of the installation process, the installer will check your hard drive with Disk First Aid to be sure there are no disk directory issues before the software is actually installed. If there are problems Disk First Aid cannot fix, the installation won't continue. At this point, if you have a copy, run Norton Utilities or TechTool Pro and see if they can fix the problem.*

13. If you want to check or pick and choose the components of your system installation, click Customize, which brings up the screen shown in Figure 2-8.

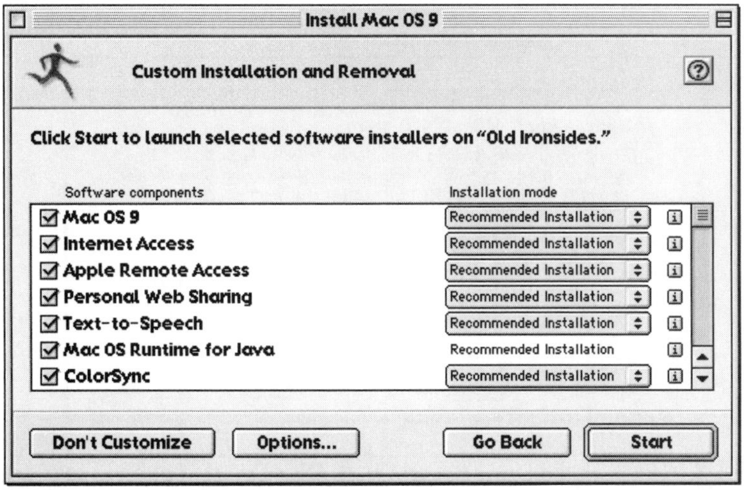

FIGURE 2-8   Click the check box to add or remove a system component

The Right Way to Do a System Upgrade

14. Review the Software components list. If everything is what you want, click the Start button to begin the installation. If you wish to remove or add a component, click the check box next to its name.

NOTE

If you wish to further customize the installation of software components, click the Recommended Installation pop-up menu to pick further options. Be sure you click the "i" icons for specifics on the effect of the choices you make, if you have any questions.

15. If you have a Mac with a non-Apple hard drive, you'll want to click Options (see Figure 2-9). Then uncheck the box labeled Update Apple Hard Disk Drivers. If you don't follow this step, you'll either have to respond to a dialog that your drive can't be updated or, worse, confront a problem with the drive if the Apple installer tries the update anyway. Click OK to continue.

NOTE

If your hard drive isn't formatted with Apple's Drive Setup program, you may want to contact the manufacturer of your disk formatting software to make sure it's compatible with your newly installed system version.

16. Once your system installation is done, click Quit to close the installer program.

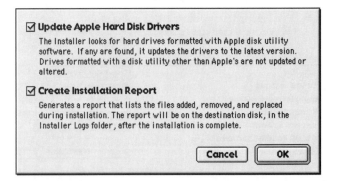

FIGURE 2-9   Uncheck the Update Apple Hard Disk Drivers option if you install on a non-Apple hard drive

17. If you changed your Startup Disk Control Panel settings, locate the control panel on your CD (in the Control Panels folder) and select your original destination disk as the startup disk.

18. Choose Restart from the Special menu.

The first part of the system installation is finished, but you have more to do before you can get down to work with your new System Folder. Now you've got to start the merge process.

How to Merge System Folders

When you complete your clean system installation, you'll have a System Folder and a Previous System Folder. The latter is simply your original System Folder, which Apple has "deblessed" (made inactive) as a consequence of your installation. Now that it's there, what do you do about it?

I have seen situations where folks have just left it there, doing nothing with it, and not taking advantage of its value. If you prefer, you can simply reinstall all your third-party control panels and extensions, redo all your program and Internet settings, and be done with it. If you can accomplish this task in a reasonably short amount of time, it may be the best choice.

But for most of us, it's better to simply merge the System Folders, moving over the non-Apple files and certain preferences files from your Previous System Folder to the new one.

This is not a trivial process, and you may expect it to take anywhere from a half hour to a couple of hours to do right. You'll also have to check the contents of each folder within your System Folder to be absolutely certain you are copying over the things you need and not the things that will replace newer system components or cause further trouble.

Here are the steps to follow:

1. Retrieve the Apple System Profiler report you made before the clean installation. Now open the Previous System Folder and the new System Folder, and place the directories side by side to compare them.

2. Choose View as List from the Finder for each folder, and make sure the name is selected (see Figure 2-10 for the result). This will make it as easy as possible to compare the two.

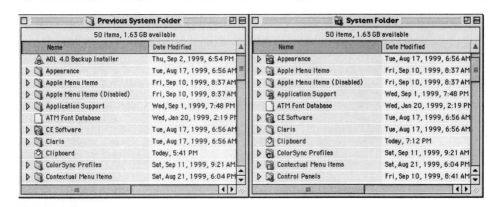

FIGURE 2-10   On the left, a Previous System Folder; on the right, a new System Folder, ready to be merged

3. Check for any folders in your Previous System Folder that aren't duplicated in your new System Folder. Hold down the SHIFT key and select each of them.

4. Hold down the OPTION key, then drag those folders to your new System Folder. When you perform this action, a plus sign (+) will appear on the mouse cursor.

NOTE *You are holding down the OPTION key so that you are copying, not moving, the files to the new System Folder. That way, if something goes wrong, you can revert to your Previous System Folder.*

5. If you have any custom sounds you've added, double-click on the System file icon in your Previous System Folder to bring up the directory of keyboard layouts and sounds.

6. Remove those sounds, hold down the OPTION key, then drag them to the System file in the new System Folder. It'll take a few seconds for the process to complete itself.

7. Next, open the Apple Menu Items folder in both the Previous and new System Folders and compare the contents. OPTION-drag over the files not duplicated in the new System Folder.

8. The next step gets a bit more complicated. Consult your copy of the Apple System Profiler report to see which items in your System Folder are from Apple and which aren't.

9. For each folder in your two System Folders, OPTION-drag the non-Apple files from your Previous System Folder to the new System Folder, with the exceptions of the Preferences and Fonts folders.

10. Go to the Fonts folder of each System Folder. Select all the files from your old Fonts folder and OPTION-drag them to the new one. Not to worry, you won't be able to replace any fonts that are duplicated (you'll get a message they're in use).

11. After your fonts are replaced, open the Preferences folder, and OPTION-drag the non-duplicated files to the new Preferences folder.

12. If you have Internet access, OPTION-drag Apple's Internet Preferences, Modem Preferences, and the TCP/IP Preferences files to the new System Folder, and OK the message to replace the ones that are there. In addition to these basic files, you'll also want to OPTION-copy folders with the name America Online, Eudora, Explorer, or Netscape, or bearing the name of any other Internet software you use. When you copy these additional files, stored program settings, bookmarks, downloads, email, and other files will be brought over to your new System Folder.

NOTE *If you cannot locate the preferences files for all of your Internet software, use the Find feature to bring up Apple's Find or Sherlock screen to find a list of the files you need.*

13. Locate the Remote Access folder and open it.

14. Drag the Remote Access Connections file from this folder to the Remote Access folder in your new System Folder.

15. Double-check the items you've transferred. You may have to move a file from here and there, if you missed any.

16. If everything is all right, choose Restart from the Special menu.

17. Once your Mac has restarted, make sure it works properly. If all went well, you should be ready to enjoy your new System Folder.

How to Merge System Folders

NOTE *Do not delete the contents of your Previous System folder until you're sure your new installation went well. Otherwise, you'll end up having to do another clean installation.*

What If the Clean System Installation Goes Badly?

It doesn't happen too often (thank heavens), but sometimes reinstalling your system software only makes matters worse for your Mac. Should this happen, you can go back to using your Previous System Folder. This is why you should copy rather than move your files during the merge process.

The following process is quite drastic. You'll have to be prepared to restore all of your programs in addition to reinstalling system software. It's only recommended as a last resort.

NOTE *If you have an iMac or iBook and did not install much or any third-party software, you can use your System Restore disk to put everything back the way it was. And, if you back up your files, the Restore process can be set to erase your hard drive. This is as clean an installation as you can get. For other new Macs, the Restore disk simply puts back the original System Folder and related components.*

Here's what to do next:

1. Restart your Mac if it crashed. If you cannot get it to start, restart with your system CD, holding down the "C" key (as noted in the previous section) to get it going. On newer Macs, you need to press the OPTION key to bring up a screen on which you can select the CD as the startup disk.

2. Go to your new System Folder on your startup drive, and remove the System file.

3. Select the folder's icon and rename this folder "Obsolete System Folder."

NOTE *Renaming an icon simply involves clicking on the name to select it, waiting for the name to highlight, then typing in the new name and pressing RETURN or ENTER to save it.*

4. Go to the Previous System Folder, select the icon, and rename it back to System Folder.

5. Open and close the folder. This has the effect of "blessing" the former Previous System Folder, so your Mac can start again.

6. Restart and verify that you're up and running again.

7. Trash the Obsolete System Folder.

8. Either continue to use your original System Folder or go ahead and try the clean system installation process again, as outlined in the earlier section entitled "The Steps to a Clean Installation." But this time, rather than merge the Previous System Folder with the new System Folder, first verify that your Mac works properly.

9. Once you've done that, reinstall all of your third-party control panels and extensions. If you have application software that includes system components, you'll have to reinstall them as well.

NOTE   *The newest Microsoft Office and Internet applications are designed to run a "self-repair" routine if you launch them with missing System Folder components, so you shouldn't need to worry about them. These programs are designed to take care of themselves (though I've heard of a case or two where a complete software reinstallation was needed).*

10. Once you've reinstalled everything, you should recheck your Mac's startup process and your programs to make sure everything works properly. Prepare to have to revisit a program's preferences and your Internet settings.

If the foregoing process doesn't work, there are some more options:

■ **Check your hard drive.**   While Apple's Disk First Aid should be able to ferret out disk directory problems that may affect your Mac OS installation, don't hesitate to give it another go-around. If you have one or more of the commercial disk repair programs on hand, such as Alsoft's DiskWarrior, Symantec's Norton Utilities, or MicroMat's TechTool Pro, let them do their stuff. It's always possible these programs will find a problem Disk First Aid missed. Once you run these programs, give the system installation another try.

How to Merge System Folders

■ **Reformat your hard drive.**　This is a drastic step, but if you have a backup (or can use a Restore disk to put everything back), this may be the best way to clear up lingering problems. It's not quite as intimidating as it sounds, so long as you can back up everything. But prepare to spend the better part of an afternoon to accomplish the task (or an entire day if you have a Mac with several big hard drives and lots and lots of files).

■ **Have the Mac checked by a dealer.**　If you've tried everything possible to get your Mac to run in a stable fashion, have the hardware checked. It simply isn't normal for a Mac user to have to go through so much grief to get the computer to operate as it's supposed to.

Clean System Merging: The Easy Way

The process just described is a little complex and requires lots of attention to detail. But it isn't the only way to do a clean installation of your system software.

Fortunately, there is a way to actually help you automate the process, so you don't have to get a case of blurry eyes trying to figure out what goes where and when.

The solution is a special feature of Casady & Greene's popular Conflict Catcher program (see also Chapter 18). The stock and trade of Conflict Catcher is its ability to help you diagnose possible system extension conflicts, but the program can also help you merge your disparate system elements after a clean installation. Here is how to do it:

1. Do a clean system installation, as explained in the earlier section entitled "The Right Way to Do a System Upgrade."

2. Install Conflict Catcher after restarting with your new System Folder. This process works best if the program is installed on both the current System Folder and the Previous System Folder.

3. Restart your Mac, and hold down the SPACEBAR, which brings up the Conflict Catcher window, shown in Figure 2-11.

4. Choose Clean-Install System Merge from the program's Special menu.

NOTE

Conflict Catcher's "Clean-Install System Merge" feature is based on Conflict Catcher 8. Sorry, this feature isn't part of earlier versions of the program.

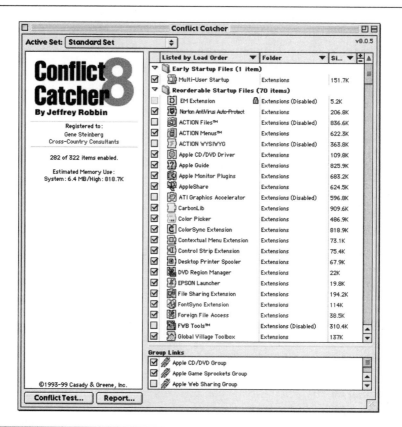

FIGURE 2-11   Conflict Catcher offers a large set of system management features

5. You will then see a dialog, shown in Figure 2-12, in which you confirm you're running the new System Folder. Click Yes to continue.

6. In the next dialog, you'll be asked to select, from the list, your present System Folder, and the one from which you want to merge. Click on your Previous System Folder (if that's what you'll be using) where requested.

7. You'll then be brought back to the prior dialog box in which you'll see the name Previous System Folder.

8. Click on the Compare Folders button. Over the next few minutes, Conflict Catcher will go to work to seek out the differences between

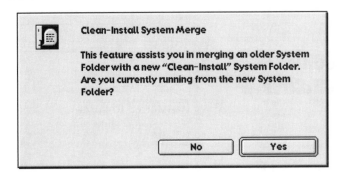

FIGURE 2-12   Conflict Catcher is readying its Clean-Install System Merge process

the two System Folders. As soon as its work is done, you'll see a screen containing a list of the items in your Previous System Folder that aren't duplicated in the new one.

NOTE   *As part of its scanning process, Conflict Catcher will check for corrupted files in your Previous System Folder. If you see a dialog about it, go ahead and let Conflict Catcher attempt to fix the files.*

9. Look at the list, selecting the check boxes for each item that you *don't want* to copy to your new System Folder.

NOTE   *If you're not sure about a specific system extension, don't worry. Just click the name, and Conflict Catcher will consult its reference file and let you know what the item is used for (it has a database of thousands of entries and gets it right most times).*

10. If you want to customize the merging process still further, click on the Options button. The key option is whether to Copy Items or Move Items. In the latter case, the files will just be transferred to the new System Folder. In the first case, copies will be made. You'll want to consider the first option, in case your new System Folder isn't performing as you'd like and you want to use the original ("Previous") System Folder again.

11. The next option is helpful in setting up preferences for your new System Folder. It's called Merge System File Resources, and it'll transfer the

Owner Name, Computer Name and (if it applies), the password you placed in your File Sharing Control Panel, your printer selection, and your selected sounds. Once you've made the settings, click OK to begin the final leg of the journey.

12. On the next screen, click Merge Systems.

13. After the files you selected are transferred to the new System Folder, you'll return to the main Conflict Catcher screen. Here you can recheck the results of the merge process. Confirm the settings, click Continue Startup, and you're just about there.

14. If everything looks good, click Continue Startup. Your Mac's startup process will continue where it left off, with one possible exception. If the merge process added items that load before Conflict Catcher, you'll be asked to OK a restart instead.

CAUTION *If you access the Internet through a regular Internet provider, be sure that you also transfer your Internet Preferences, Modem Preferences, Remote Access folder, and TCP/IP Preferences. In addition, you'll want to locate preferences files and folders with such names as America Online, Eudora, Explorer, and Netscape (or any other Internet program you use). These files contain such critical items as program settings, bookmarks, favorites, email, downloads, and other important files. You need these settings to seamlessly connect to your provider without having to do the setups all over again.*

The Magic and Mystery of Preferences Files

The biggest hurdle to overcome in merging a Previous System Folder with your new, clean System Folder is what to do about the preferences files.

When you want to customize your program to show a specific set of toolbar options, to use an autosave or auto-backup feature, display fonts in WYSIWYG fashion, or a host of other options, you will look for some sort of preferences or settings feature.

Most programs store their preferences in a separate file, not in the application itself.

And it's not just the programs you install that have preferences settings. More and more of the things you customize in your Mac system software generate some sort of preferences file. At first it was just the Finder, but now there are preferences for a host of functions.

How to Merge System Folders

NOTE *This list of Mac OS system preferences applies strictly to a fairly normal System Folder running Mac OS 9.*

Here's a list of the Apple preferences encountered on a recent trip to a Mac's Preferences folder:

Apple File Security Prefs	Finder Preferences
Apple Menu Options Prefs	General Controls Prefs
Apple Video Player Prefs	Hot Keys Preferences
Apple Help Prefs	Internet Preferences
AppleCD Audio Player Prefs	Key Caps Preferences
AppleShare Prep	Keychains
AppleTalk Preferences	Keyboard Preferences
AppSwitcher Preferences	Launcher Preferences
ASLM Preferences	LiveUpdate Preferences
ASP Preferences	Location Manager Prefs
Calibrator Prefs 256	Mac OS Preferences
ColorSync Cache	Memory Preferences
ColorSync Preferences	Monitors Preferences
Control Strip Preferences	Modem Preferences
Custom Desktop Patterns	Mouse Preferences
Date & Time Preferences	Navigation Services
Desktop Pictures Prefs	Network Browser Preferences
Display Preferences	Printing Prefs
Energy Saver Preferences	Remote Access
Expansion Manager Prefs	Sound Preferences
Extensions Manager Preferences	Software Updates Pref
FBC Indexing Preferences	System Preferences
File Sharing	TCP/IP Preferences
File Exchange Preferences	Users & Groups Data File

So if you decide to do a clean system installation, you have all those Apple program preferences to worry about. You could, of course, just decide you'll redo all the settings from your Mac, but this could be time consuming, and, when it comes to the settings you use to get on the Internet, not always so easy.

The best solution is to make a backup of your Mac's Preferences folder when you feel you've got the settings down pat, so you can quickly restore it should the need arise for a clean system installation.

Upgrading Is Next

As you can see, the process of handling system problems and reinstalling your system software isn't quite as intimidating a process as it seems to be. If you follow the steps in this chapter, you'll get through it most times without serious fuss.

In the next two chapters, we'll cover the highways and byways of hardware upgrades, from RAM to CPU cards. You'll also learn when to decide if the best upgrade for you is actually a brand new Mac.

How to Merge System Folders

Chapter 3

The Mac Upgrade Guide: Peripheral Cards

I begin this chapter with a bit of trepidation. There are so many hundreds of possible Mac system and hardware combinations, it won't be possible to cover every conceivable installation situation specifically. Instead, I'm going to focus on general areas you need to look out for when you do one of these upgrades.

You'll learn about the kinds of products that are available and the steps to take to be sure your upgrade installation goes as easily as possible—and what to do if your upgrade doesn't work as it should.

Adding Expansion Cards

While some Macs, such as the original compact models and the iMac, are designed to support RAM upgrades and not much else, most desktop Macs are set up to support peripheral cards. These cards can be used to handle a variety of features that will take your Mac to greater heights of usefulness. They include:

■ **FireWire cards**   The very same high-speed peripheral bus that is standard issue on new desktop Macs can be added to older models. As explained in Chapter 15, FireWire is free of many of the common ills of SCSI. You don't have to set ID numbers or worry about termination. Some very small FireWire devices even draw power from the FireWire port, so they don't need a separate AC power supply. In addition to handling such products as hard drives, CD writers, and scanners, FireWire capability lets you capture video from a DV camcorder—all without need of a special video capture board; of course, you do need video editing software. You'll learn more about this in Chapter 19.

■ **Graphic cards**   Even if your Mac has built-in graphics hardware, you may want to look at a graphics card for a second monitor or for speedier performance. Some graphic cards offer special support for games, for example. And some of these cards also support simple video capture, so you can copy desktop video productions right to your camcorder or VCR. As this book was written, one graphic card maker, IX Micro, was selling a single card that supported two monitors.

■ **Network card**   While all new computers in Apple's line have built-in 10/100Mbs Ethernet networking capability, you may want to add high-speed (or any Ethernet) capability to an older Mac. Such network cards are relatively inexpensive, but can help reduce network bottlenecks. If you are part of a large office network, you'll also want to look into a gigabit Ethernet card, which can offer greatly improved file transfer speeds (but, as you'll see in Chapter 17, they're still expensive).

- **SCSI accelerators** These peripheral cards can give your Mac a faster SCSI port, the ability to handle extra SCSI devices, or even an SCSI port for Macs that don't have them. If you are performing tasks that require ultra-fast hard drives, such as image editing or video production, such products are useful. Since Mac and PC SCSI accelerator cards are virtually the same, except for ROM chips and driver software, there is a plentiful variety available.

- **Serial port cards** Fed up with juggling modems and serial printers and dealing with software that may be flaky? You can add extra serial ports with an expansion card. This feature is also useful if you have a Mac with USB instead of the older type of serial port (though there are USB-to-serial adapters available too).

- **USB adapter cards** If you want to join in the USB revolution and add digital devices, input devices, scanners, and other USB peripherals, these cards are useful. They are also valuable if you want to move a USB device from Macs that support the feature to older models that don't.

- **Video capture boards** New Macs have FireWire, which lets you directly input and output video from a camcorder or other video device with FireWire ports. But if you have an older video device from which you'd like to capture video, you'll need one of these cards. Some of these products are quite cheap, a couple of hundred dollars or less, useful for a simple family function or just having a good time. Other video capture boards give you broadcast-quality video and are actually used for commercial video editing.

NOTE *Expansion cards typically come in 7-inch and 12-inch sizes. Some Macs, such as those from the Performa series, cannot support the larger cards. Before you purchase one of these products, check the technical specifications for your model (or look inside and see if there's room in there for a bigger card).*

Adding Expansion Cards

Peripheral Card Installation Tips

Installing a peripheral card on your Mac is no more difficult than adding RAM, and sometimes less difficult, especially if you have one of those Macs that require complete logic board disassembly and removal for RAM and cache cards.

CAUTION

When you order a peripheral card for your Mac, make sure you get the right type. Older Macs, mostly those that came out before 1995, used an expansion bus called NuBus. Some models only had a processor direct slot (PDS) for upgrade cards. Newer Macs use PCI slots (making them compatible with an expansion bus that is also used on PCs). Also, don't take the cross-platform issue too literally. You shouldn't buy a PC-based peripheral card and assume it'll work on a Mac. You may have to get special driver software or swap out a ROM chip to get it to run.

Once you've got the card you want to add to your Mac, here are the steps to follow:

1. First, be sure to install any software that's required for your peripheral card to run. For example, graphic cards use special drivers to provide video acceleration and custom features, such as the capability to switch resolutions with a single set of keystrokes.

2. Shut down your Mac and all attached peripherals.

3. Be sure to disconnect *all* cables, aside from the power cord, from your Mac.

4. Unscrew the case and remove it. You may have to slide out the logic board to gain access on some Performas. Consult your manual or Apple's technical information database for instructions that apply to your Mac if it's not immediately obvious from the layout.

NOTE

On some Mac OS clones, you'll actually have to remove a cover at the bottom of the computer to access PCI slots.

5. To drain off static electricity, touch the power supply (it's usually a big rectangular box with drilled holes, often having a label indicating its power capacity). If you have a wrist strap, attach the other end to the power supply.

6. Remove the power card or turn off the power strip (if it's attached to one) before going to the next step.

7. Locate an empty slot for your peripheral card. If you are using a six-slot Mac with a PCI slot, consult the manufacturer's directions about which slots to use. Some cards work best in the upper slots, some in the lower. And some setups require placing cards with similar functions in adjacent slots, such as for video capture and SCSI acceleration.

NOTE   *The reason there's an upper/lower slot issue is that because of the limits of the technology, Apple had to provide two PCI buses on their six-slot computers. Moving data between the two buses can be an issue.*

8. If you are installing a PCI card, you'll probably have to remove a Philips-head screw and perhaps a rear cover to install the card.

9. Holding both sides of the peripheral card, seat it carefully in its slot, making sure you align the pins properly. If the card has an external connection jack, you'll know which direction it points to without having to check the pin layout. Press it firmly until it seems to click into place. Check visually to make sure it's seated at both ends.

10. If you need to tighten it down with a screw, make sure the leading edge of the card aligns with the screw slot, then screw it in. This isn't always easy, as you may have to tug on the edge of the card to get it to align with the slot.

NOTE   *On some Mac OS clones, you may actually have to bend the top of the metal plate at the edge of the peripheral card very, very slightly (don't break it) to be able to screw it in. Just make sure you don't unseat the card in the process.*

11. Repeat steps 5 through 8 if you install more than one peripheral card.

12. When you're done, close everything up, and be sure the case is good and tight.

CAUTION   *Don't try to run your Mac with the case open.*

Adding Expansion Cards

13. Close the case and attach screws or nuts or whatever is used to tighten the case.

NOTE

Don't be surprised if you have to spend a few minutes moving and aligning the case to the chassis on some models. If you don't fit everything together precisely, you may not be able to get the screws back in.

14. Once everything is closed tight, reattach the mouse and keyboard and then the AC cord. Leave the peripheral jacks alone for now; you just want to make sure everything works properly.

15. Turn on your Mac and zap the PRAM. This is done by holding down the COMMAND-OPTION-P-R keys at startup and waiting for two or three startup chords to sound. If your Mac boots properly, you'll want to test a function that accesses the peripheral card's features, such as checking graphic display speed, for a graphics card.

NOTE

Zapping the PRAM will reset a number of Control Panel settings, such as display settings, mouse tracking speed, network settings, and startup disk selections, to their system defaults. You'll need to change them where necessary (except for Mac OS 8.5 or later, where only the Startup Disk Control Panel needs to be configured after you restart).

16. Once you've determined that everything works properly, go ahead and shut down your Mac, and reinstall your regular peripherals.

What If It Won't Boot?

It doesn't happen terribly often, but there's always the possibility of something going wrong. If you have a problem with a peripheral card or CPU upgrade, you may see a gray screen and that's it.

If you encounter a problem of this sort, here are some steps to follow:

■ Shut down your Mac, and recheck the upgrade card. Go through the entire installation process, removing and reinserting the CPU or peripheral upgrade card.

- For a CPU card, press and hold down the cuda switch (as described in the next section) for 30 seconds or so, which resets the logic board to accommodate the new card.

- Close the case and try restarting, zapping the PRAM again, as described in the previous section.

- If your Mac still won't boot, shut everything down, open your Mac and remove the card you installed. If you need to replace it with one you removed (such as a CPU card), do that as part of this process.

- Close your Mac and again try to boot the computer. If it works this time, you may simply have a defective or incompatible unit. Contact the dealer or manufacturer for assistance. The easiest solution may simply be that the manufacturer has released a driver or firmware update for the card to address some incompatibility. This was especially true when Mac OS 9 was released. Some graphic and SCSI cards had problems that caused manufacturers to scramble in order to fix various problems.

Installing Accelerator Cards: The Good, the Bad, and the Ugly

Beginning with Apple's PCI Power Macs, a new wrinkle was added to your upgrade options: the removable CPU card.

The theory is great: you can upgrade your CPU to a faster version as easily as you could add a graphic card, SCSI card, or any other expansion card. You plug it in, and when you restart, your Mac suddenly becomes much faster. It's like getting a virtually new Macintosh for a very modest price (assuming the price you pay for your CPU upgrade is modest). Just how, though, do the theories stack up to cold, hard reality?

Here's some things to watch out for and expect when you add a new CPU card:

- **You need to install the software first.**   Most CPU upgrade cards use some kind of software to either turn on the card's cache feature or activate certain custom features. Some of these features may allow you to speed up the cache to provide slightly more spirited performance. Check the upgrade card's installation manual or instruction sheet for information about what software needs to be installed.

If you are using a CPU upgrade that requires software, you'll want to check for updates whenever you upgrade your Mac system software.

■ **Be careful about jumper switches and dials.** Some CPU upgrade cards are fitted with little jumper switches and dials. These adjustments allow you to configure the upgrade for optimum performance. They will set the speed ratio of the CPU card to the logic board bus speed or the speed of onboard cache, if any. The instructions that come with your upgrade should explain just what sort of changes are wrought by these adjustments. For the most part, it's best to stick with the standard setup. Whenever you do anything to increase the clock speed of your Mac's CPU beyond its rating, you may experience unstable performance, such as frequent crashes. If you opt to try for these changes, you should make them in small increments, checking your Mac's performance for a day or so before moving on. Other than crashes, a symptom of turning the setting too high is the inability to boot, or booting without your Mac's regular startup tone.

■ **You may have problems with SCSI chain devices.** This doesn't happen too often. Most accelerator card manufacturers carefully test their products, but when you upgrade to a different CPU family, such as from the older 604e to a G3 or G4, you can expect some side effects. In several instances, for example, backups to a tape drive were unreliable when some G3 upgrade cards were used. Over time, the manufacturers updated their software to clear up this problem, but even if you have the latest and greatest, you should definitely test performance of all your peripheral devices after installation.

A few months before Apple introduced its Power Mac G4 line, they issued a firmware update for the Blue & White G3 models. Officially the update was supposed to improve performance on the PCI bus. Unofficially, it also rendered these computers incapable of using G4 upgrades. I won't get into the political issues of why it happened, except to say that the companies who produced those G4 upgrades managed to deliver their own firmware updates that were designed to eliminate the CPU upgrade block.

■ **Don't forget the "cuda" switch.** PCI Macs and Mac OS clones, such as the 7500, 8500, 9500, and so on, have a special CPU reset switch on the logic board called *cuda*. In order for your Mac to properly recognize the CPU upgrade, you have to press this switch and hold it down for 10 to 20 seconds. The instructions for CPU upgrade cards are sometimes clear about this subject, and sometimes not. But this little amber-colored switch is located somewhere in your Mac's logic board (where depends on the specific model, so I can only tell you that you need to look carefully for it). A side effect of pressing the cuda switch is that your Mac's date display will return to default (1956), and you'll have to change it back.

■ **New system upgrades may leave you behind.** Even if the card works just fine, there's no guarantee that Apple won't release a system version that will not support the upgrade card. A case in point is the client version Mac OS X, which Apple claimed (long before the software was due to ship) will only support models that ship with a G3 or G4 CPU. Even if you add a G3 to a Mac with an older PowerPC chip, it may not work. That's because the computer's ROM still reports the original CPU type that shipped with the Mac, and that's what Apple's software installers check when a system installation is done. If the ROM says you don't have a G3, it doesn't matter what kind of CPU card you installed.

■ **A new Mac may be a better choice.** Even if you can get a CPU upgrade for your Mac that speeds up performance by a factor of several times, the rest of the computer won't be changed. You will still have the same old CD drive and the same old hard drive. If you have an older Mac, you can bet both are relatively slow compared to what Apple offers in their recent product lines. When you consider what it may cost to upgrade those items, it begins to add up. Maybe it's time to hand off that older Mac to another member of your family (or try to sell it), and buy a new one.

NOTE *I don't want to entirely throw cold water on getting a CPU accelerator for your Mac. If you have a lot invested in RAM and compatible peripherals, such an upgrade may extend the life of your computer, and then it makes a lot of sense to give it some serious thought.*

A Brief Look at the Types of CPU Accelerator Upgrades

The means to upgrade your Mac with a faster CPU varies from model to model. I've collected this very short list of the sort of upgrades that are available:

■ **PDS cards** Some Macs have a slot called the processor direct slot (PDS). Whatever you plug in there accesses the same logic board features as your

Installing Accelerator Cards: The Good, the Bad, and the Ugly

Mac's CPU. Where this feature exists, there is apt to be a CPU upgrade card of some sort that fits in it.

■ **Cache slot upgrades**   In the next section, I cover the subject of cache cards. But in some Macs, the very same slot used for a cache card can serve for a CPU upgrade card. Once installed, the CPU upgrade will replace the functions of your Mac's onboard CPU.

■ **CPU card**   Beginning with the first generation PCI Power Macs and some Mac OS clones, you can replace the CPU simply by removing one card and putting in another. For a while, such upgrade prospects proved expensive, but as the cost of G3 CPUs went down, you could find some real bargains in such products. Some manufacturers have now begun to put so-called ZIF adapters in a CPU card, so they can standardize on a single design for CPU upgrades. See the next bullet point for an explanation about ZIF.

■ **ZIF slot**   Short for zero insertion force, a ZIF slot is part of the G3 and G4 Power Macintosh line. To install a CPU module, you simply undo a heat sink, then lift a small latch to loosen the module. You lift it up, replace it, close the latch, reseat the heat sink, and you're done. If there's a downside, it's that all those pins beneath a ZIF module are delicate and can be easily bent, so be careful if you do this sort of upgrade.

Installing a Cache Card

There are caches and there are caches, and it's very easy to get them mixed up. To be perfectly blunt about it, a cache card is a cheap way to make some older Macs run faster.

NOTE   *I should explain at the outset that this information applies to pre-G3/G4 Macs. The newer Macs (with the exception of one specific entry-level G3 PowerBook) all have CPUs that include an L2 (backside) cache.*

Following is an explanation of the various types of caches available and what they can do for you. Once you know the facts, I'll then talk about how to decide whether getting a cache card is the right thing for you to do:

■ **Disk cache**   Nope, it's not something on your disk, it's a small amount of memory the Mac OS sets aside to store frequently accessed data *from* the disk in RAM. So if that data (a program, system software instructions, or a document file) is called upon again, performance speeds up. That's because RAM is much faster than a hard drive. Apple sets aside 32K of disk cache for each 1MB of RAM you've installed on your Mac. You can fiddle with these adjustments, but the clever folks who have worked on the disk cache component of your system software have made it more and more efficient as years go by. For Mac OS 7.6 and later, the default setting should work fine.

NOTE *Over time Apple has made the disk cache work better. While anything over 4MB on pre-Mac OS 8 systems was probably too much (and might actually slow things down), the situation has improved for the various flavors of Mac OS 8 and Mac OS 9. For example, my Power Mac G3/400 has 256MB of RAM, and Apple's default disk cache setting is 8160K (which seems to work quite nicely, thank you).*

■ **Drive cache**   Hard drive manufacturers take the same basic idea behind the disk cache and install RAM on a drive to speed up performance. There's nothing you can do to change anything about it, since it's part of the manufacturing process. But when you buy a hard drive, you may want to look at models that have larger built-in caches (they typically range from 256K to 2MB).

NOTE *The fact that one model of hard drive has a little bigger drive cache than another doesn't always mean it runs faster. Clever designers may eke better performance out of a smaller cache than from a larger cache that's not so cleverly designed. You might want to check out the product reviews in your favorite Mac computing magazine, as they will sometimes do performance comparisons.*

■ **RAM disk**   This is not a cache at all. A RAM disk simply sets aside a portion of RAM to work as a hard drive, sort of the reverse of what's done with virtual memory (which sets aside disk space to mimic RAM). If you have gobs of memory, you may want to visit your Memory Control Panel and try a RAM disk and see if it makes the things you place on it (such as a Web browser cache) run faster.

■ **Web browser cache**   This sort of cache can be used to speed up your Web performance, by storing your Web art on your hard drive. When you call up a site, the browser checks the graphics on your hard drive first and

Installing a Cache Card

retrieves them if the ones on the site itself haven't changed. I'll cover the topic in more detail in Chapter 22.

■ **Font cache** This piece of memory stores information about the fonts you use. You'll find a font cache in Adobe Type Manager (ATM). ATM uses the cache to store information about the characters in the font and uses that information to render clean screen images. Other font caches may be found in the software that comes with a graphic card. Notable examples are the GA or HawkEye Control Panels from Formac, a West German Mac peripheral manufacturer. They include an adjustable font cache ranging from 256K to 4096K. This program comes with graphic cards from such companies as Formac, MacTell (well, at least until this company went out of business in late 1999), and Number Nine. And, yes, it does provide a slight speedup on font display.

■ **Cache card** Way back in 1989, when Apple first released its IIci, there was provision for a so-called L2 (or level 2) cache, containing high-speed RAM that stored frequently used instruction data crunched by the CPU. The net effect was an average 10 to 25 percent performance boost (sometimes more, particularly on Macs without accelerated graphic cards), which made your Mac seem a lot zippier. On the early IIci, the cache was optional (it was later added as standard equipment). On other Macs, such as the IIfx and later the Power Macintosh 9500 and 9600, the cache was soldered onto the logic board.

■ **Backside cache** This is the foundation of the great performance of the G3 and G4. The L2 cache sits on the CPU module itself, operating at a speed much faster than the logic board (usually half that of the CPU itself). You thus get the maximum possible performance boost. Because of the nature of the design of these chips, it's not possible to swap out a smaller cache for a bigger one. What you get, you get (unless you actually replace the CPU with a faster one or one with a bigger cache).

Should I Get a Cache Card?

If your Mac is capable of supporting a cache card, it's a great way to boost performance to a noticeable degree and save a few dollars. But is it for you?

My response is that it depends. If you have a G3 or G4 Mac, then it really doesn't apply. The only way you can speed up your computer is to replace the existing CPU module with a faster one.

Macs that can use cache cards include the original IIci, a number of models in the LC and Performa series, Quadras, earlier generation Power Macintoshes, and Mac OS clones. Some models in these product families have cache cards soldered onto the logic boards, and that pretty much prevents you from installing a replacement cache card.

As of the time this book went to press, most Power Macintosh and Mac OS clones were eligible for a G3 CPU upgrade of one sort or another (check with a manufacturer or dealer to be sure one is available for your model).

The difference between a cache upgrade and a CPU upgrade is tremendous. If your Mac is eligible for a G3 or G4 upgrade, you may be able to increase the processing speed of your computer by several times at prices beginning at less than $200. When you compare that to the prospects offered by a cache card, the choice seems clear-cut: get the CPU upgrade card.

That is, if your Mac is eligible. And as far as Power Macs go, a good number of these models can support upgrades. Even where upgrades were not available when this book was being written, it's likely some enterprising manufacturer might soon find a way to do it at an affordable price.

Installation Tips

Installing a cache card is not terribly different from installing a RAM upgrade. Here's the basic information you need to install a cache card on almost any Mac that can handle this sort of upgrade:

1. Before attempting to install a cache card, go to the Apple menu and run Apple System Profiler. Look at the memory overview category to check whether a cache card is present or not and if so how big it is.

NOTE *In order to see whether a cache card is installed, you need to use Apple System Profiler 2.0 or later. Older versions of this program won't show evidence of a cache card. You can download the updated version directly from Apple's Web site at http://asu.info.apple.com.*

2. After you confirm that your Mac is ready for your cache card, shut it down and shut down all attached peripherals.

3. Be sure to disconnect *all* cables but the power card from your Mac.

Installing a Cache Card

4. Carefully unscrew the case and remove it. In some Performa models, you'll have to slide out the logic board to gain access. Consult your manual or Apple's technical information database for instructions that apply to your Mac if it's not immediately obvious from the layout.

> NOTE
>
> *If need be, take paper and pencil and set down just what you removed and from where. This will help guide you to an easier reassembly process.*

5. Touch the power supply (it's usually a big rectangular box with drilled holes, often having a label indicating its power capacity). This helps drain off static electricity. If you have a wrist strap, attach the other end to the power supply.

6. Unplug the power cord or (if it applies) turn off the power strip.

7. Locate the cache slot. Normally it'll be off by itself at one side of the RAM slots.

8. If you are removing a smaller capacity cache card, grab the edges and lift it out. You may have to tug a bit, but the upgrade should be removable without too much difficulty. On some models, you may have to press retaining clamps on each side to loosen the module.

9. Position your cache card module so the pins precisely match the layout of the ones in the slot (they'll only install properly in one direction).

10. Place the cache card in position and snap into place. You may have to gently move a retaining clip aside to insert the module, then press the top of the card to seat it properly.

> CAUTION
>
> *Try not to walk around between steps, especially on a carpeted floor, where you may give yourself a new dose of static electricity. Best to do your bathroom visits before you begin.*

11. Once the cache card is in place, reinstall the logic board or any other parts that are required in the reassembly process.

> CAUTION
>
> *Don't attempt to operate the Mac until you have closed the case. Even if it runs, you may risk a shock if you touch something (which could also damage the Mac's logic board or other parts).*

12. Close the case and attach the screws or nuts or whatever is used to tighten the case.

NOTE   *You may have to struggle a bit to properly align the case to the chassis on some models. If you don't fit everything together precisely, you may not be able to get the screws back in.*

13. Reattach the mouse and keyboard and then the AC cord. Leave the peripheral jacks alone for now; you just want to make sure everything works properly.

14. Turn on your Mac. If it starts all right, go right to the Apple menu, and launch Apple System Profiler. Check the memory overview setting to be certain the cache card is running and that it is the proper capacity.

15. If the cache card isn't listed, shut everything down, and repeat your installation steps to make sure that the cache card was properly installed. If it still doesn't work, contact the vendor who sold you the upgrade for assistance.

Testing Your Cache Card

When it comes to a RAM installation, it's easy to check About This Computer to make sure that the RAM is being recognized. With a cache card, you can check to see that it's there and running with Apple System Profiler (so long as you have version 2.0 or later), but the performance change may not be readily apparent.

The first thing you'll notice with a cache card is the speed of graphics display. Your Mac's screen may refresh a little faster. If you have any concerns or questions about performance, you can use a benchmarking program, such as Norton System Info, which is part of Symantec's Norton Utilities, or MacBench, the benchmarking standard for *Macworld* magazine. You can download a copy of MacBench from ZiffNet's Web site at http://www.zdnet.com/zdbop/macbench/macbench.html. If you want to do CD-ROM and graphics and video tests, however, you'll also have to order their test CD.

If the cache card is working as it should, you should see some degree of performance improvement in CPU and graphics scores.

Installing a Cache Card

Summing Up

Although some Apple products, such as the iBook and iMac aren't eligible for much in the way of upgrades, quite a few are. With a little judicious selection and careful attention to installation, you can gain new features and better performance with your upgrade product.

In the next chapter, I'll review the other part of doing an upgrade, which even an iBook or iMac can handle—a RAM upgrade.

Chapter 4

The Mac Upgrade Guide:
Dealing with RAM
Upgrade Pitfalls

In Chapter 3, I covered the basics of installing expansion cards, CPU upgrades, and cache cards on your Mac. In this chapter, the topic is RAM.

Although the process of installing RAM on your Mac isn't always easy, you should be able to come through those installations a champ. I have installed RAM in probably one or two hundred Macs over the years (including PowerBooks and iMacs) and have never lost a patient.

However, there's also that old adage that if something can go wrong, very likely it will go wrong at one time or another. I have written this chapter to cover the possible pitfalls of a RAM upgrade and what to do should the worst happen.

Yes, It's All Right for You to Add a RAM Upgrade

In the old days, Apple gave you a stern warning. You could void your new product warranty if you added anything but an expansion card or internal drive to your Mac.

Fortunately, that policy has been liberalized (and certainly it's moot if the warranty has expired). For the newest models, Apple will even give you detailed instructions on how to do a RAM upgrade. For the iBook, they put a little label inside the computer itself, so you can see where the upgrade module fits. The lone exception to the rule are those long-retired compact Mac models, such as the Plus and Classic. Opening the case exposes you to the high-voltage video display chassis, and there is a potential shock hazard. Even the manufacturers of displays and televisions warn you not to poke your hands in those places.

CAUTION   *Although just about any Mac can receive a RAM upgrade, take care if your Mac is under warranty. If your Mac is damaged as a result of installing a RAM upgrade, Apple is off the hook. It's your problem. But if you take care in installing the upgrade, this shouldn't be anything to worry about.*

How to Avoid RAM Upgrade Damage

Mac RAM installations are fairly straightforward, once you get past the process of removing the necessary parts to get to the RAM slots. As I said in the previous chapter, you need to take a few precautions to make sure you don't fry your Mac's logic board in the process of installing any other sort of upgrade inside your Mac. That's because all of these electronic components are quite delicate and susceptible to damage by the elements and static electricity.

That's why I recommend using a wrist strap if your memory chip supplier includes one (and if you get one from another purchase, keep it on hand). If you don't have a wrist strap, it's not a catastrophe. Touching your Mac's power supply (after it's shut down, of course, but with the power cord still in place) should be quite enough to drain static electricity.

Here are some other considerations:

- **RAM retaining clamps are delicate.**   Depending on the kind of Mac you have, the little clamps that lock your RAM in place are either plastic or thin metal. Either way, they are delicate, and if you push, tug, or bend them, they can break off. These parts are not replaceable; if you break them, the RAM slot may not be usable, and you'll have to replace the logic board if you need to install that extra RAM.

- **Orient the RAM properly.**   Each RAM module has something in its design to let you know in which direction it should be placed. You may find separate sets of pins with different widths, for example. Just make sure the pin layout on the module exactly matches the one in the slots, and you won't go wrong. It is possible to force it in the wrong direction, and pay the price of damaging your RAM or the slot. On older RAM SIMMs, there will be a little pinhole to match up against a little pin on the Mac's RAM slot, so you'll know you've pointed it in the right direction.

- **Don't be embarrassed to ask for help.**   While the newest Apple computers are designed for simple RAM installations, the same isn't true for some of the older models, as explained in the previous chapter. Those models were not, shall we say, upgrade friendly. If you have doubts, it's better to pay a professional to do the work for you. Many dealers charge a fixed rate for RAM upgrades, regardless of the complexity. A local Mac user group may be able to assist as well. The small amount you pay is a lot less than what it would cost if you damaged something.

How to Avoid
RAM Upgrade Damage

TIP

A RAM supplier's Web site may also have information on installing upgrades. For example, The Chip Merchant (http://www.thechipmerchant.com) has a series of FAQs at their site that cover common Mac RAM installation questions and troubleshooting. NewerRAM (http://www.newerram.com), originally part of Newer Technologies, has a set of RAM installation instructions in Adobe Acrobat format.

Checking RAM Compatibility

When you install RAM, it doesn't put up a warning label to let you know that you've installed the wrong chip. The only surface indication is that the pins line up and it fits, and that's about it. Arcane items such as voltage requirements and the design elements of the module are not things you can easily detect except, perhaps, for a packing slip or a box or container from the vendor. And, more often than not, the packing slip doesn't contain information that's easy to translate. The only way you can test your RAM after installation is to actually boot your computer.

However, if you have the wrong kind of RAM, that may be too late. You could risk damage to the module or perhaps the logic board by installing the wrong type. So I must emphasize that, before you attempt installation, you check the original packaging or invoice to see if it has the proper labeling. If in doubt, call the dealer and ask what you need to do to confirm you have the right product.

Not All RAM Is the Same

Wouldn't it be great if all RAM chips were the same? When you buy a new Mac, you could simply move the module from the old model to the new, thereby extending your investment.

Alas, this is not to be. There are a number of different types of RAM available for Macs of one sort or another, and you cannot mix and match. What works with one model may cause problems with another, even if it looks exactly the same.

Here's a very basic guide to the kind of RAM that's available. Your best approach, when you buy RAM, is to make sure your dealer knows exactly which make and model you have, so there's no room for confusion. Some RAM modules may come in packaging that lists the make and model it's designed for, but since most of the time Apple uses industry-standard RAM for many of their newest models, the label may not be informative.

CAUTION *Using RAM that is not suitable for your Mac could damage the module itself or your Mac's logic board. If you have the slightest doubt about whether the memory upgrade is suitable for your Mac, check the technical specifications that came with your Mac or ask your dealer for assistance.*

■ **SIMMs** Short for Single Inline Memory Modules, this is the original RAM technology. Various versions of these modules worked on just about every kind of Mac from the original compact Macs (except for the earliest models through the Mac Plus) up through the first generation Power Macintosh models. When you buy SIMMs for these models, make sure you get the correct number of modules. Most installations require you install either two or four at a time.

■ **DIMMs**   Beginning with the PCI Power Macs, the second generation, Apple went to something called DIMMs (Dual Inline Memory Modules). The larger, 168-pin DIMM modules could be installed in single units, though some Power Macs and Mac OS clones benefit from interleaving, if you install identical DIMMs in matching memory banks (Bank A and Bank B).

■ **EDO RAM**   Not all DIMMs are created equal (as you might expect). One of the variations, EDO (Extended Data Out), is designed to give nearly the same level of improvement as interleaved RAM, but it only works in a small number of Macs and Mac OS clones.

CAUTION   *To make matters doubly confusing, Apple has offered models that use either 3.3-volt and 5-volt EDO RAM. You cannot mix and match. Double-check the RAM your Mac needs when you place your order.*

■ **SDRAM**   The first generation Power Macintosh G3 and PowerBook G3 models incorporated still another variation on the memory theme, SDRAM (Synchronous Dynamic Random Access Memory). The word "synchronous" means that the clock speed of this sort of RAM chip synchronizes with the Mac's CPU. Obviously, the size of a RAM upgrade module that fits a PowerBook won't work on a desktop Mac.

■ **SO-DIMMs**   This kind of RAM module (Small Outline Dual Inline Memory Module) runs on both G3 PowerBooks and first generation iMacs. You'll need to check with your dealer as to which sort of RAM is required for your model.

■ **PC 100 DIMMs**   Beginning with the Blue & White Power Macintosh G3 line (and the second generation, or slot-loading, iMacs), Apple went to a type of SDRAM that would support the 100Mhz system bus. PC 100, as the name implies, is a standard for RAM used on PCs as well. As with other types of RAM, you need to make sure you buy a module that supports the model you have. Not all PC 100 DIMMs are created equal.

Checking RAM Compatibility

CAUTION *Watch out for so-called composite SIMMs, which are made up of a large number of small chips (16 or higher) to provide the rated capacity. Having lots of little chips on a single module is cheaper to make and can save you a few dollars, but it can also cause timing errors and possible crashes. Apple doesn't recommend composite memory for any of their models.*

I have not tried to cover all subdivisions of RAM types available on various Macs, and won't even attempt to predict the future. As soon as Apple standardizes on one type of RAM module, it seems they are apt to find still another kind for another model line.

How Do I Know What to Add?

There are many ways to skin a cat, and many logic board layouts to confront, not to mention the kind of RAM chips you need.

If you still have it, the first and best resource is the original manual that came with your Mac or the technical information booklet. If neither is available, check out Apple's AppleSpec database, which is available to view or download directly from their Web site at http://www.info.apple.com/applespec/applespec.taf.

Another helpful resource is a RAM vendor, NewerRAM (at http://www .newerram.com). Not only do they provide a wealth of information at their Web site about the various sorts of RAM available for Macs (and those long-gone Mac OS clones), they also offer a free program, GURU (see Figure 4-1), an easy way to check on the RAM needs of your Mac. You can download the latest version of GURU directly from their Web site, or check this book's CD.

The Benefits of Interleaving

Some Macs, notably some Quadra models and second generation Power Macs (the first models with a PCI peripheral bus), benefit from a technique known as *interleaving*.

When you install identical RAM modules in groups of two or four (depending on the model), the entire memory bank is addressed by the computer's logic board as a single unit. The net effect of this technical hocus-pocus is that your Mac runs a little faster (usually from 5 to 10 percent). If you install RAM of unequal size, you lose the benefit.

None of the current Macs, with their ultra-fast G3 or G4 CPUs, benefits from memory interleaving.

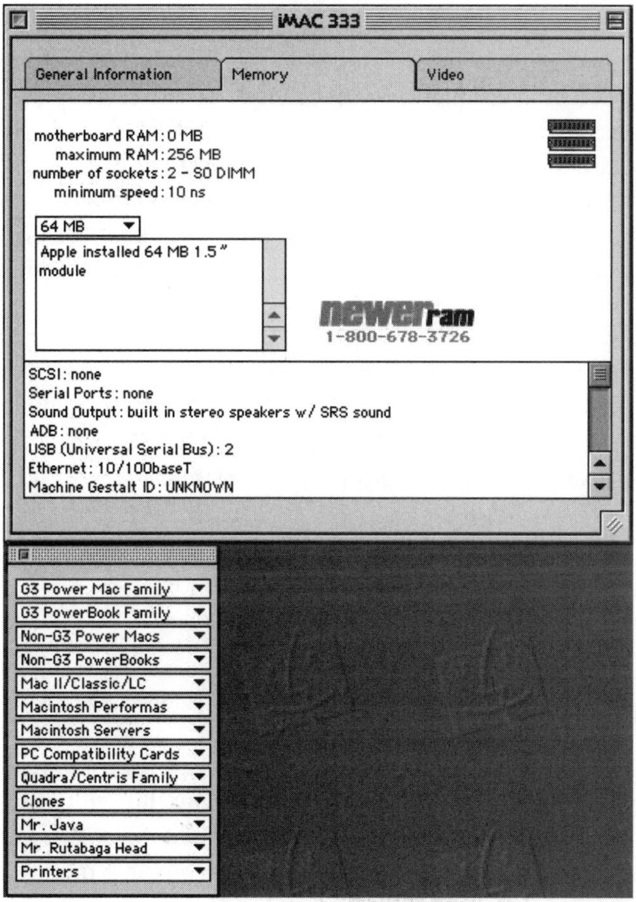

FIGURE 4-1   NewerRAM's GURU software gives you a wealth of information about the RAM your Mac needs and how to install it

Why the Price Difference?

RAM prices are volatile, sometimes more so than the price of oil on the world market. You'll find upgrades selling for $100 one week, and maybe quite a bit more the next. You'll also find widely varying prices from vendor to vendor.

Market conditions in Asia, where a large amount of the world's RAM chip supply is produced, can also affect the process, in addition to natural disasters (such as the major earthquake that occurred in Taipei at the time this book was written).

So the question arises: Does it make a difference? Isn't memory a commodity product?

Here's a simple guide to memory purchases. Most of the world's memory chips are produced by the same basic set of manufacturers. They are generally produced to meet a similar set of specifications. But it's up to the RAM vendor to test the modules and make sure that they do indeed work as advertised.

When you buy RAM, don't hesitate to shop around, and don't hesitate to negotiate with a dealer, if you're making a large system purchase. Not all prices are fixed and a dealer may be happy to sacrifice a little profit on a large order to keep a customer.

If you're buying RAM from a dealer that strictly specializes in RAM and other upgrades, you'll want to subject them to the same sort of scrutiny you subject any business from whom you want to make a purchase. Check them out with the Better Business Bureau or consumer agency in their home city. Check online message boards, in newsgroups or on AOL or CompuServe, and see what other customers have to say about these vendors.

You should also consult the product warranty. Some vendors offer "lifetime" warranties, which means they are honor-bound to replace the RAM upgrade module if it fails.

Adding RAM Upgrades to Regular Desktop Macs

You'd think with the easiest-to-use operating system, Mac users would have a relatively easy task when adding a RAM upgrade. But this isn't always the case. Apple doesn't seem to have given due consideration to the consequences of their design decisions in laying out the internal workings of some models.

Here are potential pitfalls:

■ **Nightmare installations**   The Blue & White Power Mac G3, the Power Mac G4, and the earliest modular Macs (such as the II series, the IIcx, IIci, and so on) were conveniently designed for simple RAM upgrades. Not so some of the minitower models, beginning with the Quadra 800, and continuing through the 8500 and 9500 series. In order to upgrade RAM on those models, you had to disconnect several sets of wiring harnesses and actually remove expansion cards, the CPU card, the on/off switch, and the logic board itself. This job was a royal pain and a half. I've done the task dozens of times and I recommend the task to nobody. This is one set of designs where you may want to have your dealer take on the headache (and the risks) of the RAM installation.

The folks who designed this impossible-to-upgrade case departed Apple long before the company designed the easy-to-upgrade successors, the 8600 and 9600. When these two models were first opened up before an audience of Apple supporters, to show how easy upgrades were, they all applauded.

■ **Sharp corners**   This one seldom gets into any documentation, but the insides of many Macs have little metallic fittings and chassis components with rather sharp corners, and it's not hard to rub your finger against one of these pieces and get a nasty cut. You'll find that Mac OS clones (especially the ones from Power Computing), which often had slightly redesigned PC clone cases, are the worst offenders. Take it from me, it never hurts to have a package of bandages at hand. I remember a few instances when Mrs. Steinberg threw a fit, with plenty of justification, when she found blood spots on the carpet from an injury I sustained while handling one of these tasks.

NOTE *Before you do your RAM upgrade, be sure you have your toolkit handy. Depending on the make and model, you'll need a regular flat-edged and Philips-head screwdriver. If the memory vendor supplied such a device, be sure to put the wrist strap on either hand, then attach the clip at the other end to your Mac's power supply as soon as the case is opened.*

A Basic RAM Upgrade How-To

Once you get your RAM upgrade, you only need to make a few simple preparations and you're ready to begin the installation process.

TIP *The latest versions of Apple System Profiler will report on your Mac's actual memory configuration. Before you go to the bother of opening the case and encountering a surprise, check the listing on the opening screen, under Memory Overview, which displays your Mac's built-in memory setup, so you can see which slots are filled and what size RAM is being used.*

The following steps are presented as a general set of guidelines, since almost every Mac model family has a different set of instructions that apply to them. But if you follow the process with care, you'll be able to handle a RAM upgrade on just about any Mac to come down the pike:

1. Shut down your Mac and all attached peripherals.

Adding RAM Upgrades
to Regular Desktop Macs

2. Disconnect *all* cables from your Mac except for the power cord (you'll see why in a moment).

3. Unscrew the case and remove it. In some Performa models, you'll have to slide out the logic board to gain access. Consult your manual or Apple's technical information database for instructions that apply to your Mac if it's not immediately obvious from the layout.

> **NOTE** *If the disassembly process is really complex, such as those dreaded older Mac minitower models, have a paper and pencil on hand to write down what you removed and from where. This will help guide you to an easier reassembly process. (Don't forget the bandages for your cut fingers.)*

4. Touch the power supply (it's usually a big rectangular box with drilled holes, often having a label indicating its power capacity). This helps drain off static electricity. If you have a wrist strap, attach the other end to the power supply.

> **NOTE** *Beginning with the Power Macintosh 7200 and 7500 series and continuing with the 8600 and 9600 minitowers, Apple provided a convenient pop-out chassis to make RAM upgrades easier. This technology became even simpler beginning with the Blue & White Power Macs, where you can generally install a RAM upgrade in a minute or so.*

5. Go ahead and remove the power cord; don't have the unit plugged in as you complete the process (or at least turn off the power strip, if the unit is attached to one).

6. If necessary, remove any parts that surround the RAM slots. Some Apple models require removal of expansion cards, CPU cards, and the logic board itself. Some Mac OS clones require removal of a hard drive assembly or other components to get at these slots.

7. Locate the empty slots for your RAM upgrade. If they are already filled, you may need to recheck the configuration (see the tip earlier in this section about running Apple System Profiler first).

8. Position your RAM upgrade module so the pins precisely match the layout of the ones in the slot (they'll only install properly in one direction).

9. Place each RAM module in position and snap into place. On some models, you have to insert at an angle, making sure the RAM is seated in the slots, then snap into the upright position. In either case, you may have to gently move a retaining clip aside.

CAUTION

Don't force the RAM module into place. You risk damaging the slot or the delicate pins that enclose it, which would require a logic board replacement.

NOTE

If the empty slot is between other RAM modules, you may want to remove the module in front of the one you want to install, to make installation easier.

10. Repeat steps 7 and 8 for each RAM module you intend to install.

CAUTION

It's a good idea not to walk around between steps, especially on a carpeted floor, where you may give yourself a new dose of static electricity. Best to do your bathroom visits before you begin.

11. Recheck the RAM modules to make sure they are properly seated.

12. Reinstall the logic board or any other parts that are required in the reassembly process.

CAUTION

In general, it's a bad idea to even try to run your Mac without closing everything up. While some modular models do run with the case off, you risk a possible shock hazard and damage to delicate components if you touch the wrong thing when it's running.

13. Close the case and attach screws or thumb-nuts or whatever is used to tighten down the case.

NOTE

Don't be surprised if you have to spend a few minutes aligning the case to the chassis on some models. If you don't fit everything together precisely, you may not be able to get the screws back in.

14. Reattach the mouse and keyboard and then the AC cord. Leave the peripheral jacks alone for now; you just want to make sure everything works properly.

Adding RAM Upgrades to Regular Desktop Macs

15. Turn on your Mac. If it starts all right, go right to the Apple menu, and open the window labeled About This Computer (or About This Macintosh for earlier system versions). Verify that the built-in memory is equal to the total amount installed.

16. If the RAM installation is successful, shut everything down (if necessary) and reattach your peripheral components, such as hard drives, scanners, and so on. After your memory upgrade has been installed, it's a good idea to spend some time running your favorite programs to make sure that there are no mysterious performance problems.

Adding RAM Upgrades to the iMac

While Apple has made moves toward simple RAM upgrades in their product line, the first generations of iMacs were a throwback to the bad old days.

In order to upgrade iMac RAM on these units, you literally have to tear it apart, first by removing the back cover, then by pulling off cable harnesses and extracting the logic board. As clever as Apple's industrial design is from the outside, on the inside, it's a hassle to upgrade.

Fortunately, Apple resolved such headaches in clever fashion with the second generation or "slot-loading" iMacs. With these models, you easily access a RAM or an AirPort networking card slot simply by opening an access panel at the bottom of the unit. You don't even need a screwdriver—you can use a quarter to turn the screw to release the panel.

But here are some things you'll want to consider if you choose to upgrade your first generation iMac's RAM:

■ **Look for the offers of free RAM.** This is definitely designed to get you off the hook. Many dealers offer free RAM upgrades when you buy a new iMac. Some add a small service charge, but whatever it is should be a great price to pay for your freedom from having to handle this task. Of course, unless you're buying a closeout first generation iMac, the installation fee doesn't make a lot of sense, since you can do the job yourself in minutes.

■ **The rear cover can be difficult to remove.** The first part of the RAM upgrade process on those first generation iMacs is to loosen and remove a Philips-head screw and lift off the back cover. In my experience, they tend to stick, and you may find yourself dragging hard on the pull handle to get it apart. The iMac's polycarbonate case is sturdy, however, so if you have to give it a couple of stiff tugs, don't fret.

CAUTION *Once you get the rear cover off, place your iMac screen face-down on a soft cloth or paper towel to prevent it from being scratched.*

■ **Move the cables out of the way.**   Once you've pulled off the back cover, you have to remove several sets of cables from jacks on the logic board. After the cables have been unplugged, spread them aside to give enough room to pull the logic board assembly out. This is a slightly awkward process, as the cables tend to catch on the edges of the chassis.

■ **Pull the logic board assembly out carefully.**   The chassis includes the hard drive and CD drive as well, and you'll want to take care in removing everything to avoid the possibility of damage to any of these delicate components.

■ **Don't tighten the screws too much.**   After you install your RAM upgrade on an iMac, you have to replace a heat sink. Screw everything in hand-tight. Don't use a power screwdriver and don't make things too tight. If the threads are stripped, you'll be in for a repair bill if you need to take things apart again (either for a larger RAM module or in case the RAM upgrade doesn't function properly).

■ **Put everything back together before testing.**   It's all right to leave the back cover off while you test your RAM upgrade for proper performance. But everything else should be placed back in position and screwed together.

■ **Consult About This Computer.**   Go to the Apple menu and bring up the About This Computer window to check that the amount of built-in memory is correct. If the numbers don't add up, shut down, take everything apart, and reseat your RAM upgrade module. If the RAM still isn't recognized, remove it, pack everything up, and contact the dealer from whom you got the RAM upgrade.

NOTE *If you want further information on installing RAM on a first generation iMac, you can retrieve two handy technical information documents from Apple's Web site on the subject. The URL for the first part is http://til.info.apple.com/techinfo.nsf/artnum/n43012. The second part of the instructions shows up as a link on the first page, but is available separately at http://til.info.apple.com/techinfo.nsf/artnum/n43013.*

Adding RAM Upgrades to the iMac

Adding RAM Upgrades to iBooks and PowerBooks

The PowerBook is another Apple product line where upgrades have traditionally been, shall we say, a little dicey. It's not that it is so hard to open a PowerBook's case. But up until the so-called "Wall Street" PowerBook G3 arrived, you needed to use special screwdrivers, of the Torx 8 and Torx 10 variety (with six sides), to undo the screws.

> **NOTE**   *An earlier version of the PowerBook G3, which used the same chassis as the PowerBook 3400, still required Torx screwdrivers to open the case for RAM installation.*

Why Apple would choose such an unusual form factor is anyone's guess, but nonetheless that's the way it is, to quote the famous phrase of a former TV news anchor.

Fortunately, with the arrival of the upgraded PowerBook G3 product line and the iBook, Apple got the idea and took steps to make RAM installations simple. They even provide step-by-step instructions in the manuals, or in the case of the iBook, inside the unit itself.

Here are some basics about PowerBook RAM installation:

- **Turn it off.**   Many of you keep your PowerBooks in Sleep mode most of the time. Before you do a RAM installation, don't forget to bring the PowerBook back to life, and shut it down. Then remove the battery and any expansion bay or PC card peripherals before you attempt your RAM upgrade.

- **Protect the screen.**   On some PowerBook models, you will be lifting the keyboard and placing it atop the delicate LCD display. Protect the screen with a paper towel or soft cloth before you rest the keyboard against it.

- **Watch out for paper-thin cables.**   The consequence of the clever miniaturization of the PowerBook is ultra-small components. This is especially true for the connection cables inside, which are paper-thin and subject to easy damage.

- **Look for a loose video cable on G3 "Wall Street" PowerBooks.**   Some of the G3 PowerBooks using 13.3-inch screens suffered from weird screen defects, such as a white vertical band appearing at one end of the display. The cause was traced to a loose video cable. Since the RAM upgrade on these models sits at the left of the video cable, make sure the cable is plugged in tightly while you've got the case opened.

NOTE   *If weird screen symptoms don't disappear when you reseat the video cable, contact Apple's customer service department or your dealer for service. In some instances, the cable may have to be replaced with a newer design (I know, it happened to me).*

- **Don't misplace those screws.**   On many PowerBooks, you will be removing screws from the bottom of the case. Sometimes the screws seem to stick in there, so you have to shake the PowerBook a bit to get them to fall out. And they are easily misplaced. A paper towel or ashtray is a great place to put these little parts so you have them when you need them.

- **Don't force the RAM to fit.**   As I said, the PowerBook's guts are more delicate than other Macs. Don't try to force the RAM module to fit. If you have a problem, contact your dealer for assistance. Even the most complex PowerBook RAM installations can be done by your dealer in less than a half hour, and they shouldn't charge you more than a very basic service fee if you'd rather have them do the job.

- **Don't try to use a PowerBook with an open case.**   You should put everything back together before you attempt to use your PowerBook with its new RAM upgrade.

- **Check About This Computer when you're done.**   As soon as you complete your PowerBook RAM installation, boot your PowerBook or iBook and go right to the Apple menu. Choose About This Computer and check to make sure that the numbers listed for your laptop's built-in memory are correct. If not, shut everything down, open the case, and remove and reinstall the RAM upgrade. If it still doesn't work, contact your dealer for assistance.

How to Know If RAM Is Properly Installed

How to Know If RAM Is Properly Installed

RAM installation is usually an either/or process. If you have seated the modules properly in their slots, your final test is to boot your Mac. If it starts up, you know (well, usually) that you've properly installed the RAM upgrade.

However, it's not always clear-cut, and sometimes a slight misalignment of the module in the slot will allow your Mac to boot most times, but sometimes you'll encounter intermittent startup problems. My case history for this chapter covers one such incident, which actually occurred to one of my clients only a few weeks before I wrote this chapter.

Case History

Intermittent Startups

The problems were vexing to my client. After installing a RAM upgrade, sometimes the Mac wouldn't start at all, and on occasion, all that was heard were the dreaded "chimes of death" (see the next section), as if someone was trying to tune up a musical instrument.

It was clear the Mac was telling the client that there was a hardware problem of some sort. I was assured the RAM was installed correctly, and that the problem was rare. On the other hand, the Mac would crash just a little too often to be normal, so I suggested it wouldn't hurt to check into the situation.

The client was cautious. This was the Mac he used to write advertising copy and press releases; if it went down even for a short time, he'd blow his deadlines.

When I arrived at the client's small suburban office, I shut the system down and pried the cover off the Mac, an entry-level PowerPC that was several years old. I inspected the RAM chips, and noticed that one of the four modules didn't seem to be seated fully. As a precaution, I removed, then reinstalled, all four modules, making sure each component was firmly seated in the slot. I restarted the Mac, and it worked just fine.

Then the client proceeded to work with a few programs that had been generating those awful crashes, and the crashes were gone. I shut down the computer several times, then rebooted with no return of the awful symptoms.

The problem was gone, never to return. That ever-so-slight degree to which the RAM wasn't inserted properly was enough to cause unstable performance.

Interpreting the Signs That Something Went Wrong

When your Mac boots, it goes through a basic routine of self-testing. The hardware is checked, and then your Mac's hardware looks for the presence of a working System Folder. At this point, you'll see your Happy Mac face, which tells you that the first part of the process is done.

But if something is drastically wrong, the boot process will come to a screeching halt (and you can sometimes interpret that phrase literally). Instead of a normal startup process, one of the following symptoms may occur:

■ **Chimes of death**   Your Mac's screen will remain dark, and you'll hear several musical tones. They usually signify that the RAM test has failed. This is a catastrophic failure, meaning that one or more RAM chips is not properly installed or is defective. On some models, the sound will more closely resemble that of a car crashing.

NOTE   *Other less common causes of this problem include defective logic boards, CPU cards, or video RAM. But if the symptoms accompany the installation of new RAM, that's the first place to look for a solution.*

■ **Sad Mac**   There are a bunch of Sad Mac messages, but they all signify some sort of hardware related issue. Sometimes it's hard drive related, sometimes related to RAM problems.

NOTE   *A Sad Mac screen sometimes occurs when you've got a SyQuest cartridge inserted in one of their removable drives. The fast solution to this problem is simply to eject the cartridge and restart.*

■ **Gray screen**   This sort of problem usually relates to something other than the RAM, such as a problem loading a hard drive device driver, a graphic card problem, a SCSI-related conflict, or another hardware issue. But if it follows a RAM installation, you'll have a likely cause for the problem.

■ **Dark screen**   This symptom may indicate bad RAM, but if the symptom isn't accompanied by one of those dreadful sounds I mentioned earlier, it could signify other problems. These include a logic board, CPU card, or power supply failure, or a bad PRAM battery. Problems with your Mac's graphic card (loose or defective) can also contribute to this symptom, not to mention problems with your Mac's display. I cover this subject in more detail in Chapter 3 and Chapter 10.

> **NOTE** *Before you concern yourself over the hardware, first tighten everything up, and if that doesn't help, go ahead and replace the PRAM battery. It is a common cause of such problems, and the PRAM battery is cheap enough to replace.*

Startup Failure Solutions

Sometimes just restarting your Mac may be sufficient to get things working properly, but more often than not, you need to do a little sleuthing to locate the cause of the trouble.

Here are some things to check:

■ **Your new RAM installation** Remove and replace your Mac's RAM upgrade module. Visually check to be sure each module is properly installed. It should be a pretty snug fit, and the pins should be fully or mostly seated in the RAM slot. If anything looks a little loose, you may get total failure or an intermittent failure (see my Case History for this chapter for further details). The best solution is just to remove the RAM and reseat the module, making sure it's seated properly. You'll feel a little "clunk" when it snaps in place. If you run into a real problem making it fit properly (and sometimes it takes a somewhat energetic push), remove the module and check with the dealer to make sure it's the right type for your Mac. As I said, you can't visually inspect for internal differences; all you can do is make sure the pins line up with the slots and the chip is pointed in the right direction.

■ **Failure of another component** Even if you took care in draining static electricity during your RAM installation, if one of the hardware components on your Mac is poised for failure, this could be the time for it to occur. You'll want to remove your RAM upgrade and, if necessary, restore your previous RAM module or modules. Once you slap everything together again, verify for proper operation. If the Mac still refuses to boot, contact your dealer about possible service.

The Difficult Symptoms of Intermittent RAM Failures

When your Mac refuses to boot, at least you know there's a problem, and you have some areas to explore to solve it. But not all RAM-related problems are so easy to spot. In fact, most times, the failure will only rear its head at random, thus making the process of figuring out a cause ever so difficult.

If you've looked at a RAM upgrade or two, you've seen that it has at least several memory chips on it. If even one of those chips fails, completely or in part, you'll begin to experience strange symptoms on your Mac. You'll encounter crashes for no good reason. You'll try each and every one of the diagnostic steps I've covered in this book, to no avail.

Routine test procedures just won't show anything wrong. Your Mac will seem to be working just fine, except for those rare, unexpected crashes.

But if the onset of those symptoms follows a RAM upgrade, you'll have an indication that this may be where to look for a solution to the problem.

A Convenient Method for Testing RAM

Apple dealers use a program from the manufacturer called MacTest Pro to do their RAM tests. It's quite thorough, but slow as the blazes. Figure on it taking from 20 to 40 minutes per MB of RAM, depending on the speed of your Mac. Imagine how long a typical desktop Mac loaded up with 256MB or 512MB of RAM would take if you ran this sort of test on it.

Fortunately, you don't have to be a dealer to test your Mac's RAM. Your option is a handy program from MicroMat called TechTool Pro. As I explain in Chapter 13, one of the important components of TechTool Pro is its ability to check and repair hard drive directory damage and optimize the drive.

NOTE   *There is a free version of this program, called simply TechTool, which is designed to zap your Mac's PRAM and rebuild the desktop. (You can find TechTool on this book's CD.) The advanced diagnostic features are reserved for the retail version of the product. In addition, Apple will give you a modified version of the program, called TechTool Deluxe, if you sign up for the version of their AppleCare extended warranty program that was introduced in October 1999.*

Among the many features of TechTool Pro is the ability to test your Mac's RAM and report if there are any problems. You have a number of test options, depending on how extensive a test you want to run.

Interpreting the Signs
That Something Went Wrong

Here's how they work (this description applies to version 2 or later):

TechTool's RAM tests run most efficiently if you boot your Mac with extensions off. This is done by restarting and holding down the SHIFT key until you see an "Extensions Disabled" message. If your Mac successfully completes the test, go ahead and restart normally.

Running a Fast RAM Test

1. Launch TechTool Pro.

2. Choose Standard from the Interface menu (the choice will be grayed out if that option is already selected).

3. Uncheck all diagnostic options except for RAM. This will produce a screen such as the one shown in Figure 4-2. The test will also include the PRAM, ROM, and VRAM.

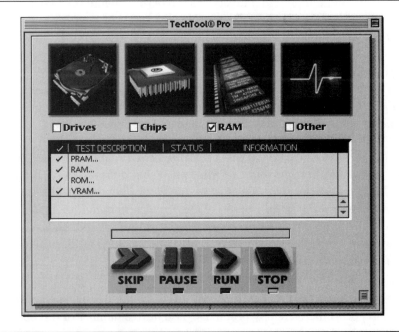

FIGURE 4-2   This is TechTool Pro's Standard interface, ready to run a series of RAM and related tests

4. If there's a problem with your Mac's RAM or any of the other components being tested, you'll see an onscreen dialog explaining what is wrong and what MicroMat suggests you do to solve the problem. If the Mac is all right, you'll also see a report to that effect (see Figure 4-3.). You can read the report on your Mac's screen or save or print it for later review.

Running an Extended RAM Test

1. Launch TechTool Pro.

2. Choose Expert from the Interface menu (the choice will be grayed out if that option is already selected). This option will produce the screen shown in Figure 4-4.

FIGURE 4-3   Looks like the author's Mac is in tip-top shape, based on this TechTool Pro RAM test report

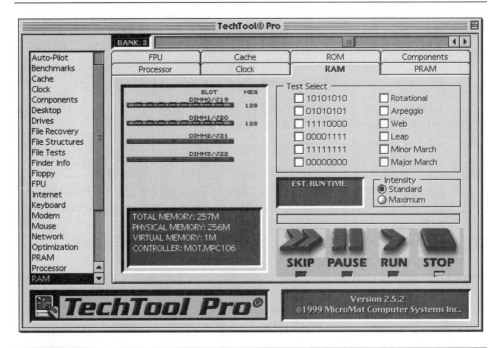

FIGURE 4-4 Choose your TechTool Pro expert test choices here

3. Scroll through the list of tests on the left pane, and click on RAM, which brings up the display of RAM test options shown in Figure 4-5.

4. In the upper-left corner of the RAM test pane, you'll see an illustration of your Mac's memory configuration. This is an alternate way to see what your Mac has (in case your Mac has an older system version without Apple System Profiler at hand). Check the Standard Intensity setting for this test.

5. Click on all test cycles, except for Minor March and Major March. While these tests are useful, they are also so intensive that it would take many hours to complete them (in the spirit of Apple's MacTest Pro). They're recommended strictly as a last resort, in case the regular test cycle produces no result and you still have problems.

NOTE *The Maximum test suites are even more intensive and can take days to complete. The shorter tests ought to be sufficient to get you a useful result.*

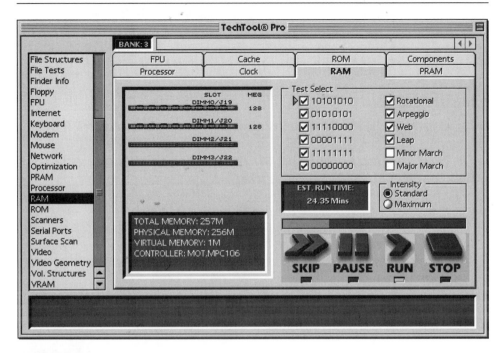

FIGURE 4-5   Choose your RAM tests from this window (which shows the test already in progress)

6. To begin the tests, click Run. You'll see an estimate of the time it takes to finish the process. The estimate shown in Figure 4-5, 24.35 minutes, is based on a Blue & White Power Macintosh G3/400 with 256MB of RAM. I won't attempt to predict how long it'll take on an older Mac with a similar memory configuration.

NOTE   *If the test seems to be taking up too much of your time without any result, you can use the Pause or Stop buttons to bring the process to a halt. When you choose Pause, you can resume it later on wherever it left off (so long as you haven't quit the program).*

7. Should TechTool's extended RAM test find a problem, you'll see an onscreen dialog explaining what is wrong and what to do to handle the problem.

If your Mac is still displaying weird symptoms, and the RAM tests and all your other diagnostic measures produce a big zero, contact the dealer from whom you purchased the RAM for further assistance. At that point, the complexity of the problem may be beyond what you can diagnose in your home or office.

Coming Next

In this chapter, you learned ways to ensure your RAM upgrade is successful, and how to handle problems should your RAM installation go awry.

In the next chapter, we'll take our Macs on the road. You'll learn how to prepare for your trip, what you need to take, and, just as important, what to do if you run into a problem.

Chapter 5

Troubleshooting Macs on the Road

Y ou have to take a business trip to Seattle, or even Paris or Glasgow. But you need to work on mission-critical documents for the business presentation, or perhaps finish that special piece of artwork to make the meeting go just right.

Or you're preparing, at long last, to take the family on a vacation and you need to stay in touch with your company or personal email. Maybe you just want to have a computer game along in case the kids get bored and need something to do when it's raining or Mom and Dad are busy getting ready for a day of fun and frolic.

In this chapter, I'll give you some hard-won advice on how to maximize use of an Apple iBook, PowerBook or Duo—and what to do if things go really wrong.

The Care and Feeding of Laptops

It's sometimes hard to keep up. Apple's product lines change so often; just as soon as you get used to the features and quirks of one product, it's discontinued and another one introduced. If the automobile industry acted this way, you'd have a 2000 model, a 2000.5 model—wait a minute, we do see this sort of behavior in that industry already.

But whether new or old, laptop computers are designed for rather rugged use, far beyond that of a desktop model. That doesn't mean you can use them as Frisbees, or that they'll survive a drop onto a hard surface. But it does mean they can wobble around in a case, or be moved from here to there and back again and manage to survive.

In the next few pages, I'll cover ways to keep your Apple laptop running safe and sound and how to solve typical problems.

Do You Need an Extended Warranty on Laptops?

I normally don't recommend getting an extended warranty, because they don't offer protection commensurate with their cost. For one thing, computers are more likely to fail early in their life cycle or too late for the warranty plan to do any good. Also, such warranties are generally a big profit item for the dealer, which is why they offer them, and they do not necessarily save you enough in potential repair costs to cover what you pay.

On the other hand, laptop computers are subjected to more extreme use than desktops. Therefore they are far more vulnerable to problems. While no warranty will cover you if you drop your laptop or damage the expensive LCD display somehow, other components could fail. If the warranty is inexpensive enough it may be worth it. For example, the version of Apple Computer's AppleCare Protection Plan available when this book was written extends your new product warranty for three years, and offers toll-free technical support, extra online support, and a special system diagnosis CD (based on MicroMat's TechTool Pro).

Cleaning Your PowerBook's Display

Yes, I know. Those LCD screens are flexible and flimsy looking, and you wonder what to do if they get a little smudged. Fortunately, they can be cleaned easily. All you need do is turn off the computer, then take a clean, soft, lint-free cloth or paper towel (such as Bounty or Viva) and dampen it slightly.

CAUTION *Don't even think about spraying any liquid onto the LCD screen. I don't need to say any more.*

Wipe the screen gently, don't bear down. If the screen remains dirty, give it another shot.

According to Apple Computer's technical information document on the subject, you may even try applying a mild glass cleaner to the cloth or paper towel (and that's one that doesn't have alcohol or ammonia on the ingredients list) or check your dealer and see if they have a cleaning kit designed for LCD screens. One such product is Klear Screen from Meridrew Enterprises. You can check out the product at their Web site: http://www.klearscreen.com.

NOTE *These steps apply in equal fashion if you have an LCD display for your desktop Mac.*

Making Your Battery Go Farther

Although battery technology has improved over the years and Apple has found newer and better power management schemes, the fact of the matter is that batteries last just so long, and then they give up the ghost. However, that's no consolation if you're not near an AC power source (such as in the middle of a transatlantic flight where you hoped to finish your work or that new DVD before landing).

Obviously, there are no perpetual motion machines for iBooks and PowerBooks (and the now-departed Duo)—well, at least not yet. So in this little section, I'll give you some advice on how to conserve battery life and what preparations you might take to get a longer lifetime out of your Apple laptop.

The Care and Feeding of Laptops

Here are some suggestions on how to handle the situation:

■ **Put in a second battery.**   If you have a PowerBook 3400 series or one of the G3 models, you have two expansion bays for extra drives or batteries. While you may need one of them for a CD, DVD, or removable drive, if you don't have immediate need of these items, you can remove them and put a second battery in that slot. You get more than double the battery life. I say more, because the expansion bay drive isn't draining any extra juice from the battery.

■ **Remove everything but the battery.**   Following the preceding suggestion, even if you have two expansion bays, there's no reason to keep both of them filled.

■ **Turn off AppleTalk.**   You're not hooked up to a network (unless, of course, you are communicating with another Apple computer using an AirPort wireless networking module), so go to the Chooser and turn off AppleTalk (a restart shouldn't be needed). Now some of the system checks the computer does when AppleTalk is loaded won't drain power. Just remember to turn it back on when you're ready to network with another Mac or printer.

■ **Turn off virtual memory.**   A nice feature of Apple's power management system is the ability to shut down unused laptop subsystems, such as your hard drive. But with virtual memory on, the hard drive must be powered up and accessed to swap unneeded data from the memory. While some programs, such as Microsoft Word, do like to read the hard drive whenever possible, anything you can do to let the hard drive sleep will extend battery life.

TIP   *If you don't need to use special formatting when writing a document, you can write it in SimpleText first, then open it in a full-featured word processor later on when you can return to AC power.*

■ **Use the Energy Saver Control Panel.**   Apple already builds some useful power conservation features into its Energy Saver Control Panel (see Figure 5-1). It's available directly from the Control Panels folder (from the Apple menu) or with a handy Control Strip module. The standard settings are perfectly fine to give a useful combination of sleep settings for the computer, the display, and hard disk. If you want to customize the setting, click the Show Details button (as displayed in Figure 5-2) and experiment to your heart's content (just remember to make sure Battery instead of AC Adapter is listed in the pop-up menu). You'll do best on the road to keep your hard disk sleep interval, the setting at the bottom of Figure 5-2, as short as possible. If you use software that constantly accesses the drive, there isn't a whole lot you can do anyway.

NOTE

If you have a version of the Mac OS without an Energy Saver Control Panel, look for a control panel labeled PowerBook, which will have a similar set of controls.

TIP

You can check whether the hard disk is spinning by examining the Control Strip for your PowerBook or Energy Saver settings, and, if need be, you can use the Control Strip to manually spin it down.

- **Reduce backlighting.**   If your Apple laptop has an adjustment for backlight (and some only offer adjustments for brightness), you can reduce it as much as possible. Don't use a screen saver, as screen savers will access the hard drive to call up those fancy desktop patterns.

- **Reduce brightness.**   Well, I wouldn't suggest you start squinting to see the screen, but bring it down as much as you can without making it hard to see.

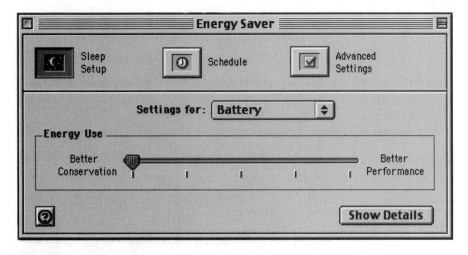

FIGURE 5-1   Move the slider to the left to engage your Apple laptop's power saving capabilities

The Care and Feeding of Laptops

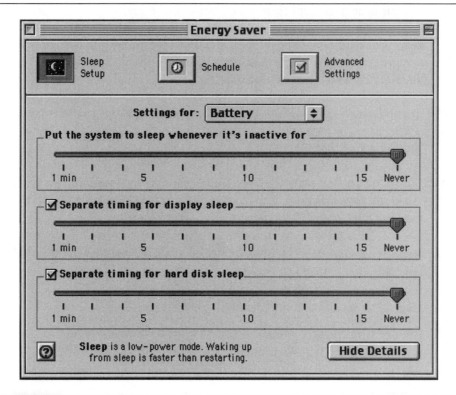

FIGURE 5-2 Click a check box and move a slider to get the setting you want

- ■ **Don't use a dark desktop pattern.** It may look nice on the screen, but dark pixels are "on" when it comes to LCD screens, which means they use more current than light pixels (which are considered "off"). You can choose your desktop patterns in the Appearance Control Panel.

- ■ **If the option is available, allow processor cycling.** Every little bit helps, and if the processor is asked to do less work, it'll use less juice. Processor cycling is available as an Advanced Setting in the Energy Saver Control Panel. Older versions of the PowerBook Control Panel will have a two-position switch labeled Easy and Custom to get the extra choices (you have to also hold down the OPTION key to see the processor cycling selections). Just bear in mind that when you select processor cycling, your PowerBook becomes a lot slower. It may, however, make the difference when it comes to the PowerBook's battery surviving long enough for you.

■ **Don't surf the Internet.**   If you're logged on while under battery power, consider getting off as soon as you can. The modem, whether built in or on a PC card, will extract more power to do its stuff. In addition, Internet access will deliver files to your hard drive (even such a simple thing as accessing a Web site, unless you've created a RAM disk for your Web cache).

■ **Remove PC cards.**   You can lessen drain of the battery's power simply by removing the PC card modem, networking card, or other such device.

■ **Disconnect expansion devices.**   System resources that access FireWire, SCSI, or USB can drain power, even if those devices are connected to a separate power supply (or may have their own battery power source). My suggestion is that if you don't need them, power down and remove them.

■ **Play it low.**   When you run your PowerBook's or iBook's speakers loud, it may sound better, but it also increases current draw. Headphones draw less power. So if you want to watch *Armageddon* or *The Fifth Element* on your PowerBook's DVD player, and still experience all the great special effect sounds, consider that a good headphone from your favorite stereo store will sound much, much better than the tiny speakers on your computer.

■ **Try a RAM disk.**   If your computer has lots of extra memory, consider setting some aside for a RAM disk (the setting is made in the Memory Control Panel and requires a restart). You can run programs from the RAM disk, save files to the RAM disk, even use it for your Web cache (if you're not using AOL, that is), and these operations will allow you to keep the hard drive in Sleep mode. Just remember to select the option to save the contents of the RAM disk to your hard drive on shutdown, so you don't lose anything if you have to turn off the computer for any reason.

PowerBook/iBook Trials and Tribulations

When it comes to diagnosing system problems, most of the factors that cause incompatibilities with Apple laptops are the same as those that affect other Macs. System extensions may cause crashes, or one application will interact badly with another.

The troubleshooting steps I described in Chapters 2 and 18 apply in equal measure to the PowerBook and iBook user. However, these computers have their own little quirks that are worth some extra special emphasis.

■ **Crashes when awakening from Sleep mode**   This has been an ongoing problem in the Apple laptop line. You use Sleep mode for its extra convenience, so you don't have to endure a full startup mode to get the computer up and running. But sometimes it just doesn't work. The computer freezes while the screen is starting to display, or it doesn't come up at all. The usual steps to follow are the same as diagnosing any system-related conflict. Restart with your Mac OS Base extension set with Extensions Manager (or Conflict Catcher). Follow the steps outlined in Chapter 18 for isolating system-related conflicts.

■ **Automatic Sleep mode doesn't work**   If you have an older PowerBook and you're connected to a networked computer, or doing regular Internet log-ins (such as an automatic AOL session), you may encounter this problem. If so, the Mac OS will detect the network activity and not slip into Sleep mode at the specified interval. The solution is to dismount your networked drives, and turn off the automated sessions. You can also turn off your networking access simply by switching off AppleTalk in the Chooser or the Control Strip.

■ **Trackpad doesn't track properly**   It's great to be able to mouse around with your finger, but sometimes the clever little device misbehaves. The cursor moves along in ragged fashion or not at all. The usual solution is just to make sure your fingers are dry, not wet or greasy. So even if your hands are sweating because of that approaching deadline, wipe them off before you track and just use one finger (two fingers fighting each other for mouse motions doesn't help). If performance still isn't right, check your Trackpad Control Panel settings (see Figure 5-3). Make sure mouse tracking speed is what you want (the settings in the Mouse Control Panel have no effect on Trackpad speed).

■ **Battery won't charge**   If you've had your PowerBook for a while, it may just be that the battery needs to be replaced. But if you have a new battery, there may be another cause. Failure to charge has been put at the doorstep of a bad fuse on the logic board, and, in some cases, a problem with the AC power supply.

FIGURE 5-3   If the cursor moves too slowly, select a speedier version in this control panel

■ **Memory effect problems** Older PowerBook models with NiCad batteries may suffer from something called the "memory effect." If you continue to charge the battery without fully discharging it first, the battery seems to retain the memory of this shorter life cycle and won't last as long before it needs to be recharged. Whatever the cause, the usual remedy is to run the PowerBook down completely, past all the warning notices that it's about to shut down, right until it shuts itself off. That should restore the battery to its normal capacity. The lithium ion batteries available on recent Apple laptop computers are immune to this effect.

Changing Batteries on an iBook

Switching batteries on a regular Apple PowerBook or Duo is a snap, literally. Batteries easily pop out for fast replacement. However, Apple does it differently with the iBook.

In order to replace the battery on an iBook, you need to get a coin and loosen the retaining screws on the battery door. A quarter-turn counterclockwise is enough to open the door. Then you can pop out the battery, replace it, and tighten the screws.

■ **PowerBook 5300/190 problems**   This generation of PowerBooks seemed doomed from the start. Just as they went into production, Apple had to stop using lithium ion batteries because of a possible fire hazard (the issue was later resolved, but such batteries were never used in that product line). Apple also established an extended repair program to address such issues as the screen bezel separating, as well as problems with the AC adapter and power supplies. My PowerBook 5300ce made two trips to Apple's own repair center before it settled down and began to work properly (a friend who bought the PowerBook from me had to send it back to Apple for another repair session before he, too, finally found another owner for it). As this book was written, the extended repair program was in its final years, so if you still have one of these models and experience any of these troubles (or something that seems related in some fashion), you may want to have Apple arrange for service.

■ **Problems with PC cards**   Those little credit-card-shaped devices, PC cards (also known as PCMCIA), are a relatively inexpensive way to extend the capabilities of PowerBooks. With older PowerBooks, they are used for modems and Ethernet connections. But they have their quirks. The usual way to eject them is to drag the PC card icon to the trash. But sometimes that doesn't work; they get stuck in their slots (it's a tight fit, always). So if it happens to you, try a restart. If that fails, try this: insert a straightened paper clip into the little hole next to the PC card slot and push it in far enough to press the little button inside (the process is the same as force-ejecting a floppy disk). In most cases, this should be enough to eject the card. If not, there's a more drastic way recommended by Apple (and only as a last resort, as you could damage the PC card). Try prying the card out with your fingers or a pair of needle-nosed pliers. If you get the card out, go ahead and take that paper clip and push it into the slot to release the spring (and cross your fingers).

CAUTION   *Even if your PC cards can be placed and removed without trouble, there's still another issue, one that may prevent them from working, period. The latest PowerBooks have a PC Card Bus slot, which is a later revision of the PC card standard. Older PowerBooks don't. If in doubt, check your documentation or the manufacturer of the PC card to see which models are supported.*

■ **Too hot for lap use**   You're working on your trusty PowerBook. It's placed on your lap (well, it's a laptop computer, right?). And your thigh gets very hot. Is there something wrong? The fact of the matter is that the hard drive is generally at the lower left of the PowerBook, and a lot of heat can build up there. If it gets to the point where it's painful, you may want to have the unit checked. But even a properly functioning model will seem quite warm there. It's great on a cold winter's night.

Power Manager Woes

Another common problem with Apple laptops is a corrupted Power Manager. Symptoms may include failure to boot, failure to charge a battery, or the inability to wake from Sleep mode. The Power Manager directs a number of basic functions of the computer, including backlighting, energy saver settings, battery charging, and serial port access. Resetting the Power Manager is done differently from model to model. Here's a brief list of the steps involved in the process for recent models:

PowerBook G3 Series (Wall Street Edition)

1. Shut down your PowerBook.

2. Press the SHIFT, FN (function), CONTROL, and power keys—all at the same time.

3. Count five seconds.

4. Restart your PowerBook by pressing the power button.

PowerBook G3 Series (Lombard or Bronze Keyboard Edition)

1. Shut down your PowerBook.

2. Go to the rear of the computer, and locate and press the reset button. You'll find it right between the modem and external video ports.

3. Count five seconds.

4. Restart your PowerBook by pressing the power button.

PowerBook/iBook
Trials and Tribulations

iBook

1. Shut down your iBook.

2. Locate the reset button, which is placed at the base of the iBook's display. Take a straightened paper clip and press the button.

3. Count five seconds.

4. Restart your PowerBook by pressing the power button.

Older PowerBooks Summarized

There are various ways to reset the Power Manager on older models, depending on the kind of PowerBook you have. The processes described are just part of the equation. For many models, you actually need to disconnect the battery and power adapter.

There's not even a reset button on some of these computers. You have to use two straightened paper clips and press both reset and interrupt buttons at the same time for 10 to 20 seconds. On these units, the buttons are usually found inside the rear door.

For more information, pay a visit to Apple's Web site and read their technical information document on the subject. Here's the URL: http://til.info.apple.com/techinfo.nsf/artnum/n14449.

Protecting Your Laptop Against Theft

Although crime rates around the USA are supposed to be down, there is one element where they remain at an especially high level—and that's laptop computers.

According to a survey from Safeware, a company that specializes in insurance policies for computer users, some 303,000 laptop computers (I don't have a breakdown among manufacturers here), with a total value of $906,546,000 were stolen in 1998 alone. When you consider that it takes months for Apple to sell that many PowerBooks, you can see the breadth and depth of this problem.

Obviously, this is a great advertisement for getting good insurance, and it's nice to know that more and more firms are recognizing the need to provide computer coverage, especially for home office users.

Case History

Is It Dangerous to X-ray a Laptop?

Over the years, I had read differing opinions about whether my PowerBook could be damaged by the mandatory airport security check. What about the hard drive, I thought? Could the integrity of the data be affected?

For several years, I took the paranoid approach. I asked the security people to do a physical examination instead. All they need to do is have you open the computer, power it up so they see it start and show text of one sort or another, and they'll be satisfied that it's not a repository for contraband or dangerous weaponry.

> **NOTE** *The best thing to do if you must submit your iBook or PowerBook to this sort of check is simply to keep it in Sleep mode, so you can get it up and running quickly.*

On one trip, I noticed the pilot boarding the plane with his laptop (no, it wasn't one of Apple's, but I wasn't going to enter into a platform war discussion with someone who had my life in his hands). I asked him if he ever subjected his computer to a special security check.

No way, he said. He just ran the thing through the X-ray machine and he hadn't had a problem, ever.

Of course, how could I be so dense? I write science fiction stories, so I should have known the elementary scientific principles at hand here: X-rays aren't magnetic. How could they affect the data on my drive? All right, I got the message this time.

On the return trip, I just put the PowerBook's case on the conveyer belt. After the security check, I went to the waiting area, and quickly awakened my precious little computer to be sure it was all right. I suppose I was acting like Jack Nicholson's character in that fabulous movie *As Good As It Gets*. Then again, the character *was* a writer, right?

I repeated the maneuver on a few subsequent trips and finally just gave up checking and rechecking. I've never had an ounce of trouble, ever. And nobody

Protecting Your Laptop Against Theft

I know ever has either. Even Apple Computer, in a technical note on using Apple's products overseas, says that "X-rays and other magnetic radiation associated with X-ray machines only pose a slight potential danger." The only possible risk, they assert, might be to removable media (such as floppies, Zip drives, and SuperDisks). My suggestion is to just let the security machines do their stuff and don't worry about it. Even my old-fashioned film cameras have come out of the experience without any damage to the film.

Despite having an insurance policy at hand, it's far better, obviously, not to have to use the policy. I've experienced a handful of thefts over the years—one a camera, and three times an attempted car theft. Forget about the fact that the lost or damaged items can be repaired or replaced. You feel violated, helpless, and if the item stolen contained valuable information you need for your work, there is the time you must spend recreating all of it, if you can. That's why I recommend, over and over, the need to back up your files (see Chapter 14)—and I'll say it again at the risk of boring you, because it's so very important.

True, there's not much you can do if you're held at gunpoint or surrounded by a gang of thugs, unless you're a kickboxing expert, of course. But there are things you can do to help protect you against theft of your iBook or PowerBook—and there are things you can do to help get the thing back if it's taken.

Here are some suggestions:

■ **Be careful in public places.**   If you're at an airport terminal, a car rental establishment, or hotel lobby, for example, don't leave the laptop on the floor or table, even for a second. It wouldn't take long for someone who stalked you to dash on through the crowd and slip away with your computer (even if it's protected in an undistinguished fabric case). Don't put it down. If you have a case with a carrying strap or handle, hold on to it, tight as you can. Yes, I know that a PowerBook or iBook in a big case can put the weight of the world on your shoulders, but a few aches here and there are far more comfortable than the pain you'd endure if your computer is stolen from you. If you must set it down, sit on the strap, rest your hand on the case, keep a wary eye on it. And, although laptop cases are convenient, you may be better off putting the case itself into a regular overnight bag or suitcase, so it's not obvious to the onlooker just what you have there.

NOTE   *The striking, colorful design of the Apple iBook makes it a theft magnet. While its convenient fold-down carrying handle makes it easy to carry, you are better off putting it in a case of some sort so it doesn't attract attention.*

■ **Consider a hardware registry.**   A popular iBook/PowerBook Web site, O'Grady's PowerPage, has established a special PowerBook Registry database. It's designed to be a central repository of information that'll help the authorities recover your computer in the event of theft. Check out the site and consider registering there. Here's how to do it:

1. Get the serial number. You'll usually find it at the rear (especially if it's a unit where ports are hidden behind a door) or the belly of the unit. If the serial number isn't obvious, check the original box for the information.

2. If your PowerBook isn't on Ethernet, go to the AppleTalk (or Network) Control Panel, and make sure it's selected.

3. Locate the Ethernet hardware address. You can dig it up by launching Apple System Profiler (from the Apple menu).

4. When Apple System Profiler is open, click on the Network Overview arrow (so it points down) on the main System Profile screen.

5. Then click on the AppleTalk arrow (again so it points down), and you'll see a listing for your iBook or PowerBook's Hardware Address.

6. Access the Hardware Registry Web site (see Figure 5-4) at http://www.ogrady.com/registry.

7. Enter both pieces of information where indicated on the Hardware Registry page.

8. Click the register Apple hardware link.

9. On the next screen, enter your name and address information plus the system information requested.

10. When you're ready, click the submit record button. The information you've entered will become part of the site's database.

Protecting Your Laptop Against Theft

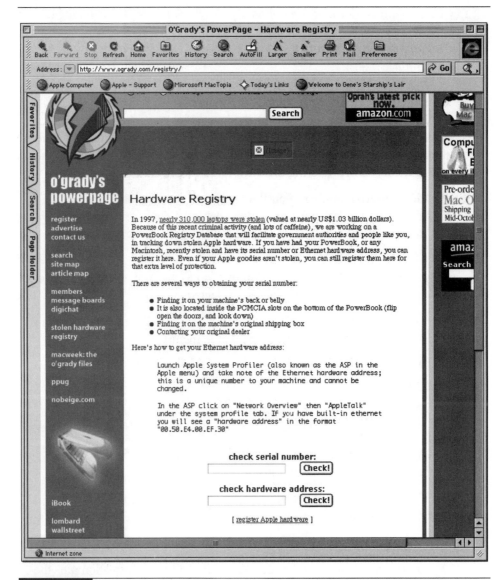

FIGURE 5-4   Enter your laptop's production information in the space provided

Protecting Your Laptop
Against Theft

NOTE *O'Grady's Hardware Registry isn't just for laptops. You can also place information about all your desktop computers in the same database (you submit one listing at a time). Just be sure you enter the correct CPU type on the Submit page.*

■ **Get insurance protection.** It used to be difficult to get meaningful computer coverage on a home insurance policy, but that is no longer the case. In addition to the company who provided the theft statistics I quoted here (Safeware, a specialist in insuring computers), regular insurance companies such as Farmers Insurance Group offer low-cost riders that cover computers (even for tenants). Be sure your policy is sufficient to cover replacement value of your computer, peripherals, and software (and this can all add up). Make sure there's also coverage for your computer and software when you travel.

■ **Store your laptop in a safe when you leave your hotel.** I wouldn't for a moment suggest that the staff in a hotel has skullduggery on their minds, or that it's easy to break into your room. But it is a fact that your door will be left open when they're doing their cleaning, and I've seen enough movies showing folks casually walking into a stranger's room under such circumstances to be at least wary of the process. So I recommend you check with the hotel and see if they have a room with a safe or can provide secured storage when you're not in the room. At the very least, insist that housekeeping staff close your door when they are making your room ready for you upon your return.

Using Your PowerBook as a SCSI Drive

In the days of the PowerBook Duo, you could slip it into a Duo Dock and make it into a desktop computer, more or less. But even other PowerBooks, at least until SCSI capability disappears, can do double duty as an extra hard drive on your desktop system. This is useful for fast file synchronizing or backup, in the event you don't have a fast network connection.

Here, briefly, is how you set it up:

1. Get hold of a PowerBook SCSI Disk Adapter cable. Make sure you get the right cable, as Apple, in its infinite wisdom (I seem to use this phrase often), also designed an almost identical-looking regular SCSI cable, which is used to attach a SCSI device to a PowerBook. Dealers tend to confuse this, so make sure the words "Disk Adapter" are on the package. You can also get a SCSI Dock connector at your dealer, a little module with a plug at one end and a SCSI port at the other, and a switch for either SCSI mode.

2. On your PowerBook, go to the Apple menu, and access the Control Panels submenu. Choose the PowerBook SCSI Setup Control Panel.

3. Choose a SCSI ID that doesn't conflict with the one on your desktop computer (this is critical).

4. Shut down your PowerBook (don't put in Sleep mode, please) and your desktop Mac.

CAUTION *Before you turn off the PowerBook, make sure that the Password Security Control Panel or any other password protection on the computer is disabled. Otherwise, you will run into problems trying to access the drive on another Mac.*

5. Attach your PowerBook's SCSI Disk Adapter cable to the SCSI port on your Mac or the one on your last attached device (you may need an adapter plug if it has a different type of SCSI jack).

6. Turn on your PowerBook. Within a few seconds you should see a SCSI icon on the PowerBook's screen.

NOTE *If your PowerBook starts up normally with that cable connected, it means you have the wrong cable, and it's not going into SCSI disk mode. Should this happen, power down and replace the cable.*

7. Boot your Mac normally. The PowerBook's disk icon should show up normally on your desktop Mac. If it doesn't, power down and recheck your SCSI setup. SCSI ID and termination conflicts may be present. Should this happen, consult Chapter 15 for further advice on the subject.

The Apple Laptop Travel Guide

Forgetting something? When you need to take your Apple Duo, iBook, or PowerBook with you on a trip (business or personal), you'll want to make sure you have the right stuff, in case of a problem or simply to make your computer run properly in most situations you'll encounter.

The first time I had to take a PowerBook on the road, it was for a purpose that wasn't very pleasant. My wife needed some surgery, and the physician and hospital were in another state, some 250 miles away. Unfortunately, I was also in the middle of a writing deadline, and deadlines aren't concerned with such fine points as family needs.

So I packed my PowerBook, scanner, removable drives, extra keyboard, mouse, modem, and backup tape drive in the trunk, and the entire Steinberg clan took off.

The hotel's housekeeping staff was no doubt startled to see my makeshift home office, but it worked. I was able to spend several hours a day keeping up on that project, with plenty of time for hospital visits. I even managed to take my son for an occasional sightseeing tour, so the trip wasn't quite so boring for him.

A little advance travel planning will do wonders toward making your computer do all the work it can do.

- ■ **Check overseas phone and voltage requirements**.   If you plan on traveling to another country, congratulations. Apple's products are labeled as "universal," designed to work in many international environments. Power requirements generally run from 100 to 250 volts, and current ratings of 50 and 60 Hz. You may, however, need a special adapter plug to access a power line in a particular locale. In addition, Apple won't officially certify products designed for the USA market for overseas use, although that doesn't mean you can't use them with the proper adapters. Before you visit another country, you may also want to check out a dealer who specializes in international connectivity products. One prime example listed by Apple Computer is TeleAdapt, which you can access on the Web at http://www.teleadapt.com (or telephone 1-877-835-3232). Their product line includes plug adapters, modem adapters and testers, line filters, acoustic couplers for hotel phones that don't have a separate data port, and security alarm systems. One of their products, the $99 Executive TeleKit, gives you the tools you need to test and hook up your modem at an older hotel that's hard-wired, without regular modular phone jacks.

NOTE
Apple portable computing products introduced to the market since January 1, 1998, are protected by a worldwide warranty. That means if your recent Apple laptop needs service, you can visit any local service installation during that period for warranty repairs. As far as older models are concerned, well, they'd be out of warranty anyway.

■ **Don't break it in on the road.**   If you have a brand new iBook or PowerBook, you should use it as much as you can before you travel. That way you can check for possible problems that you can fix before your departure. Even with Apple's product warranty (or perhaps an extended warranty), you wouldn't want to have to spend the time away from home diagnosing a system-related problem or having to wait for a repair.

■ **Don't forget a spare battery and charger.**   Even if you don't expect to stretch the limits of the battery, you should be prepared in case of an emergency. For one thing, laptop batteries have a finite life cycle, and may have to be replaced after a year or two of use. Also, if they go bad prematurely, you will be left in the lurch if there isn't a power plug at hand. If you intend to travel to a region with uncertain weather conditions, or visit older hotels with older electrical systems, don't be surprised to encounter a prolonged power outage. In addition to a spare battery, it wouldn't hurt to get a battery charger so you always have a fully charged spare ready to roll. You can get batteries, chargers, and other accessories for recent Apple laptops from VST Technologies (http://www.vsttech.com).

■ **Send your backups to yourself.**   No, this isn't a request that you start talking to yourself, though I have felt that way at times when I've forgotten to take something I really needed on a trip. When you write critical documents that you cannot afford to lose, and you have online access where you are staying, send the file in an email to yourself. That way, in the event your original file is damaged, or if your computer is damaged or stolen, you can retrieve the file when you need it. If you don't want to clog up your mailbox with the added material, see if your online service offers an extra mailbox. For example, AOL gives you up to seven screen names (mailboxes) on each account. EarthLink offers a free second mailbox if you upgrade to their optional EarthLink Gold service; otherwise there's an extra cost, depending on how many extra mailboxes you need.

■ **Protect your laptop from extreme weather.**   Don't assume your rugged-looking iBook or PowerBook is immune. If you intend to travel into an extreme environment (winter weather or the tropics), pack your laptop carefully, perhaps using a hard-shell shipping case designed for the purpose (check your dealer for product offerings). Keep it away from heat, extreme cold, or moisture. The supplier of international connection adapters I mentioned earlier, TeleAdapt, also has a device called a CoolPad, which keeps the PowerBook elevated from a desk to give it better air circulation (though frankly this is a far greater problem with Intel-based notebooks than Macs, because the Pentiums usually generate more heat).

■ **Bring a backup drive.**   The reasons that you back up at home or office are doubly important on the road, when there is added risk of damage by the elements or possible theft. You should bring along an extra drive with enough space to store duplicates of your important files, then keep it separate from the laptop computer (so the loss of one doesn't necessarily include the backup device). An expansion bay drive for a PowerBook, be it a Zip, SuperDisk, or hard drive, is an excellent choice. The iBooks and G3 PowerBooks with the "bronze" keyboard also have USB ports for extra drives and other devices. Your choices are similar: Zip drive, SuperDisk, hard drive, plus CD writers and tape drives. One USB-based CD writer, the Que Drive (pronounced "kay," and I have no idea why) comes with a convenient carrying case that can easily fit into a large laptop case or an overnight bag.

TIP   *Another extra drive option is FireWire. Chapter 15 covers the differences between FireWire and SCSI. The Newer Technology FireWire to Go PC card will allow a PowerBook G3 to use FireWire drives.*

■ **Consider a portable inkjet printer.**   If you must produce printed copy, take a look at the products available and see if one is small enough for travel. If you want to save space, you could arrange to fax yourself a copy with your fax modem (but bear in mind a hotel will charge a per page fee for faxes). Another option is to see if there's a local service bureau or printer who could print your documents for you.

■ **Make sure you can access your online service on the road.**   The national services, such AOL, CompuServe, AT&T WorldNet, and EarthLink, have

The Apple Laptop Travel Guide

thousands of local access numbers for you to select, and often a reasonable percentage of those are outside the USA. It's a good idea to collect these numbers before you travel, so you're ready to hook up when you arrive. If you have a local ISP without access points outside your state, consider a Web email service, such as Microsoft's Hotmail or Yahoo mail. On the other hand, if you intend to do a lot of traveling, you may want to rethink your ISP choices for this very reason.

TIP

Before you leave, it's a good idea to create separate dialing profiles in Apple's Remote Access or PPP Control Panels for each locale to which you're traveling. It's done by choosing Configurations from the program's File menu, duplicating your current setting, and then entering the new information (after which you rename and save it). If you're an AOL or CompuServe member, you can create custom connection (location) profiles in the software provided by these services.

NOTE

AOL has a Web-based email system, NetMail (also called just AOLMail), which is designed to provide access to your AOL email if you don't have access to their regular software. You'll find more information at the company's Web site: http://www.aol.com/aolmail. EarthLink was about to introduce a similar service at the time this book was written.

■ **Don't forget an accessory kit.**   In addition to having an extra battery and charger at hand, there are some other items you might want to take along. You'll want to take extra disk media, a SCSI terminator (in case you use an extra SCSI device), a long modular phone cord (in case your computer is far from the phone job; again, TeleAdapt can help you here, with one of their roll-up cords), and maybe even a spare AC adapter.

NOTE

For PowerBook Duo owners: Apple's departed notebook computer was great for tight spaces. But it didn't catch on with enough folks to sustain the market line. The considerations for a Duo are the same as other Apple laptops. If you take your Duo on the road, consider whether you need a Duo MiniDock or just a Duo Floppy Adapter, so you can use a floppy.

■ **Consider a separate keyboard and mouse.**   If you plan on spending extra hours on the computer, consider getting a regular desktop keyboard and mouse. Laptop keyboards and input devices (whether the trackpad or the little trackball on the very first PowerBooks) can be an acquired taste, and not everyone takes to them for long sessions. I have found the feel of the iBook's keyboard to be closer to that of a regular keyboard than any Apple laptop I've used (but that's just a personal opinion).

NOTE *As our fearless technical editor, John Rizzo, reminds us, keyboards are big for a carrying case. But they'll fit nicely into a suitcase or overnight bag.*

■ **Choose a case carefully.**   While a thin, attractively designed case may look just great, it may not have enough room to meet your needs. Before you buy a case, try to see it in person (I realize this is a problem if you do a lot of catalog and online shopping). See if there are extra bins and pouches for the extras you need, such as disks, removable drives, and adapter cables. Also check to see if the laptop compartment is well cushioned in case of a bumpy trip. Since Apple's newest PowerBooks have larger screens, they could be a tight fit in older cases. If you do see the accessory case in person, check the product specifications for extra features, dimensions, and so on, so you can be reasonably assured it'll do the job. Order it well enough in advance of a trip so it can be returned in case it's not suitable.

More to Come

In this chapter, you learned how to make your mobile computing experience safer and more productive. If you want to keep abreast of the latest news and views on Apple laptops, may I suggest you point your Web browser to Jason O'Grady's excellent site, PowerPage. The URL is: http://ogrady.com.

In the next chapter, I'll cover a subject near and dear to my heart, as an old-time commercial typographer, and that's fonts. There's a whole lot more to a Mac's font handling capabilities than just a few letters and numbers.

The Apple Laptop Travel Guide

Chapter 6

The Weird World of Fonts

You cannot use a Mac without fonts. Even the basic window and menu bar displays on your Mac use fonts of one sort or another.

One of the big factors that attracted the graphics industry to the Macintosh platform was the easy availability of fonts and the invention of the PostScript page description language, PostScript fonts, and laser printers.

One would think, then, that fonts would be as easy to handle as other Mac files, but that's not really the case. The proliferation of fonts and new font formats has created a nightmare. The more fonts you have, the more difficult it is to keep them organized.

The purpose of this chapter is to cover the whys and wherefores of font organization and troubleshooting. You'll discover how best to keep up a large font library and how to handle the common problems that affect their use.

TrueType vs. PostScript Fonts: What's the Difference?

In the beginning, fonts came in bitmap form. You had a different font for every size, and what you saw on the screen was reproduced on the page, at least to the limits of those old ImageWriter printers.

Things changed when the clever folks at Adobe invented something called PostScript, which takes the elements of a page and reduces them to math. Accompanying PostScript were PostScript fonts. If you wanted scalable fonts (fonts that would print in all sizes at the full resolution of your printer), you had just one choice, PostScript.

The Anatomy of a PostScript Font

In the old days of traditional computerized typesetting, your fonts came in two parts. There were the actual letterforms themselves, which would be on a thin piece of film or on a floppy disk. Then there was a second part, a printed circuit card or floppy disk that recorded the width values of the fonts. This was the information that told the computer how wide a particular character was supposed to be.

When scalable font technology was introduced by Adobe, they followed the very same design motif. There was a screen font (or bitmap) font, which provided clear display of the font on your screen in a single size, and also contained the width values (or metrics) of a typeface. So the letter M on a proportional font was always wider than the letter I. To the left is a typical PostScript screen font icon. Notice there is always a size in its file name.

The second part of the equation was the printer font, which contained the font "outline" information that allowed the font to be reproduced on your printer in any size you selected. This is the component of the font that scales to whatever size you select, yet retains the same high output quality. To the left is the printer font icon for an Adobe font. Other font manufacturers would often make their printer font icons resemble a printer.

In order for the font to work, you had to install both parts. The screen fonts usually came in several sizes merged together in a file called a suitcase. By giving you extra sizes, the font manufacturer could give you better screen display (at least when you selected those specific sizes). Beginning with Mac OS 7, you would simply double-click on a suitcase file to examine its contents.

In 1989, Adobe came out with a clever solution to give you clear screen display in all available sizes: Adobe Type Manager (ATM). ATM was designed to work with a single bitmap font plus your printer font to generate screen images in the sizes you selected. An added benefit was the ability to use PostScript fonts with non-PostScript printers. Without ATM, whenever you selected a size for which a bitmap font wasn't available, screen display would become extremely poor because the Mac's QuickDraw display technology would try to fill in the missing pieces.

In order for PostScript fonts to work, you simply dragged both files to the closed System Folder icon, and the Finder would put them in the Fonts folder (which was introduced with Mac System 7.1).

> **NOTE** *There are other ways to organize fonts that bypass the Fonts folder, but they require installing software that manages a font library. I'll cover that subject in the last section of this chapter.*

PostScript fonts come in two forms. Type 1 is the most common type. In addition to the fonts you install on your Mac, Type 1 fonts are also installed on PostScript printers.

The other type of PostScript font is Type 3, not used as much these days, except for special applications (such as custom logo designs). Type 3 fonts are not as efficiently designed as the Type 1 variety. The file sizes are larger, and they exact greater amounts of printer memory to work; their biggest benefit is the ability to make fonts with grayscale fills and complex characters based on PostScript illustrations. Unfortunately, ATM doesn't support them.

For the rest of this chapter, when I refer to PostScript fonts, I'll be concentrating strictly on the Type 1 variety.

TrueType vs. PostScript Fonts: What's the Difference?

TrueType Fonts Hit the Scene

Back in 1990, the entire subject of fonts on a Mac became more confusing when Apple came up with TrueType. The story goes that Apple resented paying Adobe big licensing bucks to use PostScript fonts, so they decided to come up with their own alternative. And in theory it's a better alternative, because each TrueType font is a single file, containing both screen and outline portions. You don't have to worry about missing one file or the other.

NOTE

The irony of the arrival of TrueType is that, although a Mac innovation, it was rapidly embraced on the Windows platform, where it appears to have greater popularity, even to this day.

TrueType is a scalable font format too, with the font scaler built into your system software. As a result, you can view and print on any printer connected to your Mac without having to worry about PostScript or Adobe Type Manager. This is a great plus if you have a regular inkjet printer hooked up to your Mac.

And, like a screen font, a TrueType font can live by itself or be placed in a font suitcase, along with other fonts. The icon to the left is a typical TrueType font. Notice the multiple letter A, which indicates the font is scalable, and the lack of a size in the font's name.

Bookman Hd BT

The Printing World Gives TrueType a Thumbs Down

TrueType fonts sounded great on paper. And indeed they had distinct advantages over PostScript fonts, such as the ability to work on non-PostScript printers and the ability to give clear screen display without needing a separate ATM-type program. But they wrought havoc in the commercial printing world. The expensive imagesetters that printers and service bureaus used to make high-resolution output of documents were designed to work best with PostScript fonts. So even though the Mac operating system could handle TrueType with aplomb, those expensive output devices would choke at the presence of a TrueType font. Sometimes the processing stage would halt, or the output wouldn't produce acceptable results.

And the solutions weren't cheap. In some situations, the actual imagesetter processor's hardware had to be updated to recognize the existence of TrueType, at a cost of hundreds or thousands of dollars. In other cases, it was just a downloadable update. But in either case, it took time for the industry to accept the reality of TrueType.

Even today, PostScript fonts are still the industry standard in the publishing industry. Although the high-end output devices usually work in a satisfactory manner with TrueType, your best approach is to check with your commercial printer before you use such fonts in your documents if you intend to take them beyond your office laser printer.

On the other hand, if you confine your printed output to inkjets and laser printers, or you want to exchange fonts with Windows users, you are apt to fare better sticking with TrueType. Not having to deal with separate bitmap and printer fonts and ATM will definitely make life easier.

Introducing OpenType

As if coping with the vagaries of PostScript and TrueType fonts weren't enough, there's another font format on the horizon—OpenType. Developed jointly by Adobe and Microsoft, OpenType promises to end some of the confusing side effects of the existing font structure.

If OpenType spreads, it'll cure a whole lot of ills. For one, the format covers both PostScript and TrueType fonts, and the actual font file can support either format or both. In a sense, it's a merger of both formats, and there will be no need for separate screen fonts if you opt for an OpenType font with PostScript support. It's all in one file.

Another great OpenType feature is the ability to embed such fonts on a Web page, which helps provide a uniform look and feel for Web pages across browsers and computing platforms.

In addition, OpenType will support extended characters, such as ligatures and fancy letterforms, and improved character kerning. The latter will go a long way toward making the appearance of type much, much better as well.

So What Does OpenType Do for Me?

It won't change your existing fonts in any way. You'll continue to use them as you do now. But once OpenType fonts start appearing on the market, you'll be able to buy them and enjoy the increased convenience and additional features they offer. Of course, that assumes there aren't any problems in Apple supporting the new format (and that is by no means certain as of the time this book went to press).

The Sad Tale of QuickDraw GX

In the early 1990s, Apple announced a new set of technologies that, on paper, seemed just wonderful. It was called QuickDraw GX, and it was designed to not only update the Mac's image display model, but also how fonts and printing were handled.

TrueType vs. PostScript Fonts: What's the Difference?

When it came to fonts, the character limitations would be history. You'd be able to get and use fonts with all sorts of extra characters, such as swashes (little effects and flourishes that decorate a letter), extended ligatures (such as the combined "ffi" letter combination that you see in high-quality books) and more. Font organization, especially with PostScript fonts, would be eased, since the printer and screen fonts would be combined into a single file (yes, just like TrueType fonts).

QuickDraw GX would also revolutionize the way graphics programs were developed. The core programming routines that covered display and rotation of your drawings would be done behind the scenes by the Mac operating system. All programmers would have to do would be to call up these routines, rather than have to reinvent the wheel and program their own graphic elements. It would make for smaller, less RAM-hungry programs with consistent performance.

And then there was printing. All printers would get desktop icons. Rather than work with the clumsy old PrintMonitor, you could simply drag and drop jobs to the specific printer you wanted to use, and even move documents from one printer icon to another to equalize the load. You could pick different printers from your Print dialog box (no more regular trips to the Chooser).

That was just the beginning. There would be extra printer features, such as the ability to automatically place watermarks on a page, print several small-sized pages on a single sheet of paper (thumbnails), and more.

The theory was truly intriguing, and dedicated graphic designers no doubt waited patiently for the reality. When it finally showed up in the mid-1990s, the reality was not quite as impressive as the promise. QuickDraw GX took up several megabytes of RAM, especially on the then-innovative PowerPC models. It was buggy, it was the source of regular crashes, and software publishers moved at a snail's pace to adopt the technologies. Some blamed the fact that it wasn't a cross-platform technology (and the biggest graphics programs are designed to work about the same in the Mac and Windows environments). Only a very few QuickDraw GX-savvy programs ever came out.

Finally, Apple got the message and scuttled the technology—well, except for those desktop printer features, which are now, in large part, included with your latest system software. Yes, you can drag and drop documents on printer icons, and even move them from one printer to another. You can select from among PostScript printers in the Print dialog, and there are little watermark features that are part of the latest LaserWriter 8 drivers.

So, basically, we got a large part of the QuickDraw GX printing technology, but the rest went the way of OpenDoc and other failed Apple technologies that looked great on paper but somehow never worked in the real world.

NOTE

OpenDoc was designed to change the emphasis from the application to the document. You'd create a single document, then OpenDoc would let you use the parts necessary to provide the features you needed (such as a word processing part, a graphics part, or an image editing part).

Still Have Quickdraw GX Installed?

Despite the drawbacks just described, it may very well be that you went ahead and used QuickDraw GX anyway. Perhaps you are using one of those very few programs that required QuickDraw GX, such as Lightning Draw and the QuickDraw GX-aware version of the old desktop publishing program, Ready,Set,Go. I don't want to dump cold water on your decision. But it is a fact that Apple isn't supporting the technology, nor can you expect the developers of these programs to keep up to date.

While there's nothing wrong with using old software if it works all right, just be aware of the fact that you may be stuck in a time-warp if you decide to ever get a new Mac or new version of the Mac OS.

NOTE

A case in point is Mac OS 9, where all vestiges of QuickDraw GX support are gone.

A Quick Survey of Multiple Master Fonts

Another font technology that hasn't gone a long way is Adobe's Multiple Master Fonts. To explain what this is all about, it may be worthwhile mentioning how fonts were designed in the old days.

Way back when, fonts would be optimized to look good in a single size or a small range of sizes. For example, in relation to their size, you'd make letters tall and wide for text, to enhance readability, and small and thin for headlines, where you wanted close-knit spacing for optimum appearance in very large sizes.

Font manufacturers actually produced two or more versions of each font to meet these needs. At one time there was even a separate font master for each point size, which simply meant you had to buy lots of fonts to get a reasonable number of point sizes.

With Multiple Master Fonts, Adobe tried to expand upon this scheme by developing a single set of fonts that you could modify in a wide number of ways, to provide the best possible optical appearance. You could even design your own variations on the basic core design, by manipulating the basic letter shapes to be thicker, thinner, condensed, or expanded. The limit was your imagination.

Of course, if anyone tried to match your font alteration for a specific task, it would be a nightmare in the making, since the usual directories of font designs that

TrueType vs. PostScript Fonts: What's the Difference?

graphic artists use wouldn't accommodate any such possibilities. And forget about picking them out in a font menu, as the variations were named by adding some numbers to the actual font's name.

Fortunately, or unfortunately, depending on your point of view, the technique hasn't really gone beyond a small set of Adobe font products—that is, except for its emergence as part of Adobe's font substitution technology. Take ATM and a core set of four Multiple Master Fonts, and a database of Adobe designs, and you can simulate many font designs (at least in terms of spacing if not the actual look). This is a great convenience if you just want to get a general idea of how a document looks, without having to go out and get all the fonts you need.

Adobe Acrobat also uses font substitution technology to replace fonts that aren't embedded in the Acrobat file and give the document a look resembling (though not quite matching) the original design.

Finding Damaged Fonts

Except in rare circumstances involving hard drive directory damage, you will seldom run into a damaged document. But damaged fonts are another story entirely. Seems as if they turn up at the worst of times, when you need a font to finish a document. Worse, the problem is not always easy to trace, and can be easily diagnosed as having a totally unrelated cause.

The Symptoms

When a Mac application is launched, among the things it does while you see the program's startup screen is load a list of available fonts. If one of those fonts is damaged, the program can crash on you right off the bat. In other cases, your program may work just fine, but the font won't print properly, or your printer will hang trying to handle the job.

It's not always the case that fonts are responsible. For one thing, the symptoms may also have other causes, such as a system extension conflict, a damaged or incompatible program, or a corrupted preference file.

But if you follow through with the standard array of diagnostic steps I've outlined throughout this book and come up with a big fat zero, it's time to consider the possibility that your problem may be font-related (and this happens a lot more often than you may expect).

The Cure

A damaged font isn't obvious. The icon doesn't change. It may install just fine, but betray itself by the telltale symptoms just listed above.

Here are some ways to check your fonts for damage:

- **Try Norton Utilities or TechTool Pro.**   Both programs will check for damaged files as part of the process of scanning your Mac's drive for directory problems. If one or more fonts come up as damaged, delete them and reinstall the fonts.

- **Use a font management utility to diagnose the fonts.**   Adobe Type Manager Deluxe, Alsoft's MasterJuggler, Diamond Soft's Font Reserve, and Extensis Suitcase 8 FontAgent can all scan for damaged fonts. Use the built-in capabilities of these programs to find the offending files and then replace them with fresh copies.

NOTE   *Mac OS 8.6 users face a special font problem. Mac OS 8.6 introduced a unique conflict with Apple's Font Manager, the system software component that handles fonts. Very old fonts didn't have something called FOND, which is the technical name for the font family resource (such as saying the font belongs with the Times or Helvetica families). If the font doesn't have this information, Apple's Font Manager creates it, and for 8.6 what is created can result in a crash. If you have a new Mac and you don't have any of these very old fonts (most of which date back to the 1980s), there's nothing to worry about. Otherwise, you'll want to look at Apple's Support Web site for a file called Font Manager Update at http://asu.info.apple.com/swupdates.nsf/artnum/n11489.*

- **A virus program works, too.**   The popular virus detection programs Network Associates' Virex and Symantec's Norton AntiVirus will report damaged files to you as part of their scans for virus-related activity.

NOTE   *I recommend up-to-date commercial virus software for the ultimate in protection against computer viruses. But if you have a copy of the old free virus program Disinfectant around, you will be pleased to know it will check for damaged files as part of its scanning process.*

Finding Damaged Fonts

Coping with Font Conflicts

When system extensions conflict, the results are usually predictable. Applications quit, the Mac freezes. The things you need to do to fix those problems are pretty straightforward. The previous chapter and Chapter 18 cover the subject in more extensive detail.

But font conflicts don't manifest themselves in so clear a fashion. They are not the same sort of conflicts that affect regular software, the kind of conflicts that cause system crashes and other untoward behavior. Rather, they are conflicts that result in improper display and printing of your documents, and they can be a bear to handle, unless you organize your fonts carefully.

Case History   Futura vs. Futura

I was working with a graphic design studio with a bank of those high-end printers, called imagesetters, that are used to prepare final copy for offset printing. One of the services offered was to provide high-resolution prints for a number of clients.

A normal job request came down, a newsletter using the Futura typeface. The client had provided laser prints, so we could compare the original with the end result. And that's where the problem began.

On the screen, before the document was sent to an imagesetter, we could see that everything was all wrong. The line breaks were different, and the look of the lettering was different as well. Sizes didn't match. We ran a laser print, and it only confirmed what we saw on the monitor.

There was nothing unusual about the list of fonts used in the document. They specified several different styles of Futura in several different sizes. So we phoned the client and learned one more thing. Their version of Futura came from a different source than ours. We used Adobe's fonts. Shown here is the regular Adobe version of Futura Bold, in 24 point, a popular typeface used for ad display.

Attack of the Rockoids is Coming!

Their fonts came from a company called Bitstream. The Bitstream variation is similar, when shown in 24 point, but notice how the actual width of the letters and even the size differ slightly from the Adobe version.

Attack of the Rockoids is Coming!

Should it have made a difference? Yes indeed. Even when the names are the same, each font vendor will have its own idea about how the design is executed. The width values of the letters may differ; even the actual size of the letterforms may be a little larger or a little smaller. This means that 12 point from one manufacturer may be a bit smaller or larger than 12 point from another manufacturer. When the two factors combine, you are creating the climate for a font catastrophe.

The final result was that the client was asked to supply their own fonts with their work. This is a common practice with service bureaus that handle this sort of job. If you supply your own fonts, there's no problem in matching things up.

NOTE *Even though font publishers have stringent licensing requirements for their products, most will allow you to send your fonts to a service bureau, so long as the fonts are not used to output any other client's job.*

The other suggestion is this: If you intend to share a document with another company and need to make sure everything looks the same, check first to make sure their fonts are the same as yours. If not, request they acquire the fonts or bring them with you if you need to work on a document at their site.

Coping with Font Conflicts

More Font Troubles and Solutions

In addition to mixing the same fonts in PostScript and TrueType form, or simply having a font from the wrong vendor, there are other problems with fonts that can be just as aggravating. In the next few pages, I'll cover some of the usual problems and the usual suspects.

Bitmapped PostScript Font Screen Display

You write something on the screen, and instead of the letters appearing reasonably clear and sharp, the edges are jagged, and it looks like your font consists of a set of large rectangular bricks.

Attack of the Rockoids is Coming!

Here's what to check:

- **ATM requires PostScript printer fonts**   If you're using Adobe Type Manager to clean up font display, you have to make sure that both the bitmap (screen) and printer fonts are in the same folder. ATM doesn't have any way to look for your printer fonts in another location. Remember, too, that ATM cannot help you print a document with PostScript fonts on a non-PostScript printer without the printer fonts.

> **NOTE**   *If you're using a font manager, such as Adobe Type Manager Deluxe, Alsoft's MasterJuggler, or Extensis Suitcase, you still have to keep printer and screen fonts in the same folder for them to work properly.*

- **Missing printer fonts**   Double-check to make sure that you indeed have the corresponding printer fonts for your PostScript font sets. Screen fonts are easily acquired, even from Adobe's Web site, but they don't help if the printer fonts aren't there as well.

- **ATM not installed**   When it comes to PostScript fonts, you'll only get clear display on your screen if you install Adobe Type Manager. Fortunately, the bare-bones version (with the "Lite" moniker) is freely available with Adobe's Acrobat Reader or direct from Adobe's Web site. If you installed Acrobat Reader and ATM isn't around, check the folder in which Acrobat Reader is installed. For some unaccountable reason, it's often placed in a folder called Fonts, which has nothing whatever to do with the Fonts folder inside your System Folder. Once you locate ATM, drag it to the closed System Folder icon, restart, and all should be right with your font display (assuming the fonts are correctly installed).

- **Reinstall the font**   If the font is correctly installed, and you have ATM in place, try reinstalling the font. The original could be damaged.

■ **Check for font conflicts** Even if the font is correctly installed, mixing PostScript and TrueType versions of the same fonts (such as PostScript Times and TrueType Times) or having several versions of the same face from different manufacturers may produce some very untidy side effects with your screen display and printout of a document. Read the section entitled "A Look at a Font Manager" for suggestions on software that can help you deal with this dilemma.

Bitmap Printing

Poor screen display may be something you can live with if you can get good quality with your printed documents. But if the output quality is bad (even if the screen display is good), then it is intolerable. Here's how to address the problem:

■ **ATM needed for non-PostScript printer** Those inkjet printers from such companies as Canon, Epson and HP do great work on photos and regular artwork, but when it comes to PostScript, they just don't speak the same language. They work just dandy with TrueType fonts, but to use PostScript fonts on such printers, you have two choices. The simplest is just to install ATM (it's free with Adobe Acrobat Reader or at Adobe's Web site, as I mentioned earlier). If you want to handle PostScript graphics (also known as EPS), you'll want to consider PostScript software, which turns your Mac into a real raster image processor (RIP). You can get one of these programs from such companies as Barmy, Epson, or Infowave.

NOTE *PostScript graphics are simply those created in a program and saved in Encapsulated PostScript (ESP) format. This file format lets you place or import graphics into your document and get the highest possible print quality.*

■ **Missing PostScript printer font** Even if you have ATM installed, you cannot get good quality printouts unless the PostScript printer font is correctly installed in the same folder as the screen font.

■ **Font conflict** If you have mixed PostScript and TrueType versions of the same font, or two fonts of the same name from different vendors, your Mac may just give up and not download the proper font information to your printer. Instead of just getting poor letter spacing, the actual characters themselves may be bitmapped. The solution is to organize your font library (using the suggestions later in this chapter) to make sure you are cautious when you mix or match.

Coping with Font Conflicts

Fonts Missing from Font Menu

You can't very well use a font if it's not appearing in the font menu. Here are the likely causes of this problem and what to do about it:

- **Screen font missing**   Yes, your PostScript printer font may be in the Fonts folder, but it doesn't live in a vacuum. Font menus on Mac programs are also based on the presence of the bitmap (screen) font. So if you install a new font and don't see it listed on the menu, double-check to be certain the bitmap font is properly installed (it can either be a separate file or placed within a font suitcase).

- **Software won't dynamically update font menus**   Some programs, such as QuarkXPress or Adobe's InDesign and PageMaker, are cleverly designed to know when you install new fonts. The font menus will update automatically, though it may take a few seconds for the deed to be done. But many programs are not so smart about such changes. If a newly installed font doesn't appear in the font menu, quit the program and launch it again. If that doesn't work, just restart your Mac.

- **Replace preferences for font menu modifiers**   The programs that modify your font menus to organize and clean up display keep preference files as a database of the fonts you've got installed on your Mac. These programs include Adobe Type Reunion Deluxe, MenuFonts, and ACTION WYSIWYG Menus (a demonstration version is included with this book's CD). If you're adding or removing fonts and the font menus don't reflect the changes, locate the preference files (in the Preferences folder inside the System Folder) and remove them. Restart your Mac, and the programs will rebuild their font displays.

NOTE   *If the preference files for a font menu modifier program aren't obvious, look for a folder with the name of the publisher (such as Power On Preferences for the ACTION Utilities product line).*

- **Reinstall the font**   Even if you've checked your font and it comes up undamaged, reinstall it anyway. Font damage is usually easy to detect when it's a printer font, but if a single screen font size in a font suitcase is damaged, programs such as Norton Utilities and TechTool Pro just won't pick up on it.

Font Has Missing Characters or Square Boxes Instead of Letters

This is one problem that has a fairly easy solution. Some low-cost font packages, from companies such as FontBank and KeyFonts, didn't come with the complete character set. You'd get all of your letters and numbers, but such characters as a percentage sign or a copyright symbol were missing. In addition, some fonts are all capital letters, with nothing but square or rectangular boxes in the lowercase positions.

Whether this is a cost-based decision or is due to some other cause, I won't hazard a guess. But it can be downright annoying.

If you're not certain whether the font you have has the full character set, use Apple's KeyCaps program (which is installed in the Apple menu) or my favorite, a shareware program, PopChar Pro, both of which will check the letters available on a specific font.

Fortunately, if a specific character symbol isn't available from one font, there's nothing to stop you from switching to the Symbol font or another typeface and using the character from that font instead.

Can't Delete Font in Fonts Folder

This happens every so often. You decide you really don't need a specific font, so you try to trash it. You open your Fonts folder, and attempt to drag the font to the desktop or trash, but you get a message that you can't do so because the file or folder is damaged.

NOTE *You also can't delete a font if any applications are open, so check your application menu. However, in this case, the Finder will put up a very clear message as to why the fonts can't be moved.*

Here's what to do if this happens to you:

1. Check your Mac's drive directory with Disk First Aid or a commercial hard drive repair program, such as Alsoft's DiskWarrior, MicroMat's TechTool Pro, or Symantec's Norton Utilities. I'll cover the process in more detail in Chapter 13.

2. After the hard drive is checked, and any disk directory damage repaired, open your System Folder, and drag the Fonts folder onto your Mac's desktop (don't delete it!).

Coping with Font Conflicts

3. Restart your Mac. The process will create a brand new, empty Fonts folder inside the System Folder.

4. Open the old Fonts folder on your Mac's desktop and remove the font you want to trash. This should work properly this time (if not, try step 1 again).

5. Select all of the remaining fonts and drag them to the closed System Folder icon, then OK the message from the Finder to place them in the Fonts folder.

6. Trash your old Fonts folder.

7. Empty the trash.

This process has worked for me every time I've been unable to remove a font. I won't necessarily say it's caused by a corrupt Fonts folder or a corrupt font or hard drive directory damage. It can be one or all of these, but at least you'll be able to start fresh with a brand new Fonts folder.

Font Organization Tips and Tricks

Fonts are everywhere. They come in low-cost packages, and they are included with various and sundry software boxes from Adobe, Corel, Microsoft (even with their free Internet applications), and elsewhere. In years past, if you wanted a lot of fonts, you had to pay a pretty penny for them, or get low-quality knock-offs that offered poor quality or were missing some of the more obscure characters.

Today, without a substantial investment, you could end up with hundreds or even thousands of fonts from here, there, and everywhere. So what do you do with all of them? Just install them on your Mac and use when necessary? It's not that easy.

Mac Font Folder Limits

Apple has thoughtfully (or otherwise) limited the size of your Fonts folder to 128 separate font resource files (at least through Mac OS 8.6), which are defined as files containing bitmap fonts or font suitcases. PostScript printer fonts don't count in this figure.

Apple isn't just trying to shortchange the dedicated font user from having a variety of fonts around. There are simple reasons why it's not a good idea to have too many fonts installed at any one time. For one thing, many programs have limits as to how many open fonts they can handle. It's typically 256 fonts, where there's a limit at all.

In addition, if you try to open up more than a few hundred items on your Mac, the operating system's own built-in limits come to the fore. You may experience out-of-memory messages or messages that too many files are open.

The solution is simply to keep your font menus as short as possible, and only activate the ones you truly need. After all, it is hardly likely you will need to run 50 fonts per page, unless you're writing a ransom note.

Mac OS 9 Brings Font Capacity Relief

With Mac OS 9, Apple has addressed some big limits in font handling capability. For one thing, the 128 font resource limit is gone, replaced by a limit of 512.

In addition, they've increased the maximum number of open files from 348 to 8,169. Now you may not see the significance here, because you hardly expect to be running 348 open files at the same time, but it's an easy limit to reach.

When you boot your Mac, all those things in your System Folder needed to make your Mac run count up to over 100 open files. Many programs are made up of little components that run when you double-click a program's icon. Software with the abiiity to handle plug-ins or add-on modules to enhance their features contribute to this. So you can see that even opening three or four programs will get you up to that limitation, when you add in all the fonts you have available.

These changes in Mac OS 9 can mean greater stability for your Mac, since you won't run out of system resources to handle extra open applications, and you have the ability to run more fonts than you ever thought possible.

NOTE   *The arrival of Mac OS 9 also made a number of programs, including Adobe Type Manager, incompatible because of these changes and others. Fortunately, most of the problems were quickly addressed with program updates.*

On the other hand, having a font menu with 512 separate listings on it (even if your programs could handle a font menu that big) could be an unwieldy thing to handle. So I still recommend a font manager program, which, by the way, forms the topic of the next section.

Font Organization
Tips and Tricks

A Look at a Font Manager

The dilemma of having to load and unload a lot of fonts was especially cumbersome in the days before Mac System 7 came out, when you had to use a clunky program called Font/DA Mover to move screen fonts in and out of your System file. Half the time, the program would crash your Mac, especially when you needed to do a lot of font adjustments in a single step.

A clever programmer, Steve Brecher, created a solution. It was called Suitcase (see Figure 6-1), and it was designed to open and close fonts, regardless of whether they were truly installed in the System Folder.

NOTE   *You'll find a demonstration version of Suitcase on this book's CD.*

It worked by fooling "Mother Nature" (in this case, the Mac operating system) into thinking that the fonts were indeed in their proper location, the Fonts folder. Some call the program a clever hack, but I won't use that term.

So all you had to do was create a special folder for your fonts, then use Suitcase (or one of the other programs that perform this function) to switch your fonts on and off like a light switch.

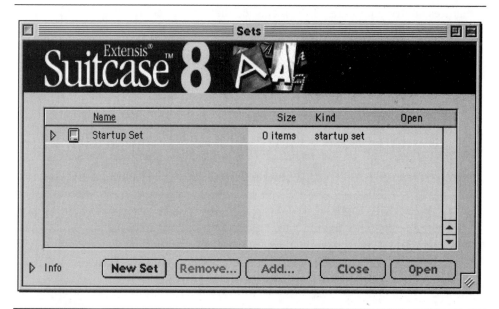

FIGURE 6-1   The latest version of Suitcase, now published by Extensis, can be used to organize even the largest font libraries

The fact of the matter is that it was a terrific way to keep your font menus lean and mean and deal with large numbers of fonts, without having to go through the usual installation process.

In addition to Suitcase (which, after going through three publishers, is still going strong), there's Adobe Type Manager Deluxe (see Figure 6-2) and Alsoft's MasterJuggler.

The Font Reserve Alternative

Another font management program, DiamondSoft's Font Reserve, works by putting your entire font collection (except System Folder fonts) in a single, huge database. The program then goes through them and figures out your font conflicts and whether any fonts are damaged.

The advantage here is one of organization. You simply add the fonts to the program's database file, and it sorts them all out for you. It works best, as do the other font management programs, with a large library. The larger your font library, the more valuable one of these programs will be to keep it in tip-top shape.

NOTE   *A special limited-function version of Font Reserve is included on this book's CD.*

A Handy-Dandy Font Organizing Routine (Using a Font Manager)

If you've got a lot of fonts and need to activate bunches of them at a time, here are some suggestions on how to organize them so you don't run into conflicts and problems launching your applications.

This routine assumes you will be using one of the font managing programs described earlier. Otherwise, feel free to ignore these suggestions:

- **Keep the System Folder's Fonts folder small.**   When you have a font manager, you don't have to put all your fonts in the normal place. The font manager software will do those chores. Just keep your basic set of Apple-installed fonts in your Fonts folder, the ones that you see on your screen beneath icons, in the menu bar, or in titles. These include: Charcoal, Chicago, Capitals, Gadget, Geneva, Impact, Monaco, New York, Sand, Symbol, Textile, and Techno. You may also want to leave fonts that you use all the time, such as Courier, Helvetica, and Times. The rest can be placed elsewhere.

Font Organization Tips and Tricks

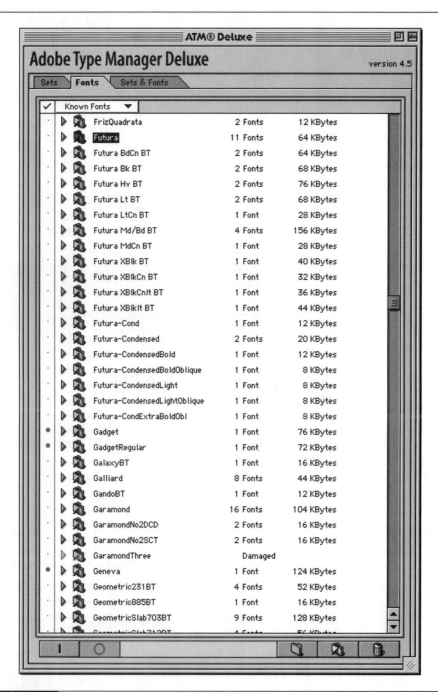

FIGURE 6-2 Adobe Type Manager Deluxe not only cleans up the display of PostScript fonts on your Mac, but also lets you activate or deactivate them

NOTE

If you're using Adobe Acrobat, you'll also want to have these fonts installed in your Fonts folder: AdobeSerMM, AdobeSanMM, Adobe Serif MM and Adobe Sans MM.

■ **Put the rest of your fonts in another folder.** Aside from the essential fonts, put the rest of your font library in a brand new folder, which you can call Resources (or anything you like that makes sense to you, such as Other Fonts, and so on). This folder doesn't have to be in the System Folder. It only has to be on a hard drive that is mounted on your Mac when you need the fonts.

■ **Sort fonts by font manufacturer.** This makes sorting easy if you have a big font library. Within your Resources folder, create folders bearing the names of the manufacturers of your fonts, such as Adobe, Bitstream, Monotype, and so on. By doing this, it'll be easier to keep tabs on possible font conflicts, which occur when you have more than one font of the same name open.

TIP

If you can't tell who made the font by looking at the icon, use the Finder's Get Info command and look for a copyright notice. There are no guarantees you'll find one, but it's worth trying.

■ **Set aside separate folders for each type family.** This is also a good tip for a huge library. After you subdivide fonts by font manufacturer, set aside a separate folder for each type family. Put Helvetica in one folder, Times in another, and so on. Just remember to try not to mix fonts of the same name from different vendors.

■ **Be cautious about TrueType fonts for professional output.** Before you decide whether to use a TrueType font, contact the printer or service bureau who will be handling your high-resolution output. Be guided by what they say in terms of font compatibility. And, of course, feel free to seek another firm if the one you call first doesn't give you the services you need.

■ **Be cautious about specifying PostScript fonts for your Web site.** Just as TrueType fonts aren't a good idea for professional output, the reverse is true on the World Wide Web. The likelihood that a large number of folks will have the fonts you specify is slim, since the basic system fonts for both Macs and Windows-based computers are TrueType. If you keep to those basic TrueType fonts, you'll stand a good chance of providing the best quality font display for the largest number of Net surfers.

Font Organization Tips and Tricks

■ **Disable fonts you don't need.**   Enjoy the convenience of the font menu manager. Disable any font you have no need for, so your font menus are kept short and your application launch times are as brief as possible.

A Handy-Dandy Font Organizing Routine (Without a Font Manager)

If you don't have a large font library (that is, more than 100 to 200 fonts), there's probably no need to buy a separate program to manage your font library. But you'll want to keep a few things in mind as you set up your libraries:

■ **Combine font suitcases.**   If you have a lot of fonts from the same family, combine the font suitcases. That way you'll see fewer files in your Fonts folder, and you'll get around the 128-font resource limit imposed by Apple Computer.

NOTE *As I explain earlier in this chapter, Apple's font limits have risen to 512 beginning with Mac OS 9. But you'll still want to keep your Fonts folder small, so you can easily see what you have available.*

■ **Remove fonts you don't need.**   If you don't intend to use certain fonts, you can move them elsewhere. You may want to create a folder labeled Fonts (Disabled), which corresponds to the folders in which disabled Control Panels and Extensions are placed. Put the fonts you don't need in those folders.

TIP *If you're using Casady & Greene's Conflict Catcher to handle your System Folder, you'll be pleased to know it's just as capable when handling the contents of the Fonts folder (though it requires a restart for any changes in font lineup to take effect). You'll find a demonstration version of Conflict Catcher on this book's CD.*

Quit Applications Before Removing Fonts to the Fonts Folder

Unlike font management software, you cannot remove a font unless all open applications have been quit first. If you think you've closed all programs, yet still get the message, check to see if you have any special icon palettes on your Mac's desktop, which are commonly used to launch programs and documents. One example is Apple's Launcher. Yes, it is an application, too, and you can quit it simply by clicking the close box.

Once you quit all open applications, you should be able to remove fonts. If you still get a message that applications are open, restart your Mac and try again.

Or just open Extensions Manager, choose a Mac OS (whatever version you have) Base Set and restart. That should close any hidden or background applications your Mac is using.

Coming Next

In this chapter, you learned about the various font formats on your Mac, how to manage your fonts, and how to deal with font conflicts.

In Chapter 7, I'll cover the trials and tribulations of dealing with graphic files, with special emphasis on Web-based graphics, and sharing files with Windows users.

Font Organization Tips and Tricks

Chapter 7

Dealing with Graphic File Headaches

Y ou'd think that the number one problem a computing consultant deals with would be system-related problems. Considering that application quits and crashes are part and parcel of the personal computing experience, this would seem to be a very logical assumption.

But one of the most vexing problems I deal with on a regular basis is the matter of graphic files. The advent of the World Wide Web and easy Internet access has made it easy as pie to send and receive files. Since the way files are handled differs from one computing platform to the other, it makes for a corresponding number of problems.

The most common complaint is that folks you send your graphic files to cannot read them, or that you cannot read the files they send to you.

A Quick Review of Graphic File Formats

There are dozens of graphic file formats that exist across the various computing platforms. Fortunately, some of these formats are not often used cross-platform, so there isn't much likelihood that you'll encounter many of them. If you do, a shareware program mentioned later in this chapter, GraphicConverter, may serve to help you deal with some of the most arcane types of graphics.

In this section, I'm concentrating on the types of files you're apt to encounter on a regular basis on your travels on the Internet or when exchanging files with your contacts who use the other platform. In addition, I'll list the DOS file extensions that apply to these files, so if you're converting the file to Windows you can attach the appropriate file.

NOTE *Dealing with graphic file formats isn't the only source of trouble in handling cross-platform issues. I'll cover the subject in much more detail in Chapter 11.*

■ **ART (.art) files** This is a graphic file format used by AOL for processing Web-based images. It's designed to speed delivery of Web pages to AOL members by compressing graphics in this proprietary format. Unfortunately, this feature can result in the loss of quality on Web-based images, and definitely kills any animation that might be present in the original picture. That, in itself, is a real downer, since well done animation is one of the great joys of visiting a Web site. In addition, you need AOL's software to actually open such images. Even the full-featured GraphicConverter software doesn't read the format. Worse, the file's name isn't changed by the conversion process (so it'll still retain its .gif or .jpg file extension, for example), and you won't know it's in the wrong format until you try to open it. If you're an AOL member, the best way to avoid these problems is simply to turn off the option to compress Web graphics. It's a WWW preference in AOL's software.

- **AVI (.avi) files**   This is a Windows-based movie format, designed to compete with QuickTime. QuickTime 4.0 handles such files with aplomb.

- **BMP (.bmp) files**   The Windows answer to PICT. When you use the print screen feature under Windows, the image you capture is saved in this format. Since it is a bitmap format, you can scale it downward (with increased resolution), but when you scale upwards, the size of the dots grow larger, and thus image quality suffers.

- **EPS (.eps) files**   The term is short for Encapsulated PostScript. EPS files contain PostScript instructions that require a PostScript printer to produce good quality output. On a non-PostScript printer, all you get is a low-resolution PICT version. EPS files are normally created by high-end illustration programs and are imported into desktop publishing or word processing documents. This is the only vector format that I'll list here; it's a format that you can scale in any size and still have it reproduce at the full resolution of your output device.

- **GIF (.gif) files**   This is another compressed graphic format, which originated with CompuServe. GIF stands for Graphic Interchange Format. Such files have advantages and disadvantages. The advantage is that they are suitable for Web-based animations, but you are limited to 256 colors (a far cry from JPEG). In addition to their Web capabilities, GIF files tend to work better with text than JPEG.

- **JPEG (.jpg) files**   One of the popular file formats used for Web-based artwork. The term stands for Joint Photographic Experts Group, and the file uses compression to save storage space. The compression technique is called *lossy,* because portions of the file are removed, though it takes a lot of compression to reduce image quality to a noticeable degree. However, the quality loss isn't near as great as in the GIF format. JPEG files work great with photographs, less well with graphics that contain text.

- **MOV (.mov) files**   This is a format for QuickTime movies. You can open it with QuickTime Player or any other program that can read QuickTime files.

**A Quick Review
of Graphic File Formats**

- **PCX (.pcx) files** This is a PC format used for bitmap graphics, and it's used for PC Paintbrush and other programs. There are four basic variations of this format, but only the version 5 format supports 24-bit color.

- **PICT (.pct) files** This is the native Macintosh bitmap file format. When you save images to the Mac clipboard, or make a screen capture (using such shortcuts as COMMAND-SHIFT-3 and COMMAND-SHIFT-4), the files are saved in PICT format. This is, by the way, the format I used when I captured screen images for use in this book. It suffers from the same shortcomings as any bitmap image format; it scales down nicely, and quality is lost proportionately as you scale upward. This format is not recommended if you wish to send a file to a Windows user.

- **PNG (.png) files** The promoters of this format called it a successor to GIF. PNG is short for Portable Network Graphics format, and it's designed to offer better file compression and improved image quality (including support for 24-bit color). PNG format is supported by Web browsers that are compatible with HTML 4.0; other browsers just get the GIF variation of the image.

- **SGI (.sgi) files** This is an image format used for SGI (formerly Silicon Graphics) computer systems. Since SGI workstations are often used in the creation of high-level graphics and movie animations, you may from time to time run across such image files.

- **Targa (.tga) files** The format was first used by Truevision for their Targa and Vista video capture boards. It's a bitmap file format for high quality graphics, used in a number of 2-D and 3-D programs.

NOTE *The Targa capture boards are now marketed by Pinnacle Systems. If you wish to explore desktop video editing in more detail, you'll want to read Chapter 19.*

- **TIFF (.tif) files** The term is short for Tagged-Image File Format. In case you were wondering, the "tagged" aspects are the enhancements made to improve the appearance of the image. TIFF files are commonly used for photographs and other high-quality images. And, need I add, a full-color TIFF photograph can be many, many megabytes in size (which is why such programs as Photoshop require huge amounts of RAM to work efficiently with them). TIFF files are commonly used for creating high-quality printed materials.

- **WMF (.wmf) files** The term is short for Windows Metafile Format, and it's used for exchanging graphics among Microsoft Windows programs.

How to View PC Graphics on a Mac

As Apple's system software has come of age, the tools to handle files of different formats have grown more robust. For example, Apple's File Exchange, the descendant of both Mac OS Easy Open and PC Exchange, lets you easily map Windows file extensions to corresponding Mac files. As a result, you can easily open those files simply by double-clicking on them—that is, so long as you have a Mac program with which to view the files.

Fortunately, most of the graphic files you're apt to receive are easily read by one or more programs you already have on your Mac.

These are some examples:

- **Adobe Photo Deluxe** Although it's considered a low-end image editing program (because of its low price) it is quite capable of reading and saving files in a number of graphic formats, both PC and Mac-based. You'll find this program bundled with many of the lower-cost scanners from several manufacturers. In fact, you may already have a copy if you have one of those products.

- **Adobe Photoshop** This is the premiere image editing program, used by professionals in the graphic arts industry. It can read most of the graphic file formats I've described here, including EPS files. A number of scanners include the full or limited function versions of Photoshop as part of the package. If you're lucky enough to get this program, you'll find it a valuable tool to process graphic files of all kinds.

- **GraphicConverter** This is a favorite of mine. It's a popular Mac shareware program (used extensively to handle the figures for this book), which is capable of reading dozens and dozens of types of graphic files on the major computing platforms (including Unix). I won't begin to list the formats that are supported; the program is updated several times a year with still more supported file formats and more features. A notable exception are EPS files, which require a separate program to rasterize the images (see the previous bullet about Photoshop).

■ **PictureViewer**   This program is part of QuickTime 4, and it's capable of reading graphics in such formats as BMP, JPEG, MacPaint (similar to PICT), Photoshop, PICT, PNG, QuickTime, SGI, TGA, and TIFF.

■ **QuickTime Player**   This program can handle the same range of graphic formats as PictureViewer, plus QuickTime movies, Windows-based AVI movies, and many more. Counting the audio and video formats, QuickTime Player can read more than 30 file formats.

> **NOTE** *In addition to working directly via a QuickTime program, File Exchange will let you select a QuickTime translator to work with another program to help you view a file. The choice will always be labeled "with QuickTime translation."*

■ **Your Web browser**   New Macs and system upgrades come with both Microsoft Internet Explorer and Netscape. Either program can handle the basic image files, such as GIF and JPEG, plus the Windows BMP format.

> **NOTE** *I've made no attempt here to cover all the programs that can read various graphic file formats. There are far too many to list. Instead I'm concentrating on the ones most often available. If you have other software in these product categories, simply check your documentation for the file formats that are supported.*

As you see, your Mac is probably well equipped to deal with graphic files. Regardless of whether they come from a Web site, email or another source, here's how you'd view such files:

1. Locate your graphic file.

2. Double-click on the graphic.

3. If File Exchange produces a dialog asking you to select from a list of applications that can read the file, choose an appropriate program (use the ones listed earlier as a guide).

NOTE *When you select a file to use when opening a document in File Exchange, the program will remember your choice and religiously use that same program each time a similar document is opened. If you wish to remove that choice, make sure the Always Show Choices When Translating Files option is checked. Older versions of Mac Easy Open labeled this option Always Show Dialog Box.*

4. Click the Open button to launch the application you select and open the document. If all goes well, you should see your picture file on your Mac's screen in short order.

A Quick Review of Problems in Opening Graphic Files

Even if you have the right programs, it's possible that you will run into trouble when it comes to opening a graphic file. Here are some common symptoms and their solutions:

- **Application not found message** If you get an alert that an application can't be found to open the document, check your Control Panels folder to make sure that File Exchange or its pre-Mac OS 8.5 ancestor for file translations, Mac OS Easy Open, is installed. If it's not there, use Extensions Manager to reactivate the program, or, if it isn't available, reinstall it from your system software disks. Chapter 2 covers the subject of system installations in more detail.

- **Wrong application opens** If the act of double-clicking on a file opens a program other than the one you selected, make sure the Always Show Choices When Translating Files option is selected. Then just select a different program to open the document from the list. If you have an older version of the Mac OS with Mac OS Easy Open, you'll find a handy Delete Preferences button on the opening screen that will accomplish the task. If it still doesn't work, rebuild the desktop.

NOTE *You rebuild your Mac's desktop by restarting, then, before the Finder loads (after the last extension icon appears on your screen), hold down the COMMAND-OPTION keys and OK the dialog to rebuild the desktop (this action must be repeated for each drive volume you use on your Mac).*

How to View PC Graphics on a Mac

■ **Try the Open dialog box**   If all else fails, try opening the application first, then go to the File menu, choose Open and select the file from the list (you'll probably have to navigate to the correct folder or disk). If the file doesn't show in the Open dialog box, use the program's Insert or Import or Place feature, if available. If the program can open a particular type of graphic file, one of these commands ought to work.

Preparing Mac Graphics to Work in the Windows World

Wouldn't it be nice if all graphics files worked the same way on both Mac and Windows computers?

Alas, it is not to be. On the Mac, a file's format is automatically recognized by the Finder, assuming the file's attributes are intact, of course, using the invisible desktop files that record a file's type and creator code.

For other computing platforms, including Windows and Unix, you have to, in effect, tell the operating system what sort of file it is by using a three-letter extension at the end of the file's name (files saved by applications on those operating systems are already correctly named). Otherwise, the operating system won't know how to handle the files. I'll cover the subject of cross-platform file issues more thoroughly in Chapter 11.

NOTE   *Naming a file is half the battle; the file actually has to be saved in the proper format for it to be opened properly. Otherwise, the file may come up as damaged or in the wrong format when someone on another computing platform tries to access it.*

So, for example, a JPEG file, a format commonly used in Web graphics, must have a .jpg extension to the file name so the folks who aren't using Macs can access the file. Here's how you can set up your files so users of Windows won't run into trouble in trying to use those files.

CAUTION   *When sending files to Windows users, try not to use Mac-specific formats, such as PICT. It's very easy to change the file format to something that is compatible without losing image quality.*

File Is in Correct Format

If the file has already been saved in a format that can be read under Windows, just follow these steps (if the naming isn't correct):

1. Click on the file's name to select it and press the RETURN key.

2. Add the proper file extension to the end of the file's name. For example, if the file is called rockoids and it's in JPEG format, you'll rename it rockoids.jpg.

Now you can send your file to Windows users and they'll be able to open it with any program that can read such files.

> **NOTE**
>
> *Under Windows, when your document is correctly named, it'll recognize the file as associated with a specific program, so you can double-click on the file and have it open in the proper program. If double-clicking doesn't work, Windows users should be able to see the file by using the Open command from the File menu.*

File Is in Wrong Format

If the file you have is not already in a format that can be conveniently read by a Windows-based computer, you'll need to not only rename it, but convert it to a format that does work. Here's what to do:

1. Open the file in your preferred graphic program.

2. Choose Save As from the File menu, which will bring up a screen where you can select the format in which to save the file. If the program has no such feature, such as Apple's PictureViewer (shown in Figure 7-1), choose the Export command instead (if available).

> **NOTE**
>
> *The QuickTime Pro upgrade, giving you all the extra export and basic video editing capabilities, is $30. However, if you buy a new Apple computer or a retail Mac OS upgrade, you'll be entitled to a free upgrade to QuickTime Pro when you register your new product.*

Preparing Mac Graphics
to Work in the Windows World

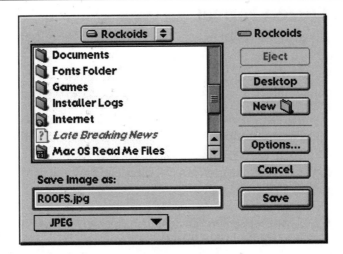

FIGURE 7-1   PictureViewer, part of Apple's QuickTime, lets you export files in a number of popular formats (if you upgrade to the Pro version)

3. Choose the file format from the list. Notice that PictureViewer will automatically pick the file extension for you.

4. Click the Save button to convert the file and change its name.

Now you should be able to send that file to the Windows users of your acquaintance with reasonable assurance they'll be able to open the file without encountering any problems.

Summing Up

In this chapter, I covered the ways to effectively handle graphics problems, so you can freely exchange images with Windows users. This is only a subset of the issues you'll have to consider should you wish to share files with Windows users or if you are on a cross-platform network. I'll cover the subject in much more detail in Chapter 11.

In the next chapter, you'll learn how to install, configure, and troubleshoot your printer.

Chapter 8

Making Your Printer Sing

There's hardly a Mac out there that doesn't have a printer attached. The paperless revolution promised at the dawn of the personal computer era seems far, far away. Today, you not only print your normal word processing documents, but also Web pages and even those electronic manuals that substitute for real printed instruction books for most products these days.

But with so many choices, it's hard to know where to begin or what to do when you install your new printer and find it's not working as it should.

I've put this chapter together to cover typical problems when working with a printer and ways to get it to work properly again.

Installing a Personal Printer

It's amazing what a couple of hundred dollars will buy you in a new printer these days. Such companies as Canon, Epson, and Hewlett-Packard offer great quality full-color printers that can work in a home or small office. Like consumer VCRs these days, they are so cheap that if they break down, there's little problem in replacing them with the latest and greatest successor in that manufacturer's product line.

Here are some things to consider when setting up one of these personal printers (including inkjet models and USB laser printers):

- **Don't forget to install the printer's software.**   Since Apple left the low-cost printer market, don't expect to find many usable printer drivers on your Mac. Use the installation disks provided by the printer's manufacturer. Check the setup instructions carefully in case the installer places drivers for several models on your Mac. For example, Epson printers come with serial (or USB) drivers and drivers that work with models with a network card (for LocalTalk and/or Ethernet). The latter will have an "AT" in the name you see in the Mac Chooser, so be sure to select the correct one.

- **On older Macs, don't forget to turn off AppleTalk.**   A serial printer, such as most lower-cost inkjet models, won't work on the printer port with AppleTalk activated. If you are forced to use AppleTalk for another printer that requires LocalTalk, you can handle this dilemma in two ways. One is to connect the printer to your Mac's modem port (if it has one), but then you may have to share it with your modem if you use an Internet or online service. You could, of course, buy a "port sharing" program or a switchbox to get around this. Or just hook it up to the printer port, and make sure AppleTalk is turned off in the Chooser. For Macs with USB ports, this problem no longer applies (thank heaven).

> **NOTE** *Another symptom of failing to turn off AppleTalk when trying to use a serial printer attached to the printer port is a "serial port in use" message. But, usually, you won't be able to retain the printer port setting for such a printer if AppleTalk is left on.*

■ **Remove packing materials before use.**   Be sure that the cardboard, plastic, and/or tape fittings are taken off before you put the printer into service. The delicate inner workings of a low-cost printer are easily damaged.

■ **Be careful about third-party or recycled ink cartridges.**   My conclusion about this is the same as recycled toner (discussed later in the chapter). Quality tends to be inconsistent. In one example (and I won't mention the brand name in case I just got a bad product), my inkjet printer required repeated head cleaning operations before I could get reasonable quality. By then a large amount of ink was spent, and the money I saved by buying a cheaper cartridge was not worth it.

> **NOTE** *Head cleaning is a process where the ink is systematically sprayed through the printer's nozzles to clean the pathways. It's done automatically when you install new printer cartridges, and you can do it using the printer's software if print quality declines.*

Installing a Network Printer

It used to be that networked printers cost several thousand dollars, and they were only suitable for a large office. However, prices have come down to the point where a network-capable laser printer costs no more than the lowest priced personal laser printers of just a few years ago.

> **NOTE** *I define a network printer as any model that comes with a built-in LocalTalk and/or Ethernet port so you can hook it up to a network consisting of Macs, or PCs and Macs.*

Even if you're using such a printer at home, the ability to seamlessly network with a second Mac may make this sort of product something to seriously consider. Here are a few things to remember when installing and using a network printer:

- **Use Apple's LaserWriter 8 driver unless the printer uses a custom printer driver.**   Check the documentation to see if that custom driver is necessary to ensure compatibility with the printer's unique features. Even if you stick with Apple's driver, it doesn't hurt to run your printer's installation disks anyway, as the installer will also usually install a PPD file for the printer (see the section entitled "What's a PPD File and What Do I Need It For?" later in this chapter). Basically, Apple's LaserWriter 8 supports most popular PostScript printers. There's also the added advantage of good compatibility when Apple updates its system software, since the update will, if need be, include a new version of the driver. That's not always true about the alternatives, such as Adobe's PS Printer (also known sometimes as AdobePS).

> **NOTE**   *As this book was written, version 1.0 of Adobe's desktop publishing program, InDesign, was released. This program requires the AdobePS driver (supplied on the installer CD) and a PostScript printer (supporting Level 2 or Level 3 PostScript) to output your document directly (otherwise you have to convert to Acrobat or PDF format first). Consider these requirements if you decide to use this program.*

- **Be sure to remove packing materials before use.**   Manufacturers include all sorts of little doo-dads to protect the printer during shipment to dealers and end-users. These include cardboard and plastic inserts or pieces of tape. Be sure to check the printer thoroughly to make sure all this material has been removed before you try to run the printer. You will probably have to open various doors and compartments on the printer to locate all of the material (the instruction or setup guide usually explains where to find them). If you fail to remove everything, you may experience paper jams or erratic performance (not to mention the potential to damage the unit).

- **Rock toner cartridge back and forth before installing.**   By properly distributing the toner, you can be sure that you'll see even print density on your documents.

- **Be careful about recycled toner cartridges.** While such products are often advertised as offering superior quality or longevity, my experience has been inconsistent. One cartridge works fine, the next is unusable. And print quality may differ considerably from the manufacturer's normal range. If you are not preparing your documents for reproduction or for client review, and don't need the absolute best quality, you can save money by buying recycled. In this case, try to stick with a company that offers you consistent performance from cartridge to cartridge.

- **Consider a used printer.** You can often get older top-of-the-line laser printers from Apple, HP, and other companies for $200–300, in perfectly usable condition. Many of these printers were designed for large office environments, with life spans of hundreds of thousands of copies before requiring major overhauls. If they haven't been abused, you can expect them to work reliably, year after year without a problem. You should, however, test the printer thoroughly to make sure print quality is good, the unit doesn't make weird scraping or scratching noises, and the paper doesn't jam.

USB vs. Network Printers: Is There a Difference?

A new generation of printers has come to market. In the old days, you hooked up a printer to your serial port (printer or modem or combined), or the Ethernet port. However, new Mac computers, ranging from the iMac and iBook to the Power Macintosh G4, don't have serial ports. In addition to Ethernet, they use USB ports for printer connections and other peripherals.

So is there really a difference? Why buy one over the other? It largely depends on your needs and the performance level you want to achieve. I'll describe some of the differences in the following sections.

Network Printers

A network printer, typically supporting the Adobe PostScript page description language, will usually have its own built-in CPU and memory, meaning it doesn't use your Mac's CPU to run. More important, such printers can be shared across a network by other Macs, and they will be able to correctly handle the output from PostScript programs, such as Adobe Illustrator and Macromedia FreeHand, or documents containing PostScript or EPS graphics with top quality.

USB vs. Network Printers: Is There a Difference?

NOTE *When I say a network printer "usually" has a built-in CPU, I mean that it's not done all the time. Some printers and high-resolution typesetting machines actually use a Mac or PC to handle CPU chores.*

In general, most networked printers are laser printers, black and white or color. Other networked printers are high-end inkjets or color printers with other technologies (such as dye sublimation) or imagesetters, which provide output on paper or film for the printing industry.

NOTE *Apple's Printer Share software (formerly GrayShare) does let you share an Apple StyleWriter printer across a network, but it also uses the host Mac (the one to which the printer is attached) as the processor, which means your Mac's performance suffers when others access that printer.*

USB Printers

While some USB printers have come to market supporting PostScript, these printers are simply the descendants of the regular printers you'd attach to your Mac's serial port. We used to call them QuickDraw printers, because they supported Apple's native image display language, and could support bitmap or TrueType fonts.

USB printers are not designed to be shared among Macs, although you can get USB switchboxes, which allow you to switch them to work with whatever Mac needs them at the moment. In addition, such printers use your Mac's CPU horsepower to process the files that are being printed, and that means performance may suffer somewhat while a document is being printed.

Both USB and serial printers are low cost and deliver great quality, especially when it comes to color photos. For personal use, and limited production needs, such printers make a lot of sense.

Even better, some models, such as a few of Epson's and HP's color inkjets, can be adapted to network use later on by installation of an Ethernet network card. But you still have to consider whether or not you need PostScript, which, as it happens, forms the subject of the next section in this chapter.

PostScript: What Is It? Why Do I Need It?

Back in the 1980s, Adobe Systems invented the PostScript language, which reduces the elements of the printed page to math. PostScript is device independent, which means it can work with a printer at its maximum possible level of quality, ranging from a cheap laser printer to the most expensive imagesetters used by the printing industry.

If you just intend to use PostScript fonts with your documents, you don't need a PostScript printer. Adobe Type Manager (which comes free with Adobe's Acrobat Reader) or Adobe Type Manager Deluxe (a retail version that also manages font libraries) can process PostScript fonts and make them work perfectly fine on a non-PostScript printer, such as one of those ever-popular color inkjet models.

If, however, you plan on using PostScript (or EPS) graphics in your document, you have no choice. To get the highest possible quality, you need to buy either a PostScript printer or one for which you can add one of those PostScript software programs (which are mentioned in the section entitled "Using PostScript Software for an Inkjet Printer"). Otherwise, the output quality suffers. All those fancy graphics will appear as low-resolution bitmapped images (not very nice).

Is It PostScript or a Clone?

Just as Apple produced TrueType fonts to, in part, avoid paying licensing fees to Adobe for PostScript font technology, there are printers out there that use PostScript page description emulation technology rather than license Adobe's brand.

The telltale sign is in the printer's specifications. They will list the printer as "PostScript compatible" or talk of various printer language emulations, including PostScript, but won't specifically say anything about Adobe PostScript.

In previous years, this was a problem. You bought a printer that used a PostScript clone, and you were in for trouble. Simple documents, complex documents—sometimes they wouldn't print properly, even though they would work just fine with a printer that used true Adobe PostScript.

Worse, quite often you could not predict which documents would print properly and which wouldn't. Output quality would be inconsistent. Halftones, the dots that make up a photograph, would reproduce poorly at times, and other times it would take extended amounts of time to process even the simplest documents.

However, the quality of the clones has improved, and you don't hear too much anymore of troubles with such printers. I won't argue for or against a PostScript clone, except to say that current HP printers use clone technology, and I haven't had reports of any problems, either with my own clone printer or the ones used by many clients.

If you are, however, considering buying a very old clone printer, I would still urge caution. New printers have become inexpensive enough to make the decision to upgrade not nearly as difficult as it used to be.

Using PostScript Software for an Inkjet Printer

This seems to be the ideal combo. You buy a cheap color inkjet printer, then get yourself a PostScript program, such as Adobe PressReady, Birmy PowerScript, Epson Stylus RIP, or Infowave SuperScript. All you have to do is install the program and you'll have a genuine Adobe PostScript printer.

Does it really work that way? What are the tradeoffs?

Let me give you the good stuff first. These programs do work! They actually let you use a supported inkjet printer and output your PostScript graphics. And the quality can be first-rate.

In operation, you normally set up one of your Macs as a server, and the other Macs on your network work as clients, accessing the server Mac for printing. But there are potential liabilities (and solutions) with these programs:

- **They're RAM hungry.**   Figure on giving a PostScript program (or RIP, Raster Image Processor) a good 15 to 20MB of RAM to do its stuff—and that's just the minimum setting. If your Mac doesn't have enough to handle this program and your regular software at the same time, you'll want to consider a possible RAM upgrade.

- **They have to be running for you to print.**   You can't just print your document; you have to launch the software RIP first and keep it running while your document is running. If you quit the program prematurely, your documents will stop then and there, even if they're halfway through your printer.

- **They will slow down your Mac.**   As with an inkjet printer, a software RIP program uses your Mac's CPU for processing (unlike a regular PostScript laser printer, which has its own CPU and memory). Everything you do will bog down until the printing process is done. This can be downright annoying if several Macs are accessing the one that is handling double-duty as a print server.

- **You'll get slow printer performance.**   Don't expect miracles. Depending on how fast your Mac runs, you can expect it to take minutes (sometimes many minutes) to handle a document that may normally output on an inkjet printer in less than a minute.

■ **You can expect some bugs.** In my experience, these software RIPs can be buggy, especially if you are working in several programs at once. You'll want to restrict the number of programs you run while such a program is handling the printing chores.

■ **Consider a dedicated Mac to run a software RIP.** This is, in a sense, the same way some imagesetters are run. You set aside one computer to do nothing but process print jobs. That way, you don't run into any performance issues, and the job doesn't bog down any production machines. This is an ideal task for an older Mac due for retirement, but first check the minimum requirements of your PostScript software. For example, the latest version of Epson's Stylus RIP software requires a Power Macintosh with System 7.6.1 or later. So your older 680x0 Macs won't cut the mustard.

Which Driver Do I Use?

You are ready to set up your printer, and you open the Chooser and you gasp. There are so many choices. What to do?

Sometimes the answer is obvious. If you have a laser printer, you choose LaserWriter 8 (unless you're using a system version that predates the arrival of LaserWriter 8 back in the mid-1990s). That is, unless you have a printer that requires a custom printer driver, such as Adobe's PS Printer (now known simply as AdobePS).

If you have another sort of printer, you'll want to look over the items in the Chooser for something that resembles the model you have (see Figure 8-1).

While some printer drivers are clearly labeled, such as SC 900(AT) for the AppleTalk versions of the Epson Stylus Color 900 series, other drivers may not be quite so easily identified. The best solution is to check your printer's documentation to see what to pick.

NOTE *When you install some inkjet printer software, such as Epson and HP, you'll often find drivers for both serial and AppleTalk versions of the printer. The latter will usually have an AT designation in the level; don't use that one unless you do have a model with LocalTalk or Ethernet ports.*

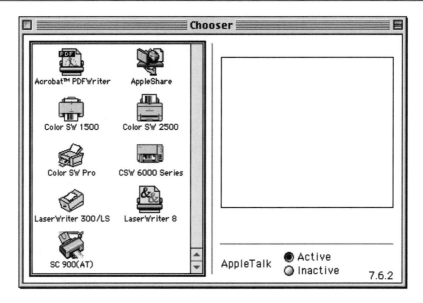

FIGURE 8-1   Which printer should the author use for his Epson 900N inkjet?

What's a PPD File and What Do I Need It For?

You buy a fancy new laser printer and it has a number of handy features. These may include extra paper trays, so you can print documents using various paper sizes without rushing to pull paper in and out. Some printers can even be set to duplex, which means you can automatically print on both sides of the paper.

Other printers may include special resolution or image enhancement technology to provide sharper printing or handling photos. Some have the capability of adjusting printer resolution.

In addition, some of the more sophisticated desktop publishing and graphic programs need to know about your printer to give you the best possible print quality.

But your laser printer driver doesn't automatically realize that your printer can do all those wonderful things. The clever folks at Adobe came up with something called a PostScript Printer Description (PPD) file, which is a text document that tells the driver what your printer can do.

If you feel ambitious and want to see just what this file contains, you can open it in SimpleText or any program that can read plain text files, such as Word. See Figure 8-2 for an example of a PPD file for a large office printer from Hewlett-Packard (the 8000 series), which is typical of the breed.

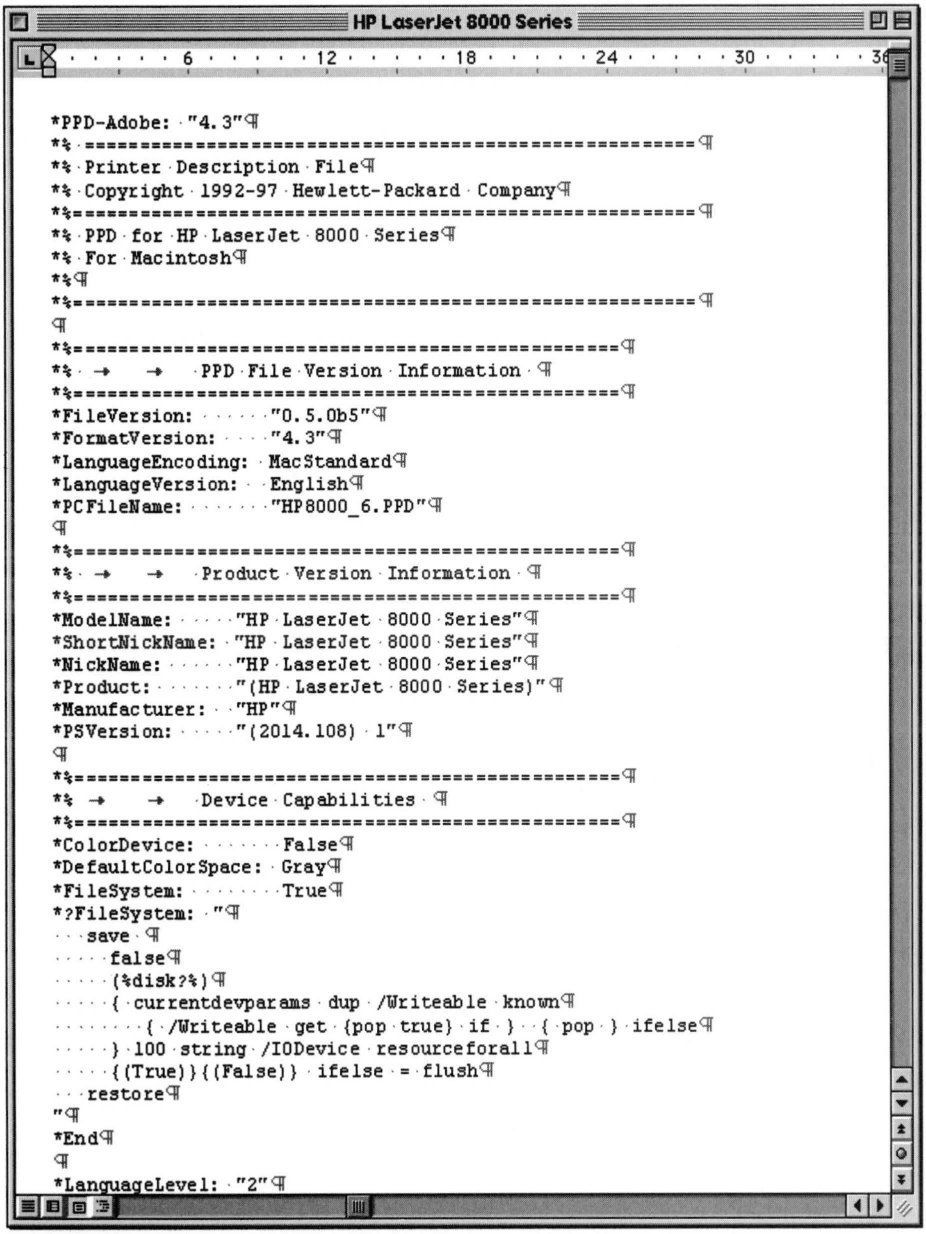

```
*PPD-Adobe: "4.3"¶
*% ===========================================================¶
*% Printer Description File¶
*% Copyright 1992-97 Hewlett-Packard Company¶
*% ===========================================================¶
*% PPD for HP LaserJet 8000 Series¶
*% For Macintosh¶
*%¶
*% ===========================================================¶
¶
*%==========================================================¶
*%  →    →    PPD File Version Information ¶
*%==========================================================¶
*FileVersion: ······"0.5.0b5"¶
*FormatVersion: ····"4.3"¶
*LanguageEncoding: ·MacStandard¶
*LanguageVersion: ·English¶
*PCFileName: ······"HP8000_6.PPD"¶
¶
*%==========================================================¶
*%  →    →    Product Version Information ¶
*%==========================================================¶
*ModelName: ·····"HP LaserJet 8000 Series"¶
*ShortNickName: "HP LaserJet 8000 Series"¶
*NickName: ·····"HP LaserJet 8000 Series"¶
*Product: ·······"(HP LaserJet 8000 Series)" ¶
*Manufacturer: ··"HP"¶
*PSVersion: ·····"(2014.108) 1"¶
¶
*%==========================================================¶
*%  →    →    Device Capabilities ¶
*%==========================================================¶
*ColorDevice: ·······False¶
*DefaultColorSpace: Gray¶
*FileSystem: ········True¶
*?FileSystem: "¶
··save ¶
····false¶
····(%disk?%)¶
····{ currentdevparams dup /Writeable known¶
·······{ /Writeable get {pop true} if } { pop } ifelse¶
·····} 100 string /IODevice resourceforall¶
·····{(True)}{(False)} ifelse = flush¶
···restore¶
"¶
*End¶
¶
*LanguageLevel: "2"¶
```

FIGURE 8-2   The author's printer uses this PPD file for custom options

What's a PPD File
and What Do I Need It For?

How to Install a PPD

In order for your laser printer to work its best, you need to make sure the proper PPD file is selected and installed by the printer driver. Here's how to set up your printer driver to work with your printer:

1. If you aren't setting up an Apple printer, locate your printer's software floppy or CD and see if there's an installer or PPD file available.

2. If you locate an installer file, run it. The action may include just a PPD or, in other situations, a complete set of software that includes a laser printer driver and printer utilities of one sort or another.

3. If the PPD file is a separate item, select the file and drag it to the closed System Folder. The Finder should tell you it's going to go into the Printer Descriptions folder, within the Extensions folder. If you don't see that message, place it there directly yourself. You don't have to restart your Mac for the PPD to be recognized.

4. If you run the installer, you'll most likely have to restart your Mac.

5. Once you've restarted, go to the Chooser and select your laser printer driver, as I've done in Figure 8-3.

6. Click on the printer's name in the Chooser window, which will bring up a Create button.

7. Click Create to begin the setup process.

8. The contents of the Printer Descriptions folder will be compared against your printer's characteristics to see if a matching PPD file can be located (see Figure 8-4). If one is found, you'll see another message, Building Desktop Printer (see Figure 8-5). If the correct PPD is found, you do nothing but wait till the process finishes.

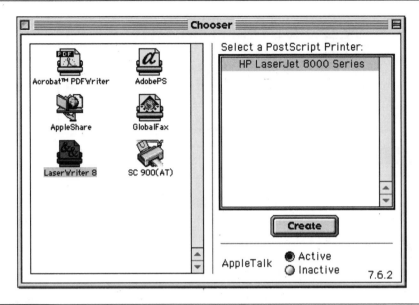

FIGURE 8-3 Click on your printer driver's name to select it

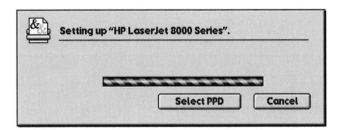

FIGURE 8-4 LaserWriter 8 is checking to see if the proper PPD file is available

What's a PPD File and What Do I Need It For?

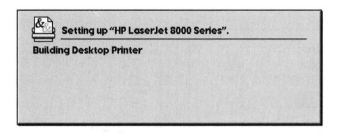

FIGURE 8-5 Success! Your desktop printer icon is being created

If the correct PPD is found, there's nothing more to do than print your documents. However, sometimes, for one of many reasons, you may find that the driver cannot locate a PPD file, or you get a message that you have to change something on it.

Here's a brief listing of what you can do next:

■ **Need to select printer options** If your printer comes in several configurations, you may receive a dialog in which you have to pick the options that apply to your printer. An example is shown in Figure 8-6. You may have to check your printer's documentation or print out a test or configuration page to see the installed options. Once you've done that, just

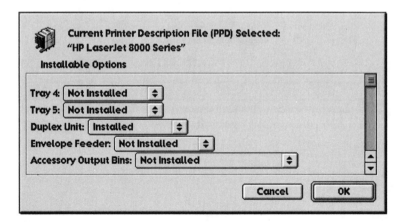

FIGURE 8-6 Choose your printer's installed options if you see a screen similar to this

select the options from the menu, click OK, and the process should finish up in a few seconds.

■ **PPD file not listed**   If a matching PPD can't be found, the printer driver will put up an Open dialog box (see Figure 8-7) showing the existing Printer Descriptions folder. You'll then have to pick the correct make and model from the scrolling list, or choose one that's a close match.

■ **Choosing a generic PPD**   This may be your final choice. The correct PPD file isn't shown in the list, and you cannot find one on the manufacturer's disks. Until you can search for a solution, select this option. It'll allow you to print regular documents on standard paper sizes, such as legal and letter-size. You won't be able to use your printer's custom options for now, but you'll be able to get your documents completed.

> TIP
>
> *Here's a great all-in-one source for a PPD file: Adobe's Web site, http://www.adobe.com/prodindex/printerdrivers/macppd.html. Last time I checked, more than 80 printer manufacturers were represented there, and the list is updated regularly.*

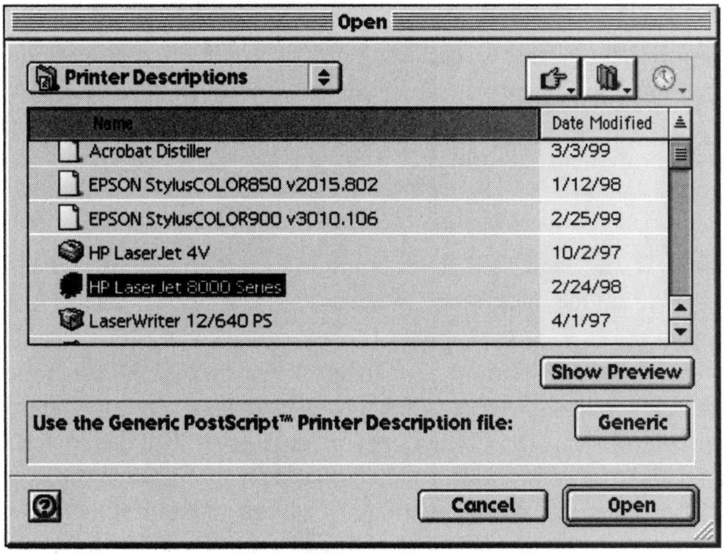

What's a PPD File and What Do I Need It For?

FIGURE 8-7   You need to select a PPD file from this list

Solving Common Printing Problems

It's a sad fact that most printers don't always know how to tell you when they've got a problem. More than likely they'll put up messages that simply don't make very much sense, and you're left pulling your hair out trying to figure out why your document can't be printed.

An example: You are happily printing away when you see a dreaded flashing icon in the Finder's application menu. You switch to your Finder's desktop and see a message about a printer problem. Sure enough, when you double-click your desktop printer icon (or bring up PrintMonitor) you learn the job could not be printed because of a "PostScript error."

So you go back and recheck your document, or restart your Mac and try again, only to confront the same message.

There are two things you can do to see the real error message as the printer driver processes your document:

- **Change your job logging options.** When you choose Print from the File menu, you'll find a pop-up menu on your laser printer driver (usually labeled General). Click on this menu and choose Job Logging (see Figure 8-8). Check the Summarize On Screen or Print Detailed Report option, so you can see a real message as to why your document won't print.

- **Keep desktop printer window open.** Double-click on your desktop printer icon to bring up a printer status window, which will show the progress of your job. If you're using PrintMonitor, just locate it from the application menu and bring it up, so you can see what's happening with your job.

Over the next few pages, I'll cover common printer problems, what they signify and the usual means to solve them.

- **For most printer-related problems** Try printing your document again if at first you don't succeed. For whatever reason, a second attempt sometimes just works (without rhyme or reason). If it doesn't work, go ahead and turn off the printer, then turn it on again. Sometimes the mere act of resetting the printer (which also clears its memory banks) will help cure the problem and your document will print just fine.

- **Inkjet printer lettering breaks up** An inkjet printer should give some visual indication (or flash a light) when a cartridge needs to be replaced.

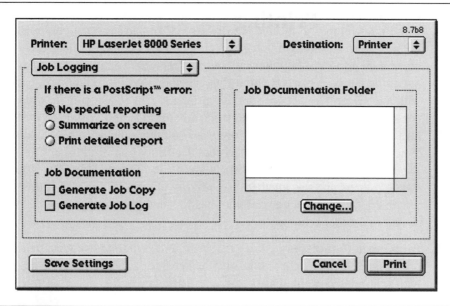

FIGURE 8-8   Select your job logging choices from this screen

Epson printers, for example, will stop running. But if you see faint lines in letters or photos, you may just have to clean the print heads. Check the documentation for your printer on how to run a cleaning operation. You may have to do it from your Mac, using the printer driver, or perhaps there's a cleaning switch on the unit's front panel. For example, Epson printers include a Utility icon in their printer driver dialog boxes, which you access for maintenance functions. Some HP printers offer similar features in a separate utility program that's installed as part of the regular software installation.

■ **Inkjet printer text out of alignment**   Try a higher resolution setting and see if the situation improves. Also see if your printer has an adjustment to align the printer heads for best performance. The printer utilities that can clean the print heads will often have a print-head alignment feature of one sort or another.

■ **Inkjet with network card loses connection when you send a job to another printer**   The network cards on these printers have different capabilities in terms of managing a print queue. I have noticed, for example, that HP's JetDirect Ethernet cards can accomplish the task without a whimper. I've successfully sent jobs to an Ethernet-equipped HP inkjet printer and, while it's working on the document, selected another networked printer for another job, without missing a beat. On the other hand, the network card on some Epson printers will lose communication with the printer if you choose another printer to handle a document while it's still at work. The job stops dead in its tracks, and you often have to turn off the printer to reset it before you can output the document again. When you're not faced with a critical deadline, you might want to experiment with the network card's ability to manage jobs after you switch printers and see whether there are any glitches of this sort. If there's a problem, just make sure the inkjet has finished printing before you switch to another printer.

■ **Bitmapped font display**   For PostScript fonts, you may be missing the printer font. You'll want to consult Chapter 6 for advice on how to deal with font-related problems.

■ **Bitmapped graphics**   If you are using an inkjet printer or other printer without PostScript, don't try to use PostScript (or EPS) graphics with your document. The printer won't be able to handle anything but a low-resolution preview image (same as your regular fax software). If you want PostScript graphics, you can consider buying a PostScript software program for such a printer, but, as I said earlier, such programs have their own limitations.

■ **-8133 Error**   This is nothing more or less than a generic PostScript error, which tells you there's a problem, but doesn't quite tell you what it is. More than likely, the printer has run out of memory to process your job. You may want to go back to your original document and see if you can make it simpler, using fewer fonts, maybe simplifying the graphic elements in it (if any). If you're using a heavy-duty graphics program such as Adobe Illustrator or Adobe PhotoShop, look for options to "split paths," which help make the document easier to handle, especially if you're planning on using a high-end imagesetter for your document. Turning the printer off and on again, or just trying to print the document again may also help.

■ **Vmerror**   This is one of the easier to understand messages, but not always easy to fix. It's telling you that a PostScript printer doesn't have enough memory to handle your document. At this point you can consider either simplifying your document (fewer fonts and graphics) or checking to see if you can add more RAM to your printer. Older Apple printers, such as the LaserWriter NT, couldn't handle RAM upgrades and often ran out of memory with complex documents. But most newer laser printers can be upgraded inexpensively.

■ **Limitcheck** This is an error that indicates the graphics in your document are just too much for your printer to handle. Your choices here include using fewer graphics or the "split paths" option, if available, to make your document easier to work on.

TIP

If you are using imported graphics in a desktop publishing program, such as Adobe InDesign, Adobe PageMaker or QuarkXPress, perform special functions, such as rotating, in the original program before you import the graphic. That will simplify the printing process; it may take longer if your publishing program has to do the rotating.

■ **Mac crashes when printing** This can be the result of a system extension conflict. Consult Chapter 18, which covers the process of diagnosing system-related problems. But if all other steps fail, you may also want to consider reinstalling the fonts used in a document. A damaged font suitcase can also cause your computer to crash at some point during the print process.

■ **Printer resets itself when processing a document** This is the printer's equivalent of a system crash. Something has overwhelmed the printer's memory and caused it to stop working. The usual step to take now is simply to try printing your document again. Most of the time this is quite enough to get your document printed. If the printer still acts up, consider trying your document with fewer fonts and simpler graphics. As a last resort, you may want to reinstall the fonts you're using in the document; damaged fonts can also cause this problem.

■ **Banding and moiré effects on photos and artwork** This may be a limitation of your printer that you cannot do anything about (other than changing your design to use solid colors rather than fill patterns). You can check your program's Page Setup dialog to see if your program has any way to adjust printer output. High-end graphic programs may; regular word processing programs won't. You may also want to consult your printer's documentation to see if there are any settings you can use to improve the print quality.

Solving Common Printing Problems

NOTE   *A moiré effect consists of unintended regular, geometric patterns across the image.*

- **Edges of printed document cut off**   You may have exceeded the margins of your printer, but as a test, you can double-check the Page Setup box in the program you're using. For the latest LaserWriter print drivers, a setting of Letter (Small) or Legal (Small), means you're not getting the largest possible size. Choose the plain old Letter or Legal. But on some lower-cost printers, with limited memory, trying to print a legal-sized document to its full dimensions may be too much for the printer to handle. You may want to reduce the size of your document's printed area (it can also be scaled down in the Page Setup box).

- **Undefined Offending Command error**   This is another of those generic PostScript printing errors that really doesn't tell you what went wrong or how to solve it. It is similar to the -8133 error and you should take the same steps to fix it. Simplify your document, using fewer fonts or graphics. Use the "split paths" option for high-resolution graphics, if your software supports that capability. You can also try, in succession, restarting your Mac, turning the printer off and then on, and printing the document again to see if the problem repeats itself.

- **Font substitution on laser printers**   Sometimes your carefully constructed document, with a number of font styles, will come out with sections in Courier, that old typewriter style font. Should this occur, consider using fewer fonts in your document. Also check your Page Setup box and look for an option labeled Unlimited Downloadable Fonts under PostScript options (available from the pop-up menu, as shown in Figure 8-9). Make sure this option is not checked. Sometimes what it does to help (allow you to use more fonts in a document on a printer that has limited memory) actually causes a font substitution instead. This is especially true if you are printing a document that contains an imported graphic that, itself, uses fonts different from the ones in your regular document. Read Chapter 6 for more information on dealing with font-related hassles.

CAUTION   *If you are printing from a Mac other than the one the document was created on, be sure you install the very same fonts (from the same manufacturers) on that Mac too. If you don't, you will neither see nor be able to print your documents in the correct face. Chapter 6 covers this subject in more detail.*

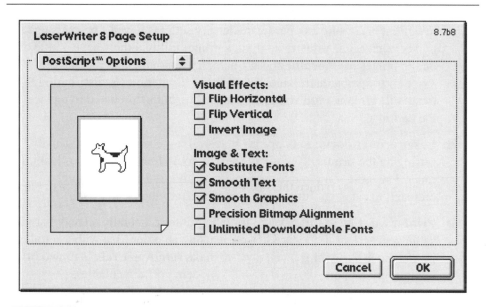

FIGURE 8-9 These printer effects in a Page Setup box can be turned off without harming document quality

TIP

If you continue to get font or Courier substitution when printing a document with an imported graphic containing text, try this: Use the same font somewhere in the text portion of the document. Just a single character or word space with that font will be sufficient to ensure it's downloaded to the printer so the graphic will reproduce properly.

■ **Laser printer documents develop splotches or smears**   This may be the symptom of a bad toner cartridge, which is easy to replace. Or it may represent a problem with the fuser assembly, which is part of your laser printer's imaging engine. Your first step should be to replace the toner cartridge before looking into the hardware. If the printer is under warranty, contact your dealer or the manufacturer for further service if replacing a cartridge doesn't solve the problem.

■ **Laser print quality fades at one side of the page or another**   Try removing the toner cartridge and rocking it back and forth. Run a few pages and see if the situation improves. If it doesn't, replace the toner cartridge. This is also a symptom of spent toner.

■ **Laser print documents get very light** A classic indication that toner is low. First make sure any hardware density settings haven't been changed by accident. Some printers do it via a printer utility, others have a little dial on the printer itself. If that doesn't help, try removing and rocking the toner cartridge back and forth a few times. Sometimes redistributing the toner will get you a little bit longer toner life, but be prepared to replace the cartridge.

■ **Laser printer documents are all black** First check the toner density setting on the printer. If that's correct, it could be a symptom of leaking toner. I suggest you remove the toner cartridge and replace it, but be prepared to clean out little clumps of toner from the printer itself.

■ **Printer can't be found** Make sure the printer is actually on and that your cable connections are secure. If you're using an older Mac with a serial printer (such as an inkjet) you need to make sure AppleTalk is turned off on your printer port (or use the Mac's modem port if available).

TIP

First generation (beige) Power Macintosh G3s had a bug where networked printers would, at random, disappear from the network. Apple released a system extension, LocalTalk PCI, which was supposed to address this problem. But it appears to have largely vanished with Mac OS 8.5 and later system versions.

NOTE

If you're using a switchbox for serial connections, and your Mac doesn't recognize your printer, be sure the switchbox is set to the right connection.

Hints for Faster Printer Performance

Today's printers offer photo-quality reproduction, and the ability to produce documents you can take directly to your commercial printer and get excellent results.

But despite the promise of faster and faster performance, there are times your printer will just bog down and take seemingly endless amounts of time to handle your documents. Is it something you did, or is the printer just not doing what it should do?

Case History

The Case of the Damaged Font Suitcase

This happened to me in the early 1990s. I was working with a large graphic art studio, and we had to produce a critical document for an important client. I had printed the document on the office laser printer, and it looked just perfect. So I decided it was time to send it to the company's expensive imagesetter.

I brought up the PrintMonitor window. The document contained nothing more complex than a few paragraphs of text in several different styles of type. Piece of cake, I thought.

I watched and watched some more. And nothing happened. PrintMonitor put up a "processing job" message and just sat there for about half an hour. In frustration, I cancelled the job and restarted the Mac. Then I tried printing again, and the same problem occurred. At this point, the studio's management came over and began to fret and worry about the delay. Constant phone calls from their client didn't help their collective blood pressures. They even tried printing the document from another Mac with the very same result.

So why did it work perfectly on the laser printer and not on the imagesetter?

The solution was something we couldn't diagnose directly, because the Macs we had in that studio were all running quickly and reliably, with only a rare system crash. Many larger printers and imagesetters actually come with their own hard drives, so you can store PostScript printer fonts on the output devices themselves. This speeds up performance, because there's no delay in sending the font information to the printer.

On a whim, I decided to remove the fonts that document required from the imagesetter's hard drive, and downloaded them again from the copies I had on my Mac. With fingers crossed, I printed the document again.

Within less than a minute, the imagesetter gave forth its regular beep sound and began to print the document without any problems at all. It seems that one or more of the printer fonts were damaged. But since they were located on a printer's disk, there was just no way to diagnose the problem except to actually replace the fonts.

Solving Common Printing Problems

If you are dissatisfied with the level of performance your printer delivers, consider this:

- **Clean up your document.**   If your documents contain a lot of fonts and complex graphics, your printer has to work that much harder to produce them. If you can simplify the document, you may find it'll output much faster and perhaps quality won't suffer.

- **Use a lower print resolution.**   Inkjet printers offer several resolution options, such as 360 dpi, 720 dpi, and so on. The maximum speed ratings of these products are based on the lowest resolution. If you are just printing a draft of your document, or you simply want a hard copy of a Web page for later reference, set your printer to the lowest resolution setting and get maximum speed. You'll also want to compare quality at various settings. For example, a top quality inkjet printer may only deliver its best reproduction of color photos on a special photo-quality paper, and then take many minutes to handle even a single document. If you don't want the best quality pictures, and use regular paper, you may find you can save many minutes per page by choosing a lower resolution setting.

- **Turn off background printing in the Chooser.**   This option is designed to make you more productive; you can continue to work on your Mac while printing happens in the background. But it can also make your Mac bog down terribly, especially if it's an older model. When you turn off background printing, your Mac will sit there and do nothing but print and you won't regain control until it's over. Since that process gets 100 percent of your Mac's attention, your document is printed more quickly. It may be a good choice if you need to print a long, complex document and you are on your lunch hour. Turning off background printing also sometimes helps when you cannot print a document in the normal way.

Hints and Tips for Upgrading a Laser Printer

The symptoms are typical: your printer seems too slow or it chronically runs out of memory when processing large, complex documents. Is there an answer?

It depends. Many of those out-of-memory messages are related to your system software and are not necessarily the result of a problem or an indication your printer lacks anything.

Here are some options you might consider, though, to enhance your printer's performance:

- **RAM upgrade**   At the time this book was written, RAM was still inexpensive compared to what it was years ago (but had risen above the lowest levels because of supply and demand). RAM upgrades for many popular printers cost less than $100. A RAM upgrade will give a laser printer the ability to handle more fonts in your document, or speed processing of documents with complex graphics. This is especially true of the lowest-cost models, where RAM allotments are kept to a minimum to keep prices down. On the other hand, the more expensive laser printers generally have more than enough RAM for normal use out of the box. Some years back, I did an office printer survey for *Macworld* magazine. Their test laboratory actually tested several office laser printers with or without RAM upgrades, and found little performance difference between the two. The other consideration: on some printers, you may have to completely disassemble the unit to find the logic board and RAM slots. The time and energy may not be worth the bother, especially if you need to pay a dealer to do the job for you.

- **Duplexing**   The ability to duplex on a printer means it can print on both sides of the paper in a single operation. This is useful if you want to save paper or you want to print a small number of books for office manuals or other purposes. I haven't seen a downside, other than the increased possibility of a paper jam due to the highly complex paper paths.

- **Extra trays**   If your printing needs require different paper sizes or large amounts of paper, this is a worthwhile option, if not always a cheap one. If you're using a printer with extra trays in a home or home office, prepare for spousal protest. My wife says my laser printer (with a duplex unit and extra trays) looks like an ugly beige washing machine.

- **Optional hard drive**   Some printers are set up to allow installation of a hard drive for font storage. Since print times slow down as fonts are downloaded to a printer's memory, if you handle lots of documents with a large number of fonts, having a hard drive attached to the printer may be useful. On the other hand, compared to the cost of regular hard drives that you connect to your Mac, a printer's drive may be an expensive proposition. In addition, you may be forced to buy the manufacturer's disk upgrade rather than just install a regular hard drive, because of special drive formatting requirements.

How to Fix Paper Jams and Feed Problems

A printer has a lot in common with a copy machine, especially if it's a laser printer. And as with copiers, paper jams occasionally. Sometimes it's the printer's fault; a little wheel or gizmo has worn out and paper won't travel through cleanly. Or perhaps you just didn't install the paper properly, and it folded on itself as it fed through.

When you face a problem of this sort, here are some suggestions on how to solve them quickly:

- **Be careful when you remove paper stuck inside the printer.** Whether it's a low-cost inkjet printer or an expensive laser printer with multiple trays, the parts used generally consist of a complex array of levers, rollers, and springs, and it's very easy to damage or loosen one of these parts. So be careful, and don't push and pull things unnecessarily to extract the paper. Generally the manufacturer's instruction manual will give you suggestions on removing paper jams. Some printers may even have a small diagram located inside the unit that shows you how to clear a jam. Once the paper is removed, check to make sure that little pieces aren't left (as they can often cause further jams).

- **Smooth and fan paper before you place it in the paper tray.** A jagged batch of paper can often result in paper feed problems. And it's not just the low-cost inkjet printers that are sensitive. More expensive printers may also be sensitive to such problems.

- **Don't mix paper types with inkjet printers.** The paper transport mechanisms of these low-cost printers are as inexpensive as the rest of the product. Having paper of different thicknesses can cause the possibility of a paper jam. This is especially true if you're using so-called "photo quality" paper for the highest quality reproduction. Some printer instruction books recommend you remove regular paper first before putting the glossy stuff in the paper tray.

■ **Be especially careful with envelopes.**   Each printer varies in its ability to handle envelopes. Before you use an envelope, make sure the flap isn't bent or stuck together and consult the manual for the proper orientation (it isn't always obvious). If you live in a humid climate, make sure the gum isn't damp. You wouldn't want to have to extract that stuff from one of your printer's paper-transport rollers. If your printer cannot handle envelopes properly, see if a special envelope tray is available as an option, or consider addressing envelopes the old fashioned way.

How to Fix Paper Jams and Feed Problems

Chapter 9

Troubleshooting Mice, Joysticks, and Keyboards

In the old days, it was simple. Your new Mac often came with just a mouse, and you bought whatever keyboard you wanted (though it was often just an Apple keyboard, extended or otherwise). The original compact Macs had a small keyboard, true, but things got better beginning with the Mac Performa series when Apple included one of their low-cost AppleDesign keyboards as part of the package. The practice soon spread to the entire desktop product line.

NOTE   *The 105-key Apple extended keyboard and similar products essentially mimic the style of the typical PC keyboard, with added scrolling keys, such as HOME, DOWN, PAGE UP and PAGE DOWN, and 15 function keys. The original Mac keyboard had none of these.*

Nowadays, it may seem there may be no reason to buy an input device at all. After all, Apple already gives you what you need to get started. But there are a number of reasons, in addition to replacing defective units, why getting another input device may be important to you.

NOTE   *An input device is defined as any product you use to input something on your Mac, such as a keyboard to input letters, or a pointing device, such as a mouse or trackball, to input clicks and move your cursor to the desired position on your screen.*

Choose Your Own Input Device

The new style iMac-inspired keyboard and mouse isn't everyone's cup of tea. The rounded mouse, for example, is cute but confusing to use, since you don't always know which way is up by feel alone (unless you remember to grasp the cord every so often to be sure). Even though Apple has placed a little lip at the top of the mouse on some of its newer models, it may not be enough. And the keyboard, while nicely designed for such a compact product, puts page navigation keys in an awkward place (at the top) and is missing several features that users of the extended style keyboard are used to. These include those extra function keys, and the DOWN key (to take you to the end of a document window).

In addition, you may want to consider buying a trackball, a special "ergonomic" keyboard because of a wrist injury, a joystick for games, or a graphic tablet for drawing. As a result of these needs, there is a growing demand for after-market input devices, as well as devices that can be used to offer enhanced capabilities.

Here's a brief list of the sort of input devices now available:

- **USB mouse extension**   If that round mouse is getting you down, you can buy a little plastic fitting, such as the iCatch from MacSense or the UniTrap from Contour Design. Either device clips on to that clumsy round mouse and makes it look and work just like a regular mouse. Both products come in the usual variety of iMac and G4-inspired colors.

- **Standard mouse**   If a plastic attachment doesn't suit, you can buy a complete normal-sized USB mouse for your iMac or Power Mac. Or you can get a plain old ADB mouse to replace the one used on older Macs. There are a wide variety of options. Some of the less expensive styles more or less mimic the form factor of the standard Apple ergonomic mouse, such as the Macally single-button mouse. Macally also has a cute alternative, the iSweet, which includes five separate covers, to match your iMac's color scheme. Unfortunately, the initial shipment didn't take into account the graphite color scheme of the Power Mac G4 and iMac DV Special Edition.

NOTE   *The following products all generally come in both ADB or USB versions, but you'll want to check with your dealer or the manufacturer for a complete list of their offerings.*

- **Multi-button mouse**   Such companies as Adesso, Belkin, Interex, Kensington, Logitech, Marlow Data Systems, Macally, Micro Connectors, MicroSpeed, XLR8, and even Microsoft offer a whole array of mouse products that offer two, three, or four buttons. The supplied software adds extra functions to these buttons, which let you automatically launch applications or bring up Apple's Contextual Menu. The latter function, in effect, mimics the right-mouse button on a Windows mouse. Some models even include a scrolling wheel, letting you dial your cursor's position for ultra-precise movements.

NOTE   *A regular USB mouse designed for the Windows platform may often work just fine on a Mac without any extra software. The multi-buttons, though, will not provide any extra functions unless you can find a Mac driver for the product. As this book went to press, Microsoft had just shipped new software for its USB IntelliMouse products so they could function in the Mac environment.*

**Choose Your Own
Input Device**

■ **Trackballs**   A trackball is, simply stated, an upside-down mouse. The little ball that moves is at the top rather than the bottom, so instead of moving the entire pointing device, you just whirl the trackball. Some folks find moving a trackball to produce less wrist strain than a traditional mouse; others just find it more convenient. Whatever your preference, you'll find a reasonable selection of trackballs from many of the same manufacturers as a regular mouse-type product. They start with the famous Kensington Turbo Mouse, one of the earliest trackballs, which is still being produced, and that company's Orbit, a smaller trackball that some prefer (including your long-suffering author). Most trackballs have two or four switches, which can be programmed via software for additional functions.

■ **Joysticks**   This product is designed to turn your Mac into a true gaming machine. You use the joystick to handle the traditional cursor movement chores, or to perform functions required by a regular game. I have one client who actually preferred to use a joystick over his regular mouse, and he had no interest in computer games of any sort.

■ **Graphic tablet**   If you want to use your Mac for graphic design work, you may find that having a mouse or trackball emulate a pen and pencil may not provide the precision you need. A graphic tablet literally uses a pen-like device that you use to draw your pictures on a flat panel that mimics the function of a drawing pad. They are pressure sensitive, which means that the lines you draw on the tablet become thicker and wider as you bear down. If you purchase a device of this sort, of course, you may still prefer to have a regular mouse around for regular pointing chores.

NOTE   *One of my publisher's fearless editors suggests that a graphic tablet is also very useful for cutting and pasting parts of images in such programs as Adobe Photoshop. It makes it far easier to trace the sometimes convoluted outline of a picture in order to select it.*

■ **Trackpads**   If you like the approach used on the iBook and PowerBook, where your fingers walk on a trackpad to provide cursor movement, you may be able to find a standalone version you can hook up to a regular Mac. I say "may" because none of the trackpad products I had seen demonstrated through the years seem to have made it into the Mac catalogs I consulted while writing this book. If you do run across one of these devices, it may be worth a try—that is, if you like this input device approach.

- **Wrist and mouse pads**   While not pointing devices, these are accessory products you may find useful. Both are designed to orient your wrists in a position that's designed to relieve stress. I won't presume to recommend any of these items, except to say that my teenaged son began to use a wrist pad when he developed minor aches and pains. The symptoms have since departed, and he uses his wrist pad all the time when he's working on his iMac. On the other hand, when I have to do something on his computer, I move the wrist pad to the side. (I hate them, and my wrists have yet to complain about it, so maybe I am strange.)

- **Replacement keyboards**   If your old keyboard has expired, you'll find a ready market of replacements. You can buy one of Apple's models, or choose products from many of the same companies that make mice and trackballs. Most of these keyboards resemble the Apple products in some fashion, and can be considered low-cost alternatives (but try them out first).

- **Ergonomic keyboards**   This variation on the keyboard theme is designed to incur less wrist strain. Such keyboards are typically divided into three or four segments of keys, each segment fanning out at a slight angle to provide greater keying comfort. This type of keyboard is an acquired taste. I know of some folks who swear by them, but I have spent way too many years on the traditional keyboard and I usually just curse at such keyboards whenever I have a chance to try them. My suggestion is that you work with one of these devices first to see if you can become accustomed to it.

- **Combo keyboards**   One interesting keyboard alternative comes from DataDesk Technologies: the TrackBoard. This is a line of products that includes an integrated three-button trackball fitted onto the keyboard itself. Some models include a numeric keypad, while others are designed so you swap the trackball with the keypad.

ADB Input Device Cautions

Have you ever accidentally pulled the ADB plug from your Mac or mouse? You plug it back in and what happens? Most times, response is slow; your mouse cursor seems to just take forever to move across the screen. A restart will usually fix the problem, but the symptom should raise a warning flag.

The ADB version of plug-and-play requires you to shut down before you remove or attach any devices. Apple Computer gives a stern warning about this. The risk is not just erratic performance. When you plug and unplug an ADB device, there could be a brief short circuit, and that short circuit has the potential of damaging the input device or your Mac. In the latter case, that can mean replacement of the logic board (unless you have a spare ADB port to use).

If you do pull the plug by mistake, restart your Mac right away. Even if it works out all right, don't think you can do it over and over again with impunity. Although I've not personally encountered an ADB port failure as a result of plugging devices in and out, I have read the warnings and tried my best to heed them, since they are based on actual technical considerations. Just be careful!

Installing Input Devices

The arrival of USB on the Mac has greatly simplified the process of installing an input device, but that doesn't mean you can just add as many as you want, without observing a few cautions.

If you have one of the older model Macs with ADB ports, there are very specific problems that you'll need to consider before you hook them up.

ADB Input Device Installation Guidelines

When it comes to installing an ADB device on your Mac, you'll follow some of the very same steps you use when you install a SCSI device.

First, turn off your Mac; don't take chances here! Then unplug the ADB product you want to remove, and add the new devices. ADB devices are daisy-chained, one after the other. If any of the cables are too short, contact your dealer about getting an extension cord. If your unit has special features beyond that of the regular keyboard and mouse, such as programmable keys, you'll need to install some software first before you boot your Mac. You'll also want to take a few important precautions (see the next section) as to how many devices you can add in safety.

USB Device Installation Guidelines

You have lots more freedom with USB ports. You can, in theory, daisy-chain up to 127 separate devices on each USB bus. On the other hand, real-life considerations, such as the amount of bandwidth the device needs to run at full capacity, make this number largely a pipe dream. In practical terms, you can hook up any reasonable number of input devices you can reasonably expect to need. And you can add a host of other devices to the USB chain, as explained in the section entitled "How to Handle the USB Connection."

NOTE *The original iMacs and Blue & White G3 Power Macs had a single USB bus, with two ports (thus a 127-device limitation). The second generation (slot loading) iMacs and G4 Power Macs have two USB buses, hence a limit of 254 devices.*

Setting up a USB device isn't terribly hard. You plug it in to a free USB port on your Mac, iMac, or iBook. If there's no free USB port, you need a hub. With a large USB chain, there are some cautions that are explained in the last section of this chapter.

Once the unit is attached, go ahead and install any necessary software. Then restart, and you should be ready to roll. If you run into any problems, check the section in this chapter entitled "USB Problems and Solutions" for further assistance.

Case History · The Case of the Frozen Mouse

This happened to me when I visited a small advertising agency. I was busy updating several of their Macs, and one of the graphic artists asked me to help her solve a problem with a frozen keyboard. I followed her to her Mac, a model of recent vintage, and gave it a workout.

The Mac started perfectly normally, but as soon as the system software finished loading, everything was frozen. I restarted the Mac with extensions off (SHIFT key held down at startup) to no avail. Frozen tight as a drum.

I checked mouse and keyboard movement as the startup process progressed, and right after the Happy Mac face appeared, they both locked up. I plucked out a copy of the Mac's system software CD and restarted directly from the CD. Same problem. Finally, I shut everything down, and located a spare mouse in an accessory box and replaced the one installed on that Mac. Then I restarted.

The computer booted perfectly; everything worked just fine. Mouse and keyboard action were completely normal.

While you might not expect a defective mouse to affect other devices on the ADB chain, in this case even the keyboard failed to work.

Installing Input Devices

Test Drive Your Keyboard First

When you buy a new car, you usually take it out for a spin first, especially if you haven't had experience with that particular make and model. This is understandable, considering how expensive even compact cars are once you add a few necessary options to the mix.

But it's very common for folks to buy a keyboard without trying it out first. You see a nice looking keyboard at your dealer or in a catalog, the price is right and you order it, without a second's glance. When you get the item home, you may find it's not quite what you want or expected. The keys are too springy, too mushy, or awkward to the touch. You find yourself making more errors, even if you are an experienced, skilled typist. So what do you do?

Keyboard quality is a matter of personal taste. What I like, you may despise. My absolute favorite Mac keyboard is the venerable AppleDesign keyboard, the same one that shipped on pre-USB Macs. I like the soft touch and responsive action. Though I'm not a fan of the new iMac-inspired keyboard, it is designed with a similar touch. Others hate that keyboard for the very same reasons, preferring a springier feel.

The best solution, if you can, is to try out a keyboard first at your dealer before you take one home. You may have to work with several before you find the one you like, but you'll be rewarded with more comfortable keying and, no doubt, fewer typos to correct.

NOTE *Test driving isn't just meant for keyboards. If you want to use an alternate pointing device, say, a trackball or a mouse with a different design, give it a try also. Regardless of what your friends or published reviews may state, it's your personal preference that's involved here. Buy the product you like best, even if it didn't get high marks from other users.*

Dealing with Long ADB Chains

The ADB chain is designed to handle up to 16 daisy-chained devices. This would, in theory, seem to present some terrific possibilities for expansion. Imagine having a mouse for regular work, a joystick for games, a graphic tablet for artwork, and perhaps a second keyboard if you or another user needs one of those ergonomic keyboards to avoid or deal with a wrist injury.

Unfortunately, the theory doesn't always work as well in practice. For one thing, proper performance of the ADB port depends on having enough current with which to drive each attached device. If there's not enough current, you may experience erratic performance or the device may simply refuse to function.

Since each ADB device has different electrical requirements, I won't hazard a guess as to where you'll reach the limit, except to just quote Apple Computer, from their technical information document on the subject: "The practical limit is three or four devices."

If you have one of the older Macs with two separate ADB ports, you're in luck. If not, you'll need to be more judicious about the number of devices you use at any one time.

> NOTE
>
> *The PowerBook 5300 has an especially low current capacity on its ADB port, 200mA. The practical limit is one keyboard, one mouse, and that's it. Beyond that you risk activating the PowerBook's protection circuitry (which will shut the ADB port down). Or you may just end up blowing the circuit, which would mean a logic board replacement.*

ADB Device Problems and Solutions

In addition to the limitations on the number of input devices you can place on an ADB chain, there are other possibilities for conflicts and problems. Following are some of the common problems you'll encounter with an ADB device and the solutions:

- **Keyboard dead**   When you type something on the keyboard, nothing happens. It appears to be frozen, even though the mouse continues to function. Before you assume it's the keyboard, check the cables first. ADB cables sometimes loosen easily. If the ADB cable is disconnected try shutting down with the mouse, by selecting Shut Down from the Finder's Special Menu. Once your Mac is off, make sure the cables are properly connected and restart. If the keyboard is plugged in, restart your Mac with extensions off (SHIFT key held down at startup) and see if it works. If the keyboard is still dead, restart with your system CD. If that's not successful, try another keyboard cable if you have one or, if possible, another keyboard. Lacking that, contact your dealer; your Apple keyboard shares the same new product warranty as your Mac, one year. Third-party keyboards may get a longer warranty. But since a new keyboard can be had fairly inexpensive, you shouldn't fret too much over a bad unit, even if the warranty is history.

■ **Some keys aren't functional**   There may not be much you can do about this symptom. Few keyboards allow you to change individual switches. But first you'll want to remove the keytop if possible (usually a small flat-head screwdriver can be used to pry it off). Then clean out the switch assembly and surrounding area as much as possible. Sometimes a little electrical contact spray (such as the type Radio Shack sells) can be helpful. If none of this succeeds in making the key work, it's time for a new keyboard.

■ **Mouse motion erratic**   The once smooth motion of your mouse is now jerky. You move the mouse around, and the cursor either stays put, or jumps with a start to the other end of the screen. This is usually a symptom of a dirty mouse ball or trackball. On a mouse, you should be able to pry open the ring at the bottom. It'll either snap out, or you'll rotate it partway to loosen it. When you open the ring, let the mouse ball drop into your hand or on a soft surface (such as the mouse pad). You can use isopropyl (rubbing) alcohol and a cotton swab to clean the mouse ball, and also the little roller assemblies inside the mouse assembly. A trackball has a similar layout (check the instructions for removing the ball if it's not obvious) and similar cleaning steps. If cleaning doesn't help, contact the manufacturer; it's probably time for a new one.

■ **Mouse button stops working**   If you have a regular mouse, this is usually an indication that it's time to get a new unit. However, such manufacturers as Kensington can fix or replace the mouse buttons on their input devices for a small fee. Check the product warranty or contact the manufacturer for assistance. I remember one instance in which my original Kensington Turbo Mouse had a defective button, just a couple of months out of warranty. At the time they were located in New York City, not far from my office (they have since migrated to the West Coast). I brought in my Turbo Mouse and for a small service charge they fixed it and had it ready for pickup that afternoon.

■ **Defective cable or ADB port**   If all else fails, it may be the ADB port itself that's defective. On many older Macs, you have two ADB ports. If one doesn't work, don't hesitate to try the other. It's a lot cheaper than replacing a logic board. And while the AppleDesign ADB keyboard and other similar models have just one ADB port for a mouse, others, such as Apple's Extended Keyboard and Kensington's "keyboard-in-a-box," have two. One fails, there's a backup. If none of these steps work, try another cable (assuming it's not hardwired into your keyboard, as is the case with the AppleDesign keyboard) before you give up on the input device itself.

■ **PowerBook or iBook trackpad fails**   First, you'll want to consider your trackpad posture. You should use just one finger and not your entire hand when you use a trackpad. Be sure your finger is dry, not wet or oily. You may want to keep a paper towel at hand if you live in a damp climate. If you are using your trackpad properly and you still experience jerky cursor movements or the trackpad stops working, restart with extensions off to see if a software conflict is possible. Consider zapping the PRAM or resetting the unit (many PowerBooks have a reset switch at the rear).

■ **Software conflicts**   Multi-button mice and graphic tablets use special software to provide their unique functions. You'll want to keep abreast of software updates that may address your problems should something happen when you update system software.

NOTE   *When Apple first introduced Mac OS 8.5, Kensington had to update its MouseWorks software because of weird conflicts with such programs as Microsoft Word 98. And it wasn't the sort of conflict you'd trace to input device software. Among the symptoms of this conflict were missing buttons on Word's alert box.*

■ **Numeric keypad stops working**   You prefer to use the numeric keypad for number entries or special functions (such as document navigation in Microsoft's Office software). Suddenly it stops working. What's wrong? If your Mac has a regular keyboard with a NUM LOCK light, make sure it's glowing. If it isn't lit, press the NUM LOCK key on the keypad and see if it lights up and starts working again. Bear in mind that not all programs support the numeric keypad. You'll want to check the documentation or Help menu if you're not sure.

■ **Poured liquid on your keyboard**   When I worked in a design studio as production manager, I was near paranoid about keeping liquids away from the Macs, but on rare occasions someone would spill coffee or a soft drink on a keyboard. Should this happen to you, shut down your Mac and peripherals. Remove the keyboard, and turn it over onto a paper towel or cloth to drain the excess liquid. Then turn it upright and, if you can, pop off

Installing Input Devices

the keys, then use an absorbent paper towel to remove as much liquid as you can. I've heard of folks actually pouring a light stream of water onto a keyboard to wash off spilt coffee or other liquids, but I recommend caution about any such step. Just give the keyboard plenty of time to dry before you try it out. Sometimes the cleanup process works, but don't be surprised if you need to buy a new keyboard.

NOTE
Does your keyboard beep at you instead of displaying a character whenever you press a key? Check your Control Panel's folder for the presence of Apple's Easy Access software. When it's activated, holding down the RETURN key for more than five seconds will turn it on. Easy Access and another utility, CloseView (designed for those with impaired vision), are provided by Apple for folks who have disabilities. If you don't need the features, deactivate these programs if you find them on your Mac.

How to Handle the USB Connection

When Apple introduced USB for the first iMac in August of 1998, a lot of folks complained. What about all those keyboards, mice, trackballs, pointing sticks, graphic tablets—all those things that Mac users had added to their Macs, things you needed for work and play?

To add to the confusion, it was a fact that USB had already been introduced on the PC platform and hadn't gone very far. The lack of support in terms of new products on that other platform was really unfortunate, as USB is an industry standard that provides real plug-and-play. And that's something that Windows users usually only get a glimpse of.

You can attach and disconnect a USB device without having to turn off or restart your computer, except where a software driver is necessary. And you can add up to 127 daisy-chained devices per USB bus, although there are practical limitations to that figure (I'll get to this in a moment).

In addition, you aren't limited to input devices on a USB chain. There are USB storage devices (removable, regular hard drive, CD writers, and tape drives), inkjet and laser printers, digital cameras, scanners, modems, and interfaces for displays (to name some of the products that are shipping).

The iMac, Blue & White Power Macintosh G3, the G4, and the "Bronze" PowerBook G3 have two USB ports; the iBook has one. If you need to add extra devices, you can buy a USB hub to provide additional ports.

USB Has Its Limits

The USB silver lining, however, has a few clouds. A USB bus is capable of up to 12Mbps speed, but any device that hogs a large amount of that capacity will impact performance on the rest. For example, you can add plenty of undemanding products such as input devices on a USB chain, but you cannot expect a hard drive and removable drive to both function at their performance limits at the same time, since either will tax the limits of the USB protocol.

So you can expect performance to deteriorate if you copy files from your USB Zip drive to your USB SuperDisk drive or USB hard drive.

This limitation is partly addressed with the Power Macintosh G4 and second generation iMac models (the so-called "slot loading" versions), which have two separate USB buses, rather than two jacks sharing a single USB bus. These new USB designs also let you boot from a USB drive (a feature lacking in the earlier Apple USB products).

The other limitation is power. The USB bus provides enough power for a few low-power devices such as keyboards. Other USB products have their own power supplies. But if you add enough low-power devices together, they may exceed the current offered by the USB port, so you need to buy a hub to provide the extra ports and (where powered) extra current.

USB Problems and Solutions

The advent of USB on the Mac has not been without a few teething pains. But for the most part, the adoption of this peripheral bus has been fairly trouble-free.

If something is wrong, however, your Mac will put up a message about it. Here are some of the error problems you'll encounter most often:

- ■ **Not enough power to function**   As I said in the previous section, any non-powered USB device will draw current from the USB bus. If there's not enough current to power all the attached devices, your Mac will put up a warning. If you have a USB device with an AC adapter, you'll need to make sure it's plugged in and the unit is turned on (if it has a power switch, and many don't). If the device doesn't have a power adapter, try connecting directly to the Mac, iMac, PowerBook, or iBook, rather than daisy-chaining. Or consider using a self-powered hub, which should (when plugged in) provide the additional juice necessary to make the extra device function.

How to Handle the USB Connection

■ **Not enough power for all functions** This error message is a subset of the one just described. It indicates that the device is partly functional. The solutions are essentially the same. If the product has its own power supply, make sure it's plugged in and the unit is turned on. For non-powered devices, try plugging directly into the computer's USB port or use a powered hub.

■ **No driver found** When you see this message, it may be more explicit than that. It'll identify by name the USB device for which no driver is installed. While a simple keyboard or mouse won't require any added software, a mouse with extra buttons and most other USB devices require software to run. When you encounter this message, open Extensions Manager and check to see if the driver is present and active. If it's turned off, activate it by clicking on the check box at the left of its name and then restart. If you can't find any indications that the device's software is installed, you'll want to fish out the CD that came with the device and reinstall.

NOTE *Beginning with Mac OS 9, Apple's USB Driver Extension was designed to support many USB devices, including SuperDisk and Zip drives. The best way to see if your input device is supported is simply to try it out before installing the software. See if the device's special features, if any, work. If not, you'll need to install the proper software.*

■ **USB device connected to hub not recognized** Some USB hubs (early Macally designs are an example) do not open a connection port until a device driver actually recognizes a peripheral connected to it. Since USB devices are not all created the same, this may cause a problem in using some devices. If you have a spare USB port on your Mac or keyboard, try hooking up the device directly rather than to the hub (or switch things around if you can). Otherwise, contact the manufacturer for a version of their hub that keeps the ports open all the time.

■ **Liquid on your keyboard** The same possible solutions that I described in the section about cleaning a wet ADB keyboard apply here as well. Just keep your fingers crossed that the process will work (sometimes it doesn't).

NOTE

As USB support evolves in the Mac OS, you should expect to pay regular visits to a manufacturer's Web site for software updates. One convenient source of update information and links I've mentioned several times in this book is http://www.versiontracker.com.

Summing Up

Although Apple is being justly criticized for the kinds of input devices they offer on many recent Macs, it's good to know you have choices. And, as long as you don't have an older input device you need to use, the switch to USB is definitely a big improvement over the way things were.

In the next chapter, I'll cover an output device—your Mac's display.

How to Handle
the USB Connection

Chapter 10

The Display Is the Window of the Computer World

The first thing you see when you turn on your Mac is the display. Since the original, classic-style Mac, and the newer iMac and iBook have integrated displays, it's very easy to think that you are looking at the Mac itself, and not another device. It's very much the same image conveyed as when you look at your TV.

But the fact is, for most Macs, the display you see is a separate product, quite often produced by someone other than Apple Computer, with its own set of opportunities or problems (or both).

When you want to upgrade your Mac, a brand new display can give you a new way of looking at the computing world. The picture can be larger, sharper, affording your Macintosh with a much-improved workspace.

Displays, however, especially larger-sized models, do not usually arrive ready to run their best out of the box. You frequently have to spend at the very least a few minutes setting them up properly.

The purpose of this chapter is to guide you through the basics of setting up and configuring your new display. I'll also cover some of the problems you might encounter with both new and old models, and how you can make them perform at their best.

Display Selection Hints

There are dozens of manufacturers of computer displays, and the selection and specifications can easily cause your eyes to glaze over. Aside from all the buzzwords and fancy-sounding names, don't buy a display just on specs alone. It's a good idea to actually look at a display already set up and running to see if it looks right to you.

Even if all specifications are the same, color accuracy and the quality of the picture will vary from one model to the next. Even minor adjustment variations and production differences may result in distinctions between two displays of the same make and model. I'd recommend you check your favorite Mac magazine or review-oriented Web site for information about the latest products.

To help you pick the right type of display, here are some of the common terms you'll see and how they may affect the quality of the product you buy:

■ **Aperture grill** This is an alternative to shadow mask technology (mentioned later), which is typically used in Mitsubishi's DiamondTron, Sony's Trinitron, and products from such companies as Apple, Miro, NEC, and ViewSonic (to name a few examples). The technology employs alternating red, green, and blue phosphors in lines, rather than individual dots. The lines are separated by a series of thin wires, which are referred to as aperture grills.

- **CRT**   Short for cathode-ray tube. This is the conventional type of display, which uses a large vacuum tube as the screen, same as your regular television set.

- **Dot pitch**   This measurement describes the size of the little dots that make up your picture. The lower the figure, the sharper the picture (assuming all other elements of the display are well engineered). Just about anything with a dot pitch of .30mm or less should give a good quality display.

- **Flat screen**   There are two basic types of flat screen displays, and it's easy to confuse one with the other because of the common use of the term. Some of the newest CRT-based displays have a flat front surface, without the slight end-to-end curvature typical of lower-cost products. Though such displays cost more, you get a more accurate picture, free of curves or edge distortion. The other type of flat screen uses LCD technology, same as Apple's PowerBooks and the iBook. LCD displays will also sometimes be referred to as flat panel displays, and because of the price of raw materials, they can cost several times more than a CRT display of similar size.

NOTE   *Apple's own LCD display line includes the Apple Cinema Display, a costly widescreen 22-inch model with spectacular image quality. It's designed as a companion for the Power Macintosh G4 series. If you have a spare four grand to spend (the price at the time this book went to press), it is definitely worth exploring.*

- **Maximum resolution**   This is a manufacturer's specification, showing the maximum pixels per inch of which the display is capable. The typical display, however, will tend to look fuzzy at this resolution, and the text will be just too small.

- **Screen size**   This is the size of the actual picture tube used in the display. The image size you really see will typically be an inch or two less.

- **Shadow mask**   This is the more commonly used display technology, which utilizes phosphors arranged in a triangle, with red, green, and blue at the corners. The screen used to separate individual phosphor dots is called a shadow mask.

Display Selection Hints

- **Stripe pitch**   On an aperture grill display, this specification will give you an indication of the sharpness of the image. It measures the distance between two lines of the same color.

- **Viewable image**   This is the actual size of the display's picture, measured diagonally from end to end. Not that you actually tilt your head when you look at the screen, of course.

Installing a New Display

For sheer weight and bulk, the display is probably the largest purchase you're apt to make for your Mac (except, perhaps, for some of the bigger workgroup printers). Even a 17-inch CRT model, which is quite common nowadays, may weigh from 50 to 60 pounds. Large displays tilt the scales at 70 to 80 pounds. These are not trivial products that you can easily move from place to place. More than likely, you'll want them to be installed in one position and remain there until you move or redecorate.

NOTE   *The exceptions to the rule are LCD displays, which are relatively light compared to CRTs and are much, much thinner.*

Here are some preliminary steps for setting up your new display:

1. Unpack the box carefully and, if possible, keep the box in storage. If you have to return the unit for repair or replacement, you need to ship it in a container that can protect the unit. Displays are delicate instruments, and they are easily damaged in shipment.

2. Locate cables and adapter plugs, if any.

3. Check the manual for special setup advice, such as using the display as a USB hub or taking advantage of special features, such as built-in loudspeakers.

4. Shut down your Mac system.

5. Clear the desk or table on which the new display will be installed.

6. Seat the display on your desk or table.

CAUTION
If you have a larger CRT display, get someone to help you lift it, unless you pump iron and are in excellent physical condition. A display is not something you want to accidentally drop. I once observed a display fall from a shipper's dolly during delivery, cracking the picture tube. It was not a pretty sight.

7. Plug in all cables from the display to the Mac and to the wall outlet. Displays typically come with so-called PC-type connectors (called VGA, short for video graphics array), consisting of three narrow rows of 15 pins, or Macintosh style, which places the 15 pins into two wide rows. If your Mac has the older Mac-type jacks, you will need a converter connector to use a VGA cable. Fortunately, such converters are often supplied with displays or as an inexpensive option.

NOTE
Some displays come with a special AC cable that will plug directly into your Mac. The advantage is that the display will come on automatically when your Mac is turned on, and shut off when your Mac is turned off. If you are using a large display (19 inches or larger), you may want to first check your Mac's specifications as to how much power it can deliver to an external display.

8. Turn on your Mac system, including the display.

If all goes well, the picture should flash on and your Mac will begin its startup sequence. You should expect, though, to have to perform a few picture adjustments to get good performance from most displays, especially larger ones.

If the display simply won't work properly, check the last section in this chapter, which covers common display problems and the usual solutions.

Making the Picture Look Right

You've installed your new display, and now you turn it on for the first time and something doesn't quite look right. It's too dark, the picture tilts to one side, square objects are rounded. Or you have an old display and you've just gotten used to the defects. Is there no way to fix the picture without calling in a service person?

Making the Picture Look Right

Just about every computer display out there has some sort of picture adjustment capability. Sometimes it's just brightness and contrast, but at least you have a starting point. Even the little iMac has a lot more than that, if you take a look at the possibilities.

TIP   *If your all-in-one Mac or iMac seems to be missing a Geometry option in the Monitors & Sound Control Panel, open your System Folder, and see if you can find a file in the Extensions Folder called °AppleVision (including that little symbol at the beginning of the name). If it's not there, you can probably restore it by reinstalling your system software (use the Add/Remove feature for recent system versions).*

Most display adjustments are quite clearly labeled with an icon or label that specifies the kind of adjustment you're producing. Some models will even produce an onscreen display to simplify matters (see Figure 10-1). Adjustments range from the simple to the very complex, and all sorts of possibilities in between. If you follow these steps (and refer to the display's manual if there are big differences), you should be able to get top performance for your display.

NOTE   *The notable exception to the rule are LCD displays, which provide essentially perfect geometry and usually just require adjustments for brightness, contrast, and color accuracy.*

Where Are Those Adjustments?

Display adjustments are provided as a set of either knobs or buttons, the latter of which are usually accessed by calling up a menu of some sort. If you have an AppleVision display or iMac, you can also do the adjustments using the Monitors & Sound Control Panel (see Figure 10-2 for an example).

NOTE   *Beginning with Mac OS 9, Apple has again separated the Monitors Control Panel from the Sounds Control Panel (which hearkens back to the pre-Mac OS 7.5.2 variations). The look will be a little different, but the functions will be essentially the same.*

If the specific display adjustment isn't identified by a clearly labeled control, you may find a button labeled Menu, Proceed, or Select that lets you toggle or move through various types of settings.

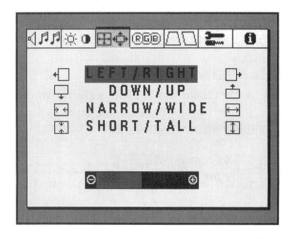

FIGURE 10-1 This is the On-Screen Manager from an NEC display. This particular model also includes built-in speakers, which explains the additional audio-related adjustments

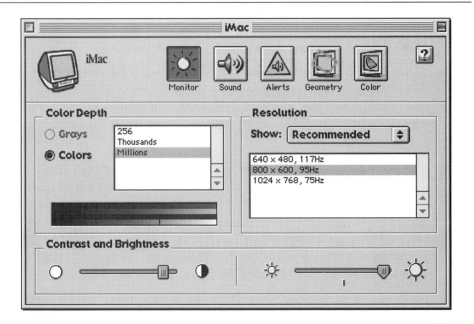

FIGURE 10-2 Use Apple's Monitors & Sound Control Panel to make your display look better

In the next few pages, I'll list some of the common and not-so-common adjustments available for a regular display and for Apple's iMac. You can easily extend these descriptions to apply to almost any available model.

Before You Adjust Anything

While brightness and contrast have pretty obvious effects, the changes wrought by geometry and other calibration settings may not be quite as obvious. Before you change anything, you might want to consider this:

- ■ **Look for a "default" or "reset" button.**   If you get too far afield and your display's picture looks worse than ever, you may want to get things back to the factory settings. Most displays have a button that will change things back to the shipping configuration. Sometimes the reset sequence may require pressing two buttons, so check the display's manual. For the iMac, a click on the Factory Settings button on your Geometry screen will do the trick.

- ■ **One setting affects another.**   The geometry settings, which affect the shape of the picture, are sometimes dependent on other settings. You fix one thing, another setting is changed as well. You should make your adjustments a little bit at a time to make sure the changes are what you want.

- ■ **Write down what you've done.**   Take a writing pad or open a word processing document on your Mac. As you make an adjustment, note what setting you started with and what you ended with. Some displays put up a numeric display as you make adjustments, so you can easily go back to the original setting.

- ■ **Avoid adjusting anything inside the display.**   Some of the settings (especially those involving the early Apple color displays) are located directly on the unit's chassis. When you open up your display's case, you will be exposing high voltage components that can give you a nasty shock. Such adjustments are best left to a service agency. Limit yourself to the adjustments you can do using the front, side, or rear controls (or your Monitors & Sound Control Panel, for some Apple products).

- ■ **Don't expect perfection, especially on larger displays.**   I have never seen a perfect CRT display, one that offers precise geometry across the screen, perfect convergence, and so on. So long as cathode-ray technology dominates, it's going to be imperfect. The larger the display, the more difficult it is for the circuitry to keep things precise. Expect a few imperfections and learn to live with them.

NOTE   *Although offering perfect geometry, LCD displays have their own display issue: dead pixels (meaning the little dots that make up the picture) may be permanently on or off. Most times, such little blemishes aren't noticeable, but if there are enough of them, a manufacturer will generally replace the unit (or the display portion, if on an iBook or PowerBook).*

■ **If all else fails, get help.**   If your adjustments still fail to get you a picture you can live with, contact your dealer or the manufacturer for assistance. Some manufacturers offer a fast replace option, which means you'll get a replacement unit within a day or two if the original is defective.

Display Adjustments by the Numbers

Now that you're ready to dive in, here's a list of common display adjustments, including the ones you make on your iMac. With this guide, you should be able to make almost any display perform at its best in just a few minutes.

The following list includes adjustments that you can make on a wide variety of displays. Some will have similar settings and labels, some won't. Armed with this information, simply go through my step-by-step adjustment scheme and you should come out with a great looking picture in a few minutes.

CAUTION   *It can take a computer display up to half an hour to warm up fully, during which time display adjustments may change. Make sure the display is on for at least this amount of time before you begin.*

■ **Color depth**   This adjustment can be made with your Control Strip, Monitors, or Monitors & Sound Control Panels. It controls the number of colors displayed by your display. For maximum color accuracy with graphic programs, choose millions of colors, if available. You may find lower color depths if your Mac's video display hardware doesn't support that resolution.

■ **Resolution**   As with the color depth setting, this adjustment is made from your Control Strip, Monitors, or Monitors & Sound Control Panels. It sets the number of pixels displayed by your display. An ideal setting for the iMac or similar-sized display is 800 × 600; for a larger display, try 1024 ×

768 or 1152 × 870. If one of these settings isn't shown, try the nearest equivalent. Not all Mac graphic display hardware displays all the resolutions you may want to try.

NOTE *If the quality of your picture deteriorates sharply when you choose a specific resolution setting, try a lower figure. It may be that the display you have isn't sharp enough to show a higher resolution.*

TIP *Does your picture turn black when you pick a new resolution setting? More than likely your display or the Mac graphic display hardware doesn't support it. Usually if you leave well enough alone for a few seconds, the Mac will revert to the previous resolution. If not, restart, and zap the PRAM (the process is described later in this chapter). Some Mac graphic display cards may require that you press a key (such as "R") at startup to reset resolution to something the display can support.*

■ **Brightness**   This setting controls the overall brightness of your display. The best starting point is halfway between the darkest and lightest settings. If you're not using ColorSync to adjust the display to a specific range, use whatever adjustment feels comfortable to you.

TIP *As the display ages, the adjustments you make may drift. You may want to redo these adjustments approximately once a year or whenever you move the display to a different place in your home or office.*

■ **Contrast**   This setting controls the image's brightness compared to the background. The usual setting is the highest, and that's what the ColorSync setup suggests. But if it seems too extreme, feel free to experiment with something you prefer.

■ **Convergence**   Your color image is made up of three colors: red, green, and blue. If the three colors aren't properly aligned to form a single combined image, text and pictures on your display may be fringed with blue or red. There will typically be a vertical and horizontal adjustment. Some displays include additional convergence settings to control each corner of your display.

■ **Size and position**   These adjustments affect the height and width of the picture on your display. An example of such a setting appears in the Monitors & Sound Control Panel on an iMac (see Figure 10-3).

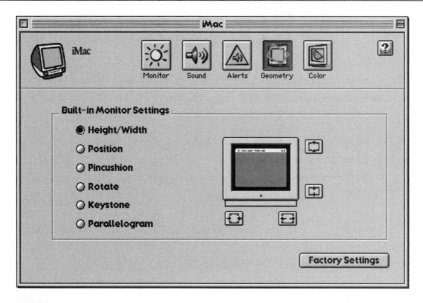

FIGURE 10-3 Click the arrows at the bottom and right side of this window to adjust the picture's size and position

CAUTION   *No doubt you'll be tempted to stretch your picture as much as possible. Depending on the type of display you have, image sharpness may deteriorate at the very edge of the image, or you may exceed the image area (in which case, the edges of the picture will be clipped).*

- **Geometry**   These settings handle the curvature and angle of your display image. Here's a list of the ones you'll find most often:

   - **Pincushion**   This setting affects the inward or outward curvature of the image at either side of the display.

   - **Pincushion balance**   This setting controls the amount of left or right curvature and is used with the preceding setting to help refine the image.

   - **Parallelogram**   This setting adjusts the left or right tilt of the side of your image.

   - **Keystone (or trapezoidal)**   This adjustment will increase or decrease the size of the image at the top or bottom, to make a perfect rectangle.

   - **Rotate**   This setting will tilt the entire image clockwise or counterclockwise.

Making the Picture Look Right

NOTE   *The tilt of the image on a CRT display depends on your display's position in relation to the Earth's magnetic pole. So if you turn the display around when moving it to a new location, expect to have to redo this setting.*

■ **Corner correction**   Some displays, especially with larger screens, let you adjust the corner geometry of the image so if one corner seems misaligned, you can hone in on a more precise setting.

■ **Linearity**   If this setting is available, you can use it to make sure squares and circles are perfectly proportioned or as perfect as a modern computer display will allow. You'll probably want to have a ruler handle to measure the results.

■ **Sharpness**   This setting controls how clear your image will look. The most accurate adjustments are done with small text. Look at the text from corner to corner to get the best compromise.

NOTE   *Since displays aren't perfect, don't expect to find your text to be equally sharp from corner to corner and top to bottom on a large display. Just try to make it as close as possible. If there's a wide variation, contact the manufacturer or dealer for additional assistance.*

■ **Moiré**   This setting controls the wavy pattern you may see on your display, especially on grayscale or color images. The setting, if available, will reduce the effect.

How to Make Your Display Adjustments

Now that you have the basics on what display adjustments do, here's how to perform the settings so you can set up your display like a pro.

Adjusting the iMac and AppleVision Displays

The venerable Monitors & Sound Control Panel (or AppleVision on earlier models) can be used to make most of your display settings onscreen. Here's how you do it:

1. Go to the Apple menu, select Control Panels, and then Monitors & Sound from the submenu.

NOTE

If you just want to make brightness and contrast adjustments, you will usually find they are on the first (or Monitor) screen of the Monitors & Sound Control Panel (otherwise they are on the ColorSync setup screen). If you plan on performing a ColorSync calibration, leave these settings alone for now.

2. Click on the Geometry icon, which brings up the screen shown in Figure 10-4.

3. Click the radio button that represents the kind of adjustment you want to make.

4. Click one of the arrows and hold down the mouse to make the adjustment shown on the icon (as shown in Figure 10-5).

5. Repeat steps 3 and 4 for each setting you want to make.

6. Once your settings are the way you like, choose Quit from the File menu to leave the Monitors & Sound Control Panel, or click on another icon to make a different type of setting.

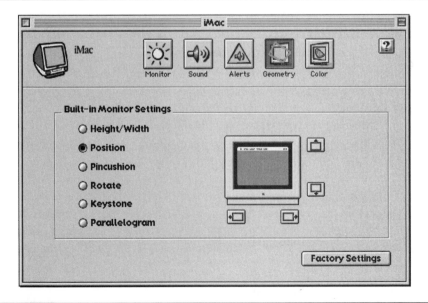

FIGURE 10-4   This screen is used for setting display geometry for the iMac and other Apple products

Making the Picture Look Right

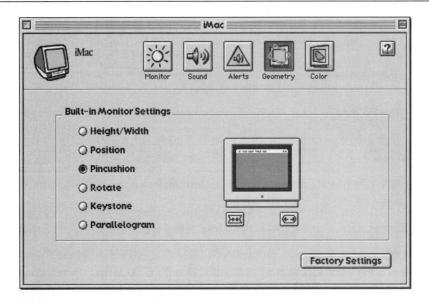

Each icon represents a different sort of adjustment to your display

Adjusting Other Displays

If you have a display from Apple or another manufacturer that doesn't benefit
from geometry settings in the Monitors & Sound Control Panel, you should be
able to make a reasonable set of adjustments.

Here's what to do:

1. Check the bottom, side, or back of the display for a control panel, knobs,
    or buttons.

NOTE   *If you cannot locate any display settings, consult your manual or contact
the manufacturer or dealer for advice. Nearly every display I've ever seen
has had at least a brightness and contrast setting of some sort (with the
possible exception of some PowerBook models that only let you adjust
the brightness).*

2. If your display creates an onscreen display panel for settings, click
    the button that activates this feature. It may be called Menu, Select, or

Proceed, to cite some common examples of an adjustment entry switch. This onscreen menu will produce a display of adjustment options.

3. Use the appropriate button to move back and forth or up and down through the settings menu. Once you select an adjustment to change, you may need to click the settings entry button again to activate it.

4. Move the adjustment buttons or knobs to adjust the setting to your taste.

5. Once you have finished making a specific adjustment, look for an "Exit" or similar button to leave the settings screen and move back to the main menu.

6. Follow steps 3 through 5 to continue to make your display adjustments.

7. Once you have completed your settings, press the switch that exits the settings panel (and it may indeed be called Exit). On some displays, pressing the adjustment entry button once you're at the main menu will exit the screen.

NOTE   *Most display settings windows are designed to vanish from the screen if you don't use them after a minute or two. So don't be surprised to find it's gone if you're called away from your display for a short time.*

Adjustment Problems/Solutions

All things being equal, the adjustments I've just described are likely to make a noticeable improvement in the way your display looks. I've seldom seen a display that won't benefit from a little tweaking here and there. Even the models with so-called "Auto Adjust" capability cannot take into account every possible installation or graphic card or how you position the display in your work area.

If the adjustments don't work, here are more things to consider:

■ **Degauss the display.**   If there's a stray magnetic field, such as that caused by putting a small magnet or regular loudspeaker too close to the display, it may distort the picture, leaving blotches at either or both sides. Click the Degauss button to restore the picture to its normal condition. If no such button is available, turn the display off for a few seconds, then turn it on (you don't have to restart your Mac).

■ **Reset to factory defaults.**   If the settings are so far out of whack, you may find it difficult to bring things back to normal. If the display has a reset

Making the Picture Look Right

switch of some sort (it may require pressing two buttons on some models), use it to return to the settings the unit shipped with. On the iMac and AppleVision displays, the setting is labeled Factory Defaults in the Monitors & Sound Control Panel.

■ **Get help.**   If you cannot get a satisfactory picture, don't hesitate to call the manufacturer or dealer for assistance. If your display is new, or refurbished, it could be defective. Most new computer displays have product warranties of one to three years.

Using ColorSync to Calibrate Your Display

As you've seen so far in this chapter, there are quite literally dozens of ways you can adjust your display. And any single adjustment may affect another adjustment in a less than favorable fashion.

But even after your picture is clear and sharp, and the squares are straight rather than circular, and the brightness is relatively equal from one end of the screen to another, it doesn't mean the colors will match.

Color matching may not make all that much difference if you just want to surf the Web, keep a checkbook, write some letters, and draw some pictures. But if you intend to actually print the documents you create, and you want to use color, having a display that has reasonably accurate color matching is quite important. And it can be a real time and money saver, especially if it helps prevent a nasty surprise when you get your material back from the printer.

ColorSync: The Limits

In the next section, I'll guide you through a typical display calibration using Apple's ColorSync technology. But before I go on, I should point out that while these adjustments will get you in the ballpark, if your work requires high-end graphic design and expensive color printing, it is probably not enough.

NOTE   *The versions of ColorSync you can use to calibrate your display come with Mac OS 8.5 or later. If you use an earlier version of the Mac OS, you can download the latest version of ColorSync from Apple's support Web site: http://www.apple.com/support.*

Here are some additional issues to consider:

■ **Calibrate input and output devices too.**   The display may be set up just right, but if you are scanning and printing in color, you'll want to make sure that these items are calibrated as well. When you install Apple's ColorSync, there will be default profiles for Apple products. If you're using a non-Apple scanner or printer, check the installation disks for ColorSync modules. These modules are typically placed in the ColorSync Profiles folder inside the System Folder.

■ **Consider calibration hardware.**   If you intend to use your Mac for high-quality graphic design and output, you may want to buy a separate calibration device, which will provide the most precise color matching. Contact your display's manufacturer or your dealer for information about these products.

Calibrating Your Display with ColorSync 2.5 and 2.6x

To calibrate your display, follow these steps:

1. Set the room lighting to your usual needs. The presence of sunlight in the room will affect the accuracy of the settings, so you may want to close the blinds for a more accurate result (unless you usually prefer to have sunlight brighten your work area).

NOTE   *If you prefer to open and shut the blinds as the workday progresses, feel free to create separate profiles for each lighting condition. One of the great features of ColorSync is the ability to create as many profiles as you need.*

2. Go to the Apple menu, select Control Panels and choose Monitors & Sound from the submenu.

3. Click on the Color icon, which brings up the Apple Monitor Calibration Assistant, as shown in Figure 10-6.

4. Choose a color profile from the list that most closely matches the make and model of your display. If it's not shown, choose a generic profile (don't worry, you'll still get a good result).

5. Click the Calibrate button, which brings up a screen explaining what you're about to do. Click the right arrow to continue (see Figure 10-7) or the left arrow to return to a previous setup screen.

6. Set your display's contrast to the highest setting.

Using ColorSync to Calibrate Your Display

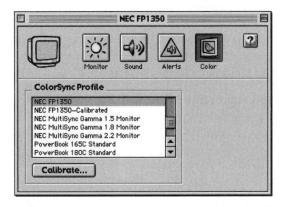

FIGURE 10-6   You'll begin your color calibration right here

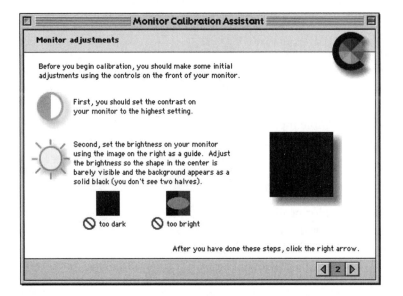

FIGURE 10-7   This screen is used to set brightness and contrast

7. Adjust your brightness setting to produce a perfect black square, with just a faint oval in the center. Click the right arrow to move to the gamma (color intensity) setting, which brings up the screen shown in Figure 10-8.

NOTE *This is a difficult setting. You need to move the sliders back and forth until the Apple illustration in the center vanishes, for the most part, in the background. You will probably want to move your chair back until you're roughly two feet from the display to get this setting right. It will never be perfect, but when you're close enough, you'll barely be able to separate the Apple shape from its surroundings.*

8. When you've finished making your color settings, click the right arrow to bring up your target gamma screen, as shown in Figure 10-9.

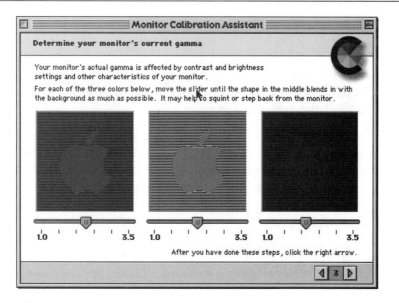

FIGURE 10-8   Take your time with the gamma setting, since it is critical to accurate color display

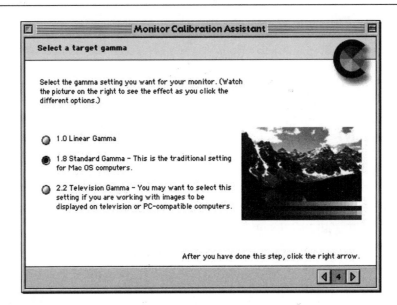

FIGURE 10-9 Choose your target gamma from the settings shown

9. Your target gamma (midtone setting) is set based on the purpose for which you're using your display. The middle setting (1.8) is the one used on most Macs. Click the right arrow to move on.

10. In the next setting, you'll select a specific display from the scrolling list. The choice you make is designed to provide ColorSync with the most accurate information about the range of colors your display can show. If you don't see the right model, pick the one closest to it. Most models within a manufacturer's line will handle colors similarly. Click the right arrow to continue.

TIP *Feel free to use the left arrow to cycle through the setup screens of the Monitor Calibration Assistant to double-check your configuration.*

11. On the screen shown in Figure 10-10, you'll check the radio box that corresponds to your display's white point setting, which adjusts the

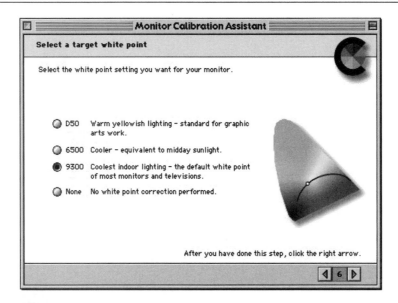

FIGURE 10-10   This screen is used to specify your white point setting

accuracy of the white image on your display. The setting you pick here will depend on the sort of lighting in your work area. Click the right arrow to move on to the final step.

12. The journey is just about over. On the final screen (see Figure 10-11), you name your profile, as I've done, then click the Create It button to make it so.

13. Close the Calibration Assistant and you're done.

> **NOTE** *Since the settings you make now will change as your display ages, you'll probably want to recheck them every few months.*

Calibrating Your Display with ColorSync 3.0

Mac OS 9 will come with a version of the Monitor Calibration Assistant that allows for a greater range of customization of your display settings. This will be

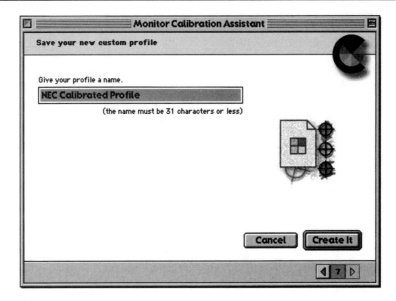

FIGURE 10-11   Give your profile a name, and then create your display's profile

useful when you're calibrating your input, display, and output devices for top quality graphic work. For regular work, frankly, this is nothing you need fret over.

The basic settings you'll follow will be nearly the same as those just described. But here are some of the key differences:

■ **Expert mode**   When you bring up the first screen of the Monitor Calibration Assistant, you click on the Expert Mode check box, which enables you to fine-tune some of the gamma and white point settings.

■ **Target gamma**   The setting, shown in Figure 10-12, lets you use a slider to make subtle gamma changes.

■ **Target white point**   You can use a slider to gain more precise control of this setting (see Figure 10-13). You can also pick a check box with no correction at all.

■ **Profile summary**   When you're finished creating your new calibration profile, you'll see a complete summary of the precise settings you specified (see Figure 10-14).

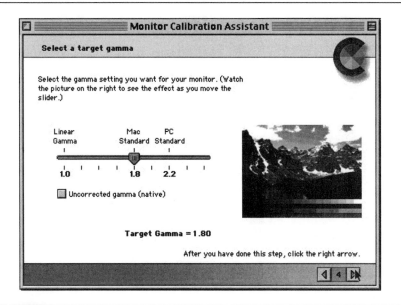

FIGURE 10-12   Click and move the slider to make precise gamma settings

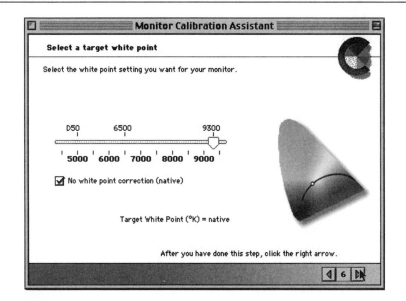

FIGURE 10-13   Fine-tune your display's white point to your special needs

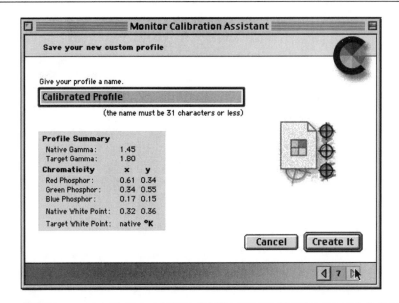

FIGURE 10-14   Take a look at the lower left for the precise numerical settings you
made to your display

Hints and Tips About Multiple Displays

There are some very good reasons to add a second display—if your work desk is
big enough. You can "mirror" or duplicate the picture on the other display: this
may be a good choice if you wish to see the material at two different sizes at the
same time.

But the most frequent purpose for adding another display is to extend your
Mac's desktop. Graphic designers and architects find this feature especially useful.
It's like having one huge display that spans several feet in width.

Whether you can support one feature or both depends on the kind of Mac you
have. Here are some hints and tips about using more than one display on your Mac:

■ **Are you limited to mirroring?**   The iMac DV has a standard VGA plug
for a second display, but it's just for mirroring. Same is true for many
PowerBooks with a video display port. Check the instructions for your
Mac to see whether such features are supported. If your computer has a

Video Mirroring Control Strip, check it to see whether you can switch between these modes.

■ **Move the menu bar to the startup display.**   You can adjust your extended desktop with the Monitors (or Monitors & Sound) Control Panel. You will see an icon for each display. For the menu bar to appear on a particular display, click and drag the menu bar on the display icon to the one you wish to use, if it's not already there. You can move the display icons around in relation to each other to set where your extended desktop goes.

■ **Can you use a TV as a display?**   Look for an RGB output on your graphic card. If it's not there, consider getting a graphic card with this feature, such as the ATI's Xclaim VR 128 from ATI Technologies, the same company who supplies the chips for Apple's onboard graphic controllers. Just remember that your average computer display is designed to deliver more accurate and sharper pictures than a television (which is why, size for size, they cost so much more). There are also outboard converters available (from such firms as Focus Enhancements) that can convert your Mac's display output to work on a regular television—and that's useful for special presentations where a very large screen is necessary.

What's Wrong with My Picture?

You have adjusted everything to perfection, but you are still not satisfied with the picture. Or the picture suddenly changes for the worse. Or you simply want to install an old display on a new Mac and something goes wrong.

Most times, a few adjustments are enough to get your display working properly again. In the final portion of this chapter, I'll cover common problems and solutions. There are so many possible Mac and display combinations that it's impossible to cover the more obscure issues. If your problem isn't addressed here or solved by the steps I've outlined, contact your dealer or the manufacturer for assistance.

An Old Display on a New Mac

Your trusty old display works just beautifully. Clear, sharp pictures. Geometry is straight. It cost you a bundle and you'd like it to last a good, long time. Then you trade in your Mac for a new model, and suddenly the display stops working. The picture is blank. Is there any hope for that old, trusty friend?

Yes, there is. The most recent Mac models can work with most Mac displays and just about any PC display with VGA support. But you may have to jump through a few hoops to get them to work. Here's what to do:

■ **PC display support**   This is really a piece of cake. So long as the display has a standard VGA port, you can buy an inexpensive Mac adapter at your local computer store. Recent G3 Power Macs and PowerBooks already have VGA jacks, standard issue, as do some graphic cards. Just plug the display in normally, start your Mac and you should be able to get a usable picture. The moral of the story is that if a computer dealer says such a display won't work on your Mac, they're probably wrong.

■ **Sync on green displays**   Older Mac displays used a technique called "sync on green," which is the process of combining the green signal with the synchronization pulse. Shorn of the technical stuff, support for this feature was removed from the onboard video of Macs beginning with the Quadra series back in the early 1990s. There are two ways around it. One is to get a graphic card that supports the feature (such as the ones from Formac and IX Micro), but that doesn't help if your Mac has no place to put a graphic card (as with a PowerBook). The other solution is Griffin Technology's Mac Sync Adapter. You can buy the adapter plug from a dealer or order direct from the Nashville-based company from their Web site: http://www.griffintechnology.com. In fact, the head of the company, Paul Griffin, built the company on selling these adapters, which give your old displays a new lease on life. The company has since expanded to support missing features in other Apple products, with ADB and serial port adapters for the iBook, iMac, and Blue & White Power Mac G3s.

Curing Common Picture Irregularities

Whether the problem occurs when you set up a new display or it shows up suddenly, more likely than not, there is a conventional solution. Following are a few common symptoms and their equally common solutions.

Faint Lines on Screen

If your display has one or two faint horizontal lines across the screen, check the specs. Displays that use aperture grill technology, such as those using Mitsubishi

DiamondTron or Sony Trinitron picture tubes, will have those faint lines on the screen. It's part of the assembly of these units and it's perfectly normal. You'll learn to ignore them after a while. If the lines are very dark or vertical, or aren't straight, have your display checked by the dealer or manufacturer.

Case History

Graphic Cards and SCSI Cards Don't Get Along

It took a couple of weeks to isolate this problem. After installing Mac OS 9, I was unable to boot my Blue & White Power Mac G3/400 consistently after I installed a ProFormance 3 graphic card from Formac, a West German–based manufacturer of high performance Mac peripherals.

The symptoms were the same: A gray screen that would never progress to the Happy Mac.

Formac's USA division tried to help. They even sent me a replacement card, but the symptoms were the same. Worse, they said their technical support engineers couldn't duplicate my problem.

Finally something occurred to me, a subtle issue that I had previously ignored as irrelevant.

Seems that my G3 also had one of Adaptec's 2930U SCSI cards so I could continue to use my old removable drives and scanner. Adaptec requires that you move a jumper on the card to allow you to boot from attached SCSI devices when it's installed on the newest Macs, and I dutifully followed their directions.

But since I don't use any of those devices as a startup drive, I just restored the jumper to its original position, and then I restarted. The Formac graphic card worked perfectly.

I left it to Formac and Adaptec to figure out just what went wrong when their two cards played together. No doubt it will have long since been resolved by the time you read this book.

What's Wrong with My Picture?

Shrinking Picture

Over time, as components on your display age, the picture may shrink. If you have a size adjustment, you can easily extend the height and width to their original size. If such adjustments aren't available, or do not accomplish the desired effect, contact the dealer or manufacturer for service.

Color Changes and Artifacts

- ■ **Black and white or grayscale picture suddenly appears.**   Check your color depth settings, either in the Control Strip, Monitors, or Monitors & Sound Control Panels. See if you accidentally switched the setting.

- ■ **Color depth changes.**   Some games will only run at 256-color setting (or on a rare occasion, 16 colors). If your display setting changes abruptly when you play a game, don't despair. It'll probably change back when you quit the program. If not, you'll need to switch it back manually, using the Control Strip, Monitors, or Monitors & Sound Control Panels. Most games, however, will put up an alert box about this, which you must OK to make the change. If the game doesn't put up an alert, but display performance bogs down, you should try setting the color depth to 256 colors anyway to see if the setting helps.

- ■ **Color changes when switching programs.**   Some programs handle the Mac's color palette differently than others, so this effect may be normal. It's more likely to occur, however, when you are using a lower color depth, such as 256 colors. The problem ought to rectify itself when you quit the program.

- ■ **Color artifacts appear onscreen.**   If you see splotches of color on the screen in a particular program, switch to another program or to your Finder desktop to see if the problem disappears. Some programs may interact strangely with certain Mac video hardware. If the problem begins to affect all of your programs and the desktop, check your Mac's video hardware or software to see if there's the potential for a problem. A call to the manufacturer's technical support department is a good idea.

Unavailable Color Depth Settings

When you install a larger display, you may face a problem. You were using millions of colors, and now, at the resolution you pick, you only have 256 or thousands available. If this happens, it may just mean that your Mac's video hardware doesn't support the setting. If your Mac or video card can handle a video memory upgrade, it's time to think about that possibility. If your Mac can support separate graphic cards, you may want to buy a new one. To get millions of colors from a 19-inch or larger display, for example, you need at least 4MB of video RAM for graphic display.

> **NOTE** *I'm using the term "video RAM" in the generic sense here. A number of different types of RAM are used for video display in various Mac models and graphic cards.*

Picture Too Large

You install a larger display and suddenly everything on the screen, from windows to text, is just too large. You will probably want to check the Control Strip, Monitors, or Monitors & Sound Control Panels for a higher pixel resolution setting. This will reduce the size of the items displayed on your screen.

Screen Blacks Out Momentarily

When your Mac is starting up, it will often load a special display enabler extension that controls the size of images on your screen. When this happens, the picture may briefly black out and then return. Sometimes the actual display size (resolution) will change as well. This particular phenomenon was also common with Mac OS 8.6 and is quite normal.

Slow Screen Redrawing

- **There are too many pixels.**   When you get a larger display, or increase screen resolution and/or color depth, your Mac's video hardware has to work harder and draw many more pixels to create a screen display. That's apt to make screen display slower. You may want to try a lower screen resolution setting (which makes images look larger) or choose a lower color depth to speed up performance. If possible, consider a video RAM upgrade, or get a new high performance graphic card.

- **The video drivers are missing.**   When you install a new graphic card, there will likely be a floppy disk or CD that contains the video drivers. These are needed to provide the onboard graphic acceleration and other features. You'll want to install them.

What's Wrong with My Picture?

■ **The video drivers are disabled.**   When you check for a system conflict, you will likely disable some control panels and extensions to see if the problem goes away. You may have disabled your graphic card acceleration software by mistake.

Unstable or Rapid Scrolling

■ Check the video cable at both ends. Make sure it's seated properly. If the cable connector is loose, shut down the system before you tighten it.

■ When you use a Mac video adapter plug, make sure the settings on it are correct. Most of these plugs with dipswitches have a label at the bottom showing settings for specific types of displays. Again, shut down your system before making these changes.

■ If these simple changes don't work, contact the manufacturer or dealer to check the unit.

Fuzzy, Blotchy Picture

■ If you are using computer speakers, move them farther away from the display. While speakers designed for use with a computer should be magnetically shielded to prevent such symptoms, sometimes it's just not enough.

■ Degauss the display. This function helps remove stray magnetic fields, which can cause blotchy effects on your display. Some displays have a special switch for the purpose, but usually just turning the display on and off (you don't have to reboot your Mac) is sufficient to provide the degauss effect.

■ If the display has a "moiré" control, try it. This will help eliminate the crosshair lines that may appear on the picture.

■ Check adjustments affecting sharpness or convergence and see if the picture is improved. If not, consider sending the display to the manufacturer or dealer for service.

Bouncing Picture, Wavy Patterns

- The most common cause is an electrical interference. If you have a vacuum cleaner or other heavy appliance running, turn the appliance off and see if the problem is gone. If it is, consider moving the appliance to another outlet and see if that helps.

- Move the display. Sometimes proximity to fluorescent lights will cause display oddities.

- If you're adjacent to an office that uses lots of appliances (such as a dental office) transport the display to a different position or to a different electrical outlet and see if it helps.

- If the regular solutions don't work, have the display checked by the manufacturer or dealer.

Missing Colors, Tinged or Discolored Picture

- **Zap the PRAM.**   Sometimes the display settings get corrupted. Zapping the PRAM is done by holding down the COMMAND-OPTION-P-R keys at startup. You then wait for at least two startup "tones" to sound on your Mac. The net effect is to restore some of your Mac's settings (such as monitor depth, mouse tracking speed, network, serial port, and startup disk choices, among others) to factory defaults. If these settings are corrupt, display irregularities and even system crashes may result.

NOTE   *Beginning with Mac OS 8.5, Apple began to use preference files for additional settings, so you are no longer forced to redo a number of standard settings when you zap the PRAM, except for your startup disk selection.*

- **Select another display resolution or color depth setting.**   Perhaps your display or graphic card doesn't support your selected configuration.

- **For IX Micro graphic cards**   If the picture has a greenish tinge, open the Control Panel of your graphic card software, and uncheck the box labeled "sync on green." That setting is only required for displays that support that feature.

■ **For AppleVision displays**   Some of Apple's 15- and 17-inch displays have a hardware defect that will cause a color problem. A common defect is a red-tinged image that appears intermittently or just stays put. If you encounter this sort of difficulty, contact your dealer or Apple's customer service department and inquire about their special warranty program affecting some of these units. If the customer service department doesn't have any information for you, insist on speaking to a supervisor about it.

Case History

The Case of the Black-on-Black Lettering

The symptom was really strange. A client was trying to type a letter on AOL, and the letters came out in black, with a black background. It was frustrating. He tried to reinstall AOL's software, checked for system extension conflicts, the whole nine yards.

On a whim, I took another look at his system setup. He was running a first generation Power Mac G3 (the beige version), and had attached one display to the internal video and another to a PCI graphic card. The symptoms appeared on both displays. The PCI-based video display card, however, had a problem. It would not recognize the graphic acceleration software. Hence it displayed pictures really slowly.

I shut down the system and removed the graphic card. The symptoms disappeared, and the client sent the defective product back to the manufacturer for a replacement. The new graphic card displayed none of these symptoms, and he was a happy camper.

No Picture

Your display is set up correctly. You have the proper sync adapter, and everything is all plugged into the right place. You turn on your Mac and there's no picture. Is it the Mac, the display, what?

Here are some likely scenarios and their solutions:

- ■ **It's not on.**   This may seem to be a simple solution. But the power switches on some displays will depress slightly when you turn them on. If you don't push them in far enough, they pop out again and your display is off. If the switch won't stay engaged, take the unit in for service. Some displays will display a small, rectangular LED light when they're on.

- ■ **The lithium battery is dead.**   Your desktop Mac has a little lithium battery that's used to power the parameter RAM (PRAM). Such settings as date and time, display resolution and screen depth, mouse tracking speed, and network settings are stored there. If the battery goes bad, not only will those settings revert to factory defaults, but your Mac may not start up at all. You'll have just a dark screen. The battery itself is fairly cheap (ten to twenty dollars, depending on the Mac model you have) and can usually be replaced in a few minutes. You can check the battery with a simple voltmeter, or just remove it for ten minutes and reinsert it (sort of a super PRAM zap). If the latter doesn't help, replace the battery.

- ■ **A graphic card is loose.**   If you move your desktop Mac around, the graphic cards may slip out of their slots slightly. Before taking everything to the repair shop, shut everything down, open your Mac and reseat the card or cards. Then power up everything and restart the Mac. This should restore your picture.

NOTE   *Some Mac OS clones, such as the ones from Power Computing, appear to have an intermittent problem that prevents a proper startup sequence, so the display remains blank. All you have to do, usually, is to force a restart, by holding down the COMMAND-CONTROL-POWER ON keys at the same time. Release the keys when you hear the startup chord. The picture should reappear; sometimes it'll take a second restart to restore good performance.*

- ■ **Video cables are loose.**   Shut down the system and reattach the cables. Sometimes cable contacts are oxidized and don't make good contact. The act of loosening or removing them and then reinserting and tightening is usually enough to fix the problem.

What's Wrong with My Picture?

NOTE *There are a few so-called "boutique" computer cables available at some dealers, with gold-plated plugs and so on. They are comparable to the high-priced connection cables you can buy for home stereos, because they cost a lot more than the regular brands and seldom provide any real benefits.*

■ **It's the wrong kind of display.** While Macs can use VGA-style PC displays in addition to Mac models, you cannot, for example, use displays designed for the Apple II or some other older computers that don't support current standards.

■ **There's a bad graphic card.** There's no way to test for this, except with another graphic card. Most manufacturers guarantee their product from three to five years, and replacement cards are fairly cheap nowadays. But until the replacement arrives, your Mac will be without a video display, unless it also has internal video.

■ **There's a bad logic board.** If the Mac only has onboard video, you've no choice but to have it replaced.

■ **The power supply is bad.** Same answer. The power supply will have to be replaced.

■ **The power supply on the display is bad.** This sort of repair may cost a couple hundred dollars at the very least, and is only done by specialists, perhaps only at the manufacturer's own facility.

NOTE *Before you decide whether to repair that old display, you may want to price out a new model. The cost of displays today is but a fraction of what it was only a few years ago. For example, the money you used to pay for a 14- or 15-inch display will now get you one with a 19-inch display.*

Summing Up

In this chapter, you discovered how to set up and adjust your new display, and how to fix problems when they occur. You were also shown how easy it is to set up Apple's ColorSync so you get more accurate color display.

In the next chapter, we will pay a visit to the Windows world, and you'll learn how to integrate your Mac in a Windows environment and how to use Windows and even PC applications on your Mac.

Chapter 11

Help with Mixed Mac/Windows Offices

There is no getting around it. The vast, vast majority of personal computers out there use Windows. Though it's true the Mac platform has made great strides in recent years, and has reclaimed a huge amount of its former glory with clever new products such as the iMac, the iBook, and the Power Mac G4, it's a cross-platform world out there.

Many offices have computer systems from both platforms, and even home-based systems may have a Mac and PC at hand.

It's hard enough getting people who speak different languages to work in harmony, but it can be done. And the same is true for personal computers. It may take a little work to make things work properly, but it can be done, and done successfully.

Making Macs and PCs Communicate Peacefully

Direct from the factory, Macs are equipped to work with many Windows files without having to install special software or translators. It's also possible to network computers from both platforms; in fact, it's not uncommon in many businesses that use a Windows or Windows NT (or Windows 2000) computer as a file and/or print server, and Macs for regular production work.

Accessing DOS or Windows Files on Your Mac

For several years, the Mac OS has included a program that helps you translate Windows files so Macs can read them. In addition, the program lets your Mac read PC floppies, and such removable media as Jaz, Zip, and SyQuest, as easily as you read a Mac disk.

Originally, the program was PC Exchange, and, since Mac OS 8.5, it's File Exchange, which also incorporates the functions of another file access program, Mac OS Easy Open (see Figure 11-1).

Here's a quick review of how File Exchange is set up:

■ **PC file mapping**   As I explained in Chapter 7, Windows file types are identified with a three-letter extension added to the file's name. For example, a file with the suffix .doc usually refers to a Microsoft Word document. When you use the Save As feature on a file on a Windows computer, the file suffix is automatically added to the name. PC Exchange uses this information to match the file up to a Mac program that can read the same sort of files.

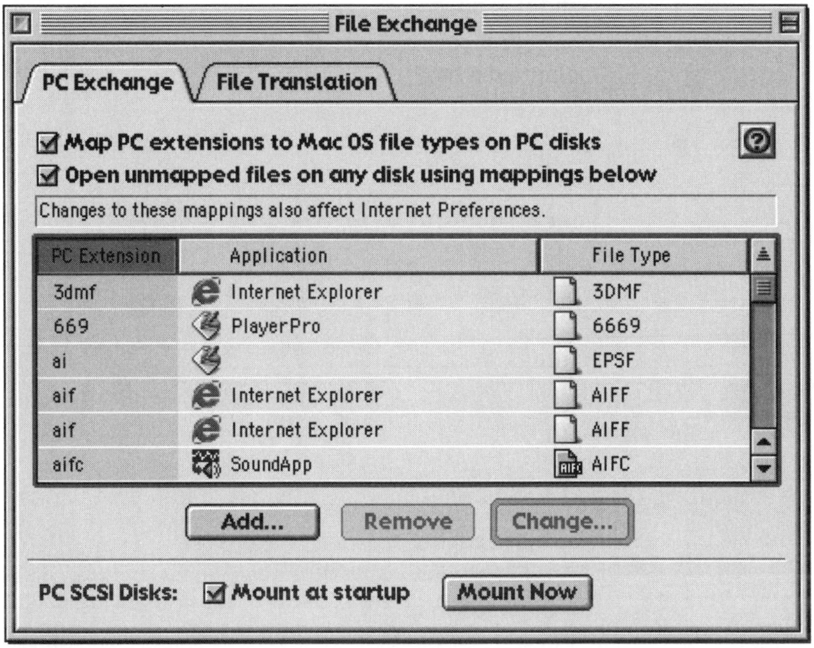

FIGURE 11-1   Apple's File Exchange Control Panel runs behind the scenes so you can easily work with PC files and disks

NOTE   *The file mapping feature of PC Exchange is shared with the Internet Control Panel, which means that the files you read from a disk, retrieve from a network, or download from the Internet are all handled in a similar fashion (assuming you have the "Open unmapped files on any disk using mappings below" option checked).*

■ **Reading PC disks**   This option lets you mount PC floppies and PC SCSI disks, such as removable media, on your Mac's desktop. In addition to being able to read and write files on these disks, you can erase disks in three formats (see Figure 11-2). Along with Mac and DOS formats, there's ProDOS, a relic of the days of the Apple II (an Apple product that came out before the Mac).

Making Macs and PCs
Communicate Peacefully

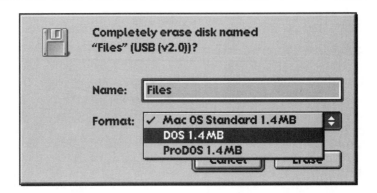

FIGURE 11-2   You can format disks in Mac, DOS, and Apple II (ProDOS) format from
this menu

- **Translating files**   In addition to finding Mac programs with which to
  open PC files, the other capability offered by File Exchange is the ability
  to simplify the process of translating documents so they can be read by
  your Mac programs (see Figure 11-3). If everything is working properly,
  all you have to do is double-click on a file, and File Exchange will locate
  a compatible program for you. If more than one is found, you'll get a list
  of options, from which you select the one you prefer.

NOTE   *When you receive a list of choices, the best option to try is a Mac equivalent
of the Windows program if you have it. Otherwise, choose a program in
the same category as the one used to make the document—for example,
a Mac word processor for a Windows word processing document.*

Solving File Exchange Problems

Apple's File Exchange usually works quite well. Troubles arise when the Mac
program you are trying to use to read the Windows document just can't translate
it properly. Here are some suggestions for dealing with problems with DOS or
Windows files:

- **You cannot open file by double-clicking on it.**   If File Exchange doesn't
  give you any choices, or you get a message that a translator can't be found,
  do this: open the application you want to use first, then use the Open dialog
  box to locate and open the file. You may have to change file-opening

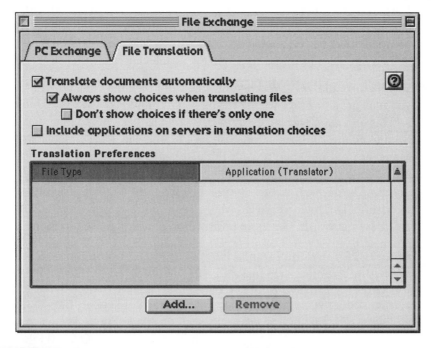

FIGURE 11-3   The File Translation feature of File Exchange locates compatible Mac
programs to convert files to a readable form

options from a pop-up menu in the Open dialog box, though. For example,
in Word 98 there's an All Files option that is very powerful and can
manage to extract the text from a great many types of files.

NOTE   *If opening files becomes a chronic problem, consider rebuilding the
desktop on your Mac. It can cure a variety of ills of this sort. The subject
is covered in much more detail in Chapter 18.*

■ **Document files have strange characters or they're garbled.**   If opening
the file directly doesn't help, look at your program's documentation and
see if there's an Insert, Import, or Place command that can be used. Such
functions will often activate special file translators a program can use to
read the special characteristics of many types of document files. If this
choice doesn't work, try to use another program to translate the file
(see the next section for details).

■ **Files aren't visible on disk.**   If you're using a Mac OS version prior to 8.1, make sure the disk hasn't been formatted in the HFS Plus format. Normally, if it is, you should see a special ReadMe file explaining how to read the file (in short, upgrade to 8.1 or later).

■ **Disk is unreadable.**   When your Mac can't read the contents of a disk, you may get a message asking if you want to initialize the disk. Don't do it! This operation will wipe out the data on the disk. While you may just want to do that as a last resort, you should first check the Extensions Manager Control Panel to see if File Exchange is activated. If it isn't, activate the program, then restart your Mac. If that doesn't work, try running Disk First Aid, or a commercial diagnostic/repair program, such as Alsoft's DiskWarrior, MicroMat's TechTool Pro, or Symantec's Norton Utilities on the disk. For more information on using these programs to repair or recover a disk or drive, read Chapter 13.

■ **CD can't be read.**   The way Apple sets up its CD software is confusing. Not only do you need the CD driver (called Apple CD/DVD Driver in current system versions), you also need a bunch of support files to read various types of CDs. These usually include Apple Photo Access, Audio CD Access, Foreign File Access, High Sierra Access, ISO 9660 File Access, and UDF Volume Access. If one of these extensions is missing, you may be unable to read a specific type of CD. Other than UDF Volume Access, which came about when Apple began to support DVD drives, make sure all of the others are active. Check your Extensions Manager. If one or more of these files is missing, run your system software installer, using (in the latest versions) the Add/Remove feature to restore your CD software.

NOTE   *If your Mac doesn't have an Apple CD or DVD drive, make sure the driver software that came with the drive is installed as well. Many of these drives come with such programs as FWB's CD-ROM ToolKit or CharisMac's CD AutoCache.*

How to Change File Mapping

If double-clicking on a DOS or Windows file brings up an application that won't do the job, you can easily change the file mapping in the PC Exchange panel of the File Exchange Control Panel.

Here's how it's done:

1. Go to the Apple menu, choose Control Panels, and select File Exchange from the submenu (if you have a Mac OS system prior to 8.5, look for PC Exchange instead).

2. Look at the PC Extension category in the PC Exchange window, and select the file extension you want to change.

3. After it's selected, click the Change button, which brings up the Change Mapping dialog shown in Figure 11-4.

4. Choose the program you want to use to translate the file.

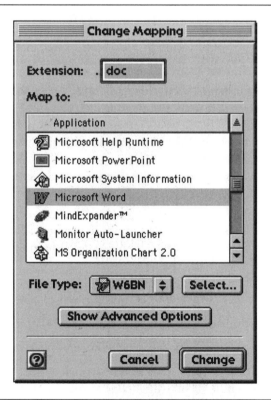

FIGURE 11-4   Select another program to open your DOS or Windows file from the list in the Change Mapping dialog

Making Macs and PCs
Communicate Peacefully

5. Click the Change button to activate your setting.

6. Repeat steps 3 through 5 to make further changes to File Exchange.

7. When you're done, click the close box.

Networking Mac and Windows Computers

When it comes to accessing a regular network printer on a cross-platform network, the issues are not complex. The printer will appear in the Chooser, and you set it up without regard to whether Windows users can access it as well.

But if a Windows computer is doing chores as a print server (that is, storing print jobs and feeding them to the printer), the situation is more complicated. The same is true if you want to share files across the network with your Windows counterparts.

Depending upon the sort of Windows network configuration you have, there are different ways to share files. These will be covered in the next few pages.

Windows Services for Macintosh

If your network uses the server version of Windows NT (or Windows 2000 Server and Advanced Server, which will be out by the time this book appears in print), you'll be pleased to know that the tools are already available for you to set up for Macs to share files and printers with their Windows counterparts. The tools come under the banner of Services for Macintosh.

Installing Services for Macintosh on a Windows NT 4 server is a very straightforward solution. Here's how to get started:

1. On your Windows NT computer, open the Network Control Panel, then click on the Services tab to display the list of Windows NT Network Services that are currently installed.

NOTE *You'll want to keep your Windows NT Server CD at hand. At the beginning of the installation process, you'll be asked for the CD, so the needed files can be retrieved as part of the setup process.*

2. If Services for Macintosh is not installed, click on the Add button to bring up a list of the available network services you can install (see Figure 11-5). From this list, select Services for Macintosh and click the OK button.

3. After Windows NT has finished installing the files, reboot the server.

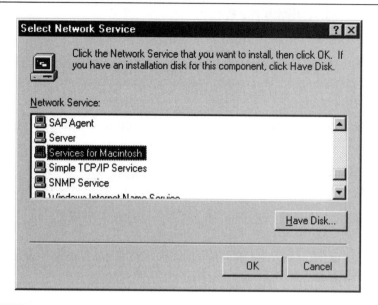

FIGURE 11-5   Choose Services for Macintosh from this dialog to begin the setup process

4. Once the NT server has completed rebooting, you will need to re-install the current Service Pack for Windows NT that you are using and reboot the server again.

NOTE   *A Windows Service Pack is a set of updates and bug fixes. During the lifetime of a Microsoft operating system, there will often be several of these Service Packs that you'll want to consider installing. For best compatibility with the Macs on your network, upgrade using Service Pack 5.*

5. After the server has finished rebooting, open the Network Control Panel again and click on the Services tab.

6. Select Services for Macintosh from the list of options.

7. Click on the Properties button to display the available options. Make sure the interface you select is the one you want to use.

8. Click on the Routing tab.

NOTE *Whether or not you need a router depends on the size of your network. This is an issue that applies primarily to larger installations.*

9. If you already have AppleTalk zones on your network, simply click on the Get Zones button. This action will retrieve a list of all the zones currently available on the network.

10. Once you see the zone list, select the zone you want to use and click on the Make Default button.

11. If you are planning on using NT Server as a router, you will need to click on the Enable Routing box and then the Seed This Network box.

12. Enter in the range of zones you want to add to the network and then add in each of their names.

13. Once you have entered this information, select the zone you want to use and click on the Make Default button.

Although the process seems a little convoluted, at least in comparison to setting up a network on the Mac, this completes the basic setup process. You have now installed and configured Services for Macintosh.

NOTE *Under Windows 2000, the setup is done via the Network Control Panel. When you bring up this control panel, you'll choose the Local Area Connection option to install your Mac networking options.*

Setting Up DAVE for Mixed Networks

You don't have to use the tools offered under Windows NT or Windows 2000 to mate your Mac and Windows computers across the network.

For small networks especially you may want to consider a Mac program that lets you directly access a Windows network: DAVE from Thursby Software Systems. You can get more information about the program and a time-limited demonstration version at the company's Web site: http://www.thursby.com.

DAVE lets your Macs connect directly to Windows NT and Windows 95/98 computers using NetBIOS (Network Basic Input Output System). Installing DAVE is as simple as double-clicking on the installer program and restarting your Mac at the end of the setup process.

Once you have installed DAVE, though, it has to be configured. There's never a free ride when it comes to cross-platform networking.

To configure DAVE, follow these steps:

1. Open the NetBIOS control panel. This brings up the screen shown in Figure 11-6.

2. Click on the Name field in the NetBIOS Control Panel, and enter the name you want your Macintosh to be known as on the Windows network.

3. Now you will need to enter the name of the Windows workgroup or Windows NT domain you want this computer to belong to. While DAVE will not allow your Mac to actually join the Windows NT domain, it will allow you to see all the servers and computers that belong to that domain.

NOTE *If you're not sure of the name of this network domain, contact your systems administrator for this information.*

4. Once you have set the computer's name and workgroup or domain, you are ready to finish up your configuration. Select the network protocol you want to use when talking to the Windows computers on your network. For most Macs, you'll set this to TCP/IP.

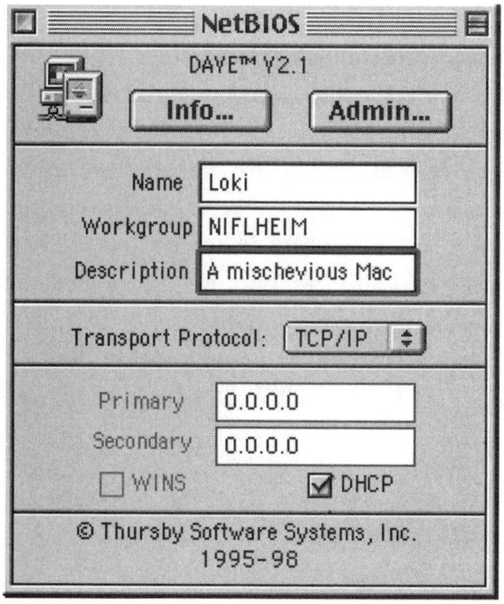

FIGURE 11-6   You use the NetBIOS Control Panel to configure DAVE for cross-platform networking

5. Continuing our settings in the NetBIOS Control Panel: If you are getting the IP address for your Mac from a DHCP (Dynamic Host Configuration Protocol) server—and that DHCP server also sends out information about the WINS (Windows Internet Naming Service) servers on the network— you will need to click on the DHCP check box. If your DHCP server doesn't send out information about WINS—or you have set your IP address in some other fashion—you will need to click on the WINS button and type in the IP address of the primary and secondary WINS servers.

> NOTE   *Once again, you'll want to carefully check your network setups before you enter information in the NetBIOS Control Panel. A single wrong keystroke may result in you being unable to link your Macs to the Windows network.*

6. Once you are finished configuring NetBIOS, open the Chooser, and locate the DAVE Client.

7. Click on DAVE to access the Windows computers on the network. For sharing print services, you'll use the DAVE Print Client Control Panel.

Troubleshooting Mixed Network Problems

On a Mac, networking is usually fairly easy. You can connect older Macs via the LocalTalk (printer) port or most any Mac via Ethernet (though some older Macs require an optional expansion card to add this feature).

At the very least, all you have to do is open the File Sharing (or its predecessor Sharing Setup) Control Panel and click the Start Button under File Sharing to activate the feature. In addition, Mac OS 9 expands the capability of networking via TCP/IP, either to your local network or via an Internet connection. I'll cover Mac network issues in more detail in Chapter 17.

The wrinkles begin when you also need to connect to Windows users on the very same network. You'll find that the setup process that works so easily on a Mac computer isn't quite so easy in the Windows environment.

Common Cross-Platform Networking Problems and Solutions

The issues of setting up a Mac/Windows network can be complex, and even if you follow all the complex dialogs and setup procedures, there is still potential for trouble.

Over the next few pages, I'll list some typical problems and solutions to make your cross-platform network function properly. As you'll see here, these are not user-friendly issues, and you may need to pore through manuals or consult a systems administrator (if your company has one) to troubleshoot the system. These are intended as basic guidelines to follow:

Make Sure Your DNS Servers Are Up to Date

On TCP/IP networks, Windows-based PCs rely primarily upon WINS and their NetBIOS Master Browsers to provide them with the capability to match a specific computer name to its IP address. But Macs, like their UNIX cousins, rely upon DNS to match a computer's name to its IP address.

DNS (Domain Name Service) is the system that, like WINS, keeps track of the names of computers and their IP addresses. However, unlike WINS, which dynamically learns the computer's name and IP address from each computer as it boots up, DNS must be manually configured. This means that the DNS server's listing of computer names and their IP addresses can become inaccurate when a computer's name or IP address is changed. So if you are having trouble connecting servers on the network from your Macs, the first thing you should check is your DNS servers to make sure they are functioning and their databases are up to date.

Check Your AppleTalk Setup and Your Routers

A router is a device that directs network traffic. When setting up a router you are, in effect, tying together two or more AppleTalk networks.

When you have trouble accessing computers outside the segment of the network on which you are located, take a look at the router or the switch that controls the link between your AppleTalk network and the other AppleTalk networks in your installation. Here are some diagnostic steps to follow:

- ■ **Check your network protocol.**   One of the first things you should look at is what network protocol you are using to reach the other parts of the network. If you are using AppleTalk, you need to make sure that AppleTalk is enabled on the adjoining segments of the network or that the routers are set to transfer AppleTalk packets through the network using TCP/IP. You will also need to ask the simple question, are there any other segments of the network that use AppleTalk?

- ■ **Check the other configuration settings.**   If there are other AppleTalk networks on your network and they are set up to communicate properly, you should look at the other settings you've used. In the old days, well, just a few years ago actually, when Macs tended to be quite chatty while communicating via AppleTalk, it was pretty common to install access lists on the routers so that certain types of AppleTalk traffic was blocked. Unfortunately, many routers still have these access lists installed despite the fact that modern Macs are nowhere near as demanding upon the network as they used to be. To check to see if an access list is blocking your Macintoshes from reaching the various resources on your network, look for access lists that would impact AppleTalk. On a Cisco router, this means looking for access lists that range from 600 to 699, as these are the AppleTalk-related access lists. Examine the various access lists and make sure they are configured in such a way as not to block your access to the resources you are trying to reach.

NOTE

When it comes to network traffic, AppleTalk is referred to as being chatty because it constantly sends out network requests asking for updates on the network setup. The problem became less severe and more manageable as Apple improved AppleTalk performance beginning with Mac OS 8, and more and more high-speed Ethernet networks were established.

- **Check the TCP/IP Control Panel.** If you are using TCP/IP to communicate, you'll want to make sure TCP/IP is configured properly on the Mac. If you are using DHCP to obtain a valid IP address for your Macintosh, you should check to see that it has acquired a proper one by opening the TCP/IP Control Panel and seeing what IP address it has grabbed. If the address you get is in the range of 169.254.0.0 to 169.254.254.255, you have a problem with the Macintosh not being able to communicate with the DHCP server. The most common cause of this problem is that the router that controls this segment of the network is not configured to forward DHCP packets from one segment of the network to another. On Cisco routers, this command is called IP Helper. As I said at the beginning, we are getting to the real nitty-gritty of network management issues with some of these issues.

- **Look at the default gateway.** If your Macintosh is communicating properly with the DHCP server and getting a valid IP address, you should check to see if the router has a default gateway set up for the segment of the network on which your Macs are residing. Forgetting to set a default gateway is a very common error that happens when a network engineer sets up an AppleTalk-only network and then goes back later to add in support for TCP/IP or other network protocols.

■ **Look at the routing table updates.**   Aside from these common problems, you should check to make sure that the router controlling access to your segment of the network is receiving regular routing table updates. These updates tell the router where to send data so that it will reach its intended destination. If the updates aren't current, your data can be sent off into "never-never land." Another common issue you should check is that the Ethernet switch to which your Mac is connected to has an up-to-date ARP cache and that the port settings for your Macintosh are set to the proper values. While modern switches are very good at determining what Ethernet speed and duplex settings are appropriate, they can sometimes choose an incorrect value or be set incorrectly by hand.

Troubleshooting a Mixed Network

The key to isolating and exterminating network problems on a mixed, Mac/Windows network is to figure out if this is a Macintosh problem, a Windows problem, or both. First, you'll want to see if the problem affects computers from both platforms.

If the problem is affecting only your Windows-based PCs, you should focus on those portions of the network that are used only by Windows. For example, Windows uses TCP ports 135–139 to handle a variety of inter-computer communications as well as file transfers via NetBIOS. If your Windows-based computers have trouble sending and receiving files via NetBIOS, make sure there are no access lists on the routers that might be interfering with the movement of this traffic.

On the other hand, if the problem is Macintosh-based only, you should look to see if it is related to AppleTalk; that is, you're having trouble sending files between Macintoshes and to AppleTalk-based printers. If your troubles are limited to AppleTalk, take a look at the routers to make sure they are properly configured for AppleTalk. You should also make sure that AppleTalk information is being properly routed over the network, so the router knows how to direct AppleTalk traffic from one AppleTalk network to another.

How to Handle Windows Emulators on a Mac

It would seem like a dream come true. All you have to do is install some software, and you convert your Mac into a Windows computer. Is the dream of having two computers a reality, or is there some hidden shortcoming that isn't being revealed in the advertising for these products?

How to Handle Windows Emulators on a Mac

Before I get into details, let me tell you that the two most popular software solutions, Connectix Virtual PC and FWB's SoftWindows, both truly work pretty much as advertised. You install these programs and you set them up according to instructions, and presto, you have a real Windows environment on your Mac.

You can use that Windows environment to run your favorite Windows programs and games. What's more, Virtual PC is designed to emulate an Intel-based computer, rather than just an operating system. This means you can go ahead and install other operating systems with the program. These include UNIX-based systems (such as the Intel version of Linux, the popular open source operating system that's giving Microsoft fits).

> **NOTE**   *Open source means that the computer code used to make the operating system is freely available for programmers to use or modify. Apple Computer has released part of its OS X operating system as open source too, under the name Darwin (though it doesn't include the proprietary Mac OS user environment).*

In addition to software, there are hardware-based solutions as well. These solutions actually put a PC logic board inside your Mac, using the PCI slot (or in older Macs, the NuBus slot). They include either a Pentium or compatible processor on a logic board with various components that allow it to interface with a Mac environment.

At one time even Apple Computer produced such products, but no more. At present, the sole hardware solution comes from Orange Micro.

How They Work

Whether you use a hardware solution or software, there is a fundamental similarity. In both cases, you set aside a part of your hard drive to make a big file that is used to emulate a PC drive. On the Mac side of the world, all you see is one very big file. When you use the Windows emulator, it's accessed as an actual PC drive.

Whether the solution is software or hardware, you enter the PC environment through an application window. You launch the program, which in turn launches Windows. You then switch in and out of this program same as any other program (see Figure 11-7).

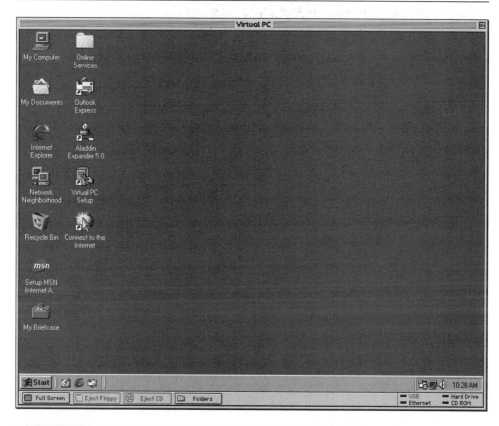

How to Handle Windows
Emulators on a Mac

FIGURE 11-7   Connectix Virtual PC runs as just another application on your Mac, but
when you click on the program's application window, you enter another
computing universe

The emulators are also set up to map the PC environment to your Mac's
various connection ports, so you can share drives, modems, network and Internet
connections, and printers. The version of Connectix Virtual PC being shipped
when this book was written also was designed to support USB.

NOTE   *Some of the older Orange Micro DOS cards also include separate
connection ports for peripherals. This lets you hook up such devices
as printers and modems without sharing the ones your Mac uses.*

A Look at Windows Emulator Performance

Just how good is the imitation compared to the real thing? When it comes to software, there is no free ride. Here are some considerations:

- **They're RAM hungry.** Windows emulation software requires lots and lots of RAM, first to cover the emulation software's overhead to do its magic, and then to act as RAM for the PC environment. You should figure on allocating a minimum of 48MB to your PC emulator for adequate performance.

- **They need big DOS files.** You should figure on allocating between 250MB and 520MB of hard drive space for a Windows emulator. And since speed is dependent on the drive you have, consider a faster hard drive if you want to spend a lot of time emulating Windows.

- **They're slow.** Even on the fastest Power Mac G3 and G4, performance won't even come close to the cheapest PC you can buy today. Connectix recommends a G3 as the slowest CPU to use with Virtual PC if you're using any Windows version. Even then, you should expect low-end Pentium performance across the board on a fast Mac, although these programs feel zippier than the raw measurements indicate because the publishers optimize such functions as pulling down menus. It's fine for doing some Internet surfing and running a word processing program. But when it comes to playing games, you may not be quite as satisfied with the level of performance.

If you have the need to run Windows programs with better performance, you may want to consider a DOS card, such as one of the products from Orange Micro. This product can bring performance close to a genuine Windows-based computer for the simple reason that it uses actual Intel or compatible hardware.

Such a product can be quite convenient, since you don't have to have a separate computer, a separate monitor, keyboard, and mouse. On the other hand, if you need some serious Windows-based computer power to handle programs that just aren't available for Macs, you should bite the bullet and consider getting a regular PC as a second computer to use when these needs arise. As I explained earlier in this chapter, with a program such as DAVE, you can actually set up a fairly inexpensive cross-platform computer network without a terrible amount of fuss and bother.

An All-Too-Brief Primer on Windows Troubleshooting

When you use a program that emulates Windows, or one of those DOS cards, you have indeed departed from the Mac operating system in large measure, and you'll no doubt be faced with an interface you have to get used to, and a new set of problems that may rear their ugly heads.

In this section, I'll cover some common Windows-based diagnostic steps. If you find your particular problems are rather more complex than I've dealt with here, may I recommend you get yourself a copy of *Windows 98: The Complete Reference*, by John Levine and Margaret Levine Young, from Osborne/McGraw-Hill. Just about any question you may have about the subject is answered in this 1,000-page book.

Windows Crashes at Startup

When your Mac crashes, a common diagnostic procedure is to restart after selecting a Base set in Extensions Manager or starting with Extensions off.

If you run into problems with Windows, you're apt to encounter a process that's roughly equivalent: Safe Mode.

If you have a severe crash, your Windows-based PC might actually start up in this mode. You can also enter it in rather a tricky fashion:

1. Restart Windows.

2. As soon as you see a message similar to "Starting Windows 98," press F8. You have to react fast to see this message, as it may zip by before you notice.

3. You'll see a Windows 98 Startup menu, and you'll be faced with six choices. Type the number **4**, then press ENTER to invoke Safe Mode.

Safe Mode supports only the very essential functions of Windows, the keyboard, mouse, display, and disk drives, and your screen size is limited to 640x480. If you successfully start up in this mode, more often than not, you'll be able to restart normally and that, as they say, is that.

Otherwise, you may have to do some further troubleshooting. We'll cover a few more steps next.

How to Handle Windows Emulators on a Mac

The Windows Variation of the Force Quit

The Windows program you are working in suddenly hangs or crashes completely. You may or may not see an onscreen error prompt. Regardless, here's a way to close the program (as I said, similar to the force quitting on a Mac):

1. When the program hangs, press CTRL-ALT-DEL (this is the DEL key on the Extended keyboard, not the DELETE key). This will bring up a Close Program dialog box.

2. Locate the name of the offending program, select it, then click End Task. That should close the program.

3. If the program isn't closed, after a few seconds, you'll get another Windows dialog asking if you really and truly want to close that program. You should OK this message.

4. Should the program finally give up the ghost and quit, it's a good idea to restart Windows. Better to be safe than sorry, especially if you need to use that program again.

5. If you cannot quit the program this way, press CTRL-ALT-DEL two times, which should force Windows to restart. At the next restart, Windows will run its equivalent of the Mac's Disk First Aid, ScanDisk. And like the feature that first premiered in Mac OS 8.5, your Windows drive (or drive image in this case) will be scanned and errors will be fixed.

NOTE   *As much as we like to credit Apple Computer with many of the major innovations in operating system flexibility, it's a fact that Apple has not had any qualms about borrowing a feature here and there from that other operating system. Running Disk First Aid after a forced restart is one example. Another example is Contextual Menus, which is similar to the right-mouse-button feature under Windows.*

A Look at Windows Troubleshooters

If you continue to run into problems in the Windows environment, you may also want to consult a set of tips and tricks provided for your benefit by none other than Microsoft. They're part of the Windows Help menu and are known by their collective name, Troubleshooters.

To access this feature follow these steps:

1. Open the Windows Start menu and choose Help. This will bring up the Windows Help menu.

2. Click on the Contents tab. This will produce a list of available topics.

3. For Windows 98, select Windows 98 Troubleshooters. This will bring up a list of topics for you to explore.

4. When you've found a suitable topic, click on it to select it.

5. On the right pane, you'll see a listing of typical problems. Click on the one that seems to apply, then click the Next button.

6. For each step of the way, you'll be asked some questions and based on your Yes or No responses, you'll be given proposed solutions. The steps described ought to help for most reasonably conventional problems.

NOTE   *Since you will be dealing with a Windows environment using Mac hardware, there are a number of hardware issues you are not apt to encounter. However, the software-related matters ought to apply to a number of the situations you will confront.*

In Defense of Your Mac

It's very true that Apple has found plenty of methods to shoot themselves in the foot. In the years before Steve Jobs returned to take over management of the company, Apple Computer managed to introduce so many related models that it took a scorecard to figure out the differences. They also squandered resources on technologies that few people bought into, such as OpenDoc and QuickDraw GX.

Although Apple's prospects have improved tremendously, especially since the iMac hit the marketplace in August 1998, there are still firms that, for this and other reasons, are seriously considering abandoning Macs and moving to the other platform.

If you are facing this situation, you will find this next section interesting. It has a rather Mac-centric view of the computing world, because that's the world I work in. But it will also give you some realistic information about the two platforms that you can use to examine the situation realistically.

In Defense of Your Mac

The Truth About Mac System Stability

No doubt you've heard the arguments. Some folks say a Mac is more stable than Windows, others say that Windows blows the Mac out of the water. As with anything as complex as a computer operating system, there are many variables at work here. There are plenty of examples where the usual assumptions just don't apply.

However, in the next few paragraphs I will cover some of the basic issues that determine stability on both platforms. The biggest difference you will notice when moving from the Macintosh to Windows or from Windows to the Macintosh is how easy it is to destabilize each operating system.

The Mac View of the Windows Environment

Mac users often find themselves aghast at how the installation of a simple application or update can render a perfectly functional Windows-based PC completely useless.

Macintosh-based applications and utilities generally don't install a large number of files directly into the operating system or replace commonly shared files with a version of their own. However, many Windows-based applications do. Since Windows utilizes a large number of interrelated files to function properly, having an installer install the wrong version of a file or delete a critical file during installation can easily render Windows inoperable.

NOTE *To be fair, I should point out that some Mac installers do from time to time toss stuff in the System Folder without regard to whether there are newer, better versions there. But more often than not, you'll just find two different versions of the same files (such as an older and newer version of AppleScript or QuickTime). It's not difficult to locate and then trash the older version.*

Likewise, the sheer number of files and the myriad ways they interact with each other make it nearly impossible to determine exactly what went wrong on a Windows computer and how best to repair it. While the addition of uninstall utilities with many applications has helped, they do not always restore the PC back to its original state. Unfortunately this means that when something goes badly wrong with Windows, you almost always have to do a completely fresh re-installation of Windows. Then you will probably have to re-install all your application and utility software in order to get the PC back to a working condition.

In the earlier section entitled "A Look at Windows Troubleshooters," I just scratched the surface, to help you deal with the basics. If you have to do a major troubleshooting task on a Windows-based PC, you're apt to find that the entire time-consuming process makes a clean install on a Mac seem to be simplicity personified.

The Windows View of the Mac Environment

Windows users coming to the Macintosh will be surprised to find that there are far fewer components to the average Mac application or utility. This means that installing and removing Mac applications and utilities is a far simpler process in general than it is on a Windows-based PC.

Macs are, as a general rule, a bit harder to crash than a Windows-based PC simply because Apple has greater control over the hardware and software, and thus the ability to make sure things work properly, than does Microsoft. Although Apple's tight integration of the hardware and operating system is sometimes criticized because it grants the Mac user fewer purchase options, in this case it works as an advantage.

In general, a great many problems that a Mac user will encounter can be traced to either a bad extension or control panel, a bad font, or perhaps a bad application or application preference file. Since the Mac OS is inherently less complicated than Windows, due to the lesser number of files in the operating system, it is usually far easier for a user to diagnose and resolve problems without having to re-install the operating system. I cover this subject in more detail in Chapter 18.

Likewise, removing a Mac application or utility is generally just a case of dragging the various files to the trash, quite a bit simpler than having to use an uninstall program. If it's a System Folder component, you'll have to restart, but that only means you'll have to wait a couple of minutes before you get back to work.

NOTE *As software publishers pack more and more features into Mac programs, it's very true that more and more components are being installed. Fortunately, when things get this complicated, a publisher will usually add an uninstall option to an installer so that you can safely remove all elements of the program without having to figure out just what they are.*

To be fair, Microsoft's industrial-grade operating systems, Windows NT and Windows 2000, are usually far more robust and significantly harder to crash than the Mac OS or Windows 95/98. While Windows NT and 2000 suffer many of the

In Defense of Your Mac

same flaws that affect Windows 95/98 users, by relying upon a large number of files and settings to function properly, they are also designed to survive most software crashes without bringing down the entire operating system.

To the average user, this means that Windows NT will, for example, either fail completely—producing what is known as the blue screen of death—or will just shrug off the error and keep on running. Windows 95/98, when confronted with a similar system error, will almost always cease to function (but, of course, that's also true of the Mac OS).

This fact of life isn't lost on Apple. For years they have been working to deliver better stability to the Mac operating system. The delivery of the consumer version of Mac OS X (which could happen by the time you read this book) is expected to provide fewer system crashes and a much higher level of reliability. This will be especially true for Mac programs that have been recompiled to support Apple's Carbon application guidelines.

Is the Mac Really Slower?

You compare the horsepower. On the one hand, you have all those Pentiums advertised with 600MHz and 700MHz CPUs and on the other hand Macs in the 400 to 500MHz range (the numbers of both ends of the equation will continue to rise over time).

On the surface, then, it would seem that Macs are noticeably slower than their Windows counterparts, at least if you just examine the megahertz figures.

But evaluating computer performance isn't as easy as that.

Since Steve Jobs took over as Apple's so-called "interim" CEO, Apple almost always introduces their new computers with a big flourish and benchmark tests that are designed to show their computers running much faster than Windows-based systems with higher CPU MHz ratings. The problem with benchmarks is that they don't apply equally to all computer functions.

For one thing, performance doesn't just depend on raw megahertz, but also on how much data the CPU can actually process, and how fast—and that is a complex issue, depending on how the CPU is designed and how it performs in the real world. Computer performance also depends, to name a few examples, on the performance level of the other elements of your computer, such as the logic board, the hard drive, the video display hardware, the CD drive, and the efficiency with which a program is created.

The fact of the matter is that some programs manage to work better on the Mac and others better with Windows (no blame is being assigned here, of course).

So every time Apple produces a benchmark showing how the Mac does something faster, a Windows user will come back with their own benchmark showing how one of their computers has excelled in one task or another.

As a practical matter, if you use your Mac strictly for such things as financial transactions, word processing, or surfing the Web, a little performance advantage one way or the other won't make you any more productive. But if you want to play high-energy games or deal with programs that do complex rendering tasks (such as image editing, 3-D design, or editing video), you'll want to eke out every possible increment of performance.

Competition is at work here. As quickly as Apple touts superiority, Windows-based systems get faster too. By managing to leapfrog each other, the performance level of personal computers continues to grow, and the state of the art hits a higher plateau. And the next Mac you buy will likely be much faster than the one it replaces.

Where to Find Mac Software

When I first bought a Mac, I included in the package much of the software I expected to use on a regular basis, so I was able to get up and running without having to buy anything extra. And today the consumer model Macs, the iMac and iBook, come with a nice selection of software you can use to get started. These include AppleWorks, Apple's great little integrated program featuring word processing, spreadsheets, database, and simple illustration components, plus the software you need to access the Internet. At times dealers will also set up special packages that include a software selection.

But one way or another, you may find that you want to expand your horizons or you need a special type of software for a particular purpose. You visit your local Mac dealer and find the cupboards bare or close to it. There are a handful of utilities, a few games, and maybe a copy of the latest Microsoft Office.

You ask the salesperson for more, and you may get this typical response, "Sorry, there isn't much Mac software available."

Did you make a mistake? Choose the wrong computing platform? Does Windows begin to tempt you?

Well, the truth is, there are thousands of Mac programs available, and not just mainstream software that's designed for a mass audience. There are dedicated Mac programs for legal offices, dentists, physicians, and other special purposes. But you won't typically find a decent section at most local dealers (though a few, such as CompUSA and Computer Town, have special Mac sections that are fairly well stocked).

Most Mac users go to mail order catalogs to buy software, from such companies as MacConnection, MacMall, MacWarehouse, and MacZone (to name just a few popular examples). When you pick up one of those catalogs, you'll find thousands of programs listed. But even a local dealer can usually order a program that isn't regularly stocked.

> **NOTE** *If your dealer doesn't have the software you need, you may want to check Apple's Web site for information on more than 15,000 available Mac products: http://guide.apple.com. The site splits the information up into a number of hardware and software categories. If the product is listed, you'll see details about how to contact the manufacturer for more information.*

So before you visit the other side of the computing platform, do a little checking first. In most cases, the program you need will be available in Mac form.

> **NOTE** *I'd like to offer a very special thank you for two colleagues who provided valuable information for this chapter. One is our fearless technical editor, John Rizzo, who maintains the popular Mac/Windows Web site (http://www.macwindows.com), and the other is Pieter Paulson, who has collaborated with me on several writing projects. Pieter is an experienced network administrator who has supported a number of mixed platform networks in his long career.*

Summing Up

The problems with making Mac and Windows computers work together in reasonable harmony are not insurmountable. Although it may take a little troubleshooting to get all the pieces to work together, it is a task that will be worth the rewards in being able to share files and printers across even the largest personal computer networks.

In the next chapter I'll deal with another issue that can rear its ugly head whether you share files with Windows users or not. And that's the subject of computer viruses.

Chapter 12

Do You Have a Computer Virus?

The show business world usually has little resemblance to the real world. And that definitely applies to how computers work. Here are two notable examples:

In the top-grossing science fiction movie *Independence Day,* one of the brave heroes, a cable TV technician, portrayed by Jeff Goldblum, used a computer virus to infect the alien's computers and make them vulnerable to attack by Earth firepower. Naturally, it's never explained just how a simple laptop computer, in this case an Apple PowerBook, could somehow interface with an alien operating system and spread a virus.

Another popular movie, *The Net,* featured Sandra Bullock as a computer programmer whose identity had been stolen by an evil industrialist. To get back at her enemy, she infected the villain's evil software with a virus.

In these two fictional cases, the computer virus was the good guy, the secret weapon that allowed our heroes to defeat the bad guys. In the real world, however, a computer virus isn't so nice. A computer virus may simply put up a silly message on your computer and be done with it. Or it may alter or damage your precious application and document files, even your system software. Worse, a virus may actually wipe out your files or erase your hard drive.

In addition to the havoc they wreak, writing and spreading computer viruses is a crime in just about any civilized location in the world. There have been notable examples through the years where virus authors were caught, tried, and convicted.

Even if just a childish prank, the presence of computer viruses is a threat to everyone, whether you use a Mac or a PC.

Are Computer Viruses a Danger to Mac Users?

On the PC side of the computing universe, virus strains number in the thousands, with more being discovered almost every day. This is one of the perils of being the majority platform.

That's not to say that Mac users are immune to such problems. In addition to the rapid spread of Microsoft Office macro viruses (as discussed in the next section), the newfound popularity of Macs, iMacs, and iBooks have brought with it the consequence of renewed interest in writing viruses for our favorite platform.

From the early days of the Mac, some very potent viruses have infected our platform, and you need up-to-date protection. No doubt about it.

Case History

My First Close Encounter with a Virus

I remember this as if it were yesterday. After migrating a design studio to Mac-based desktop publishing in the 1980s, I bought myself a Mac system for my home. I had hoped to resume my writing career and perhaps do a little telecommuting, so I could stay home and get paid for it.

It was the spring of 1989, and the hot Mac of that era was the IIcx, which sported the fastest Mac-based microprocessor, the 68030. It's hard to believe that I thought the computer was incredibly fast, but that's how technology changes.

I set up the system and worked hard and long to install software. I downloaded programs from the Internet, but the problem really originated when I brought home a small utility program (the name isn't important) from a local dealer.

I installed the program, then tried to create a new document in QuarkXPress. Now, XPress is one of a number of programs that's classified as "self-checking," meaning that it'll refuse to run if it's modified in a suspicious fashion, such as might occur when infected by a virus. I launched QuarkXPress, and got a warning about a possible virus infection. Then it wouldn't run.

Now I was startled. A virus infection was something I hadn't seriously considered on a brand new computer, and so hadn't bothered to get any virus detection software. I cleaned up all the files I could think of. I even reinstalled system software and the affected program, but it didn't work. I still got the virus warning.

Finally, I wiped the hard drive clean, and reinstalled everything from scratch. As soon as I was up and running, I logged on to an online service and downloaded a shareware virus detection program (it was Virus Detective, which is no longer being produced).

It reported that I was still infected with the nVIR virus, but was able to eradicate it from my Mac and some infected disks. And then I found the cause: that little utility I had purchased from a local Mac store was apparently infected at the factory. (They told me it was a shipping error.)

The moral of the story: Even when you buy commercial software in a reputable store, check it anyway. Sometimes mistakes are made, and there's no reason for you to have to suffer as a result. If you do find the presence of a virus on any software you buy, tell the store and the publisher immediately, and ask for a clean copy.

Are Computer Viruses a Danger to Mac Users?

The Real Dangers of Cross-Platform Viruses

The nice thing about Microsoft Office programs is that you can view and edit them on both the Mac and Windows platforms.

The nasty thing is that they make Macs vulnerable to infection by the thousands of macro viruses that infect such applications as Excel and Word. Microsoft's macro feature is valuable. It helps you easily automate repetitive steps, and handle complex formats at the click of a button (or via a simple keystroke). But with convenience comes a danger, that the very same avalanche of macro viruses may infect your Mac also.

Fortunately, on our side of the computing universe at any rate, such virus infections primarily hurt your documents, not your application or system files. As noted in the following section on Mac viruses, a common Word macro virus may somehow password-protect your document (with a password you don't know, of course) or make it impossible to save the document as anything but a template.

NOTE   *You'd be very surprised to hear the strange places macro viruses turn up. I've gotten infected documents from advertising agencies, publishers, and, in one case, a company who made DOS conversion hardware for the Mac. Most of these folks were surprised and thankful I discovered the problem (except for one company, whose name I'd prefer to forget).*

Fortunately, such problems are easily remedied. Current Mac virus protection programs will handily diagnose and dispose of macro viruses, and they are updated regularly as new mischief-makers do their dirty work.

NOTE   *It should be pointed out that a number of Microsoft Office macros on the Windows platform use Visual Basic code that isn't supported on the Mac version of the program. This lessens the danger to Mac users. But if you transfer those infected files back to the Windows platform, the infection will transfer as well, so protecting yourself from macro viruses is still very important.*

PC-Borne Viruses and the Dangers to Mac Users

It's true that a virus designed to infect the DOS and Windows operating systems won't harm your Mac, but there are notable exceptions to the rule. And they apply if you decide to emulate the PC operating systems on your Mac.

Windows Emulators and DOS Cards

When you install Connectix Virtual PC or FWB's RealPC or SoftWindows, you are definitely working in a Windows environment, even if it shows up in a separate application window.

> NOTE *In case you're wondering, Insignia sold their RealPC and SoftWindows products to FWB, the publisher of disk drive software, shortly before this book was published. The same holds true when you install a DOS card, such as the ones that Apple and Reply used to sell, and the ones manufactured by Orange Micro.*

Since you are actually running PC operating systems, those special environments are nearly as vulnerable to a PC virus as a regular PC. That means your PC application, document, and system-related files can be infected by one of those many thousands of viruses that lurk on the other side of the computing world. That means you need to get virus protection software.

> NOTE *If there's an exception to this cross-platform problem, it's viruses that affect low-level drivers and hardware that aren't part of the emulation software. So in that regard, a Windows software emulation solution may have an advantage.*

But the Mac programs mentioned at the end of this chapter won't run in a PC environment. For protection, you need to buy one of the Windows-based virus detection programs and install them. Fortunately, the very same publishers of Mac virus software, Network Associates and Symantec (and others), have virus programs for you.

If your exploration of DOS and Windows extends beyond mere curiosity and you really intend to do protective work using files acquired from others or surf the Internet, you'll want to buy virus software and keep it updated as needed.

If you want to learn more about running Windows on a Mac, please read Chapter 11.

How to Know If It's a Virus or a Software Problem

Your Mac is crashing constantly. You can't get any work done, and it's most definitely hair-pulling time. The question that may be foremost in your mind is whether some nasty computer virus is at work here, and what do you do next?

Fortunately, the instances of Mac computer viruses are small. The vast majority of Mac computing problems can be traced to more conventional solutions, such as system extensions conflicts, the need to reinstall system software, or issues with hardware peripherals, such as SCSI chain oddities.

Unless your Mac displays a classic virus-based symptom, the best advice is to look elsewhere for a solution. Many of the chapters of this book cover troubleshooting for various elements of your Mac user experience, and you'll want to read the ones that apply to your situation.

Mac Viruses and Their Effects

Some viruses just put up a silly message. Others can damage files or even your hard drive directory. Whatever the symptom, ridding yourself of the virus is paramount, because you never know whether a silly message may camouflage a more serious problem with your Mac.

The following is a brief look at some known Mac computer viruses and their most common symptoms (current virus software can detect all of these):

NOTE *I have not tried to be complete in these descriptions. I'm just summarizing the basics. And I don't pretend to cover all known Mac viruses here. In addition, some of the older viruses, such as nVIR, are relics of the non-PowerPC era, and may not be as dangerous to today's software. But since the popular virus protection programs protect you against them anyway, this is not an issue you need to consider.*

- **ANTI Virus** This virus infects primarily non-PowerPC (680x0) applications, but the damage may not be sufficient to cause a problem running a program unless the application itself has self-checking code, which means it won't run if there's an unauthorized modification. If an application is infected, it's best to replace it rather than let your virus software repair it.

- **AutoStart Worm** This Mac-borne virus turned up in 1998 after a period of quiet on the Mac platform. It's called a "worm" because it doesn't actually alter a program or document file to pass itself around. Rather, the worm duplicates itself from disk to disk on vulnerable systems. The virus itself will add invisible files to your drive, which will result in mysterious hard disk activity. Some data files may also be overwritten with random data. A fast way to protect yourself against the virus is to turn off the AutoPlay feature of QuickTime in the QuickTime Settings Control Panel or with the CD-ROM Control Strip. This won't help if you're already infected, so you need to check all your disks with virus software as well.

The worst part of it all is that a few commercial program CDs actually shipped with AutoStart, until fast solutions were found (don't worry, the disks were quickly recalled by the publishers).

NOTE *I remember a brief one-month period in which nearly half my clients could site at least one or two instances of succumbing to this irritating virus.*

■ **CDEF Virus** This virus primarily infects System 6-type desktop files, so it's not an issue with Mac OS 7 or Mac OS 8.

■ **CODE 1 Virus** The primary effect of this virus is to rename your startup drive to "Trent Saburo." It may also cause unexplained system crashes.

■ **CODE 252 Virus** This virus was designed by someone with mischief on their minds. It appears when you launch an infected application or system file between June 6 and December 31 of any year. The message it displays is as follows (and no, it doesn't erase any disks):

```
You have a virus.
Ha Ha Ha Ha Ha Ha Ha
Now erasing all disks…
Ha Ha Ha Ha Ha Ha Ha
P.S. Have a nice day
Ha Ha Ha Ha Ha Ha Ha
(Click to continue…)
```

■ **CODE 9811 Virus** The effects of this virus are rather severe. It hides your applications and replaces them with files that have gibberish titles, such as "FIDVCZWGJKJWLOI." Your desktop backdrop will also take on an aspect of electronic worms, and you may see a message stating, "You have been hacked by the Praetorians." What makes this whole mess doubly confusing is that this message only seems to affect about 25 percent of the infected installations, and only appears on a Monday. Definitely a Blue Monday.

■ **CODE 32767 Virus** This virus supposedly attempts to trash documents once a month, but hasn't spread widely.

How to Know If It's a Virus or a Software Problem

- **Flag Virus (also known as WDEF C)** This virus will infect system files and apparently overwrite a WDEF resource of ID 0 in your system, which may cause problems with some files.

- **INIT-M Virus** This virus is particularly destructive. It will appear on a Friday the 13th, and can damage files and folders. The names of files are changed to random strings containing just eight characters, and names of folders will have one to eight characters. The most serious problem, though, is that the file type and creator information (used by the Finder's desktop files to link documents to applications) are altered, and the creation and modification dates become January 1, 1904. Another symptom: The name of one or more icons on your Mac may be changed to "Virus MindCrime."

- **INIT 17 Virus** This pesky critter will spread to the System file and applications. When an infected Mac is restarted, you'll see a message "From the depths of Cyberspace." The virus can also cause unexplained crashes and other untoward symptoms, especially on older 68000 Macs, which begin with the Mac Plus and Mac SE and end with the Classic.

- **INIT 29 Virus** This very old Mac virus (dating back to 1988) can infect all sorts of files, from documents to applications and operating system components. The virus seems to be System 6 specific, and can spread very easily, though it doesn't seem to do any serious damage.

- **INIT 1984 Virus** This virus is similar in its effects to INIT M. It can also cause crashes on very old Mac models, such as the 128K.

- **INIT 9403 Virus** This is a particularly destructive strain. Once it infects your Mac, it can proceed to erase disks. Fortunately, it was only discovered in Italian versions of the Mac OS, and all current virus detection programs will eradicate it.

- **MacMag Virus** This very old virus (1987) also bore the names Aldus, Brandow, Drew, and Peace. MacMag would damage system files, and was spread via a HyperCard stack named "New Apple Products." The virus was designed to self-destruct, so you probably won't have to worry about it, unless you have a really old Mac and operating system without virus protection.

- **Macro viruses** These are rampant, because of the widespread use of Microsoft Office programs, such as Excel and Word, on the Mac. They are also cross-platform, which means that both Mac and Windows users can be infected (though the Windows platform is more vulnerable to such viruses). While Windows users can encounter corrupted system files, the most common symptoms on a Mac include mysterious password-protection of a document, and making it impossible to save a document as anything but a template.

■ **MBDF Virus**   This is a Trojan Horse virus, spread through such games as 10 Tile Puzzle, Obnoxious Tetris, and Tetricycle. Once it infects a Mac, MBDF will go on to damage both application and system files. If the system is damaged, you'd have to do a clean reinstallation.

■ **MDEF Virus**   This virus has also been given the names Garfield and Top Cat. The virus infects application files, which beep when you run them. Beyond that, there doesn't seem to be any particular damage.

■ **nVIR Virus**   Similar to Scores (which is described next), nVIR will infect the System file. Then, once you run an application, it'll be infected as well. One of the symptoms includes a voice message, "Don't panic," which you'll hear if you have Speech software installed on your Mac.

■ **Scores Virus**   This virus has also been known as Eric, NASA, San Jose Flu, and Vult. Its most notable symptom is a change of icons for your Note Pad and Scrapbook files, both located in the System Folder. Instead of having their distinctive icons, they change to blank sheets of paper with turned-down corners. And they don't change if you rebuild your Mac's desktop. Aside from spreading from application to application, after the initial infection of your system, Scores doesn't appear to do any serious damage.

■ **The SevenDust Virus**   This is a particularly threatening virus strain, and it's also known either as MDEF 9806 or MDEF 666. There are several strains, two of which may actually erase non-application files on your startup drive. One variation of SevenDust actually masqueraded as a video acceleration extension under the name Graphics Accelerator (with a nonprinting file prefix that would make it load first). What makes that doubly confusing is that there is a genuine Apple system extension named Graphics Accelerator, which is used for Macs equipped with ATI video chips or ATI graphic cards. The real extension has since been renamed ATI Graphics Accelerator, which should avoid the confusion. Besides, the latest virus detection programs will find the fake.

How to Know If It's a Virus or a Software Problem

■ **T4 Virus**   This is another one of those Trojan Horse variations, which came embedded in a game called GoMoku. Once infected, the virus spreads to your applications, including the Finder, and also tries to alter your System file. Once infected by T4, programs cannot be repaired, and the changes to the System file prevent extensions from loading at startup.

■ **WDEF Virus**   Back around 1989 and early 1990, I was working as a consultant with a graphic design studio. During a period of several weeks, just about every floppy disk we handled there had been infected by WDEF, which infects desktop files (the ones used by System 6). The net result of the virus was not serious, but it was downright annoying nonetheless. Fortunately, the advent of System 7 in 1991 and the new forms of desktop files effectively put the kibosh on that virus, since it won't affect the newer generation of Finder desktop files.

■ **ZUC Virus**   This virus was designed to infect applications, and causes the mouse cursor to bounce around erratically across the screen when you run an infected application. The virus can also alter the desktop backdrop and cause strange spurts of disk activity. It can infect Macs across a network.

Choosing and Installing Virus Protection Software

When you fight computer viruses, it's a moving target. Virus authors deliver their nasty tricks without warning, at any time. You never know when a new virus strain may emerge—witness the AutoStart virus that infected Mac users after years of the relative absence of new viruses on our favorite computing platform.

In order to protect yourself against the unexpected, the best thing to do is buy up-to-date virus protection software and keep it updated with new detection strings.

With regular software, there's no problem in using an old version, so long as it works with your present Mac and operating system version. But not so with virus programs.

The publishers are notorious for removing support against older versions after a few years, which means you are left unprotected against current strains of older viruses. And some programs are simply no longer available. Among the casualties of various software company mergers and departures are such products as Dr. Solomon's Anti-Virus ToolKit, McAfee VirusScan, and Rival (which still sells in the European market).

Even the freeware and shareware market has changed. Back when I first got a Mac, I used Virus Detective, which was retired by its author when it became too time consuming and costly to update. Alas, shareware users usually don't pay the fees to a program's author. In addition, John Norstad's venerable free virus program, Disinfectant, was similarly retired because its structure didn't allow it to recognize the latest virus infections, such as so-called Trojan Horse and macro viruses.

Comparing Norton AntiVirus and Virex

As of the time this book went to press, the remaining two commercial virus programs were Norton AntiVirus from Symantec (successor to SAM, Symantec Anti-Virus Utilities for Macintosh) and Virex from Network Associates.

NOTE   *As a point of history, the original programmer for SAM, Paul Cozza, was also the programmer for MasterJuggler, one of the early font management programs. Programming chores for both programs have since been assumed by others, and last I heard, Cozza was enjoying a fairly lucrative retirement from Mac programming, living, in part, on the royalties earned from the sale of these products.*

A quick gander at both programs will show that they are more similar than different. Both are regularly updated for newly discovered viruses, and both get regular updates to fix problems and improve performance. You will not go wrong with either selection.

Here's a rundown of what each program offers:

Norton AntiVirus

The version of Norton AntiVirus (see Figure 12-1) that shipped when this book was prepared, version 6, included these notable features above and beyond basic detection of the presence of computer viruses:

- ■ **Auto-Repair**   The program can be configured to automatically repair infected or damaged files (though this measure isn't always 100 percent effective).

- ■ **Check for suspicious activity**   The program is normally set up not just to check for known viruses, but also for activities that may indicate the presence of an unknown virus strain.

- ■ **Compressed files**   Files compressed in a number of popular compression protocols will be automatically expanded and checked by the program.

Choosing and Installing
Virus Protection Software

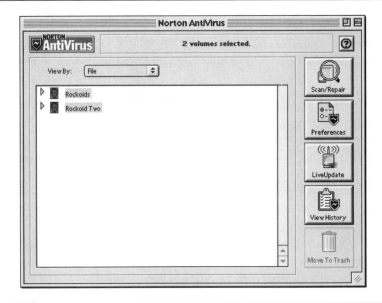

FIGURE 12-1   Norton AntiVirus provides up-to-date virus scanning technology

■ **LiveUpdate**   This feature allows you to check Symantec's Web site automatically to retrieve program and virus string updates.

■ **SafeZone**   You can set aside a location on your hard drive for automatic scanning. Whenever a file is copied to that location (either from the Internet or another drive or network), the program will check it for the presence of viruses.

■ **Scheduled scans**   You can configure the program to do a full scan of your Mac's drives at regular intervals.

Virex

The other contender in the virus protection market, Network Associates Virex, was also at version 6 when this book was written. This program (see Figure 12-2) can also scan for known viruses and the presence of virus-related activity. Here are the additional features:

■ **Control Strip and contextual menu support**   You can access Virex's features with a CTRL-click of a file, folder, or disk icon, or via your Control Strip bar.

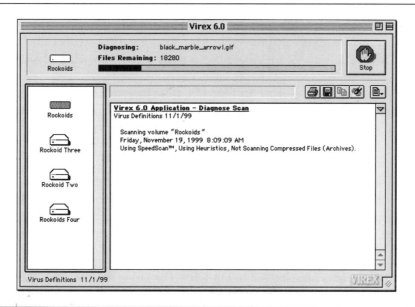

FIGURE 12-2   Virex is busy checking the author's hard drive

- **Diagnose Compressed Files**   This feature is limited to files compressed in Aladdin's StuffIt format (Norton AntiVirus, in contrast, supports several compression formats).

- **Electronic updating**   As with Norton AntiVirus, the program can be set to update itself directly from the publisher's Web site. It works in concert with the program's Schedule Editor to check for new detection strings on a regular basis.

- **Repair**   The program can be configured to repair or delete infected files without asking.

- **Scan-At-Download**   When you download files from the Internet, or retrieve them from a network, Virex goes into action to check the files.

- **Schedule Editor**   Configure the program to do a full scan of your Mac's drives at regular intervals.

- **Use Heuristics**   The program uses its internal logic to check for virus-related activity and report back to the user.

**Choosing and Installing
Virus Protection Software**

Virus Program Oddities

Virus programs are highly tied into your Mac's system software, because they are designed to carefully check for suspicious activity and the presence of known virus strains.

As a result, as Apple updates its Mac OS, from time to time virus programs are rendered incompatible. Here are some common symptoms of virus detection activity that you just have to expect (because you need the software unless your Mac operates in a closed universe):

- **Slow icon dance at startup**   This is particularly noticeable with Norton AntiVirus. The program carefully checks your system extensions for the presence of viruses, so you hear a lot more churning of the hard drive and see icons move more slowly at startup. This is a normal consequence of how such a program runs.

- **Applications take longer to launch**   The larger the program, the greater number of support files, and the longer it takes for virus software to scan everything to make sure the files are clean. Again, it's the price you pay for protection.

- **Scanning prompt when you insert a floppy or removable drive**   You can turn these options off, but viruses are commonly spread through floppies and removable media, so you want to make sure the program is configured to scan both kinds of disks.

NOTE   *Virus programs normally scan floppies automatically as part of their default settings. But since floppy disks were discarded on Macs, if you have an add-on floppy or SuperDisk drive, you need to enable a scan removable drive feature to support these devices.*

- **Mysterious crashes after installing a new system version**   Check the publisher of the virus software for possible updates. In one example, when Mac OS 8.5 first appeared, you'd get crashes whenever you copied files across a network. Both Norton AntiVirus and Virex required updates to fix the problem. Fortunately, Apple's system Read Me files will generally inform you about this.

NOTE   *The arrival of Mac OS 9 forced Network Associates to deliver a 6.0.1 update to the Virex software to quash some incompatibilities.*

Summing Up

Computer viruses can be annoying or dangerous, but with up-to-date virus protection, it's a problem you can cope with. It's a good idea, however, to tell your contacts right away if you happen to get an infected disk from them. It's part of practicing "safe hex," as one of the original virus software programmers used to say.

In the next chapter, I'll introduce you to a full-fledged hard drive maintenance and repair program.

Chapter 13

Keeping Your Hard Drive Healthy and Happy

A Mac without a disk drive is like a car without fuel. It sits there, looking just fine, especially the latest models with their innovative case designs, but it doesn't do anything else. And you didn't buy a Mac just to look at it.

In order for the Mac to do something, you have to have something to read and write data from: a disk drive.

A Brief Primer on Cataloging a Disk Drive

It was a whole lot easier with phonograph records! When you wanted to find another selection, you just picked up the tone arm and placed it on the right spot on the record (of course, you had to check the label to know where the song was). With a cassette deck, you just have to wind it to the right location, press Play and listen.

With computer drives, these basic access techniques won't work.

For one thing, a computer's drive is more complex than a record or a cassette tape. However, it uses a technology not far removed from tape. Recording tape is made up of a flexible plastic material with a metal coating. The coating is usually iron oxide, more commonly referred to as rust. You record on a tape using a little part called a recording head. This head is a powerful magnet, and it magnetizes the little iron particles as it passes over the tape. On a cassette deck, the way the tape is magnetized represents the electrical pattern of the voice or musical signal being fed to it (that's why it's called *analog*). With computer data, the input is reduced to binary ones and zeros, and it can consist of any kind of data, from music to your document files, your computer's programs or its System Folder.

A floppy disk looks like a combination between recording tape and a record. If you move aside the plastic shutter of your floppy, you'll see a flexible round disk in there. And both sides are coated with the same sort of material as your magnetic tape. A Mac's floppy drive (where you still find them) uses magnetic heads to record and read from both sides of the floppy disk (which is why older floppies are sometimes called *double-sided*).

Hard drives use a similar principle, only the magnetic coating is placed on a rigid platter. There are usually several platters in a single hard drive. As the drive spins, the magnetic heads float above the drive platters, suspended by a cushion of air, which helps prevent wear and tear to the drive. Cassette tapes, as you recall, do wear out eventually.

In order to store huge amounts of data on a hard drive, the files are put in a very small amount of space (and it gets smaller all the time as hard drive technology improves). To make the drive write and read your files faster, the platters spin much faster. It is common for today's hard drives to run at speeds from 5,400 rpm to 10,000 rpm.

Hard drives have a dangerous combination of compactness and flexibility. With data stored in an ultra-small, almost microscopic space, and spinning at a high rate of speed, even a little particle of dust can cause troubles. That's why hard drives are made in a special place free of contaminants, called a clean room.

It's All in Little Pieces Rather Than Big Ones

Another big difference between an LP or CD and a hard drive is the way the information is stored. On both the LP and CD, you have one long, spiral track that goes from beginning to end (well, actually, on a CD, it's from the end to the beginning). On a hard drive, the tracks are concentric, one inside the other. The heads use a little motor assembly to step from one track to the next.

It's hard to picture what those tracks look like, except that they are very small and not visible to the naked eye, unlike your LP record. Hard drives can have 600 tracks per square inch and more, and you can expect this number to increase over time as technology improves.

Each of those tracks is made up of little pieces called sectors. Each sector contains up to 512 bytes of information.

Erasing and Formatting: What's the Difference

When you use the Erase command from the Finder's File menu on a floppy disk, actually two things are happening. First, the tracks on the floppy disk are set up to receive data. This process is called formatting or *low-level formatting*. The second step is to write a directory on the hard drive, which sets up a blank catalog file. This process is often called *initializing*, and it's the final step of the formatting process.

With a hard drive, the Erase command only does one thing—initializing. It wipes the drive's directory (the list of files it contains) clean and installs a new one. But, as you'll learn later, that's enough to wipe out all information about your old files and write new ones on the drive.

When your drive is initialized, the formatting software puts a little invisible file on your hard drive, called a driver. This file is used to "talk" back and forth with your Mac when it wants to read and write files to the drive.

Which Formatter?

When you buy a new Macintosh computer, the drive is already formatted with Apple's own disk formatting software. Originally it was called HD SC Setup, but the current version is called Drive Setup. The software works just fine, and it allows you to do both low-level formatting and initializing. You can also divide

A Brief Primer on
Cataloging a Disk Drive

(partition) the drive into smaller pieces. However, it has one big shortcoming. If you bought your drive from another company, Drive Setup may not work with the drive.

> **NOTE**   *Officially, Apple's disk formatting software is designed to work strictly with an Apple-label hard drive. Unofficially, many current drives work fine with Drive Setup (more so with recent versions of the program), but you proceed at your own risk, since Apple won't support using their formatting utility with a third-party mechanism.*

When you install the latest versions of the Mac operating system, the installer will dutifully try to update the hard drive. If the drive was formatted with something other than Apple's software (or is recognized as a non-Apple drive), you'll see a warning notice about it.

Fortunately, this is a notice that shouldn't cause you much concern. It's just a reminder for you to make sure that the formatting software is up to date and compatible with Apple's latest versions of the Mac OS.

There's nothing wrong with buying a non-Apple drive. In fact, the dealers who sell these drives get products from the very same companies Apple uses to buy its own drives. These include IBM, Quantum, and Seagate. The drives usually come preformatted, and the dealer will give you a program (on the drive itself or on a separate floppy or CD) that you can use to format the drive whenever it's necessary.

> **NOTE**   *If your hard drive is formatted with a program other than Apple's, it's a good idea to stay in touch with the publisher of the software, so you can get their latest updates. As Apple upgrades its operating system, and installs such new file system features as HFS+, you may need to upgrade your disk formatting software. Fortunately, updating your drive with the same formatting software isn't very hard. Usually there's a feature in the program called "Update" or "Updating" that simply rewrites the device driver component on your hard drive. You shouldn't need to reformat the drive unless you partition the drive, or if there are disk directory problems that cannot be fixed by one of the disk diagnostic/repair programs.*

Partitioning: Making Little Things Smaller

With a large hard drive, you can often organize files more easily if you divide your drive into smaller pieces. The process is called partitioning. The process usually requires initializing your drive (meaning the directory is wiped out, so you need to back up your files first). Then the disk formatting software creates a number of smaller pieces or volumes from the same hard drive, each of which has a separate directory and a different name (such as Mac HD One, Mac HD Two, and so on). The partitioned drive shows up on your Mac's desktop as separate drives, with a separate disk icon for each volume.

NOTE   *Older versions of LaCie's Silverlining have a feature that sometimes lets you partition a drive without losing any files. But it can often take a couple of hours or more to run this procedure, and you still need to have a backup of your files in case something goes wrong.*

Apple's Drive Setup and just about all the third-party disk formatters can be easily set to create hard drive partitions. But remember, *you must back up your data when you partition a drive, as the directory or table of contents of the drive is wiped clean.*

NOTE   *If you'd like to explore hard drive technology in more detail, you may want to get a copy of* FWB's Guide to Storage, *by Norman Fong. The book used to be supplied with FWB's Hard Disk ToolKit formatting software, and can also be purchased directly from FWB. If you have an older version of Norton Utilities from Symantec, you'll also find a very good hard drive guide as part of the package.*

Organizing All This Stuff

With your regular cassette deck, when you search for a particular selection, you press the deck's control buttons to shuttle the tape back or forth to reach the exact point where the information is stored. This is fine for a music tape, although it can take several minutes to get from here to there. In the early days of computers, all the data was stored on huge reels of tape, and you had to wind them back and forth to find the files you wanted. Of course, you don't get very much work done if you have to wait five minutes every time you want to open a new file, launch a program, or connect to an online service.

NOTE   *In the days before floppy drives, however, we had to put up with such waits to access and edit a file. At least we all had credible excuses when the boss dropped by and asked why we weren't working.*

A Brief Primer on
Cataloging a Disk Drive

The amount of information on a computer's hard drive is incredibly large (don't forget there are at least 600 tracks per inch on a modern hard drive), so imagine how long it would take to get from one place to another if you looked for it the old fashioned way. Instead, a special place has been set aside on your hard drive to record the locations of all the files, so you can access them quickly.

Hard Drive Directories: You Can't Tell a Book by Its Cover

Data on your Mac's drive isn't all stored in one piece. It's divided into little segments, and depending on how big the file is, and how much space is available on the drive, it may be stored in different spots all across the drive.

In order to find your files, a hard drive has a directory, somewhat similar to a book's table of contents. It tells the Mac what files are available and where they are located. Before you look at the makeup of this hard drive directory, it's important to know that all this information is consulted in the blink of an eye, no matter how big your drive or where the files are located.

The File Manager

This feature is part of your Mac's system software. It is used to consult your hard drive's directory structure, locate files when you wish to find them, call them up on your screen, modify files, delete files, and update your drive's directory about all the changes that have been made.

You activate the File Manager every time you attempt to access a file. It's used when you double-click on a document or program icon, or when you use the Open or Save dialog boxes in your favorite word processing program. The File Manager is even used when you access a Web site from your Internet provider or online service, because the Web artwork is cached or stored on your hard drive.

The Master Directory Block

The first level of information in your drive directory is called the *Master Directory Block*. It's a part of a drive that is your guidepost to its contents. It records your drive's name, its size, how much of it is filled, and even where your System Folder is located (so it knows where to find it when you boot your Mac). Most important, it shows how much space is still available, so you cannot save a file that's too big for your drive to handle.

The Volume Bit Map

Once the Mac's File Manager learns how much space is available, the next thing to determine is what part of your drive is filled and what part isn't. A Mac file is made up of little pieces, and not every piece of the file is in one place. The larger the file, the more likely it'll be made of lots of pieces in different parts of your hard drive. So the *Volume Bit Map* is consulted to see which blocks have data and which don't. Once the locations are determined, the file can be written to your drive.

> **NOTE** *When a file is split into pieces at separated locations on a drive, it's considered fragmented. In theory, optimizing the drive, which puts all the pieces of a file adjacent to each other, may speed up performance. This is dealt with in more detail later in this chapter.*

Remember, all this happens in the blink of an eye, faster than you can even think about it.

> **NOTE** *When you trash a file and then empty the trash, the actual file itself doesn't just disappear, at least not then. All that happens is that the blocks that are filled with the file are marked "empty" by the Volume Bit Map so new files can be written on those blocks. This is why file recovery software can sometimes bring back files you've deleted by mistake.*

A NOTE ABOUT TREES   In the following sections, you'll see the word *tree* is often used to describe a specific disk cataloging function. That is how the file system is organized. Just imagine one large tree, with many branches, each of which has many more branches.

Extents Tree (or B-tree)

The next stage in keeping track of files is which block carries what file or part of a file. That's the job of the *Extents Tree*. This portion of your drive's catalog allows your Mac to call up the file and have it reassembled into its original form, whether you saved it five minutes ago, yesterday, or five years ago. It's very much like assembling the pieces of a gigantic jigsaw puzzle, because the pieces may be scattered all over the drive.

The Extents Tree consists of two parts. One is called an *index node,* which is used by the Mac to find the information stored. Then there's the *leaf node,* which contains the information itself.

The Catalog Tree

Now we're getting somewhere. You've seen how the files are stored; the next step is to find them. As shown earlier, the file is found in the blink of an eye, and only really large files take time to appear on your Mac's screen. In order to locate that file, the *Catalog Tree*—the Mac equivalent of a library's catalog file—must be consulted. This directory records all the information necessary to keep tabs on your file. The Catalog Tree stores the name of the file, the folder it's placed in, its position on the desktop, and how big the file is. In short, it stores all the information needed to find the file, bring it up on the screen, and make it possible for you to modify or replace the file as you continue to work on a document.

Putting It All Together

When you tell your Mac you want a file, it goes to work behind the scenes to consult the catalog, find out if the file exists, and where it exists. Then it puts it all together, and the file appears on your screen. That's well and good. Once you see your file, you may want to do some work on it, changing a word or two in a word processing file, updating your illustration in a drawing file, or moving things around or creating new pages on a page layout program.

Once you've changed the document, you will want to save it, so the latest version is available next time you need to see it or print it. When it comes time to save the file, the Mac OS File Manager has to go back and not only figure out where all the elements of the file are stored, so they can be replaced, but it has to find new locations on your drive to store the new material.

If you run out of space, you'll simply get the message that there isn't enough room to write that file. In that case, you'll have to save it to another drive, or go back to the Finder and remove files you may not need (after making copies of them, if you plan to use them later on).

When you save a file for the first time, it's similar to putting a new book in a library. A new catalog entry has to be made for the file, the catalog has to be consulted for file locations to store the new file, and the catalog has to be updated with all of this information so the next time you need that file, it's there for you to call up—again in the blink of an eye.

HFS

Apple's HFS (Hierarchical File System) is the technique used to organize these files. Using this system, you are able to store files in multiple levels for efficiency and convenience. For example, you can put folders at the top level of a drive (let's call it the first level), then store files inside those folders (the second level) and nest still more folders within the main folder, continuing with still more levels of files and folders. When you look at a diagram of this file storage system, it looks like a tree with many branches, each of which can lead to more branches.

The neat thing about this system is that you can change it at any time. If you decide you really don't want a file to be put in one folder, you can drag it to another, or make a new folder and put the file in that one instead. And all the time the Mac's clever filing system is figuring out where all this stuff goes, so you can retrieve it whenever you wish.

HFS+

There's one thing that's certain about hard drives. Each year they get bigger, faster, and cheaper. Ten years ago, an 80-100 megabyte hard drive would cost over one thousand dollars. Today, the same money will buy you a hard drive of 25GB or greater capacity.

Having drives with 250 times the capacity isn't a luxury, it's a necessity. Apple's system software and the application software you use have grown in an equal fashion. A decade ago, you could fit an entire System Folder on a floppy disk; today, all you get is a Disk Tools floppy with the minimum amount of software your Mac needs to start, plus Apple's disk maintenance utilities, Disk First Aid and Drive Setup. The actual System Folder for Mac OS 9 routinely exceeds 400 megabytes in size (mine is just shy of that) and is often much larger.

Having all this extra capacity has its downside, though. When Apple created the HFS file system, they divided a drive into 65,000 pieces or blocks. The number is the same regardless of the size of your drive. A little mathematics will show that this scheme becomes rather inefficient with a big hard drive, because the smallest amount of space a file can occupy increases in proportion to hard drive size. For that typical 8GB drive very common on new Macs, one single file, with just a couple of words in it, will fill 128 kilobytes of space on the drive.

If you have lots of little files on your drive, such as the cache files that are created when you use your World Wide Web browser, you can see that you're wasting a lot of space on that drive. This is one reason why many users partition their drive—use their hard drive software to divide the drive into smaller volumes so the smallest file size isn't so high.

Apple has an even better solution, called HFS+, which is also known as the Mac OS Extended format. The most important new feature is that, instead of dividing the drive into 65,000 blocks, the number has increased to the billions (2^{32} to be precise). The file that would be 128K under the Mac OS Standard (or HFS system) is now 4K under the new file system.

As you can see, if you have lots of small files, Apple has given you lots of extra breathing room. When you switch to the Mac OS Extended format, you'll find many megabytes of additional space.

HFS+: The Disadvantages

New Mac OS computers all ship with drives formatted in HFS+ format (even the iMac and iBook), but switching an older model isn't so simple. In order to convert

A Brief Primer on Cataloging a Disk Drive

from HFS to HFS+, you must be running Mac OS 8.1 or later, and you must initialize your hard drive under the new format. That means you will have to back up all your files first.

Apple's Drive Setup 1.4 and later and the newest versions of non-Apple disk formatting software can easily handle this process. They all offer an option to initialize your drive in Mac OS Extended format. And even if your software doesn't have the option, it's still available. Just select the drive volume you wish to convert, choose Erase from the Finder's Special Menu, and select Mac OS Extended from the pop-up menu. In a few minutes, the drive's directory will be rewritten in HFS+ format. When you copy files there, they'll be smaller.

Here are the other disadvantages to HFS+:

- You cannot use an HFS+ formatted drive as a startup disk with a 680x0 Mac. A second drive, without a System Folder, can be formatted in HFS+ format, though.

- If you're using an older version of the Mac OS, you won't be able to see the files on an HFS+ drive. Instead, you'll see a "wrapper," a blank directory showing nothing but a Read Me file from Apple telling you how to access the files (basically, that you need to be running Mac OS 8.1 or later, or the files have to be shared across a network from a computer running the new system versions).

- In order for the drive's directory to be displayed properly, you also need Apple's Text Encoding Converter Extension in the Extensions folder and the Text Encoding folder in your System Folder. If you're using Extensions Manager or a program such as Conflict Catcher to manage your system extensions, you will need to leave these items intact and not move them.

HFS+: The Future

Getting more mileage from your hard drive is not the only benefit of HFS+. In the future, there will be another benefit: bigger file sizes. The new Mac filing system has been designed to allow for 255-character file names. Of course, you'd need a really large Open and Save dialog box to accommodate file names that big, but it is the wave of the future.

Just imagine what it would be like to have a file named "This is the silly poem I wrote last week in response to a request from my boss to come up with a new advertising slogan by March 2, 2001." And even that file name leaves several dozen characters left to fill.

How to Convert to HFS+

There are actually two methods of changing your drives to HFS+. One is a serious issue, since you have to initialize the drive. The other is simple, since it can switch over your drive in place.

Here's how the two options work:

- ■ **Initializing**   To convert to HFS+, you have to start your Mac from another drive or your system CD. First, make sure all your files are backed up. Then the simplest method is to select the drive icon from the Finder's desktop, and choose Erase from the Special menu. This will bring up an option similar to the one shown in Figure 13-1. Just click on the Format pop-up menu, and select Mac OS Extended (the official name for HFS+), then click the Erase button. In a few minutes, your drive will be initialized in the new disk format, and you're ready to roll.

- ■ **Using software to convert "in place"**   Initializing your hard drive is definitely a big event. You have to be prepared to restore your files, and you'll want to devote the better part of the afternoon to the task (or maybe longer). The other way to do it is with HFS+ conversion software. Your two options (as of the time this book was written) were Alsoft's PlusMaker and Power On Software's SpaceDoctor. Both programs will, essentially, rewrite all your files in HFS+ format in place, without the need to initialize the drive and restore the files. However, no program is perfect, and you should always have a recent backup around in case something goes wrong. I cover the subject of backups in the next chapter.

A Brief Primer on
Cataloging a Disk Drive

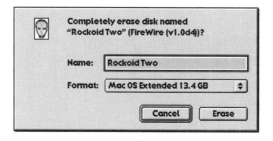

FIGURE 13-1   One click of the Erase button and you can change your drive to HFS+

What Can Go Wrong with a Drive and How to Fix It

Despite all the complexities of keeping track of thousands and thousands of files on those ultra-miniature hard drives and removable devices (such as Iomega, SyQuest, and CD-R products), most times the process works just about perfectly. You can locate and access your files in an instant and seldom encounter a problem unless you run out of room in which to store a file.

But things can go wrong—bad things—and as a result there is a potential to lose your data. As hard drives become larger, the amount of data you may lose grows ever larger and the impact far more serious.

How a Simple Shut Down Command Protects Your Drive

When you shut down or restart your Mac, it goes through a few seconds of disk action, which writes files stored in the drive's cache and the disk cache you set in your Memory Control Panel. It also does other bookkeeping chores that keep your Mac's file system up to date.

Bad things may happen if you don't do the normal shutdown routine—for example, if your Mac crashes, and you have to restart by shutting off your Mac and turning it on again. Or if you restart with the "reset" switch (which is a little switch with a triangle inside it on the front of many Macs or by the keyboard combo COMMAND-CTRL-POWER ON). If the restart process isn't done normally, all that file cleanup (which clears cached files and other data) doesn't happen. So the disk's directory may not be properly updated or may be damaged.

Sometimes a problem may be caused by forces that have nothing whatever to do with your Mac. There may be a power outage, or a spike sent across your power line (perhaps during a thunderstorm) interrupts the transfer of data to your drive. Or you simply make a mistake and turn off a power switch (something you could do on older Macs), thus shutting down your Mac before it has a chance to update the drive properly.

Whatever the reason, the files may not be properly cataloged. Even one missing or extra byte of data is enough to set problems into motion. Minor damage may not be noticeable right away, but as you continue to write or change files on your drive, you may find that files may suddenly disappear, or they may be damaged (so you can't open them).

Sooner or later, you may find not only files disappearing, but the entire drive. As I said earlier, the Master Directory Block is the entranceway to your drive's catalog. If the directory is damaged, strange things can begin to happen. One possibility is that a portion of the drive with files on it may, by mistake, be marked as being available for new files. When you write new files to your Mac's drive, the new file overwrites part or all of an older file that you still need. When you try to access that file, it won't be there. Or you'll get a message (such as a −39 or 108 error) indicating there's something wrong with the file.

Over time, the problems may become worse. One day the drive may become unreadable, and you may see a little disk icon with a question mark when you try to boot your Mac.

Other Causes of Problems

Hard drives are electromechanical devices. As I pointed out earlier, the mechanical complexity of your typical hard drive is awesome, and the drive is subject to regular wear and tear. Drive manufacturers will rate a drive as having several hundred thousand hours of useful life ("mean time between failures," they call it), but that doesn't mean all units will last that long. Some will fail much earlier. One possible symptom is the onset of bad blocks, where data cannot be written or retrieved from the drive. And accidents can happen. Your computer is dropped to the ground while its running, and there's a head crash (the drive's heads strike and damage the drive platter). Whatever the cause, hard drives can and do fail eventually. That is something you should expect, though usually they last for years without trouble.

Protecting Your Files

One of the best ways to ensure that your files are safe is to have more than one copy. It's a good idea to do a regular backup of your valuable data. If the files are mission critical (financial data, for example), you may want to have an extra copy of your files at another location, as protection against a fire or weather disaster that may damage your computer.

I'll cover the subject of backups in more detail in the next chapter.

A Guide to Partitioning Your Drive

As noted in the first part of this chapter, the HFS file system wasn't very efficient for large hard drives, such as the ones that are commonplace in today's Mac OS computers.

The bigger the drive, the bigger the files. So when you had a large hard drive, it was convenient to partition the drive, which is simply dividing the drive into smaller segments. Apple's Drive Setup and all the third-party disk formatters can do the work, but it requires reformatting the drive. Once you do that, each segment or partition mounts on your Mac's desktop as a separate volume.

You can set aside one partition for your System Folder, another for your applications, a third for document files, whatever method of organization suits your purposes.

Since Apple introduced HFS+ beginning with Mac OS 8.1, you could actually get away with not partitioning at all. On the other hand, if all your files are in smaller partitions, in theory, access times are faster. So you may still want to partition your drive (I gave it up when HFS+ came on the scene). Each of the available disk formatting programs has its own interface for doing the task. I'll show you how with Apple's Drive Setup, since that program will support all Apple products and even some non-Apple drives.

1. Back up your files first.

2. Restart your Mac using another hard drive (after selecting with the Startup Disk Control Panel) or with your system CD.

3. Locate the copy of Drive Setup on the system CD (it's generally in the Utilities folder).

4. Double-click the program to launch it.

5. After it probes your Mac's hard drive setup, it'll display a list of available devices. Select the drive by clicking on its name (see Figure 13-2).

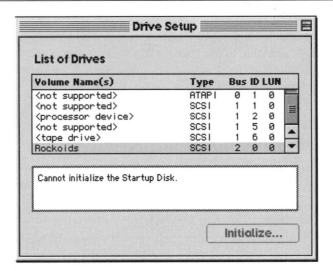

| FIGURE 13-2 | You're just about ready to partition that drive |

6. Choose Customize Volumes from the Functions menu.

7. Use the pop-up menu to divide the drive into multiple volumes, or drag the rectangles representing the drive to make them bigger or smaller, as needed.

8. Once you have selected the number of volumes, use the Initialize command to divide your drive into partitions.

NOTE   *Unless you're in a real hurry, I always recommend a low-level format (where the choice isn't grayed out). It can be selected by checking the option when you choose Initialization Options from the Functions menu of Drive Setup. This process allows possible bad blocks on a drive to be mapped out so they don't cause troubles later.*

9. Once partitioning is done, you can begin to restore files to the various partitions.

CAUTION   *It's probably not a good idea to put a separate System Folder on each partition of a single drive. For one thing, the Startup Disk Control Panel is usually unable to distinguish between partitions. You could, of course, fake the selection by removing Finder or the System file from the System Folder you wish to deactivate, but you are better off having another System Folder on a totally separate drive. Or try a freeware program, System Picker, which is designed to activate and deactivate System Folders on a single drive.*

What's a Bad Block and What Do I Do About It?

Hard drives are not perfect, and over time, one or more of the microscopic blocks on the drive may become unusable, as the drive platters age. Once that happens, minute portions of the drive may no longer be able to hold a magnetic charge. You write files and get a message about a "write error," or parts of a file already stored on your drive become damaged (a "read error") and the file cannot be accessed.

Fortunately, the hard drive diagnostic/repair programs I'll be discussing in this chapter can do surface scans to check for such problems. They may even be able to mark the blocks as "used," in other words they already have data, so new data won't be written to them.

But the best solution for this problem is to back up and do a low-level format of your hard drive. This process will wipe out all of the data, and the formatting software will generally mark bad blocks so they will be inaccessible for writing files.

Is Optimizing Truly Necessary?

The theory goes that as you add and remove files from your Mac's drive, the little pieces that files are made of become more and more scattered across the drive. This is called fragmentation, and if there is enough of it, your hard drive will take longer to access the files, thus slowing performance.

Is there a solution to the problem? Well, of course, you could initialize the drive, then restore your files in a single operation so they won't be fragmented. But that's quite an extreme step to take just to cure a little fragmentation problem.

Fortunately two of the major hard drive diagnostic/repair programs mentioned in this chapter, the Speed Disk component of Norton Utilities (see Figure 13-3) and TechTool Pro, offer a more practical solution, by optimizing the drive. The publishers of DiskWarrior have another product, PlusOptimizer (Figure 13-4), which performs the same function. These programs are designed to basically rewrite the data on your hard drive so all elements of a file are adjacent to one another, in theory speeding up hard drive performance.

So the question arises: since hard drives access files in milliseconds, does it really matter if it takes a few more to bring up a file?

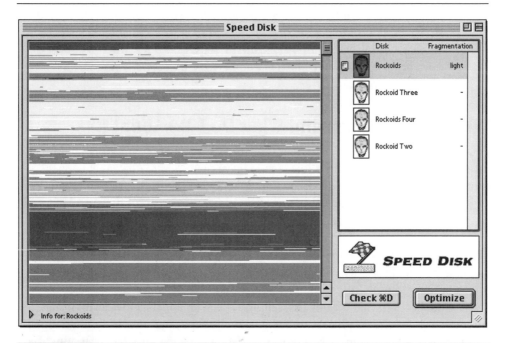

FIGURE 13-3   Although the drive's graphic display looks rather messy, Norton Speed Disk reports fragmentation as "light"

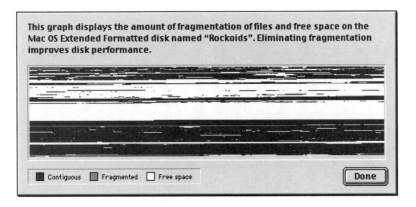

This graph displays the amount of fragmentation of files and free space on the Mac OS Extended Formatted disk named "Rockoids". Eliminating fragmentation improves disk performance.

■ Contiguous   ■ Fragmented   □ Free space   Done

FIGURE 13-4   Alsoft's PlusOptimizer also shows a graphic display of the files on the author's startup drive

Well, if you deal mostly with a small number of files, you could probably run your Mac for years and not experience any severe problem. Frankly, it'll take a lot of file manipulation to severely fragment your hard drive.

On the other hand, if you work with large image files (such as the ones you scan or create in a program like Photoshop), you may find that, indeed, a large amount of disk fragmentation develops, and occasional optimizing (about once a month) is probably a good idea.

Drive Optimizing Tips

If you decide you do want to optimize your hard drive (it's also called defragmenting or "defragging"), you'll want to make sure that you have a ready backup of your data. (See the next chapter for details on creating backups.) I don't want to alarm anyone, but I have seen accidents happen once or twice in the last 15 years and it never hurts to be careful.

Once you decide you're ready, start with these options:

■ **Check the hard drive first.**   Use Apple's Disk First Aid or one of the commercial hard drive repair/diagnostic utilities. If your drive's directory is corrupted, things can definitely go wrong while all the data is being written during optimization. While the optimizing software will normally check the drives before the process begins, it's best to be cautious. In fact, one of the commercial utilities, MicroMat's TechTool Pro (see Figure 13-5), actually includes optimization as the final leg of its standard drive diagnostic scan.

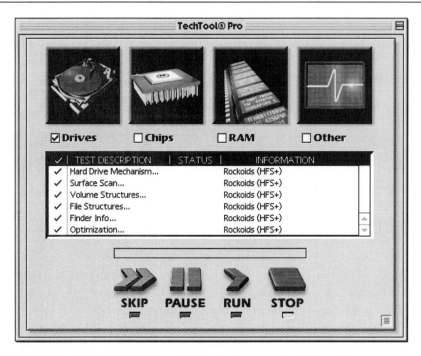

FIGURE 13-5   TechTool Pro's Standard interface shows a number of drive diagnostic
steps in addition to optimization

■ **Start from another drive or your system CD**   The commercial hard
drive optimizing programs usually come with a separate startup disk.
While, in theory, it's possible to optimize the drive without dismounting it
(removing it from the desktop), the process may not be as thorough. Only
TechTool Pro lets you completely optimize the drive while it's still
mounted (and that capability isn't supported for Mac OS 9).

■ **Recheck the drive if you crash or if there's a power outage**
If something happens to interrupt the process of optimizing your drive,
be sure to run your hard drive diagnostic/repair utility and make sure
everything is all right before continuing. The current lineup of optimization
programs have built-in safety checks to protect against this sort of thing
(such as not deleting a fragmented version of a file until the optimized
version is copied to your drive), but you should definitely check the drive
anyway. Then, if the optimizing process didn't finish, go ahead and resume
the process.

How to Cope with Drive Directory Problems

Keeping your hard drive happy and healthy is a matter of preventive maintenance. You cannot do anything to stop the forces of wear and tear, but there are things you can do to make sure your valuable files are protected:

Run Regular Diagnostics

To avoid potential problems with your hard drive, you should check it regularly with a disk diagnostic program, such as Apple's Disk First Aid, at least once a week and after a system crash.

NOTE *If you're using Mac OS 8.5 or later, you'll be pleased to notice that Apple's Disk First Aid is automatically run if you crash and must force a restart. This option, in the General Control Panel, is on by default and should be left on.*

Here's how to run a standard Disk First Aid check of your drive:

1. Locate Disk First Aid in your Utilities folder (this is where Apple's system installer usually places it).

2. Double-click on the program to launch it, which brings up the screen shown in Figure 13-6.

3. Click on the icon of the drive you wish to check (hold down the SHIFT key to select more than one volume).

4. Click Verify to check the drive's directory.

5. Click Repair to also fix any hard drive directory damage that's discovered (this is the better choice).

6. If drive damage is found and fixed, run the program again to make sure one problem didn't hide another (it happens).

7. When the program has done its work, choose Quit from the File menu to close the program.

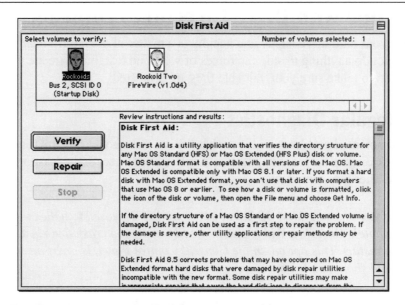

FIGURE 13-6   Disk First Aid prepares to check the author's startup drive

NOTE   *Recent versions of Disk First Aid allow you to actually repair directory damage to your startup disk without the need to start from a CD or another drive. If you don't have a recent version, check Apple's Web support site for a copy. Otherwise, you'll want to restart from your system CD and use the copy on the CD for drive diagnosis.*

Using Other Drive Diagnostic Utilities

The advantage of Apple's Disk First Aid is that it comes free with your Mac OS computer or the latest system software version.

Because it's free, though, it may not be quite as thorough as the commercial programs. They promise to catch more problems and fix them, thus justifying the purchase price.

Here's a quick overview of the available options:

■ **Norton Utilities for the Macintosh**   Symantec's Norton Utilities is one of the best-selling Mac programs, with good reason. It has been around for years in various forms (it's the survivor of the merger of three products, including MacTools and Public Utilities, from companies Symantec took over) and has provided generally reliable performance. Beginning with version 5, the diagnostic/repair component, Norton Disk Doctor (see Figure 13-7) can match Apple's ability to diagnose and repair problems on a startup drive without having to dismount it first.

■ **TechTool Pro**   This program is a descendant of MicroMat's original diagnostic utility, MacEKG. In addition to checking, fixing, and optimizing your hard drive, it'll run checks of a Mac's other systems, such as the CPU, cache, RAM, serial ports, and so on. Dozens of checks, in fact. It's a great way to check for potential hardware problems before they get out of hand.

NOTE   *Beginning with version 2.5.2, which shipped as this book was written, TechTool Pro added a Rebuild Volume feature, which appears to be designed to match the similar function offered by DiskWarrior. Norton Speed Disk will optimize a drive's directory as part of its optimization process.*

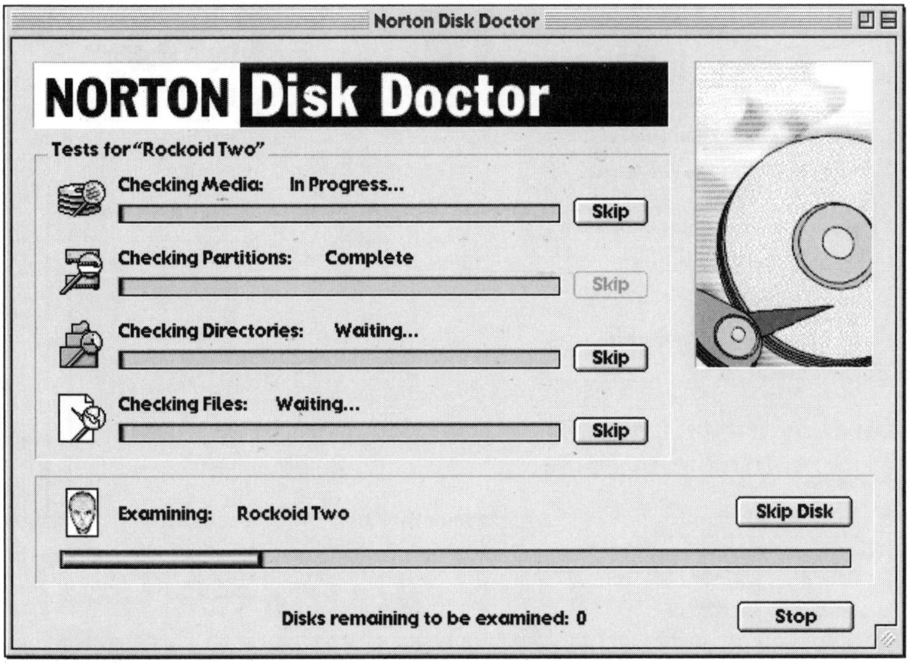

FIGURE 13-7   Norton Disk Doctor will run several categories of hard drive checks during its scanning process

How to Cope with Drive Directory Problems

■ **Alsoft's DiskWarrior**   Called a "one trick pony" by reviewers, this
program does its single trick very well indeed. The other programs are
designed to fix hard drive directory damage. DiskWarrior (see Figure 13-8)
is designed to actually create a brand new drive directory with optimized
performance and replace the old one (after fixing whatever damage it finds).
The only downside to this program is that you cannot check your startup
disk. You need to use the program's boot CD or another drive to run it.

Bundles, Dates, and Other Problems

Norton Disk Doctor will not only check for drive directory problems and fix them, it
can also check for problems with individual files. If a file is damaged, it'll report that

FIGURE 13-8   DiskWarrior has analyzed the author's FireWire drive and is ready to fix
the problems it found and replace the disk directory

fact (but all you can do is replace the file, since damaged files cannot be fixed). It'll also report some very arcane issues, such as whether bundle bits or Finder dates are correct or not. Bundle bits are only of concern if a file icon doesn't show correctly on your Mac's desktop; otherwise it's nothing important. If Norton Disk Doctor reports any of these problems, use the Fix All option in the Disk Doctor screen to repair what it finds and don't worry about any of it. TechTool Pro has a similar set of fixes, called Finder Info, and provides similar results.

It's also normal for one program to interpret a date or bundle bit problem differently than another. I call it the case of the "dueling bundles." As I said, let the program fix the problems and don't fret about it.

Does It Make a Difference If You Don't Have SCSI?

Not to the Mac operating system. All new Macs use some form of ATA hard drive, with the exception of some of the Power Macintosh computers you order via the Build-to-Order program at the Apple Store or through your local dealer. At one time, an ATA hard drive was slower than its SCSI counterpart, in addition to being somewhat cheaper. This is no longer true with the latest ATA protocols.

In addition, Apple's newest models also support FireWire, a super-fast interface developed by Apple that lets you hook up external drives without need of setting IDs or termination. You can even hot plug a device (after dismounting the drive icon by moving it to the trash).

NOTE   *As of the time this book was prepared, Apple had not updated FireWire so that you could boot from such a drive. That is expected to come, however, perhaps by the time this book appears in print. Such an update would include not only the FireWire drivers, but an update for a new Mac's firmware, so the drive would be checked for a System Folder at startup.*

Unless you are looking for a RAID setup (one in which two or more drives are used as one, which is available in FireWire or SCSI trim), there is no need to be concerned that you have an ATA drive, except for the lack of capability to add a number of extra devices. Performance ought to be similar, and the Mac operating system will handle any of these drives in exactly the same way.

NOTE   *The Power Macintosh G4 series is set up to allow you to add a second ATA drive, but that's a far cry from what the other drive interfaces permit.*

How to Cope with Drive Directory Problems

Whether ATA, FireWire, or SCSI, you can back up, reformat, optimize, or check the drive without having to be conscious of the drive interface it follows.

Case History

The Case of the FireWire Drive Slowdown

You can never quite predict the things that'll make a hard drive misbehave.

A case in point was a mysterious performance slowdown with the FireWire drives I have connected to a Blue & White Power Mac G3.

Right after installing Mac OS 9, I copied some files to one of the FireWire drives, and it took maybe five or ten times longer for the process to finish. I tried another FireWire drive with the same result.

I then subjected the drives to complete tests with all of the hard drive diagnostic programs I had at hand and they came up with a clean bill of health. It was positively weird!

Finally, I tried Casady & Greene's great extension management utility, Conflict Catcher, to see if it could pinpoint a possible conflict. I ran the program's Conflict Test and did a quick benchmark of a FireWire drive's performance after each restart. After about 15 minutes or so, Conflict Catcher flagged the USB drivers for an Imation SuperDisk drive as the culprit.

Sure enough, disabling the drivers cured the FireWire drives' slowdown. What's more, I discovered something else. Without thinking to reactivate the software, I inserted a SuperDisk into the SuperDisk drive and it worked anyway, just as it did before.

Why? Although it hasn't been documented as extensively as it should have been (at least when this book was written), beginning with Mac OS 9, Apple incorporated support for many USB devices in its USB Device Extension, which is part of the standard installation on any USB-equipped Mac. It even recognizes an Iomega Zip drive. So I didn't need the SuperDisk drivers after all, and their presence played havoc with other elements of the Mac OS (the FireWire software included). A little testing showed that having the SuperDisk drivers installed would also make the SuperDisk drive behave erratically, sometimes not work at all, even on Macs without FireWire (such as a first-generation iMac); there was also an increase in system crashes.

Yes, it's clear that performance problems can be traced to some of the most unlikely sources.

What to Do If Hard Drive Diagnostic Programs Fail

There's only so much a hard drive diagnostic program can do to fix directory damage and restore your data. It will try to rebuild or (in the case of DiskWarrior) replace the directory.

But there are situations where diagnostic software just won't work for one reason or another. It will report that directory damage cannot be fixed, or the problems will simply reappear each time you run a scan.

Here's a brief listing of those situations and possible solutions or alternatives (if any):

- **Make sure your SCSI chain is safe and sound.**   As I state in Chapter 15, using SCSI peripherals, such as drives, scanners, and whatnot, is not a cut-and-dried process. Even if you follow the rules to the letter, things may go wrong. If you have a Mac with a SCSI chain, double-check that all devices are properly connected, that termination and ID setups are correct and that all devices are left on while your Mac is in use.

- **Try another disk repair utility.**   If Disk First Aid can't fix a problem, give the job to DiskWarrior, Norton Utilities, or TechTool Pro (or vice versa). What one can't fix, the other might. Even if the disk damage is fixed properly, it never hurts to run a second scan to see if the problems return.

- **What if the problems recur?**   If you see the same disk directory problems over and over again, it's usually a good time to bite the bullet and reformat the drive (but first try the step mentioned in the next section). Directory problems can only get worse; they do not disappear.

Corrupted Device Driver

If the hard disk driver is damaged due to a crash, the drive may become inaccessible, or you may see the dreaded prompt asking if you want to initialize the drive when you boot your Mac (just say no!).

If you cannot recover the drive with a disk diagnostic/repair program, try one of the following:

For Drives Formatted with Apple's Drive Setup

1. Restart your Mac with another startup drive or your Mac OS CD. If you're booting from a CD, hold down the "C" key at startup, which will allow the Mac to boot from the CD drive.

NOTE   *If you have an iBook, a second generation iMac (the "slot loading" model), or a Power Mac G4, do the following instead: Insert the CD, restart, holding down the OPTION key until you see a display listing available startup disks. Click the CD icon, then the right arrow, and you'll boot direct from the system CD.*

2. Locate the Utilities folder on the CD and open it.

3. Look in the folder for Drive Setup and launch the program.

4. If your drive appears normally on the list of recognized devices, select it.

5. Use the program's Update function (in the Functions menu) to update the drive.

6. If the Update function isn't available, consider reformatting the drive, after checking the low-level format under Initialization Options. Be sure you have a backup for your files first, since they will be gone for good.

MAC DOESN'T START FROM A CD?   If you cannot get your Mac to boot from the CD, and it starts from your hard drive instead, open the Startup Disk control panel and select the CD as the startup disk. This process is especially recommended if you have a Mac OS clone, such as a computer from APS, DayStar, MacTell, Power Computing, or Umax, since these computers don't use Apple-label CD drives.

You'll also want to make sure that your Mac supports the system version on the startup disk, especially if it came with one of the disk diagnostic/repair utilities. Make sure the version is the same or later than the one on your Mac's original CD. If not, contact the publisher of the utility program to see if they have a later CD for your Mac. Generally they'll just charge you a modest shipping and handling charge to send a new CD, if it's available.

For Drives Formatted with Non-Apple Formatting Software

If you bought your hard drive from a dealer, more than likely it is not an Apple drive, meaning Drive Setup probably won't recognize the drive. Should this be the case, check the packaging for a formatting disk or contact your dealer about getting formatting software. Once you have acquired such software, follow this process:

1. Restart your Mac with another startup drive or (if it came with one) a CD containing your disk formatting software. If you're booting from a CD, hold down the "C" key at startup, which will allow the Mac to boot from the CD drive.

NOTE
As stated in the previous section, if you have an iBook, second generation iMac (the "slot loading" model), or Power Mac G4, follow this process instead: Insert the CD, restart, holding down the OPTION key until you see a display listing available startup disks. Click the CD icon, then the right arrow, and you'll boot direct from the system CD.

2. Locate your disk formatting software on the CD and launch it. You'll see a screen similar to the one shown in Figure 13-9 (using FWB's Hard Disk ToolKit).

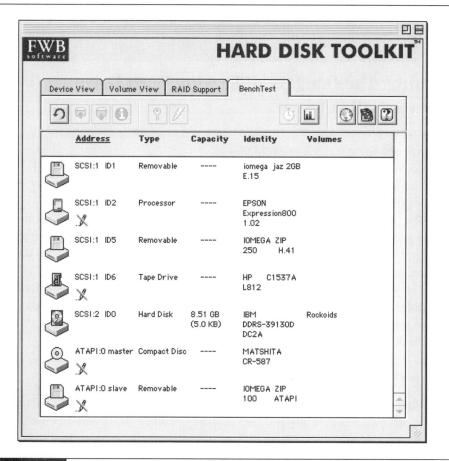

Address	Type	Capacity	Identity	Volumes
SCSI:1 ID1	Removable	----	iomega jaz 2GB E.15	
SCSI:1 ID2	Processor	----	EPSON Expression800 1.02	
SCSI:1 ID5	Removable	----	IOMEGA ZIP 250 H.41	
SCSI:1 ID6	Tape Drive	----	HP C1537A L812	
SCSI:2 ID0	Hard Disk	8.51 GB (5.0 KB)	IBM DDRS-39130D DC2A	Rockoids
ATAPI:0 master	Compact Disc	----	MATSHITA CR-587	
ATAPI:0 slave	Removable	----	IOMEGA ZIP 100 ATAPI	

FIGURE 13-9   These are the ATA and SCSI devices discovered by the program

What to Do If Hard Drive Diagnostic Programs Fail

NOTE   *Later versions of FWB's popular disk formatting software, Hard Disk ToolKit, come with a bootable CD, which will work with recent Apple system versions. If the CD you have won't work on your Mac, contact the publisher for assistance. If you're using a formatting program such as LaCie's Silverlining Pro, which doesn't have a boot CD, check the instructions regarding making an emergency disk.*

3. If your drive appears normally on the list of recognized devices, select it.

4. Use the program's Update function to update the drive.

5. If the Update function isn't available, consider reformatting the drive, using the Format (not Initialize) function. Remember that the process will wipe out any files on the drive.

Warning: The Dangers of Leaving Hard Drive Damage Unfixed

If your hard drive seems all right, despite the report of those disk utilities, you may be inclined to leave well enough alone.

True, your Mac may run fine and dandy, for now. But over time, you'll encounter such symptoms as frequent system crashes and, perhaps, one day you'll find files disappearing or damaged.

Worse, you may even experience a hard drive crash. It's not the same thing as dropping the drive on the floor. It simply means the directory has been so badly damaged that your drive is no longer accessible. You may even see a message on your screen asking if you wish to initialize the drive.

When you get to that point, it may be past the point of no return. The hard drive diagnostic/repair programs can resurrect a crashed drive, but not all the time.

The best advice is this: if your hard drive has directory damage that can't be fixed, back up your files and reformat the drive.

Drive Hardware Failures

If you find that your diagnostic software and your disk formatting program cannot find the drive (and everything is set up properly), there's the possibility the drive mechanism itself has failed. Despite those huge claims of extended lifetimes, this is something that can happen at any time. And it's also something that no diagnostic/repair program can fix.

If your drive failed, and it's still under warranty, the dealer or manufacturer can arrange to repair the unit. But they usually cannot recover your files, unless they offer that service as a special option.

If you do need to recover data that's not been backed up, prepare to pay upwards of $2,000 to recover a drive with several gigabytes of files. That's one reason (aside from the time you are left without your files) that you will want to make sure your data is properly backed up.

> **NOTE** *It's beyond the scope of this book to recommend a hard drive recovery service. One that I've read about is Drive Savers, at http://www .drivesavers.com). They claim to be able to recover files from all the major computer operating systems. In addition to recovering hard drives, they can attempt to recover files from damaged floppies and removable media.*

Summing Up

Now that you've discovered how to keep your hard drive healthy and happy, you'll want to go right to the next chapter, where I cover the steps to take to protect your files should the worst occur. It's all about backups.

What to Do If Hard Drive Diagnostic Programs Fail

Chapter 14

Foolproof Backup Techniques Explained

When it comes to safeguarding the document files you create on your Mac, one copy is never enough.

As you have seen so far in this book, the likelihood that your Mac will crash is very, very high. While most crashes are annoying, the risk that you will actually lose more than your recent work isn't all that much.

But there are times when you'll find yourself in a situation where your precious data could be lost. One typical example is when you save your document. It doesn't matter if it's your novel, an important spreadsheet, or your checkbook program. When you click Save, your software will remove the old version and replace it with the new one. But what if something goes wrong at that very moment? What if you have a power failure or your Mac crashes? What happens next?

Why Backups Are Necessary

It doesn't take a lot to make your file unrecoverable. With a paper document, ripping off a piece of a page or spilling a soft drink on it doesn't hurt very much. You can even tear it in half and fix it with tape.

But computer files are much more sensitive. The loss of even one of those bits and bytes that make up a computer file may be enough to make it impossible to open. While some programs (such as the Office 98 for Macintosh program suite) can handle slightly damaged files, there's the very real possibility that you will not be able to recover your document. It's not a large possibility, but it's ever present, and so it's a good idea to take some precautions so that you will be able to preserve as much of that data as possible.

In addition, there are other reasons why your files may be lost. Here's a brief list of the causes:

- **Software conflicts** As I explain in Chapter 2, there are plenty of software conflicts on your Mac. Some are minor, resulting in minor cosmetic or performance irregularities, but others can cause your Mac to freeze. If this happens when you're saving a document, the document may be damaged beyond repair.

- **Viruses** The newfound popularity of the Mac platform has produced a new set of virulent Mac viruses. Where some are silly pranks, others can cause crashes or perhaps corrupt your documents. Some of these viruses are designed to target users of Microsoft's Office Software for the Mac. You'll want to read Chapter 12 for more information.

■ **Hard drive directory damage**   The catalog file of your hard drive is delicate enough to be damaged by one crash too many. Over time, as your drive wears, files may also become damaged due to bad blocks, or the drive mechanism may simply fail. Whatever the reason or symptom, you may find your precious files can't be retrieved. I cover some avenues of recovery in the next chapter, but they focus more on fixing the drive directory than on getting any individual files back. The prospects for the latter are, to be perfectly blunt, rather remote.

■ **Power outage**   You are saving a file and the power goes off, thus corrupting the file (or even the hard drive). UPS devices, which provide surge protection and battery backup, can help. But they have a limited amount of backup time, and repeated outages may reduce the chance of being able to shut down your Mac and preserve your documents.

■ **Theft**   No further description is necessary. Despite the finest burglar alarm systems, we are all vulnerable to household or office theft of one sort or another.

■ **Fire**   Even heat damage or water damage as a result of fire fighting efforts could damage delicate drive mechanisms or media.

■ **Flooding**   Whether you live in an area where floods are common or not, heavy rains and other unexpected weather conditions can cause serious problems. Water damage to your computer could have catastrophic results. I faced such a threat shortly before this book was written, when heavy rains caused pools of water in two rooms of my home (fortunately my home office remained dry).

■ **Earthquakes**   A moderate quake can shake things about sufficiently to cause damage. At the very least (even if your Mac doesn't topple over), the hard drive could experience a head crash (where the read/write heads strike the surface of the drive), thus resulting in lost files.

So what do you do?

Why Backups Are Necessary

TIP

If you use your Mac strictly for play or recreation (whatever you prefer to call it), and don't create documents you need to preserve, perhaps you don't need a backup after all. New Macs come with a CD labeled "Restore," which is designed to put your Mac's hard drive in the exact shape it shipped from the factory. If the drive is corrupted beyond repair, you can use this disk to erase the drive, put all the old files back, and you've got what is, in effect, a new computer.

How Big Companies Back Up Data

Your bank, your favorite Internet provider, and big businesses around the world all treat computer data in the same fashion. They understand there are risks of losing that data, and so they back up the files on a regular basis, often using "mirroring" techniques (see the section "An Overview of Backup Media"), to make simultaneous duplicates of files on separate media. Copies are also stored offsite, in the event their computers are damaged for one reason or another.

They really have no choice. Imagine, for example, the consequences if a bank's financial data, including the information about your account, was suddenly lost, or if a company lost all its business records.

Backups: How, What, and When

There is no precise backup strategy that will work for everyone, but you should be able to use the information here to develop a plan that will be convenient and offer the amount of protection you need.

Over the next few pages, I'll cover various methods to safeguard your files. Basically, there are two ways to back up your data: manually and automatically.

■ **Manual backup** The fast and dirty way to back up your files is simple. You simply set up another drive or removable device. Then you drag the icon representing files or folders you want to copy to the other drive. That way you have the precious extra copy. The big shortcoming is that you have to manually select which files to copy over, and there's always the possibility of making a mistake. In addition, some system or program-related files are actually invisible, and since you can't see them, you can't copy them.

■ **Automatic backup** Programs such as Retrospect and other solutions I'll mention later in this chapter allow you to perform your backups at

Case History   Too Little Too Late

One morning I got a frantic phone call from a small magazine publisher. The Mac G3 on which they produced their publication wouldn't start up properly. All they saw was a disk icon on the screen with a flashing question mark. As we discuss in Chapters 13 and 15, it's a classic symptom that a startup drive with a working System Folder can't be found.

The client tried running Norton Utilities and Apple's Disk First Aid to no avail. The startup drive wasn't visible—period. Weeks of work, an entire special issue of the magazine, was on that drive and now they couldn't get to it.

"How old is your most recent backup?" I asked.

"What backup?"

The sad conclusion: I was able to help them restore the drive with a disk diagnostic program, but many of their files were lost. Had they invested in a backup strategy, they would have been able to recover all or most of their files in a relatively short time. As it was, they had to work around the clock for days to recreate everything.

A few weeks later, the client called and asked for advice on buying some backup drives, which they promptly followed. I've heard no complaints from them since that original unhappy event.

predetermined intervals. All you have to do is have your backup media in place and, if you don't need to switch media when it fills to capacity, you can go home or to dinner, and your backup will proceed without your presence.

Backup Software Choices

There used to be a number of backup programs for the Mac. In addition to Retrospect, you had FastBack and Redux, to name two popular choices. The major hard drive utilities, which then included MacTools and Norton Utilities, also included backup modules.

Times have changed, however. FastBack and its sibling, FastBack Plus, were casualties of the purchase of the publisher, Fifth Generation Systems, by

Backups: How, What, and When

Symantec. Shortly after Symantec acquired MacTools, their main rival in the disk utility business at the time, they also removed the backup utilities from that program and Norton Utilities. Then they killed MacTools as well.

Fortunately, there are good backup options, so you don't have to lament the loss of these programs.

NOTE
If you still have copies of one of those discontinued backup programs running on your Mac, and it still works properly, you may continue to use it. But do not expect to ever receive updates or even technical support from the publishers or their successor companies. If you upgrade your system software or buy a new Mac computer, do not be surprised if these programs don't perform as you expected, and you may want to acquire one of the newer backup options I'm going to discuss in this chapter.

Retrospect Express and Retrospect

Many of the backup tape drives you buy include a copy of Retrospect or its lower-cost sibling, Retrospect Express. Dantz Development has kept up to date with new Macs and new system versions. They have also added more great features with every release, which is why they get top reviews from the Mac publications. They are proven and tested in both small and large companies, so you can use them with confidence. Here's a brief overview of what these programs offer:

- **EasyScript** This feature allows you to create an automatic backup plan without knowing any programming language or how to script. When you run EasyScript (see Figure 14-1), Retrospect will guide you through the simple steps. You just answer a few questions, and you're ready to do complicated automatic backups of a single Mac or an entire network.

- **Extensive support for backup media** Whatever backup drive you pick, more than likely Retrospect will support it. Everything from tape drives to Zip drives is included (except in Retrospect Express, which doesn't support tape media). And as new drives come out, the publisher will generally provide a special update to support the product.

- **Network backups** The regular version of Retrospect also comes in a version called the Retrospect Network Backup Kit, which allows you to back up the files from an entire computer network. If you dabble in the Windows platform, you'll be pleased to know there's a Windows version with a similar set of features.

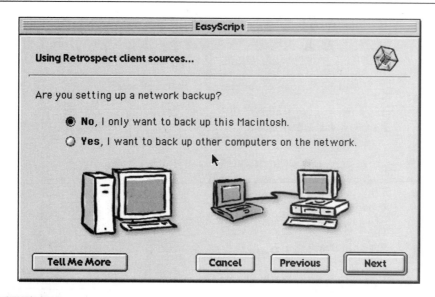

FIGURE 14-1   Just tell EasyScript what you want to do, and Retrospect will make it so

Backups: How, What, and When

NOTE   *Beginning with version 4.2, Dantz changed the name of their products to Retrospect Desktop Backup for the regular version and Retrospect Workgroup Backup for the network edition.*

■ **Internet backups**   If you want to do an online backup (and you'll need to check the limitations), you'll be pleased to know that Retrospect can handle these chores for you as well, with the same level of efficiency.

■ **Simple interface**   Once you set the program up, all features are visible from the simple tabbed interface (as shown in Figure 14-2). You don't have to consult a complex manual to get up to speed. The commands are labeled in plain English, and the online help can take you through the more arcane aspects of a backup strategy.

NOTE   *Retrospect has a useful if time-consuming technique to ensure your backup is robust. It's called "compare," and the function is activated automatically once a disk has been backed up. While you can defeat this option as a preference, I recommend that you let it run. It's an important ounce of added protection that's designed to give you peace of mind.*

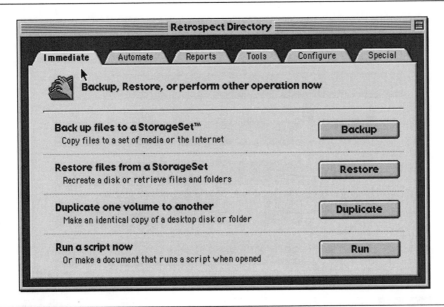

FIGURE 14-2   You can learn the ropes with Retrospect easily, using its simple, yet powerful interface

ASD's Personal Backup

If you have just one or two Macs and you want something that's simple and trouble-free, Personal Backup may be just the ticket.

As you see in Figure 14-3, Personal Backup can do pretty much all of its stuff from a single screen. Once installed, you can do "on demand" backups whenever you wish, using the program's handy menu bar command. You can also set up an automatic schedule for regular backups.

> **TIP**   *A great feature of Personal Backup is its ability to record keystrokes. That way, if you lose the file, you'll have a backup of the text that you can use to help rebuild the document. Connectix Spell Catcher, the popular interactive spelling and grammar checking software (included on this book's CD), offers a similar text capture feature, called GhostWriter.*

Connectix Speed Doubler

Speed Doubler is a popular utility designed to speed up several Mac functions. The most used features include speedier 680x0 emulation, which helps deliver

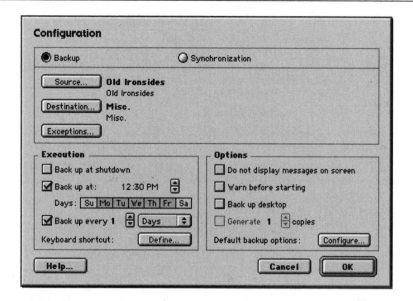

FIGURE 14-3   Easy to use and no frills, Personal Backup offers a powerful, simple
backup solution

better performance, especially if you're using older software on a Power Mac, and
faster file copying.

Here are Speed Doubler's fancy file copying features that you can use to build
a simple backup plan:

- **Synchronize**   This feature lets you compare any two folders, so both have
the latest versions of your files.

- **Smart replace**   This is a great time saver. It lets you copy only the
newest versions of files to a folder or disk. If most of the files are
unchanged, you don't have to sit back and wait for them to be
copied anyway.

- **Scheduled copies**   You can schedule a complete disk or folder
copying operation at a regular interval (see Figure 14-4). The simple

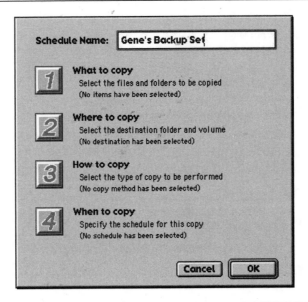

FIGURE 14-4   In just a minute you can create a simple backup plan with Speed Doubler

one-two-three-four interface is reminiscent of a dedicated backup program, and you can configure it quickly to do your bidding.

> **TIP**   *One great feature of Speed Doubler is the ability to run different copying operations at the same time, or to create extra scheduled backups to cover different files. This lets you perform such things as a simple "Smart copy" backup one day and a full backup each week.*

A Fast Look at Apple's File Synchronization Control Panel

Apple's newest consumer computers, the iBook and the iMac, come with a useful backup utility called File Synchronization. This control panel is designed to help you match up the version of a file on your computer with another one on your network (or just a backup drive). It's not anything near a full-featured backup solution, but it's quite useful when you work on two computers and need to keep your files, well, in sync. It has a simple drag and drop interface; just drag a file or folder to the control panel's screen, and it will be compared to the other version. If the one you have is newer, it'll replace the older version.

Using AppleScript to Perform a Backup

Apple has given you a powerful way to automate many Mac functions without having to buy special software or learn complex programming. It's called AppleScript. Beginning with Mac OS 8.5, a new, speedier version added the ability to perform Folder Actions, which trigger events when a file is moved to a specific open folder.

Here's how you can use this great feature to handle on-demand backup chores:

1. Make sure your backup media is ready to roll. If it's a removable drive, see if the disk or cartridge is inserted and mounted on your Mac's desktop.

2. Create a special folder on your Mac where the files to be backed up are placed. Call it anything you want, but a descriptive title, such as "Backup Source," would be best.

3. Click once to select the folder.

4. Activate Apple's handy Contextual Menus feature by holding down the CONTROL key, which will bring up a menu listing various functions that can be performed on that folder.

5. Select the option labeled Attach A Folder Action.

6. In the Open dialog that appears next, you'll be able to pick an AppleScript that applies to that folder.

NOTE   *In case the Open dialog points to the wrong folder, just navigate to the one labeled Folder Action Scripts, located in the Scripts folder within the System Folder. If you cannot locate this folder, you may need to use the Add/Remove feature of your Mac OS installer to reinstall AppleScript.*

7. Choose the script labeled "add – duplicate to folders." Your Backup Source folder will now bear a script icon to indicate it has a Folder Action attached to it.

8. Select the desktop icon of your backup disk by clicking once on it.

9. Make an alias of the backup disk icon by choosing the Make Alias command from the Finder's File menu.

10. Select the alias icon, then click on the name. Add the symbols ~! to the beginning of the disk's name.

Backups: How, What, and When

11. Now all you have to do is drag this retitled alias icon to your special Backup Source folder.

THE END RESULT Here's how your AppleScript backup scheme will work: When you drag any file or folder to your Backup Source folder, those files will automatically be copied to the backup disk. Just like that. Oh, and one more thing, for this neat AppleScript to work, the Backup Source folder must be opened. If you close it, the script doesn't function.

An Overview of Backup Media

Before you set up your backup plan, you'll want to decide where to put the files. One thing you should *not* do is copy the files to the same drive as the original. The point of the backup is protection in the event something goes wrong not just with the file but with the drive itself, whether it affects just one file or all of them.

Here's a quick overview of the kinds of backup media available as of the time this book was published, along with advantages and limitations. As time goes on, you'll find that clever manufacturers will devise variations on these themes, or even come up with ideas that are completely different from anything you see here.

- **Floppy disks** The original backup medium, especially when Macs were young. And even with newer Macs and iMacs, where you can buy an external floppy or SuperDisk drive, it's neither robust nor efficient. Imagine how many 1.4MB floppies it would take to back up the contents of even a 3GB hard drive (which is small by today's standards). The mind boggles. Aside from the inconvenience, floppy disks are prone to failure, especially if you try to use them over and over again. For a small document file or two, they'll probably do, especially to transport the file to another location. For backup purposes, you'll probably want to look elsewhere.

- **Extra hard drive** Whether the drive is located inside your Mac or attached via the FireWire, SCSI, or USB port (whatever applies), this is a useful, convenient place to store your backups. The big limitation is portability. It isn't practical to put the drive in a safe place if it must be regularly available to receive those backup files.

CAUTION *While it's easy to partition a drive (divide it into multiple segments), it's not a terribly robust way to protect your data. If a problem is serious enough to take down the drive, all partitions will be history.*

- **Mirroring data**   Special software packages, supporting RAID (Redundant Array of Inexpensive Drives), have a feature that "mirrors" or duplicates the files you save across two or more drives. That way, if one drive goes bad, there's another, identical file that you can use on the other drive.

- **Removable drive**   These products come with such names as Jaz, Orb, SuperDisk, SyQuest, or Zip, but they are all designed to perform in a similar way. The drives use a media that acts like a floppy disk, because you can remove the media when it's filled, and replace with another one to receive more files. Capacities range up to 2GB and more, similar to many regular hard drives. And, of course, you can store the media in another location for protection. Although some of these removable devices use hard-drive-based technology, they are usually somewhat slower and potentially less reliable, since the drive mechanism is more susceptible to dust.

- **Magneto-optical drive**   Such a drive uses optical disk technology (somewhat reminiscent of a compact disc), which ensures longevity. If you want to keep your backups for several years or more, this option (or a CD recorder) might be useful. The disadvantage of this technology is that it's rather slow compared to a hard drive (though faster than Zips or CD recorders), but as a tradeoff for a robust backup, it may be worth the time and trouble.

- **CD-R or CD-RW**   These two methods are based on conventional compact disc technology, same as that used with your regular audio CDs. The advantage is permanence. When was the last time any of your audio CDs failed? If you want to store your files for years and years, you'll want to think about this method. A key limitation is the fact that you need special software to "burn" or create a CD. You cannot just drag the files to a mounted disk icon and have them copy over. It can also be quite slow compared to most other backup media. Figure on it taking 15 to 45 minutes for a 650MB CD, depending on how fast the CD recorder runs. But it's a cheap way to go. CD blanks are less than two dollars each. The CD-RW variation uses more expensive media and allows you to write on the disc over and over again (usually up to 1,000 times), but older CD drives won't read the discs.

- **DVD-RAM**   This technology is based on DVD, the high-quality video disk format. You can store over 5GB of data on it when you use the higher-density media. Its major limitation is that, as of the time this book was being prepared, there is more than one way to skin a cat, and no guarantee that the media created on one drive will work on another since competing technologies exist.

■ **Tape drive**   There are several types. One of the popular varieties is DDS (Digital Data Storage), which is based on DAT (Digital Audio Tape) technology. Tapes are cheap, but not as robust as other media. And they're generally slow compared to other backup media, though newer tape drives give pretty decent performance. Finding even a single file may take a while, since the tape has to be shuttled back and forth in the drive to locate a special item (same as your audio cassette player). And this isn't the only inconvenience. With the exception of a special utility, Optima Technology's DeskTape Pro, you cannot mount a tape on your Mac's desktop. You need special backup software, such as Retrospect, to write and retrieve files.

■ **Network drives**   If your Mac is located in a business environment, you may be able to use the networked drives or servers for backing up. Some companies will have a special strategy in place for such actions, however, so you'll want to be sure you aren't putting files somewhere where they are neither welcomed nor assured of safety.

■ **Internet backups**   This new option is a consequence of the new generation of Power Macs, iMacs and iBooks, which don't have standard floppy drives. Rather than buy something extra, you upload your file to an Internet backup service, which provides secured access and stores your files. Assuming the service backs up *their* files regularly, it is a nice option, but you also have to consider how long it'll take to upload your file to this remote location. Unless you have high speed Internet access, such as a cable modem or DSL, it may take hours to transfer even a small number of document files. In addition, storage space may be very limited (typically 10MB), so the technique is generally only useful for backing up small files.

TIP   *Rather than subscribe to an Internet backup service to store your files, you could upload them to a family member or trusted friend for safekeeping on their computing systems. Of course, you would want to make sure they have a robust backup method in case something goes wrong at their end of the backup chain.*

Your Regular Backup Plan

No doubt about it, backups can be a pain. You have to stop what you're doing and remember to make an extra copy or two of your precious files. And if you're busy creating one of those files, approaching deadlines make it easy to forget something or just plain put it off until you have the time. Unfortunately, without an iron-clad strategy, that time may never come. It's so easy to say, "I'll do it tomorrow." Unfortunately, if you lose that file today, tomorrow is too late.

Here's a suggested daily backup strategy you can use, with or without extra software. All you need is a separate backup drive to which you copy files:

■ **Use a program's AutoSave or Backup option.**   Check the Preference dialogs in your favorite software to see if either or both options are available. If there's the choice to save a backup to another drive or drive partition, consider using it.

■ **Make extra copies of critical documents.**   While working on a file, drag a copy of the document icon to another disk, or just use the Save As option in the File menu to make an extra copy.

NOTE   *If you are using the Save As feature, you may want to place that extra copy on another disk, in case something happens to the original drive.*

■ **At the end of the workday, back up critical files.**   You can use a backup program for this purpose or do it manually.

NOTE   *Among those "critical files" is the Preferences folder inside the System Folder. That folder contains most of your program settings, including those involving your Internet connection.*

■ **Make full backups at least once a week.**   Over time, no doubt you've customized your Mac in many ways. You may have changed the desktop pattern, adjusted mouse tracking speed, and made a load of settings to the various programs you use. If you had to recreate all the things that make your Mac friendly and comfortable to use, it could take hours. But if you have a complete backup of the contents of your startup disk, at the very

Backups: How, What, and When

least, you'll be able to restore everything to the way it was without a lot of fuss or bother.

■ **Store backup files in a safe place.** Your backup media is subject to the same risks as the originals. In the event of fire, flood, or theft, they can be lost as well. Big firms often place a copy of their backups offsite. A secure location, such as a bank vault, might be useful if you want the maximum amount of security. But even a friend's or mother-in-law's home will do. The point is to have another copy somewhere else if the first is damaged or stolen.

■ **If you travel, take a copy of the backup with you.** Pack it in your suitcase or PowerBook carrying bag. That way if you come home to find disaster has struck, you'll be able to get up and running quickly. Computers, printers, and scanners can be replaced (good insurance is a must), but it may take hours, days, or weeks to recreate your missing data.

■ **Label your backup media carefully.** When you need to restore a file, it can be especially vexing to have to waste time searching through disk after disk to find the one you need. If possible, print out a directory of a disk's contents (clearly, you can't do this with a tape drive).

■ **Don't use the same media over and over again.** Removable media, from tapes to cartridges, may wear out over time. The best way to maximize life span is to have several disks run in rotation.

■ **Recycle media.** Older disks that contain files you no longer need can be placed back into action, but if the disks are especially old, you may find it safer to simply purchase a new set.

■ **Consider CD-based backups for long-term archiving.** While traditional disks and tapes may wear out over time, optical-based media can last for many years. If you anticipate you might need that file five years from now, a CD or DVD recorder or magneto-optical drive may be something to consider as an extra backup tool.

What Do You Back Up?

There are several strategies you can use when you decide to back up your files. Whether you do it manually or use a dedicated backup program, you'll want to consider which options provide the best combination of safety, speed, and flexibility.

- **No-frills backup.**   You have your original system software and program installation disks at hand, so you may not feel it's important to make duplicates. You can just back up your document files and your Preferences folder, the ones you make with those original programs.

- **Full backup.**   In this scenario, you back up everything on your drive. While it may take a lot of extra time to do, there's the added advantage of being able to conveniently restore your Mac to something approximating the shape it was in before catastrophe struck. This means that all of the custom settings you've done, from fancy desktop patterns to more subtle aspects of your Mac user experience, such as mouse tracking speed and a program's preference settings, are in place.

- **Incremental backup.**   You use this method to back up strictly the files that have changed since your last backup. Backup software is capable of sorting all this out in the event you need to restore your files.

Application Backup Features

In addition to backing up all your files to a central location (another drive, removable disk, or tape), there's another backup option you'll want to consider.

Some programs offer an automatic backup or automatic saving option as part of their preference settings. That way you can be assured there's a second, recent copy around somewhere in case your original file becomes damaged and unusable. I'll cover two popular choices next.

Word's AutoSave/Backup Option

If you are a regular user of Word 98 for the Macintosh, you'll find a handy feature hidden in the Preferences settings that will help you protect your valuable documents in the event of a problem. A similar preference is available for PowerPoint 98, but, unfortunately, not for Excel. Here's how to use it:

1. Choose Preferences from the Tools menu.

2. Click the Save tab, which brings up the screen shown in Figure 14-5.

3. To have an extra copy of your document, click the Always Create Backup Copy check box. Once this setting is made, you'll have an extra copy of your document file with the prefix "Backup of" in the same folder as the original.

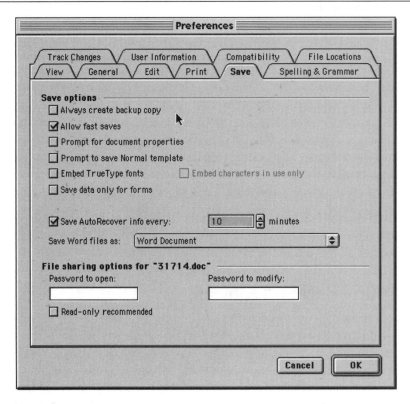

FIGURE 14-5 You can choose your Save options for Word 98 here

4. If you want to make it possible to recover a document if you crash while saving it, click the Save AutoRecover Info Every: check box, and specify the interval. Ten minutes, the default, should do just fine. Once the setting goes in effect, if you open a document that's been damaged, Word will use the AutoRecover information to restore it to its original shape (and you'll see an onscreen dialog about it).

5. Click OK to put your settings into effect.

QuarkXPress's Not-So-Secret Backup Feature

The well-known desktop publishing program QuarkXPress has a very robust, but seldom-used backup option. The feature is of vital importance, as all recent versions are known to corrupt documents on occasion. While most of these problems may be due to other causes, such as problems on the SCSI chain, they are no less vexing.

NOTE   *When I say "seldom-used," I'm not exaggerating the point. I have worked with many users of XPress, and not one of them has ever so much as looked at this particular preference. (I'm using the word XPress here to refer to the program, and Quark to refer to the company; this is the official way, although I know many people refer to the program itself as Quark.)*

The following steps will help you automatically save and back up your XPress documents:

1. Launch QuarkXPress. You do not need to open a document at this point.

2. Choose Preferences from the Edit menu, and select Application Preferences (the first one on the list). This will bring up the dialog shown in Figure 14-6.

3. Click on the Save tab, which will bring up the screen shown in Figure 14-7.

4. Check Auto Save, then pick the interval. The default is 5 minutes.

5. Check Auto Backup, then indicate how many revisions you want to have. The default is 5, but you're better off with 1 or 2. Otherwise, you'll have a lot of extra files around that you don't need.

TIP   *If you choose the option to make more than a single backup file in QuarkXPress, you may find your destination folder filled with extra copies. Every so often, it's a good idea to prune the folder of unneeded files.*

6. Select the Destination for your backup. The default, the Document folder, just compounds the risk, in case something goes bad with your drive. So click the Other Folder radio button.

7. In the dialog that appears, select the drive or folder where you want to place your backups. You may want to use the option in this dialog to create a new folder, giving it a label that makes it easy to find later on. One example may be "XPress Documents Backups" (or "Quark Documents Backup" if you prefer).

Backups: How, What, and When

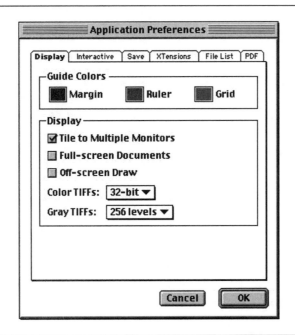

This is QuarkXPress 4.0.4's Application Preferences dialog, which is similar to the one available in older versions of the program

NOTE

If your Mac has a second attached drive, you may want to place backups there. A networked Mac or server may also be a good backup choice, but it may also slow down when doing a save operation, especially if you're not on a high-speed network. Click the OK button to store your settings. From here on, all documents you create in QuarkXPress will be saved or backed up as you specified. Auto Backup files will have the original filename, plus suffix, beginning with the number (#) sign to indicate how many backed-up files have been created.

TIP

If you run across a damaged QuarkXPress file, and even the backup doesn't work, there's another solution. MarkZWare, a publisher of Quark XTensions (add-ons) offers a product, MarkZTools, which can recover many damaged XPress documents. You can learn more about the product by visiting their Web site at http://www.markzware.com.

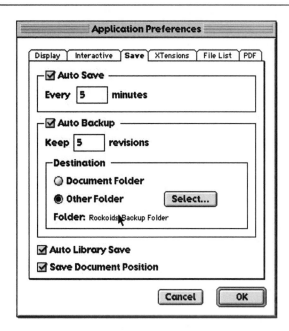

FIGURE 14-7   Choose your Auto Save and Auto Backup options on this screen

How to Restore Your Files

Whatever backup technique you use, you should make sure that you *can* restore your files should the worst occur. In schools and large companies, they often conduct fire drills to test performance in the event of a real emergency. You should consider a similar test with your backup routine. You'll want to know, in advance, that the files you're backing up are available at your beck and call when you need them.

Test Driving Your Backup Strategy

To examine the efficacy of your backup program, you should consider running a drill by actually restoring something. Here's one way you might accomplish this task:

1. If you're doing a manual backup, or a backup in "Finder" format (meaning the backed-up files appear in the same form as the originals), simply copy a few document files back to your drive, to a location different from the original. You don't want to actually replace any files; you just want to see if they are in good shape.

2. Open the files, and make sure that what you see matches the original file. More than likely, if you can open the file normally, you should have no problem.

3. If the file fails to open, review your backup plan, and the next section, to address problems with the backed-up files.

4. If you're using a backup program, such as Personal Backup or Retrospect, simply use the Restore function in the program, and select a handful of files to restore to your drive. Again, you don't want to replace any existing file, just make sure that you actually have a good copy of the files available in the event you really need them later.

If your test works, you can feel fairly confident that your backup routine is going to be successful.

What If the Backup Goes Bad?

There can be no greater source of disappointment and frustration than trying to restore your files and finding out that your backup has gone bad. You engage the Restore operation on your backup software, or simply try to copy over files you've backed up manually, and you get a message that there's a disk error or a warning that something's wrong with your backup program's "storage set."

It's frustrating, true, but it doesn't have to mean that you won't be able to restore at least some of your files. In Retrospect, for example, there are tools to fix the backup directory, known as the Storage Set. The Storage Set is your catalog of all the files you've backed up, and Retrospect needs this file to track the progress of your backup and retrieve files when necessary. While the process I'm going to describe here won't fix a bad disk, it will allow you to recover the files that are still available.

Fixing a Bad Retrospect Storage Set

If Retrospect can't recover your files, you'll see a message about it onscreen when you attempt to restore one or more files. Usually, it'll indicate that the contents of the Storage Set don't jibe with the actual backup files. Quite often this happens if your Mac crashes at some point in the backup process, though a damaged Storage Set file will trigger the same message.

Retrospect stores the Storage Set files in the same folder that contains the original application. As an ounce of protection, you ought to make duplicates of these files on another drive or removable disk. While the sets can be recreated in the event the original drive is lost, it can be a time-consuming process you will probably want to avoid.

Here's how to address the problem, using recent versions of Retrospect (this description is based on version 4.1):

1. Make sure the first or only disk of your backup is in the backup drive.

2. Launch Retrospect.

3. Click on the Tools tab, which brings up the screen shown in Figure 14-8.

4. Click on the Repair button, which produces the dialog shown in Figure 14-9.

5. The decision you make now depends on what sort of problem message you saw when you tried to restore a file. If it stated the catalog was out of sync with the backup, click the first option. If you don't have a Storage Set, you can recreate one using the data on your backup media, by clicking on whatever option in Figure 14-9 applies.

6. If your backup has additional disks, you'll see an onscreen prompt asking you to insert those disks (usually the previous disk will be ejected, but you may have to click an Eject button to do this). When you state there are no additional backup disks, the dialog will conclude with an onscreen acknowledgement that you can OK.

7. Depending on how bad your Storage Set catalog is messed up, it may take anywhere from a few minutes to a few hours to recreate or build the file. But the best prevention against a bad backup is to have more than one. That way, if a fragile disk goes bad, another disk will be available for you to get your documents back. When it comes to backups, three times is definitely a charm.

Other Backup Recovery Methods

If your actual backup disk or tape is at fault, rather than the backup catalog, there are no guarantees you'll get it back, which is why I suggested you have extra backups.

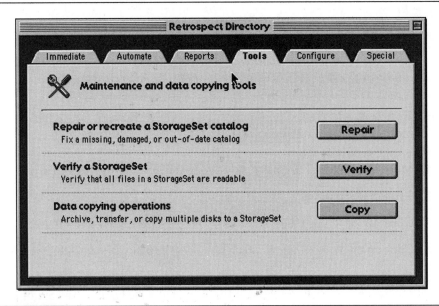

FIGURE 14-8   Choose the first option from this screen

This is especially true if your backup is on a tape, which can only be read by special software, such as Retrospect. When these disks go bad, your regular file recovery and repair programs, such as the ones I describe in Chapter 13, just won't function.

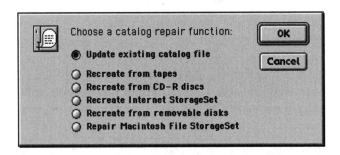

FIGURE 14-9   Decide whether to update or recreate your Storage Set catalog

> CAUTION
> *When you use a tape drive, follow the manufacturer's recommendations about using cleaning disks to keep tape heads clean. For example, DDS drives should be cleaned about every 15 hours. Retrospect can be set to remind you of this cleaning interval. If you fail to run the cleaning disks regularly, you may subject your backup to read/write errors, and the potential for corrupted or lost files.*

Abbott Systems to the Rescue

An old-line Mac utility publisher, Abbott Systems, offers two programs that can help you recover damaged or trashed documents. One of them, CanOpener, is designed to open most any document file and retrieve the contents, even if the original program cannot access it. While a complicated financial document or desktop publishing file may not be recovered in its original form, basic text and pictures can often be found.

Another program from this publisher, RescueTXT, can be used to track text on files you've accidentally deleted. This may be the court of last appeal should a stab at a hard drive recovery program, such as Norton Utilities or TechTool Pro, not be able to retrieve a file.

> CAUTION
> *Norton Utilities and TechTool Pro work best if you install them before you have a problem. Both programs will catalog your deleted files and your hard drive directory and update the catalog regularly, which makes recovery easier in the event of trouble later on. They work far less reliably if you have to use their recovery tools without having first installed the software before your drive went bad.*

You can check out the Abbott Systems product line at their Web site: http://www.abbottsystems.com.

Diagnosing Backup Problems on a Large SCSI Chain

Here are some steps to follow should you be unable to retrieve a backup from a SCSI device in a setup with several drives attached:

1. Check your SCSI chain. Make sure all attached devices are on and that termination is turned on or attached to the final device on the chain (the one at the very end).

2. If you need to move any devices to different positions, shut down your Mac, then your attached SCSI devices, then move the devices. Be sure to observe proper termination and SCSI ID settings.

3. If you still cannot get your backup device to retrieve files or run properly, shut down your Mac, then the SCSI devices.

4. Set up the backup drive as the only SCSI device on the chain. Be sure to switch on termination, or install a termination block, whichever applies.

5. Turn on the backup drive, then the Mac.

If these steps don't help, and you're using a conventional removable drive, such as a Jaz or Zip, run a disk diagnostic utility, as described in Chapter 13.

CAUTION *Before you run a disk diagnostic program with a removable drive, check the manufacturer's recommendations in the manual or Read Me file. You wouldn't want to make matters worse, unless, of course, the media is useless. In that event, even a risky method may be worth the risk.*

TIP *If you cannot make a backup drive work on your Mac, there may be an alternative—that is, if you have an extra Mac around to which you can attach the drive. Just set up the drive on the other Mac, and see if you can retrieve the file that way (you may have to install the backup software, of course). If it works, you can network the two Macs to access the files, or just copy them to another drive, if available.*

Summing Up

Backing up your data may seem an unneeded chore until you lose one of your valuable files. This chapter covered backup techniques using all types of media. One of these techniques is bound to work well in your situation.

The next chapter covers one of the principal causes of headaches and aggravation on a Mac, the SCSI chain. You'll learn the best methods to set up a SCSI chain and the telltale signs of trouble.

Chapter 15

Dealing with SCSI Chain Hassles

Compared to the failed efforts on the Windows platform, the Mac's version of plug-and-play is a superlative engineering feat. I cannot tell you how many times I've set up Mac hard drives, networks, and printers in minutes, only to face hours of debugging to do the very same things on the PC side of the platform.

But that doesn't mean the Mac is the bee's knees when it comes to freedom from setup hassles. For one thing, SCSI, once Apple's primary peripheral bus to connect such things as CD drives, hard drives, and scanners needs, shall we say, a little work to make things operate correctly. Sometimes you have to just set it up and pray that it'll work properly.

I've devoted this chapter to SCSI chain setup, diagnosis, and how to add extra devices, in the hope it'll make your encounters with SCSI voodoo less frustrating.

Fortunately, with its recent models Apple has moved totally away from SCSI except as an option. New Macs, iMacs, iBooks, and PowerBooks come with ATA drives as standard issue. In the future, you may even see internal FireWire drives, since Apple has added an internal FireWire bus to its Power Mac G4 series. So the problems you encounter here will be history once you upgrade your Mac and peripherals. But even if you have a new Mac, you may need to add SCSI capability (where possible) to handle those older scanners, removable drives and other peripherals.

At the end of the chapter, you'll also read about the technologies Apple has adopted that are free of many of the limitations of SCSI. As you update your Mac and your accessories, you'll be pleased to know there's truly light at the end of the tunnel.

How to Organize the SCSI Chain

If you follow a few basic setup procedures, you should be able to get most SCSI chains to work properly—most of the time, that is. Here are a few of the basics to consider:

> **NOTE**   *A SCSI chain is simply a collection of SCSI devices on a single SCSI bus.*

- **Keep SCSI chains short.**   In theory, you can have cable lengths with a total of over 19 feet on a plain-Jane SCSI chain, but in practice, there are limits. For one thing, that figure also includes the actual cable inside a drive mechanism, which can add up. Figure on a foot or so for every device.

High-speed SCSI chains, such as SCSI Wide, require much shorter cable lengths. Consult the information provided with your SCSI accelerator card for specifics on this subject.

■ **Don't forget termination.**   The first and last devices on the SCSI chain (regardless of SCSI ID number) need to be terminated. Your Mac provides termination at the beginning of the chain, so you only need to add it at the end. Some SCSI devices require a terminator block, but others use pushbuttons, dipswitches, or little bitty buttons to switch termination on or off. Mechanisms from APS Technology, Iomega's removable drives, and some scanners from Umax all offer a termination switch of some sort. If a quick glance at the device doesn't give you an answer as to how termination is to be set, consult the manuals or call the manufacturer for assistance. I won't even try to cover all of the confusing possibilities here.

I'll repeat this a couple of times in this chapter: PowerBooks don't generally supply enough termination power for a good performing SCSI chain (especially if there's more than a single device). The PowerBook manuals usually suggest double termination (at the beginning or middle and the end of the chain).

■ **Watch out for duplicate SCSI ID numbers.**   If your Mac has some internal devices installed, you'll need a hard disk formatter, such as Anubis, Hard Disk ToolKit or Silverlining to check for each device on the chain. You can also use SCSI Probe, which is available from many Web sites, such as http://www.versiontracker.com. Normally, the internal drive on a Mac is set at ID 0 (I've seen different ID numbers for replacement drives, though this is easily changed), and the CD-ROM drive is set at ID 3. Apple's internal SCSI Zip drives are set at ID 5.

■ **Be wary of two or more SCSI buses.**   Some PCI-based Macs and Mac OS clones have two SCSI buses: an internal chain for internal devices, and an external chain. In theory, you should be able to place seven devices on each. But some peripherals—and scanners are a big example—don't seem to recognize that there can be two devices with the same SCSI ID so long as they are on separate buses. If you encounter this problem, make sure that only one SCSI chain uses the ID number devoted to the particular offending device.

How to Organize the SCSI Chain

■ **Keep all attached SCSI devices on.** I know, you're not using that scanner, and you don't want to wear out the bulb (many of them are difficult and costly to replace). But many scanners are set to power down their bulbs after a period of disuse, and, in any case, the bulbs usually last for thousands of hours. The problem here is arcane, and involves matters of proper termination power, correct voltage on the SCSI chain, and that sort of thing. In some cases, leaving off a connected device won't do anything bad. But you may also experience unexpected system crashes and damaged files. The best advice is to keep all attached devices on. If you don't intend to use a device except on a rare occasion, power down, remove it from the SCSI chain and power up again (don't forget to change termination if necessary).

Case History

Why It's Necessary to Keep SCSI Devices On

The telephone call was frantic. A client couldn't boot his Power Mac 6500, and he had to complete a business proposal.

I rushed over to the site, ran Alsoft's Disk Warrior and Symantec's Norton Utilities (see Chapter 13). The drive had various and sundry disk directory errors that were fixed, but, sad to say, a whole folder was filled with damaged files.

After the drive's directory was repaired, I performed a clean installation of the client's operating system and had them up and running in a short time. But I noticed something amiss in his setup. He had two devices on the SCSI chain, a scanner and a Zip drive. The scanner was off. He said he only used it once a week and so he didn't think he wanted to waste the electricity.

The scanner was turned on, and the Mac restarted.

After I talked with the client a few minutes, I realized that since he had decided to turn off his scanner when not in use, his Mac crashed much more often. And there was that folder containing damaged files to deal with.

He agreed to leave his scanner on and has had no problems since then, although it took him quite a few hours to recreate the damaged graphic files.

A Handy Guide to SCSI Voodoo

In the previous section, I explained how SCSI devices are supposed to work. The word "voodoo" is used when it comes to SCSI chains, because sometimes setting things up as advertised isn't quite successful. Drives don't show up, you get frequent crashes, or data ends up damaged.

Frustrating, yes? But if you follow a few troubleshooting steps, you'll usually get things to run correctly. I say usually because there are exceptions that defeat the best efforts of humankind to resolve.

CAUTION   *Before you change anything on your Mac's SCSI chain, turn everything off. And before you reboot your Mac, turn on all attached SCSI devices first. No exceptions! You could damage your Mac's logic board or one of your devices if you try hot plugging (although there are some devices available from hard drive vendors that promise to do this sort of thing).*

- **Use an extra terminator.**   Yes, I know. I said that only the beginning and end of the SCSI chain are supposed to be terminated. But this doesn't necessarily work on large SCSI chains (with several devices and cables stretching the length limits) or with PowerBooks. PowerBook manuals usually have a special section on SCSI hookups. For other Macs, place a pass-through terminator in the middle of the chain and see if it helps improve performance.

- **Use an active terminator.**   These devices help regulate the current on the SCSI chain and will sometimes compensate for devices that don't supply proper current or electrical variations among cables. Some models will even include a power brick, which is used to help supply extra juice to help regulate a SCSI chain with a PowerBook and similar products.

- **Use cables from the same manufacturer.**   In theory, a cable is a cable, but products from different manufacturers may differ slightly in electrical specifications. It may not mean much if you have only one or two items on the SCSI chain. But on a large SCSI chain, small differences may account for a lot. If all else fails, try buying a new set of cables from one manufacturer.

NOTE   *I'm not a fan of boutique cables since (as with the cables you use on your home stereo system), you seldom if ever get better performance in exchange for the higher price you pay. Cables from major companies, such as Belkin, work just fine in any installation.*

■ **Move devices around.**   For whatever reason, some SCSI devices work best in a specific position on the SCSI chain. Sometimes a manufacturer will make a suggestion as to positioning in their manuals. An example: Some scanners work best at the very end of the SCSI chain, others work best at the beginning. You need to experiment and move things around to see if the proper combination can be found. Just remember to change SCSI ID numbers where needed (so they don't conflict) and move termination to the last physical device on the chain.

■ **Change SCSI ID numbers.**   A SCSI ID number doesn't have to be consecutive. Number 6 doesn't have to be after number 5. You can reverse the numbers if you desire (just make sure they don't conflict).

■ **Watch out for SCSI ID number 5.**   Some PCI-based Macs, beginning with the Power Macintosh 8500 and 9500 series, reportedly had problems with SCSI number 5. This problem was supposedly fixed beginning with Mac OS 7.5.3. But don't dismiss the possibility that problems might remain. Go ahead and avoid this number if you can, and see if things work any better.

NOTE   *Iomega Zip drives are designed to work either with SCSI ID 5 or ID 6. With a long SCSI chain, you may not be able to avoid ID 5.*

Do Drives Really Last for 500,000 Hours?

It's very common for hard drive manufacturers to quote incredible lifetimes for their products. They usually range from 200,000 to 500,000 hours MBTF (mean time between failures). Considering that 200,000 hours would amount to more than two decades continuous operation, more than anyone might realistically expect to use their Macs, this would be the equivalent of a lifetime warranty (imagine what 500,000 hours means?).

Yet drive manufacturers seldom warranty their products for more than three to five years. So do you take it seriously?

Well, consider this. Just because a hard drive manufacturer quotes an average doesn't mean a specific hard drive won't fail before that. Hard drives and removable devices tend to be more trouble-prone because of all the delicate mechanical parts involved. My suggestion is that you treat your drive as if it might fail at any moment (which can sometimes be the case) and have regular backups. You can also use a hard drive maintenance program to be certain there's no damage to the delicate hard drive's file directory. Chapters 13 and 14 cover these subjects in more detail.

Case History

Mixing and Matching SCSI Cables

Just a few years ago, I went through the hassles of SCSI voodoo when trying to configure a Mac with a big SCSI chain (six external devices including removable drives, scanner, and tape backup drive). The symptom was classic. I tried to copy a large file to and from any drive and the computer locked up tight as a drum.

I went through the standard array of remedies. I moved SCSI devices around, and changed SCSI ID numbers. I swapped cables, and switched a few from some extras I had on hand. Even an active terminator was used.

The SCSI chain worked if I removed any single device, but all together there was no way to avoid the problem. I checked and double-checked everything to be absolutely certain that the setup was correct. Even a second terminator wouldn't fix it.

Finally, on a suggestion from a technical support person at APS Technologies, a big hard drive vendor, I replaced the cables. All of them. Now maybe you could be cynical about it and assume they just wanted to sell me cables. Maybe so. But after replacing the old cables with the new ones, the problem was cured, immediately, never to return. The new cables did it!

Internal vs. External—What's the Difference?

Yes, they're cheaper. And no doubt that is one reason to favor an internal hard drive, but there are complications. For one thing, even if your Mac can handle more than one drive inside, you have to pop the case, remove brackets, and fiddle with hard-to-reach cables. And even when that's fairly simple, there are the drive mechanisms themselves.

Whether the mechanisms are regular hard drives or removable devices, such as a CD writer, Jaz, or Zip drive, there are other little complications to consider.

For one thing, you have to decipher a sometimes-unclear diagram to see if the proper SCSI ID and termination settings are set on the drive. You cannot always depend on the manufacturer or reseller setting up these mechanisms properly.

If you have an older Mac, you have to make doubly sure it can handle one of the big, bad hard drives available now. Some of the highest capacity models, with

10,000-RPM performance, put out a lot of heat—lots more than one of those pancake-style Macs (such as the 6100 and 6300 series) can handle without getting just too hot.

Here are some things to consider when buying an internal hard drive for your Mac:

■ **Get a smaller drive for an older Mac.**   Those thin Mac cases don't have enough cooling power from the internal fan to handle the heat generated by a big, fast drive. Before you place your order, ask the dealer or manufacturer about support for these models. And even larger Macs, such as the 800/840/8100/8500/9500 series, have problems keeping cool with large internal drives installed.

■ **Consider an accessory cooling fan.**   If you really need that big hard drive, contact your dealer and see if they can set you up with an accessory cooling fan. Such vendors as APS Technologies offer such a product, which usually attaches to the drive itself. It can make a big difference in hard drive reliability.

■ **Don't forget the bracket.**   Many Macs require the drives to be fitted with a special bracket to be installed internally. If you're not sure, ask your dealer to get you the proper bracket. You can get more information about this subject from Proline, one of the manufacturers of drive brackets and faceplates. Their Web URL is http://www.proline.com.

■ **You need a new faceplate for a removable device.**   If you want to add a SuperDisk, a Zip drive, or some other device for which you have to remove the media, you need to replace the faceplate on your Mac with one that will match the open slot on the mechanism itself. Your dealer can probably handle your needs (or check with Proline, as mentioned in the previous item). On some Mac OS clones, all you need to do is pop a small faceplate, and leave the removable mechanism with its front showing, without a cover.

■ **Make sure you can really add an extra mechanism.**   If your Mac doesn't have an extra drive bay, or it's got an internal ATA chain without SCSI capability, you may not be able to add extra devices without a separate SCSI accelerator card (see the section that follows).

Internal SCSI vs. External SCSI—Which Is Faster?

For most older Macs with built-in SCSI, there's no difference. But some of the PCI-based Macs, beginning with the 7500, 8500 and 9500 (and some Mac OS clones), the internal SCSI bus is SCSI-2 Fast, thus twice as fast as the external SCSI chain. So if you have a larger, faster drive, consider an internal model. Aside from the more annoying installation process, you stand to save from $50 to $100 on the purchase, since the drive doesn't need a case.

> NOTE *The exception to this rule is a newer Mac to which you've added a SCSI card. Even the slowest SCSI card is SCSI-2 Fast (even the ones that cost about $50), which will get you as much speed as the faster internal SCSI chains of some of the older Macs.*

Making Sense of SCSI Jumper Settings

When you install a new internal SCSI hard drive, it's often on a wing and a prayer. Even when you ask your hard drive vendor to set it up for you, there's no guarantee it was done properly, so it's best to check.

Internal drives use jumpers (small plastic pieces with metallic lined holes in them) to set SCSI ID settings and termination. Unfortunately, not all drives are made equal and not all settings are clearly explained on the drive mechanism or on the documentation (if there is any), so you may find yourself installing a drive that's not properly configured for your Mac.

> NOTE *Older hard drive mechanisms set termination with a resister pack, a long, thin part that actually plugged into the drive. While removing the pack (usually two resistors with many pins) would turn off termination, the process often broke the delicate pins, so reinstalling was usually out of the question.*

Here is a bit of advice to get you set up properly. If your questions aren't answered here, I'd suggest you call the drive vendor or the manufacturer for specifics about their products. In addition, the Web sites for the major manufacturers, such as IBM (http://www.ibm.com), Quantum (http://www.quantum.com) and Seagate (http://www.seagate.com), provide illustrations on proper setup for a specific model drive.

SCSI Termination—Off or On?

If your internal drive replaces one that's already in your Mac, you'll want to make sure termination is left on. Look for a set of jumper pins with the label "TE" under them. Make sure that a jumper is placed over the two pins in this row to keep it on; remove the jumper to turn them off.

Internal vs. External—What's the Difference?

NOTE   *Jumpers are small enough that even those of you with small, nimble fingers might find them a challenge. I find that a small needle-nose pliers (available at any hardware store) is usually sufficient to handle the tiny things. Just don't apply too much pressure or they may break.*

Typical Jumper Settings for SCSI ID

Once you've taken care of termination, there's another thing to check, and that's SCSI ID. If the drive is to replace your internal drive, you'll want to keep SCSI ID 0. If not, you'll need a jumper to change the setting.

Setting SCSI ID is simple. Where a pin is supposed to be on, you just place the jumper between the top and bottom pins. Where it's off, you put no jumper in that position.

Table 15-1 shows typical SCSI ID settings for a typical internal drive (based on a popular line of Quantum mechanisms, the Atlas II). I have included the settings for SCSI IDs 8 through 15, for SCSI Wide and faster mechanisms, which have the additional capability when used with a corresponding high-speed SCSI card.

Drive ID	Pin A0	Pin A1	Pin A2	Pin A3
ID 0	OFF	OFF	OFF	OFF
ID 1	ON	OFF	OFF	OFF
ID 2	OFF	ON	OFF	OFF
ID 3	ON	ON	OFF	OFF
ID 4	OFF	OFF	ON	OFF
ID 5	ON	OFF	ON	OFF
ID 6	OFF	ON	ON	OFF
ID 7	ON	ON	ON	OFF
ID 8	OFF	OFF	OFF	ON
ID 9	ON	OFF	OFF	ON
ID 10	OFF	ON	OFF	ON
ID 11	ON	ON	OFF	ON
ID 12	OFF	OFF	ON	ON
ID 13	ON	OFF	ON	ON
ID 14	OFF	ON	ON	ON
ID 15	ON	ON	ON	ON

TABLE 15-1   SCSI ID Jumper Settings

NOTE

*Don't have enough jumpers? Call your dealer or the manufacturer. If you
have extras, put them in an envelope and store them in a safe, easy-to-
remember place. Or just install them on any two bottom or top halves of
an unused set of pins. So long as the top and bottom aren't "linked," they
won't affect the drive's performance.*

How Do I Determine the Kind of Drive Mechanism That's Installed?

If your drive is already in a case, or it's installed in your Mac, it won't be clear
what make and model are being used. Even the model Mac you have isn't a
determining factor, as Apple will shop for drives from several vendors, and
use any that meet their basic capacity and performance specifications.

Here's a quick (and free) way to check out what hard drive you have: visit
Adaptec's Web site (http://www.adaptec.com) and check their Macintosh
download area for a copy of their version of SCSI Probe.

SCSI Probe is used to look at your Mac's SCSI chain and see which devices
are on it, as you'll see in Figure 15-1. The SCSI Buses pop-up menu at the top can

Internal vs. External—What's
the Difference?

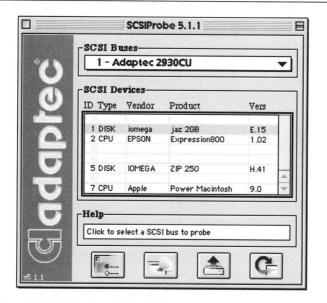

FIGURE 15-1   This is one of the SCSI chains on the author's Power Mac G3

be used to check on devices installed on a particular SCSI bus, if your Mac has more than one.

The Safe Way to Install a New Internal Drive

Once you've got the SCSI termination and ID settings configured, here's what to do next:

1. If you're installing a removable drive or other mechanism that requires a special driver, install the software before you install the drive.

2. Power down your Mac and all attached SCSI devices.

3. Remove the case, following the instructions in your manual (most recent Macs have information about adding internal drives).

CAUTION *If you don't have instructions and your Mac's innards seem too intimidating, don't be afraid to ask a dealer or local Mac user group to assist. There's no sense struggling and possibly breaking delicate cables if the process seems unclear to you.*

4. Touch the power supply or use a wrist strap to ground yourself.

5. Install your mechanism in a free drive bay, as appropriate. I won't detail the steps here, as they vary from model to model. Your owner's manual should explain how this is done. If you cannot locate the instructions, check with your dealer or visit Apple's Tech Info Library Web site (http://til.info.apple.com) and do a search for your specific type of Mac.

NOTE *Make sure you have the proper bracket assembly (if one is needed) before you attempt to install a new drive.*

6. Look for a free plug on your Mac's internal SCSI cable. Be prepared to manipulate and push and pull the cables to get them in position. There are too many models (counting Apple products and Mac OS clones) to detail the procedure or the best way to make it function. The key here is that you make sure you are not tearing the ribbon cable (it's delicate) and that you are not bending it sharply.

7. Plug the power cable (the smaller, white one) into the drive.

8. Once installation is complete, close up your Mac, restore all cables, and boot your Mac. If your new drive isn't recognized (a hard drive icon should appear on your Mac's desktop), power down and recheck the mechanism and the installation. It is possible the drive simply was never formatted (see the next section), but if you still cannot get it to work properly after trying to format the drive, don't hesitate to contact your dealer or the manufacturer for assistance.

Not Formatted?

It's a sad fact that some vendors sell hard drives for Macs without formatting them first, and sometimes they'll charge you extra for the software. Before you buy a new drive, ask the manufacturer or vendor to make sure the drive is already formatted for your Mac before you attempt to install it. Insist that they give you formatting software (even if it's an extra cost item) in case you have to reformat the drive later on down the road.

On some occasions, you can use Apple's Drive Setup to prepare (format) your drive, but with a mechanism without an Apple label this is not guaranteed.

The Safe Way to Install a New External Drive

The nice thing about an external drive is that you don't have to worry about little jumpers to set, nor do you have to play around with delicate ribbon cables.

1. If you're installing a removable drive or other mechanism that requires a special driver, install the software before you install the drive.

2. Power down your Mac and all attached SCSI devices.

3. Check the instructions that came with the drive for information on setting proper SCSI ID numbers and termination. I won't try to discuss the various combinations of pushbuttons, dipswitches, and other controls here.

4. Install the proper cables from your Mac or other SCSI device to the new drive.

NOTE *To make matters doubly confusing, some manufacturers don't take into account that a new device may not be the only one on the SCSI chain, so they'll give you a set of cables with the assumption it'll hook directly to your Mac. Be prepared to have to purchase additional cables if the product doesn't have what you need.*

Internal vs. External—What's the Difference?

5. Power on the SCSI devices, then boot your Mac.

6. Check the operation of your new device. If it's a regular hard drive, its icon should appear on your Mac's desktop. If your new device isn't recognized, power down and recheck your installation. Follow the SCSI chain configuration suggestions I made in this chapter, and if that doesn't work, contact the dealer or manufacturer for assistance.

Adding a SCSI Accelerator Card

When Apple offered Macs with built-in SCSI ports, the question of adding a SCSI expansion card was moot for most users. You didn't need one unless you needed the largest, fastest hard drives for graphics and video production.

But the newest Power Macs don't include SCSI as standard equipment. So if you intend to add a SCSI device, you are forced to go shopping for an expansion card.

Fortunately, you can buy a basic SCSI-2 card for as little as $50 from most Mac dealers. Manufacturers of such products include Adaptec, AdvanSys, ATTO, Formac, Indeo, and Orange Micro. It's an inconvenience, but one you can deal with. Besides, you may be able to find better solutions using another high-speed peripheral bus, FireWire, and be rid of SCSI hassles forever.

Single Channel vs. Dual-Channel

Why choose one over the other?

If you have slower SCSI devices, the SCSI chain will slow down accordingly, even if faster drives are connected. If you want to use both fast and slow devices and not have to buy two cards, consider a dual-channel version. It's akin to having a two-in-one card. You can put your slower SCSI devices on one channel, the faster ones on the other, and get the maximum level of performance from each.

SCSI Speeds Compared

Before you select a SCSI card, you'll want to see what sorts of drives you want to use. That is the key to the type of product you'll want to select. You wouldn't want to get something that isn't suitable for your application, and then have to buy another card later on.

NOTE
I won't describe installation of a SCSI card here. Your Mac's manual will have instructions about installing internal cards (if there are slots for them).

Here's a brief list of five popular SCSI protocols and their potential (a potential that isn't always realized, of course):

NOTE
It really doesn't make a lot of sense to buy a high-speed SCSI card with low-speed devices; they won't run any faster. You should choose the card based on the drives you have or the ones you intend to buy.

■ **SCSI-1 or SCSI-2** All Macs with external SCSI ports (and most Macs with internal ones) support this protocol, which offers a maximum data transfer speed of 5MB per second. This is just fine for smaller drives, scanners, CD drives, and many removable devices, including SyQuest and Zip drives.

■ **SCSI-2 Fast** The internal SCSI bus on so-called "PCI" Macs, including the 7500, 8500, 9500, 8600 and 9600 (the "beige" G3s are an exception), sport this faster SCSI capability. So do some of the now-departed Mac OS clones from Power Computing and Umax. Maximum speed is 10MB per second. This is good enough for larger hard drives and Iomega Jaz drives. The cheapest SCSI cards offer this capability.

■ **Fast/Wide SCSI-2** The performance level doubles, to 20MB per second. For larger, speedier hard drives, you'll want a SCSI card that provides at least this level of performance.

■ **Ultra SCSI** With a maximum potential of 40MB per second, there are few SCSI drives that'll exceed its capabilities. For anything but the most demanding tasks, this is the card of choice.

■ **Ultra-2 SCSI** This level of performance, up to 80MB per second, is recommended for desktop video and large graphic files. You'll also want to use an Ultra-2 SCSI card for RAID drives.

Adding a SCSI Accelerator Card

NOTE   *RAID (short for redundant array of inexpensive disks) lets you use two or more mechanisms to act as one, which helps speed up hard drive speeds noticeably. Among several RAID protocols, there's also one for "mirroring," which simply means that files are written to two drives at the same time. If one fails, you always have an identical backup.*

A Quick Guide to SCSI Chain Problems

The biggest problem with SCSI chains, aside from the need to be a little careful about setup, is that the symptoms of a SCSI chain problem aren't always obvious. Quite often, they'll masquerade as a system extension conflict or a problem with your system software, so you end up having to spend extra time doing a suitable diagnostic routine.

To begin with, for any system crash problems, I suggest you check over the steps I describe in Chapter 18. If they don't help, perhaps these symptoms and solutions will help you arrive at an answer.

Finder 41 Crash

This specific error is defined as the inability to load the Finder. But there is something important happening when the Finder is loading that may provide a clue to what's going on. Your hard drive directories are mounting, and if there is a problem with your SCSI chain, here's where you might experience a crash. There are several possible solutions:

- ■ Check your SCSI chain, following the steps described earlier in this chapter, to make sure the setup is done properly.

- ■ Make sure all attached SCSI devices have been turned on. If you find a device switched off, turn it on and restart. See if the problem repeats itself.

- ■ If you have an older hard drive mechanism and current Mac OS system software, be sure to update the hard drive with a recent hard disk formatter. This process rewrites the driver, which is the little piece of software on a drive that communicates with your Mac. You can't see the driver, but if the driver is damaged or out of date, the drive won't work properly.

NOTE   *The newest versions of Apple's Drive Setup will support many recent hard drive makes and models. But if you have a drive that doesn't have an Apple label or that didn't ship with an Apple product, you may need a third-party formatting program, such as CharisMac's Anubis, FWB's Hard Disk ToolKit or LaCie's Silverlining (also available as Silverlining Pro).*

Mac Freezes When Copying Large Files

This is a classic symptom of a SCSI chain problem. I suggest you refer to the SCSI voodoo steps described earlier in this chapter to address this problem. A bad hard drive mechanism can also cause this symptom, but that requires a call to a dealer or manufacturer for additional help.

Mac Freezes with Gray Screen When You Boot Your Mac

This is another prime example of a SCSI problem or a hard drive issue. Follow these suggestions, not necessarily in order, to help deal with this problem.

■ Power down the Mac and all attached devices.

■ If the drive is internal, disconnect the SCSI cable from your Mac and power up again. If the drive is external, follow the suggestions under the SCSI voodoo section to diagnose the problem.

■ If you have an internal drive, and the other steps don't work, it could be your drive has a bad partition map, which is used by a SCSI driver and your Mac to find the location of drive partitions. If (and only if) you have a second internal drive or an external drive with which to boot your Mac, there's a way to deal with this (at least sometimes). But you need to handle this carefully. Don't be afraid to seek outside help if you have any qualms about any of this:

1. Power down and open your Mac's case.

2. Locate the SCSI cable attached to the offending device and remove it. Leave the power cable inserted.

3. Boot your Mac. It should start up normally.

4. Being careful not to touch any metal parts inside your Mac (I said you had to be cautious about this), quickly push the SCSI cable into the drive's jack. This may get the drive to mount.

5. Locate your hard drive software (such as Apple's Drive Setup or whatever non-Apple program you used), and launch it.

6. Use the "update" function to update the hard drive with the problem.

7. Reboot your Mac. If it works, power down and close the case.

8. If you have a successful result, go ahead and check the offending drive with Apple's Disk First Aid, Alsoft's Disk Warrior, or Norton Utilities for possible directory damage.

9. Even if the drive checks out all right, consider backing up your data and reformatting the drive at the earliest opportunity.

10. If these steps don't help you solve the problem, consider replacing the internal SCSI ribbon cable. A bad cable can also produce similar symptoms.

The End of SCSI?

Until recently, all Apple computers had standardized on SCSI for both internal and external hard drives and other peripherals. But that began to change with the advent of Apple's Performa series, when Apple decided to move to a lower cost peripheral bus, ATA (short for AT Attachment), for internal drives and CD drives. The advantage is that such hard drives are cheaper to buy, and hence Apple lowered the cost of their Macs as well, the better to compete with the rapidly dropping costs of Windows-based computers.

From this humble beginning, the presence of ATA drives on Macs spread rapidly. Soon all PowerBooks had them, then regular desktop Macs as well (including the iMac) and, of course, the iBook.

What's ATAPI?

This variation on the ATA protocol stands for AT Attachment Packet Interface, and it's used to describe so-called non-hard-disk products, such as removable drives. These include such items as a CD-ROM drive, DVD-ROM drive, Iomega Jaz and Zip drives, and similar products.

Master and Slave

Unlike SCSI, you cannot daisy-chain a number of devices. If your Mac supports the feature, you can, however, install a second ATA device in what is called "slave" mode.

If the hard drive's ATA bus doesn't have "slave" support (and this covers pretty much all Macs prior to the Blue & White G3 series), you may find it on your CD drive's ATA bus. A quick look at your Mac's manual will explain how to add extra drives.

CAUTION

If you don't see an extra set of cable and connectors, there may be no obvious evidence to show whether or not your Mac can support ATA "slave" mode. If it's not mentioned in your manual, contact Apple or consult their technical information library (http://til.info.apple.com) for the details. A savvy drive vendor may also have the answers for you.

Once you've determined whether you can install a "slave" drive, the process is not much different from installing an internal SCSI drive. First you need to check if you need a special bracket for the drive and a special faceplate.

Then just follow these steps:

1. If your Mac doesn't have one, get an ATA ribbon cable from your dealer.

2. If your "slave" device requires a special driver to be installed (which is usually the case with a removable drive), run the installation now (so you don't have to be faced with the prospect of the drive not working later).

NOTE

Apple's latest system software includes drivers for Iomega Jaz and Zip drives, but don't expect to find drivers for any other removable device (such as an Orb or SyQuest) drive in your System Folder unless you install the files separately).

3. After installation, shut down your Mac.

4. Open your Mac following the instructions provided in your manual. Be sure to ground yourself to the power supply (or use a wrist strap, if available) before you poke around in there.

5. Check your second drive to make sure it has the proper jumper setting to enable "slave" mode. On an Iomega Zip drive, the jumper block has to be removed. Since this setting may vary from product to product, the best resource is the manufacturer or your dealer.

6. Install your second drive in an available drive bay. I won't detail the steps here, as they vary from model to model. Your owner's manual should explain how this is done. If you cannot locate the instructions, check with your dealer or visit Apple's Tech Info Library Web site and do a search for your specific type of Mac.

7. Plug in the cable at your "master" drive (if it doesn't already have it there) and run it to the "slave" drive. You may have to fiddle and move and duck

The End of SCSI?

and bob and weave around metal fittings to get this to work. There are too many models (counting Apple products and Mac OS clones) to detail the procedure or the best way to make it function. The key is to make sure you are not tearing the ribbon cable (it's delicate) and that you are not bending it sharply.

8. Once installation is complete, close up your Mac, restore all cables and boot your Mac. Your "slave" drive should be recognized.

Doesn't Work?

If the new drive or removable isn't recognized, make sure that any needed drivers are installed. If they are, shut down, open the Mac, and recheck your installation. If you still have problems, contact Apple or the drive's manufacturer.

FireWire: The End of SCSI Hassles?

Sometimes it's known by its official name, IEEE 1394, and sometimes (if you have a Sony product) i.LINK. But the original name is FireWire, and it's an Apple technology that promises to rid the computing universe of SCSI hassles forever.

What's more, FireWire is rapidly spreading across Apple's product line, and more and more FireWire products are coming to market.

The first thing you'll notice with a FireWire peripheral is that there's no SCSI ID number to be set, no jumpers or dipswitches to push and pull. Nowhere, no how. And there's no worry about termination, because a FireWire bus doesn't have to be terminated.

What's more, it's hot-pluggable, which simply means that you can connect or disconnect any FireWire peripheral, be it a CD, camcorder, hard drive, printer, scanner, or whatever without having to turn anything off. If it's a drive, you just have to remember to eject the drive icon from your desktop before you disconnect the device.

Yes, it's true plug-and-play. You finish using your FireWire device, and you unplug it and take it over to another Mac user. Or even a PC user, if they have a computer with a FireWire connection and reformat the drive to the PC disk format.

With a smaller drive, you can even use the FireWire port for power, so you don't even have to worry about finding a convenient AC outlet.

What's more you can daisy-chain up to 63 devices and use cable lengths of up to 14 feet. There are a few considerations, such as the need for a FireWire repeater hub on a large chain, but compared to SCSI, it's a revelation.

The first time I used a FireWire hard drive I made sure I tested it in the worst way possible. It was a big 14GB device from MacTell (a company that, sad to say, went out of business in late 1999), part of their FirePower product line. I simply plugged it in to my power strip, then deliberately powered up the drive. Then I connected a cable from the drive to a Power Mac G3 with FireWire port (after installing a driver for the drive of course). Within seconds, the drive's icon was on my Mac's desktop. Then I dismounted the drive icon, disconnected the drive, and installed it on another Mac with the same result.

Working with one of VST Technology's FireWire drives was also enlightening. Their lower capacity models don't need AC power; they draw the current from the FireWire port. You can learn about VST's product line at http://www.vsttech.com.

FireWire Limitations?

Though it stands head and shoulders above SCSI in convenience and ease of setup, I don't mean to tell you that FireWire is perfect. For example, the first Apple computers to ship with FireWire ports couldn't boot from the drives. So one of the advantages of an extra drive is lost till Apple has a chance to remedy this situation (it'll require a boot ROM update and a driver update, both of which may be shipping by the time you read this book).

In addition, despite the high performance capabilities of FireWire, many of the early drives barely match SCSI speeds. This is also a short-term phenomenon, being addressed by speedier device driver software and improvements to drive technology. But one thing is sure: the arrival of FireWire promises freedom from SCSI chain hassles. And that means one less book chapter to write.

NOTE
If you want to learn more about FireWire technology, visit the Apple Web site devoted to the subject at http://www.apple.com/firewire.

The End of SCSI?

Chapter 16

Making Your New Scanner Work Better

A scanner is, in effect, your Mac's eyes to see the outside world. You use it to digitize artwork and text documents so you can edit them on your computer or send them for someone else to see.

In the not-so-distant past, a scanner was an expensive luxury. Any decent model would retail at well over a grand. By the time you added an option or two, such as an automatic document feeder (for multipage documents) and a slide adapter, for example, you were approaching the two grand level. But, as with computers, the pricing has gone down a lot.

Today, you can buy some very nice scanners for not much more than $100, although the dollars add up if you want to get that slide attachment or an automatic document feeder (if they're available). Either option can fully double or triple the original cost of the product.

NOTE   *An automatic document feeder is similar to the paper bay on a printer, because it lets you scan more than one document at a time. This is quite useful if you intend to use your scanner to convert printed documents to text (OCR). I'll cover the subject of OCR in more detail later in this chapter.*

At the same time, professional-grade scanners, the ones beginning at around $1,000 or so, provide features and image capturing capabilities that approach those of scanners costing many times that figure just a few years ago.

In fact, many graphic artists manage to do some very professional work on scanners that would be quite affordable to any consumer.

The Right Way to Install a Scanner

Although scanning speed, quality, and some features may differ, scanners are usually more alike than different, so you can often follow a basic set of installation instructions to cover most models.

1. Shut down your Mac and all peripherals (this isn't critical if you have a USB scanner).

2. Unpack the scanner and remove packing materials.

3. Check the directions for unlocking the scanner's optical assembly (this is important!). The process is discussed later in this chapter.

4. If you have a SCSI scanner, verify the ID and termination settings, and configure as required. SCSI ID adjustments on a scanner may be done by pushbuttons or a little wheel that you turn with a small screwdriver (a very small screwdriver, sometimes). For more information about SCSI chain issues, see Chapter 15.

5. Attach all cables and make sure they are firmly seated.

6. Turn on the scanner and other peripherals, and make sure the scanner's "ready" light is on. If it isn't, check the section entitled "What If the Scanner Freezes?" for advice on how to cope with the situation.

7. If your scanner works all right, boot your Mac.

8. Once the startup process is complete, install your scanning software (this will generally require a restart to get it running).

9. Once your scanning software is installed, perform a few test scans on photos or printed artwork and make sure everything works as you want. If you are not satisfied with the results of your scans, consult the section entitled "Quick Routes to Better Quality Scans" for further advice.

Checking SCSI Settings and Hardware Locking Switches

The theory goes that you can place a SCSI device anywhere on the SCSI chain and as long as you make sure there are no ID conflicts, all devices are switched on, and the last physical device is properly terminated, everything should work as advertised. However, scanners tend to be rather more sensitive to SCSI chain positioning than some other products.

Before you try out your scanner, you might want to look at the manufacturer's setup instructions to see if they recommend any particular placement. For example, several Epson scanners I checked before writing this chapter were configured for SCSI ID 2. The documentation only suggested this setting as a precaution, because ID 0 is commonly used for an internal SCSI drive and ID 1 for a second internal drive.

But I have also seen documentation for Microtek scanners suggesting placement at the beginning of the external SCSI chain, and some users report best results if a scanner is located at the very end of the chain.

If the manufacturer doesn't give you guidance, follow the usual guidelines, and check out Chapter 15 for more suggestions on configuring a SCSI chain.

CAUTION *If you have a Mac with both an internal and external SCSI bus, such as the 8500, 9500, and similar models, in theory you should be able to install both internal and external devices with the same SCSI ID number. But when it comes to scanners, this doesn't always work, so if you run into problems, check to be sure no other device (even on another SCSI chain) has the same ID number.*

A Warning About Hardware Locking Switches

There's one thing the cheapest and the most expensive scanners have in common. They both contain delicate optical mechanisms that can be damaged if allowed to slide back and forth during shipment. As a result, manufacturers install a special locking switch or screw of some sort to tighten the optical mechanism down.

If you try to use your scanner without unlocking the optical components first, you risk damaging the unit, not to mention the system freeze that may happen when the scanner locks up.

So before you try out that new scanner, look over the installation instructions as to where the locking assembly is located. I have seen them underneath a scanner, at the rear, or beneath the cover. Whether or not the documentation is clear, such a mechanism will usually have a Lock and Unlock label on it, or little icons that represent the locked or unlocked position.

If you receive a new scanner that hasn't been locked in this fashion, you should contact the manufacturer or dealer right away and arrange for a replacement. If the scanner had a smooth trip to your office, it may work just fine. I had just such a situation with a new high-cost scanner I had received as a review sample for my "Mac Reality Check" column (see http://www.azcentral.com/computing for the latest edition). Despite being shipped unlocked, the scanner worked just fine, and continued to function like a champ throughout the review process (where I subjected it to a lot more abuse than most users might under similar situations).

But the manufacturer said I was lucky. They were apologetic and assured me they would have replaced the unit on the spot if necessary.

What If the Scanner Freezes?

Scanners are complex devices and work by a clever interaction between hardware and software. Among these variations, there is plenty of room for conflicts, and scanners often generate quite a few support telephone calls as a result.

There are several areas where your scanner may suddenly stop working or cause your Mac to freeze up. One is due to the regular range of SCSI chain problems, such as improper termination and SCSI ID conflicts, but that's not the only source of trouble.

Here are a few other issues that might make your scanning experience less than pleasant. I'm dividing them into SCSI and USB categories, although some of the solutions may overlap.

SCSI Scanner Problems and Solutions

If you run into one of the situations, use the following to help you out:

- **Scanner freezes when you activate software.**   This may be a SCSI chain problem. As soon as the software driver communicates with the scanner, if there's a problem in your SCSI setup, that's where the freeze may occur. But don't overlook the software. Scanning software is frequently updated by manufacturers to address conflicts with new system versions, offer improved features, or just fix bugs. A quick check at the publisher's Web site or the VersionTracker Web site (at http://www.versiontracker.com) can bring forth this information.

- **Scanner freezes during its startup process.**   When you turn on a scanner, it goes through a little self-diagnostic process. If your scanner appears to seize, and an error light or flickering light shows, it may indicate one of two things. You may have a problem on the Mac's SCSI chain that's preventing the scanner from operating (consult Chapter 15 for more information), or the scanner itself may not be working properly. As a test, power down, remove everything from the SCSI chain but the scanner, and make sure it's terminated. Then turn it on. If it still fails to run, contact the dealer or manufacturer to arrange for service.

NOTE   *You may also want to verify that the scanner's optical assembly was properly unlocked when you first set it up. Turn off your system and unplug the scanner before you check this out.*

USB Scanner Problems and Solutions

The perennial problems that afflict scanners on a SCSI chain are pretty much gone if you get one of these scanners, since the USB ports are free of ID and termination conflicts. You can even hot plug your scanner if you so choose (just remember to install your scanning software first).

What If the Scanner Freezes?

Case History

Getting SCSI Scanners to Work on SCSI-less Macs

When Apple ditched standard SCSI on Macs, they left a whole lot of products without something to connect to. In addition to external hard drives and removable devices, and even some special printers used in the publishing industry, millions of scanners no longer had a place to plug into.

One of my clients, a busy graphic studio, relied heavily on the office scanner, a mid-priced Umax, to capture photos for various brochures and package labels.

The promise of new, ultra-fast Macs finally got the better of him and he ordered his first new Mac in a couple of years, one of the Blue & White Power Mac G3 models. He also selected a SCSI card from a mail order catalog, and within a few days his new computer arrived at his office.

The installation went just fine until I hooked up the scanner. The SCSI chain was fine with just an attached Iomega Zip drive and SyQuest SyJet. But as soon as the scanner was hooked into the chain, SCSI voodoo reared its ugly head. The client used the very same cabling and SCSI settings as he did with his previous computer. The cables were short and had been recently purchased. They were top quality cables, from one of the large manufacturers.

As soon as the scanner was activated to capture a photo, the computer froze.

The large number of system extensions were reduced to just the Apple software plus the scanner extensions, with no improvement. The usual range of system diagnosis didn't change the situation (see Chapter 18 for more information on checking for system-related conflicts).

A quick visit to the Umax Web site revealed a somewhat later version. We downloaded and installed the new version, but it didn't help.

On the next restart, I went to the SCSI card manufacturer's Web site and found a newer firmware update. The update modified the card's flash ROM with code that was supposed to make it more compatible with the new generation Macs.

Sure enough, after the ROM update, my client restarted his Mac and, with crossed fingers, proceeded to scan a photo as a test. The scanner worked like a charm.

However, there are some potential pitfalls you'll want to consider with such a scanner:

■ **USB is much slower than SCSI.**   While the bandwidth requirement of a scanner isn't as much as a big, fast hard drive, you should expect it to take longer to capture artwork, particularly a large color picture. If you have one of the new "slot loading" iMacs or the Power Mac G4, you can benefit from their twin USB buses (only a single USB bus is available via the two USB ports on the older iMacs and Blue & White Power Mac G3). Just plug the scanner into one USB port, and the other devices into the other USB port to get the best possible performance. However, if optimum speed is paramount, and you have a Mac with a SCSI port or a SCSI card, consider getting a SCSI scanner, or consider a FireWire scanner if your Mac or iMac has FireWire ports.

NOTE   *FireWire capability can be added to any Mac with PCI slots, so even if your model came without this feature, you can buy an expansion card to add this capability. I cover the subject of adding expansion cards to your Mac in Chapter 3.*

■ **Scanning drivers are susceptible to conflicts.**   As with SCSI scanners, there are apt to be occasional conflicts with the software. As Apple continues to update its system software, you'll want to keep tabs on the manufacturer's Web site (or VersionTracker) for news of new versions that may address the specific problems you encounter.

■ **Scanner is not recognized.**   Check the usual steps, making sure the unit is plugged in and turned on. If you've connected the scanner to a USB hub, you may want to check with the hub's manufacturer about a revised version. For example, some older Macally USB hubs do not open their USB ports until after your Mac has begun the startup process. As a result, they may have trouble recognizing some devices for which software was loaded early in the Mac's startup process. Should you encounter a problem of this sort, contact your dealer or the manufacturer about replacing the hub.

What If the Scanner Freezes?

How to Do That First Scan with Confidence

Most lower-cost scanners are designed with software that's supposed to be user-friendly. While many people use scanners for work, scanners are also popular simply for capturing family photos and making digitized copies to email to family or friends.

In the past, the manuals that came with a scanner were much like the ones that came with your Mac: big and impressive, well-illustrated with plenty of tips and tricks to get you going, even if you're not a professional computer artist.

With low-cost scanners, printed manuals are strictly bare bones. You get some basic setup instructions and maybe a few pages about capturing an image, but that's about all. The rest of the documentation usually lies on the software CD, in electronic form. Not having to print a large book saves plenty in production costs.

Before you go through the process of learning the intricacies of the software, however, you'll want to get a good basic scan of a color photograph, just as a starting point.

The best way to get started is simply to let the scanning software do its job. Check for an Auto or automatic exposure mode. That way the scanning software will act in the same fashion as the automatic adjustments available on your camera or camcorder. While it may not be perfect for all types of artwork, such a setting ought to be enough to give you an idea how the scanner performs.

Just follow these steps:

1. Open your scanning software. If you're using Photoshop, there will be an Import or Acquire function you'll use to launch your scanning software. PhotoDeluxe has a Scanner option that you use for the same purpose.

2. Once the scanning software launches and appears on the screen, click the Preview or Prescan mode (or whatever it's labeled) to capture the image. When you activate this feature, the scanner's optical assembly will begin to travel across the length of the scanner, digitizing your artwork. Depending on the speed of the scanner, within a short time you'll see a preview of the image you captured on the left or right of your scanning software's control palettes (see Figure 16-1).

NOTE   *Some scanner assemblies work in the opposite fashion. Rather than moving the optical assembly, the paper is transported across stationary optics. One example of this sort of product is the multifunction printer, which offers copying, faxing (not all models include this feature), printing, and scanning all in one unit.*

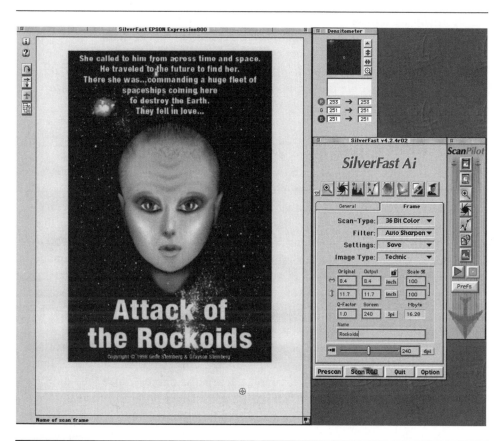

FIGURE 16-1   This image was scanned on an Epson scanner, using LaserSoft's SilverFast Professional software

3. From here, your scanning software will have several options to touch up the photo, but for the purpose of this test, locate the automatic exposure mode (it may not be obvious). With SilverFast Professional, the program illustrated here, the automatic exposure button is the fourth icon from the top on the ScanPilot palette.

4. When you're satisfied with whatever adjustments you've made, or you've selected the automatic mode, go ahead and click the Scan button (it's Scan RGB for the software shown in this chapter).

5. Within a short time (depending on the size of the image), you'll see the scanned photo appear in a document window in your photo editing software.

How to Do That First Scan with Confidence

6. If you want to save the file, do it now. Or just discard it and try another photo or piece of artwork in order to get used to the program.

NOTE *Some scanning software includes a direct save option, where you can save your image within the scanning software rather than with your photo editing program.*

Quick Routes to Better Quality Scans

Once you have put your scanner through its paces, and had a little time to get used to the software, you'll want to begin to take advantage of your scanner's features.

You may find, unfortunately, that the scans you've made aren't satisfactory. You try to print them, or just view them on the screen and they're blurry, or the color is off, way off. Each scanning program has a set of adjustments you can use to fine-tune your image. If the scanning program is bare bones, the actual image editing software (be it Photoshop, PhotoDeluxe, or something else) can do the task.

There are a few things to consider as you learn the route to top-quality scans:

- **Crop your image.** For several years, I ran an area on AOL called The Gallery, where members posted photos of themselves. You'd be surprised how many files came in showing a small picture surrounded by the huge scanner bed. Of course, we couldn't accept the photos, since they didn't meet the size requirements we set up. All scanner programs have a cropping tool of some sort, usually an adjustable rectangle that you move back and forth to cover just the part of the artwork you want to capture.

- **Watch your target resolution.** It's normal to scan at roughly twice the resolution (measured in dots per inch) that you actually need. That leaves enough room for quality loss due to editing the artwork or if you want to enlarge it somewhat. For example, if you're scanning a photo to view on your Mac, use 72 dots per inch as your guidepost, then scan at twice that, 144 dots per inch (or the closest option available in the scanning software). If you plan to print photos at a typical resolution of 120 lines per inch, scan at 240 dpi. If you scan at too high a resolution, file size goes up tremendously, and all you'll end up doing is using excess storage space on your hard drive unnecessarily.

NOTE *The file size also affects the memory required by your image editing software. The bigger the file, the more likely the software will have to swap file data from your hard drive, thus slowing up performance.*

■ **Try the automatic mode first.**   The scanner software will attempt to color-correct the original artwork. But if the preview image doesn't look right, try the scanner's color adjustments to see if you can bring it in more accurately. If the adjustments don't seem to help, go back to automatic mode, and do a final scan. Then try to adjust the image with your photo editing software. Don't forget that the color quality you see on the screen may not quite match the quality of the color in your printout. In Chapter 10, I cover the subject of using Apple's ColorSync to calibrate your monitor. Many scanners also come with color profiles and software that help you get more accurate color reproduction.

■ **Save in the correct file format.**   If you're scanning artwork for printing, the usual format is TIFF, which provides maximum image quality. If it's for your Web site or to exchange with family and friends, choose GIF or JPEG instead. If you're transferring files to Windows users, you'll also want to read Chapters 7 and 11 for information on how to live in harmony with that other computing platform.

■ **Don't make it too large.**   Scan at a higher resolution if you want to make the image very large. An example is a slide. If you need to enlarge the picture 8 or 10 times or more, you'll want to increase scanning resolution proportionately, so the quality is retained. Otherwise, the little dots that make up bitmap artwork will just get very large too, and quality will suffer.

OCR Trials and Tribulations

Back in the 1970s, when you wanted to convert a document to text for editing on a typesetting system, you either had to go through the tedious process of retyping everything or have it sent to a firm who handled optical character recognition (OCR).

OCR is a technology that uses various forms of computer logic to recognize and convert printed text to a file you can edit. In those days, equipment that performed this task was very expensive, far beyond the budget of the average user.

Today, the technology has advanced to the point where many scanner makers give you OCR software as part of the package, for no extra cost. As stated in the section in this chapter entitled "Stuck with Bundled Software?" you can buy an OCR package if your scanner didn't come with one or you don't like the accuracy level of the one you have.

One thing I'll say at the outset: no OCR program is letter-perfect. No matter how good the program or the source document, you will almost always have to go

How to Do That First Scan with Confidence

back and fix something in the translated file. Worse, such errors are unpredictable, not the typical ones a human typist will make. So it may take spell checking or proofreading to find the mistakes.

But here are some things you can do to get the maximum possible OCR accuracy:

■ **Use a clean document with large, readable type.**   Small type, unfamiliar or artistic typefaces, smudges, and pen and pencil marks will confound the OCR program and will make accurate recognition difficult. Material in 10 or 12 point type in a common typeface such as Helvetica or Times will be easiest to handle. If you must edit the text, try doing it on your Mac after you've recognized the material.

■ **Avoid faxed originals if possible.**   In the past, some fax software packages actually came with OCR components, but not anymore. The reason is that a fax provides poor text resolution. It may be fine for reading, but not so fine for OCR software to recognize accurately. If you must work with a fax, insist the person who sends you the material use the "fine" resolution mode where available. Also, large type and easy-to-read faces (such as Helvetica and Courier) tend to offer the best chance of accurate performance.

■ **Keep the scanner bed clean and orient the paper properly.**   Smudges on the glass or paper tilted one way or the other will also give the scanning software fits. Although such programs as Caere's OmniPage Professional are designed with techniques to straighten tilted copy, the results never seem to be quite as accurate.

■ **Watch out for thin paper or newsprint.**   If text is visible on the back of the document you're copying, the OCR software will capture that text too, resulting in gibberish. If you must use this sort of document, try backing it up with a few sheets of paper to make it more opaque. If your OCR software has a brightness control, turn it down slightly and see if you can get better quality; it may just work if the actual text you want to scan is clear and dark.

NOTE   *Some OCR programs simply launch your scanning software to capture the image, before they extract text from it. If you have this sort of program, the actual brightness setting will be made in the scanning software.*

■ **Dot matrix is a hassle.**   The small dots that make up the characters can also confuse the OCR's built-in logic. If the OCR program has a dot matrix option, try that (although in my experience it only does a little bit better that way). Another trick is to make a photocopy of the document, which will tend to smooth out the little dots and make recognition more accurate.

■ **Use the training feature.**   Some programs are trainable, which means you can flag common errors and save the corrected characters in a special preference or dictionary file. These files tend to have a limited capacity, but they can help you resolve the common mistakes and save wear and tear on your blood pressure.

■ **Try the OCR software's spell check feature.**   You can usually spell check your recognized document before you save it in its final format. This will help you flag many of the mistakes on the scanner's preview screen, and it may also help you adjust its training feature to recognize those mistakes (assuming the scanning software has a training mode).

Twain vs. Plug-In: Any Difference?

Scanner software comes in several forms. You may get a simple standalone application that you can launch just like any program and do your scanning chores. More often, though, the software comes as a plug-in (add-on) for an image editing program such as Adobe PhotoDeluxe or Adobe Photoshop. To activate the software, you'd need to use the Import or Acquire function.

Another type of scanner driver uses something called TWAIN, which, strangely enough, stands for Technology Without An Interesting Name. With a single TWAIN scanning driver, you should be able to work with any program that supports the technology, without having to install extra copies or get special versions for those programs.

In practice, there aren't a whole lot of programs that support TWAIN these days. Adobe's PhotoDeluxe and Photoshop recognize TWAIN drivers, but two of their other major programs, Illustrator and InDesign, do not, nor does another desktop publishing heavyweight, QuarkXPress.

In practice, this is not anything to be concerned over. Whether the scanning software comes as a program plug-in, a TWAIN driver, or both, if it works to your expectations, that is all you need be concerned about.

How to Do That First Scan
with Confidence

Stuck with Bundled Software?

Your new scanner comes with a CD filled with bundled software, beginning with the scanner drivers, and usually including an image editing program and possibly an OCR program. You could very well be perfectly happy with the programs you get.

But you are not forced to use those programs. For example, if you receive Adobe's entry-level image editing package, PhotoDeluxe, you can choose to install a much more powerful alternative, Photoshop, instead. Such OCR programs as Caere's OmniPage Professional and ScanSoft's TextBridge and TextBridge Professional work with most popular scanners.

As far as the basic scanning software is concerned, if you feel the one provided with your scanner is, well, a little too basic for you, perhaps you'd like to try something more powerful. You can consider such programs as LaserSoft Imaging's SilverFast (which is bundled with some Epson scanners) or Second Glance Software's ScanTastic (which is also used to make some HP scanners compatible with Macs).

Summing Up

Whether you just want to capture a family photo, or edit a complicated legal document, a scanner can be an almost indispensable option for your Macintosh. In this chapter, I gave you some tips and troubleshooting techniques to help you get your scanner and software to work at top efficiency.

In Chapter 17, you'll learn the secrets of getting the best possible networking performance from your Mac, from sharing files with a family member's iMac to sharing files with users of that other platform (a subject also covered in Chapter 11).

Chapter 17

Overcoming the Network Hassle

From the very first day the Mac was unleashed on the world, it was set up for networking. At first it was just with Macs and laser printers. You could share the office printer among all Macs. But the ability to print a file was only half the battle. What if you had to make a copy for another user on another Mac? In the old days, you just took out a floppy disk or media from a removable hard drive, and walked over to the other user. Sneaker net is good exercise, of course. Keeps you healthy if you get enough of it, but it's time consuming if you have to send and receive files on a regular basis from one or more coworkers.

That's where computer networks became important. In the days of System 6, you could either use Apple's AppleShare software and establish one computer as a central repository of files (a server), or use one or more unsupported programs that would make it possible for you to share files directly with other users. But the personal file sharing feature we take for granted today wasn't available.

File Sharing Basics

Throughout this chapter, I'll offer hints and tips to get the best possible network performance on your Mac. But first let's pause for a few basics on file sharing with a Mac.

The Fast Way to Share Files

If you just want to open up the contents of your drive to a family member or coworker without any limitations to access, here's what to do:

1. On the Mac from which you want to share files, click on the File Sharing Control Strip and choose Turn File Sharing On. A little sharing icon will flicker on the Control Strip, then stop flickering when it's activated. The first time, it may take a few minutes to get going, but after that, switching it on takes just seconds.

Case History

The Heady Days Before Personal File Sharing

My first taste of the ability to share files came before Apple released System 7 and introduced file sharing for the masses.

Back in the late 1980s, Michael R. Peirce, a programmer from Claris, created an unsupported free program that served as a worthy precursor to personal file sharing. It was called Public Folder. It allowed you to set aside a single folder on your hard drive as a drop box, into which you would place files that would become available across your network, and retrieve files sent to you from other computers.

> **NOTE** *Unsupported means what it says. It's available for use, but the author or publisher won't give you technical support if you have a problem.*

For a piece of free software, it worked just fine, except for a rare system crash during the file transfer process. It didn't do much for everyone's daily exercise program, but it was convenient—though, as with any LocalTalk file transfer, it wasn't the quickest way to get a large file from one place to another.

When System 7 arrived and Mac users began to update, Public Folder outlived its usefulness.

As for Peirce, he has moved on to a successful career as a private software developer. He first formed Peirce Software in 1989, but one of his most popular commercial products was probably Peirce Print Tools, a set of enhancements for QuickDraw GX. Although the product was orphaned, Peirce continues to develop shareware software, including DeskPicture, ShareDraw, Smoothie, and AppSizer.

Peirce, by the way, was also the original programmer of Apple's Trackpad Control Panel and did troubleshooting and bug fixing on the trackpad itself before it made its way into the PowerBook line.

File Sharing Basics

NOTE   *If you aren't using the Control Strip, go to the Apple menu, choose Control Panels, and select File Sharing from the submenu (or Sharing Setup, if it applies). Then click the Start button.*

2. Once sharing is activated, anyone on the network can access the contents of your drive (which is why you will want to consider specifying access privileges, as explained later). To access the shared Mac, open the Chooser and click on the AppleShare icon, which displays the name of the network Mac (see Figure 17-1).

NOTE   *Under Mac OS 9, you can access a shared Mac across the Internet simply by entering the Server IP Address that appears on that Mac's File Sharing Control Panel.*

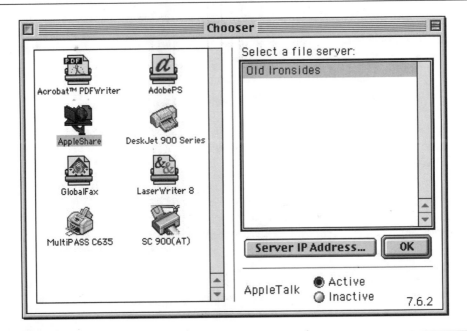

FIGURE 17-1   You can use the Chooser to log on to the Mac to which you want to connect

NOTE
If you use Thursby Systems, Inc.'s DAVE or Windows NT/2000 with Services for Macintosh installed, you can also access Windows-based computers in the same fashion.

3. Click the OK button to continue. If there's more than one networked Mac shown, select the one with which you want to share files.

4. On the Connect screen, enter the name and password established on the other Mac's File Sharing Control Panel, then click the Connect button (see Figure 17-2).

NOTE
If you are using Mac OS 9, you can use the Add to Keychain feature to store all your access passwords for automatic retrieval.

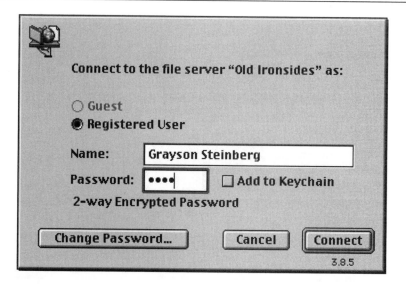

File Sharing Basics

FIGURE 17-2   You need to enter the correct information here to access the shared computer

5. On the next screen (see Figure 17-3), select the networked volume's name, then click OK to deliver that volume icon on your desktop:

Old Ironsides

> **NOTE**
>
> *If the other computer will be turned on before your Mac, and you want to always share files with it, click the check box at the right of the drive's name, so it's always opened after your Mac starts up.*

> **NOTE**
>
> *By shared volume, I'm referring to the items that are being shared. They are not necessarily entire drives. They may also be one or more folders or one partition of a drive. Turning on file sharing on a Mac without customizing access will, in essence, share whatever drives are connected to that Mac.*

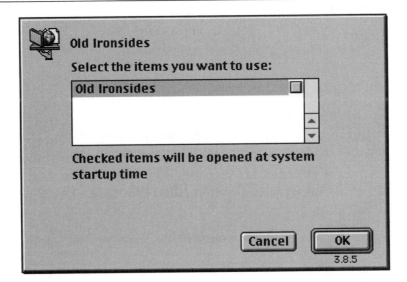

FIGURE 17-3   If the Mac you are accessing has more than one shared volume, they'll all appear on this list

6. When you want to turn off file sharing on the other Mac, click on the Control Strip again on that computer, then select Turn File Sharing Off (the selection toggles). You'll see a dialog in which you specify the interval before sharing is switched off. This gives other users accessing the shared Mac time to finish up before it leaves their desktops.

NOTE *If you do not have the Control Strip available, just bring up the File Sharing or Sharing Setup Control Panel, then click Stop to switch off file sharing.*

This technique is basically the easiest possible method to use file sharing. It makes the entire contents of the shared Mac available to anyone who logs in on the network.

Setting Users & Groups Privileges

If you need to limit the access of other users to a networked Mac, you need to set up access privileges. This will let you control which users can log on and which cannot.

The settings are made by opening the File Sharing Control Panel, and clicking on the Users & Groups tab (see Figure 17-4) under Mac OS 9. For older versions of the Mac OS, Users & Groups is a separate control panel, but the choices are the same.

You can add users individually or by group (if you want to grant similar access to more than a single person). Another feature of Users & Groups is Guests, which allows you to grant automatic access to a shared Mac without having to enter the correct name or password (but you can limit this access, as I'll explain next).

Granting Access Privileges to Shared Macs

Here's how you set privileges:

1. Activate file sharing using either the Control Strip or File Sharing Control Panel.

2. Select the folders or drives you want to share.

3. Go to the Finder's File menu, choose Get Info and then Sharing from the submenu. If you are using a version of the Mac OS prior to 8.5, there's a

File Sharing Basics

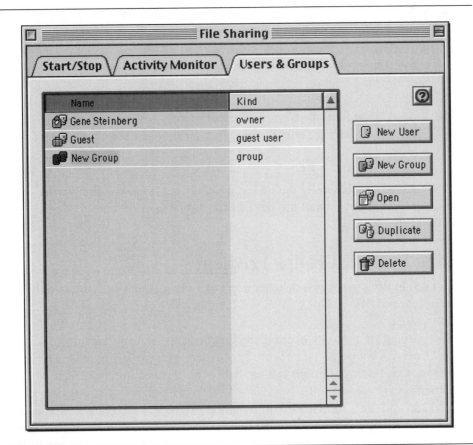

FIGURE 17-4 You can control access to your Mac from this screen

separate File menu command labeled Sharing. You'll see a separate Sharing Info window for each item you are sharing (see Figure 17-5).

4. If you want to prevent moving, renaming, or deleting the file, click the first check box.

5. Click the Share This Item And Its Contents option to specify specific privileges.

6. By default, the person listed as Owner will have the ability to read and write files (notice the corresponding icons under the Privilege column).

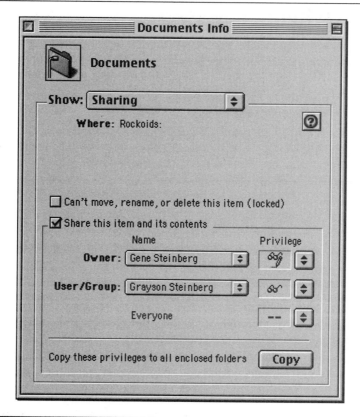

FIGURE 17-5   Grant sharing privileges on these screens

7. Click on the name of the User or Group you want to grant privileges to, and then select the Privilege from the pop-up menu. In the example shown in Figure 17-5, I've given this user read access only (meaning files cannot be changed).

8. Under the Everyone category, specify the access level you want. In this case, other users have no access to these files.

9. If you want to copy those privileges to folders within the folder or drive you select, click the Copy button. If there are lots of files and folders, it may take a while for this process to complete.

From here on, only those who are granted proper access rights can read or write the files on your shared Mac.

Networking Without a Network

You have an old Mac and a new one, and you want to transfer the files from the old computer to the new one. But the changes in Mac networking ports are confounding you. The old Mac has a LocalTalk port, which was standard on Macs for years. The new one has Ethernet. Worse, the new Macs are without floppy drives, so even that cumbersome method of copying files and taking them to the new computer can't be done, unless you go out and buy an extra drive. What to do?

You can buy a LocalTalk-to-Ethernet adapter, such as the AsanteTalk from Asante. It works very well—I've installed the product for many of my clients, and they are all pleased to be able to use their older networked devices with the new Macs.

NOTE　*Don't get the wrong impression. When you convert LocalTalk to Ethernet with one of these adapters, your printing and regular networking doesn't get any faster. You cannot bypass the speed limitations of LocalTalk this way. But it does allow you to mate the two technologies.*

But that solution may not make much sense if this is a one-time-only procedure. Why buy something you'll only be using once?

There is another solution if both computers have modems (all new Macs, except a few of the G3 and G4 models, have internal modems as standard equipment, and it's an option on the rest). You can literally have one computer call up the other, directly, without having to involve the phone company.

Oh yes, you do need a terminal program to make this connection. We'll use AppleWorks (or the older version, ClarisWorks) for this description. But if you have another program, such as Microphone Pro or ZTerm, it'll do the trick as well.

Here's how you do it:

1. Take a standard telephone cable and connect the two modems.

2. Launch AppleWorks (or ClarisWorks). If you don't get a new document dialog box on the screen, choose New from the File menu to bring it up (see Figure 17-6).

3. Select Communications, which brings up a blank document (see Figure 17-7).

4. Follow these steps on both Macs. Choose Connection Settings from the Settings menu, which brings up the screen shown in Figure 17-8.

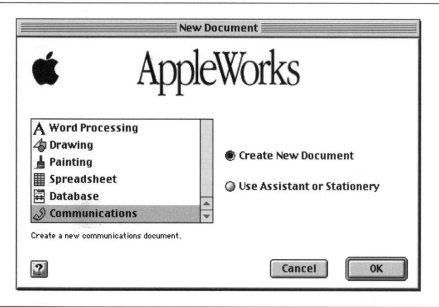

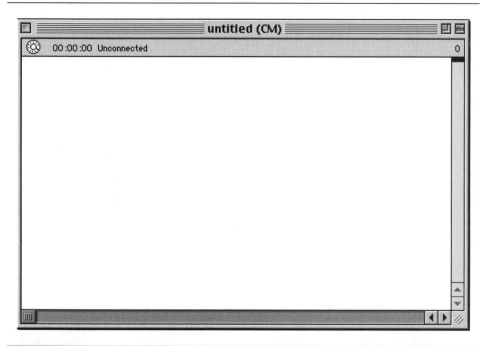

FIGURE 17-7   This document screen will display the status of your file transfer session

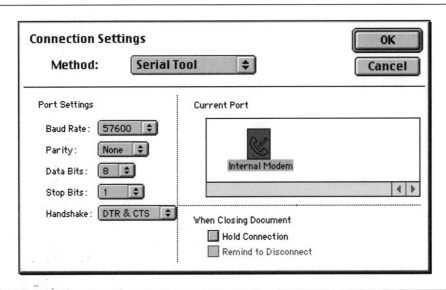

FIGURE 17-8   The settings are entered on this screen

5. Enter the following settings on this screen (just as shown in Figure 17-8):

> **Method:** Serial Tool
> **Baud Rate:** 57600
> **Parity:** None
> **Data Bits:** 8
> **Stop Bits:** 1
> **Handshake:** DTR & CTS
> **Current Port:** Internal (or whatever port your modem is hooked up to)

6. Hang in there—there's another set of settings to make before you can transfer those files, and it also has to be done on both computers. Go back to the Settings menu and choose File Transfer Settings (see Figure 17-9).

7. Now choose these options in the File Transfer Settings window:

> **Protocol:** XMODEM Tool
> **Method:** MacBinary
> **Transfer Options:** Standard

8. Once your communications settings are done, go to the Mac that will be receiving the files (which I assume will be your new one), and choose Preferences from the Apple(Claris)Works Edit menu.

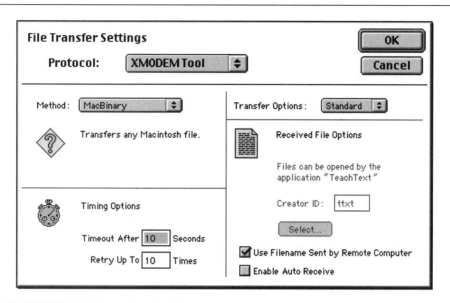

File Transfer Settings

Protocol: [XMODEM Tool ⬍]

[OK]
[Cancel]

Method: [MacBinary ⬍]

Transfers any Macintosh file.

Timing Options

Timeout After [10] Seconds
Retry Up To [10] Times

Transfer Options: [Standard ⬍]

Received File Options

Files can be opened by the application "TeachText"

Creator ID: [ttxt]

[Select...]

☑ Use Filename Sent by Remote Computer
☐ Enable Auto Receive

FIGURE 17-9   You need to make these settings so the files are sent in the proper format

9. Select your Communications preference screen from the pop-up menu, and, when it appears, click on the Receiving Folder button.

10. You'll see a dialog box for selecting the receiving folder. Make your selection, which will return you to the preference screen.

11. Click OK to store your selection.

12. Now you're nearly ready to begin the file transfers. First, choose Open Connection from the Session menu.

13. Go back to the sending computer and type **ATD** in the terminal window.

14. Return to the receiving computer and type **ATA** in the terminal window. Once this is done, the two modems should start talking with each other and you'll soon see a connection speed (which corresponds to what the modem supports).

15. On the sending computer, choose Send File from the Session menu and select the file you want to send in the dialog box. OK your selection to start the file transfer process.

Networking Without a Network

16. Returning to the receiving computer, choose Receive File from the Session menu. The file received from the other computer will be placed in the folder you designated for receiving them.

17. Repeat steps 15 and 16 for each file you want to send.

This process isn't going to win any prizes for file transfer speeds, but if you have the patience and time to do it, you won't have to waste time and money buying adapter modules you'll never need to use again.

Fixing AppleTalk Network Troubles

Your Mac networks via AppleTalk or perhaps TCP/IP. These capabilities are part of your standard Mac OS installation, so you don't have to do a thing to get it. Using AppleTalk, files are transferred, however, via LocalTalk, the original Mac method, or Ethernet, which first coexisted with LocalTalk, but now has replaced it entirely on all recent Apple computers.

AppleTalk is basically a very robust network protocol. But from time to time, you will find that it no longer works as it should. When trying to figure out why you are having troubles with your AppleTalk network, here are a few simple troubleshooting techniques to help you solve the problem:

■ **Is it just one Mac or all of them?** The first thing you should do when troubleshooting your AppleTalk connection is to find out if the problem affects only your Mac or if it is a group problem. If it is just one Mac, make sure the cables are connected and that AppleTalk is turned on (open the Chooser to see). Check to see that the right network connection (LocalTalk or Ethernet) is selected in the AppleTalk Control Panel; this is understandably confusing if you have a LocalTalk printer and an Ethernet network for sharing your Macs. If the settings are correct, move the Mac to another location on the network. If it now works, it could be your cabling or, if it applies, your network hub or switch.

NOTE *You should not have to put up with a split network setup. You can easily get a LocalTalk-to-Ethernet adapter module, such as the AsanteTalk, so your LocalTalk Macs or printers mate with your Ethernet network. No more network switching! Apple also has a free LocalTalk Bridge Control Panel that's designed to accomplish the same purpose, but it is not necessarily the fastest way to go.*

TIP   *Larger networks will use a "ping" utility to check a network. Such a program works in a fashion similar to sonar or radar. It will send a signal across the network, and wait for an echo from the devices on the network. Using this information, you can look for dropped packets, which would indicate a problem on a specific device. One such program is MacPing, a shareware program that you can access at http://www.versiontracker.com.*

■ **If the hardware is at fault**   Look at the cables. If there's no obvious physical damage, swap the cables with the ones on another Mac, or use a spare. If the cable checks out, look at your network hub or switch. Check to see that the link and activity lights for the port you are looking at are lit and show activity. If the lights are on, but no activity appears to be happening, try moving the network connection to another port on the hub or switch and see if both lights become active on the new port. If the port is functioning properly, you should see the link light come on, provided that the Mac is plugged into the network on this connection. You should also see a small amount of activity, indicated by the flickering of the activity light. Another good test is to look at the port you disconnected the cable from. If the link lights do not go out once you remove the cable, you can assume the port is probably defective. If the Mac still does not work on a new port, you need to try either a different network hub or switch to see if that works.

■ **Serial printer issues**   When Apple removed serial ports on Macs and went to USB, many of the headaches of working with a network yet using a personal printer went away as well. But if you have an older Mac with a standard serial port, you'll face the old bugaboo about having to turn off AppleTalk when the printer is hooked up to the printer port. And that, of course, conflicts with use of your network, where AppleTalk must be on. One possible solution is to see if the printer's manufacturer has a network card. For example, Epson and HP supply Ethernet and LocalTalk network modules for some of their products. Another solution is to attach the printer to the modem port, then use a switch or port switching software, if you need to work with several serial devices (such as a modem or another serial printer).

■ **More than one Mac has the problem**   If your Mac is one of many that cannot access the network, check the components they have in common. Normally, this is the network hub or switch where all your network connections are brought together. When a large number of computers all have network trouble, you should first look at the hub or switch to make

Fixing AppleTalk Network Troubles

sure it is still alive. In almost every case, you will discover that either the hub or switch has failed or that someone has misconfigured the switch. If the hub or switch has failed, you will need to replace it with a good one. If the programming on the switch has been changed, you will need to get the original programming restored so that all your Macs can once again access the network; consult the manual that came with your networking hardware on how to check and change the setup.

■ **Check Ethernet drivers for Ethernet cards**   When your Mac has an Ethernet card installed to provide basic Ethernet networking or support for a faster standard, make sure the software provided by the manufacturer is installed. Such products generally require custom drivers and will not run just with Apple's Ethernet extensions. If you've upgraded your Mac system software, you may want to check the company's Web site to see whether newer software is required.

File Sharing Headaches

Even when the network is working just fine, hardly a day goes by when I don't receive a call from someone who has a problem getting file sharing to work properly. For the most part, the solutions are simple. Setups aren't correct, preference files are damaged. Some of the problems are more obscure and take some troubleshooting to resolve.

Here's a mixture of both—problems and solutions to help you understand the file sharing hassle:

Can't Turn on File Sharing

You switch file sharing on, and, whoops, it won't activate. You get the dreaded message that file sharing can't be enabled. Here are some ways to resolve the problem:

■ **Enter or reenter your Network Identity information**   In order for you to share files, your Mac has to have an owner's name. When you set up your system software, Apple's Mac OS Setup Assistant takes you through the process. If you removed the information or never used the Assistant, you'll need to enter an Owner Name and Computer Name (see Figure 17-10) before you attempt to activate file sharing. If you already have something

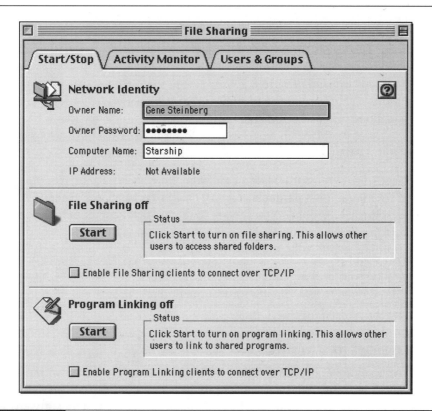

| FIGURE 17-10 | You must fill in the first and third text fields here before you can use file sharing |

there, type in the information again. And don't forget a password, particularly if you need to restrict user access.

■ **Trash File Sharing preferences**   If the preceding process doesn't work, go right to the Preferences folder, inside the System Folder, locate the File Sharing folder and trash it. Then restart.

| NOTE | *If you've never activated file sharing on your Mac, there won't be a folder there.* |

■ **Trash Users & Groups data file**   This will mean you'll have to reestablish the settings, but if all else fails, this may be a way to access file sharing.

■ **Zap (reset) the PRAM**   Hold down the COMMAND-OPTION-P-R keys at startup, and wait for two or three startup tones to sound before releasing them. This step will clear network and serial ports. I've seen it, on rare occasions, clear up network problems. Just remember that if you're using a Mac OS version prior to 8.5, you'll need to redo a number of system settings, including mouse (or trackpad) speed, network and serial port selections, and perhaps display resolution. And no matter which Mac OS you have, you'll also have to reselect a startup drive in the Startup Disk Control Panel.

■ **Check for extension-related conflicts**   In Chapter 18, I cover the process of figuring out if a particular control panel or extension is causing a performance problem. You'll want to review that chapter before you do anything more drastic (such as the next suggestion).

■ **Reinstall the Mac OS**   This seems a drastic step, but if all else fails, it may be your next approach. Since I cover the subject fully in Chapter 2, I'll refer you to that chapter for information on the best way to reinstall your system software.

Can't Connect to a Networked Computer

If your problems are at the other end—you cannot connect to the networked computers—you'll find that some of the previous suggestions, such as checking for extension conflicts, resetting the PRAM, and reinstalling system software are things to consider. But first you'll want to look over these problems and solutions:

■ **Guest access option grayed out when accessing shared Mac**   In order for you to allow guest access, you need to grant access privileges to a file, folder, or drive. Check the section earlier in this chapter entitled "Granting Access Privileges to Shared Macs" for information on the simple steps to follow to set this up.

■ **AppleTalk is off**   As mentioned in the earlier section entitled "Fixing AppleTalk Network Troubles," AppleTalk has to be on to network (unless you're networking via TCP/IP). Open the Chooser and make sure it's on. If you must use a serial printer on an older Mac, check the item concerning serial printer issues in the previous titled "Fixing AppleTalk Network Troubles" for more advice.

■ **Wrong username and password**   Quite often when you access a shared Mac, the Registered User dialog will display your name and password, not the information from your networked computer. You'll need to reenter this information. You may also want to verify the information first, especially if the password is complicated.

■ **Recheck your access privileges**   Make sure the owner of the shared Mac has granted you access privileges. If not, you won't be able to access the shared disk or disks. Even if you can network with that Mac, you'll still want to double-check that you can see the files you need to work on and read or write to them, as necessary.

SyJets and File Sharing

Although SyQuest has gone belly up, a successor company (SYQT, Inc.) still sells the products and arranges for repair. While the SyJet drive, a 1.5GB removable device, still performs well for many users, it seems to have a conflict with file sharing, at least on some Macs. If you have a SyJet cartridge in the drive when you turn on file sharing, you'll get a message that it cannot be enabled. The solution is to eject the cartridge, switch file sharing on, and when it's activated, reinsert the disk.

Getting Started with Ethernet

Ethernet has become the standard method of networking Macs these days. The older, slower LocalTalk connections have been removed, along with serial ports and ADB ports.

Before I explain how you work with Ethernet, it is useful to discuss the background of this high-speed networking standard that has come to dominate the Macintosh universe (yes, even the new AirPort wireless networking system has an Ethernet link).

A Brief Ethernet History

Ethernet was developed at Xerox PARC laboratories in the mid-1970s by Bob Metcalfe, who later was one of the founders of 3Com, the manufacturer of modems, networking hardware, and the Palm Organizer.

NOTE
As you no doubt recall, this is the very same place where Apple founders Steve Jobs and Steve Wozniak were inspired to develop what later became the Mac operating system.

At the start, Ethernet was designed as a high-speed network standard for large network-based printers. I remember, in fact, when I would add Ethernet cards to various Macs to communicate on a network with color printers and imagesetters. Over the years, Ethernet developed from being used in sophisticated network setups to the most common network format around.

Ethernet has supplanted LocalTalk for Mac networks in recent years. In fact, every Apple computer you buy has Ethernet as standard equipment. And a number of Windows-based computers also include Ethernet either as part of the original installation or as a low-cost upgrade.

Today's Ethernet Standards

The most common types of Ethernet you will encounter in your home or office are 10BaseT and Fast Ethernet, also known as 100BaseTX. Fast Ethernet was first approved in 1996.

New Mac computers, even the iMac and iBook, support both standards and will automatically switch from one to the other, depending on what's supported on the network. These types of Ethernet use low-cost twisted pair network cabling, which simply looks like thick modular phone cable.

The 10BaseT Ethernet standard supports transmission speeds up to 10 megabits per second, 100BaseTX at 100 megabits per second. Compare this to LocalTalk speeds, which run about 230,000 bits per second. This begins to add up, especially when you want to transfer large files, or send large, graphic-heavy documents to a printer.

A Realistic Look at Speeds

This business about being able to transfer data at 10 or 100 megabits per second has to be qualified. Obviously, you cannot send any files faster than your Mac's hard drive can read them, nor receive files any faster than your drive can copy them. If the network is busy transferring data among different computers and printers, there will be a slowdown, as capacity isn't unlimited (call them packet collisions), and processing overhead from your computer's system software will also add a performance bottleneck.

At the very least, you can expect real-world Ethernet data transfer rates to be several times that of LocalTalk on a 10BaseT connection, and quite higher (though not 10 times higher) for the Fast Ethernet setup.

The Quadra Had It First

While Macs until very recently had LocalTalk connections as regular issue, Ethernet came later. The first Mac to have an Ethernet port right on the logic board was the Quadra 700, released in 1991. Since then, most Quadras and all subsequent desktop Macs, with the exception of some of the Performa models, have offered Ethernet. When the iMac was unleashed on the personal computing world in August 1998, it was the beginning of the end for LocalTalk. The iMac didn't have it, and, instead, supported both 10BaseT and 100BaseTX.

NOTE   *Older Macs had non-standard Ethernet ports, called AAUI (short for Apple Attachment Unit Interface, though it was used on some Windows-based computers as well). In order to connect to an Ethernet network, you need a special interface module, called a transceiver. Beginning with the so-called PCI generation of Power Macs (7500, 8500, 9500, and so on), Apple has incorporated RJ-45 Ethernet jacks, which don't require a special interface module.*

Just about any older Mac that doesn't have built-in Ethernet, except some PowerBooks, can be upgraded to Ethernet with an add-on card for about $25 to $100.

The Future of Ethernet

As with CPU processing speeds, Ethernet technology isn't standing still. The newest technology is called Gigabit Ethernet and, as the name implies, it's capable of data transfers that are 10 times faster than Fast Ethernet.

The Gigabit Ethernet standard was first set up by a task force in 1996 and is slowly impacting large corporate networks, educational institutions that require the fastest possible networking.

It's not something, however, that will turn up on a personal computer any time soon. For one thing, Gigabit Ethernet cards still can cost upwards of $300 each, with switches and hubs reaching the low four figures (I hesitate to be specific on pricing as they change often).

Getting Started with Ethernet

It'll probably be a while before the technology becomes more prevalent and pricing reaches a point where the products are cheap enough to be incorporated on a Mac's logic board. And that assumes you'd be able to use the tremendous level of performance.

But as Macs and hard drives approach faster speeds at an accelerated clip, the time will come when Gigabit Ethernet just might turn up as a regular connection on a Mac computer.

Common Sense Ethernet Advice

If you have an older Mac and were used to networking with LocalTalk, I'm sure Ethernet may seem somewhat intimidating to you, with all the complex buzzwords about BaseT and so on.

However, actually setting up an Ethernet network is quite simple, no more difficult than connecting a cable here, a cable there, and making a couple of settings.

Ethernet—The Fast and Dirty Method

If you have only two computers or just want to connect your Mac to a printer, you don't need anything more than a single Ethernet cable. But not just any old Ethernet cable (unless you are going to get hold of a hub (a central connection module). Instead, you need to purchase an Ethernet crossover cable. A crossover cable is, as the name implies, different from a regular Ethernet cable because the first two wires (typically black and yellow) are swapped with the last two (typically red and green) at one end of the cable.

CAUTION   *Sad to say, not all dealers understand what a crossover cable is, so be certain you are getting what you asked for (prepackaged cables will have the proper label). If the cable isn't covered with a rubberized fitting, and has a clear plug, you can also visually inspect the cables at both ends, to make sure that the proper cable is being provided.*

Ethernet—The Regular Way

If you intend to connect more than two computers or combinations of computers and printers together, you will need either an Ethernet hub or an Ethernet switch. Both the hub and switch are designed to connect all your Ethernet devices together so they can communicate with each other. What's more, they don't depend on having all devices on at the same time. All you need to turn on are the actual devices that will be networking and file sharing on the Macs that will be making files available to other computers. This means you can turn on a single Mac and a single printer to get some output, and any two Macs to share files, without regard to whether anything else on the network is running. When any of them are turned on, their presence will appear in the Chooser under AppleShare or when you select the appropriate printer driver.

NOTE *The big difference between a switch and a standard hub is that the switch creates virtual circuits between the two Ethernet devices that are talking. A hub creates a single circuit that is shared by all the various Ethernet devices.*

Activating Ethernet

After you are finished connecting your Macs and printers, you will need to configure your Mac to use it. On new Apple computers, Ethernet connections have generally been established by default in the AppleTalk Control Panel, so you shouldn't need to do a thing to create your connection. You just have to make sure the two networked devices you need to use are both running, and that they are selected in the Chooser (or Network Browser, which provides file sharing services for Mac OS 8.5 and later).

If you have an older Mac that also supports LocalTalk, the issues become more complex, as you normally need to switch to your Ethernet port (since LocalTalk is the default).

The main thing you need to do is make sure that the speed and duplex options are set correctly for your network and that the Ethernet frame type is also set correctly. On Macs with only 10BaseT connections, you cannot change the speed or duplex options on the Mac. However, if you are accessing your network via the TCP/IP Control Panel, you can choose between using the 802.2 Ethernet frame type, the default, and the 802.3 frame type, known also as Ethernet II, the frame type frequently used on Novell networks.

AirPort Networking Basics

Apple's AirPort wireless networking system ushers in a new area of connectivity, especially for home and small office users. Rather than have to go through a complex process of wiring nooks and crannies of an office, under the carpets or inside the walls, you can situate your Power Macintosh G4, iBook, or iMac (second generation model) wherever is convenient for you.

Getting Started with Ethernet

You do not even have to be near a telephone line, as the AirPort Base Station can serve as a network router for your Internet connections too. AirPort's maximum range is 150 feet, but that's far more than you'd need for most setups, unless you place computers on another floor or at different ends of a larger office.

NOTE   *The ability to log on to the Internet and share a connection doesn't work with AOL's dial-up numbers. However, you can access AOL, so long as you connect first through a regular ISP.*

In addition, the Base Station has a regular RJ-45 Ethernet jack, so you can attach it to a regular wired network. That keeps your wireless installation connected with a regular Ethernet network.

Setups Are Easy

Once you have installed an AirPort card on a Mac that supports the feature, and set up a Base Station (if needed), you just install Apple's AirPort software. The AirPort Setup Assistant can be used to configure your network setup. While you're connected, a handy Control Strip module will report on signal strength, so you'll know if you're close enough to get solid networking performance. The display is not unlike what you see on your cell phone's display. You can also use the Control Strip to switch your network configuration.

In use, AirPort networking is no different from a regular wired network. You can share files, surf the Internet, and play games, as you prefer. About the only area where it may fall down is in speed. Apple rates AirPort at 11 megabits per second, somewhat faster than a traditional 10BaseT Ethernet connection. If you're using Fast Ethernet, you may see an impact, but otherwise you'll never see any particular difference. The possible exception is when you're at the extremes of its operating range, where it's always possible AirPort will step down to a lower speed to maintain signal integrity as signals degrade.

NOTE   *The AirPort Base Station is designed to support up to 10 users with good performance. If you plan a larger network, you'll want to fit it with extra Base Stations and set up extra access points for them. These are the equivalent roughly to zones on a regular computer network.*

Is AirPort Exclusive to Apple?

True, Apple Computer has been known to embrace unique standards, which create hurdles when third-party companies try to be compatible.

But AirPort is based on a worldwide standard, IEEE 8l2.11. In theory, any company who makes a product that's compatible with the standard could make it work with an AirPort network. An example would be Farallon's SkyLINE.

A PC that has wireless networking ports that support the 8l2.11 standard ought to be able to network with AirPort, though the considerations of cross-platform network connections would still have to be followed. There's no free ride in this sort of setup.

Networking via TCP/IP

While AppleTalk networking isn't going to disappear just yet, it's not the only option available for you to network your Macs. Another is TCP/IP, the same protocol you use when connecting to your Internet service provider. Beginning with Mac OS 9, Apple lets you use the same technique to share files with another computer anywhere on the Internet.

TCP/IP, short for Transmission Control Protocol/Internet Protocol, is set up via your TCP/IP Control Panel. It lets you access another computer or printer on your network, using its IP address (the unique information that identifies the specific device to which you want to connect).

If your Mac is part of a large network, this information will be established by your systems administrator and you'll want to consult that person about proper setups. In such installations, the network server, for example, would typically assign the IP address dynamically.

But you can also use TCP/IP networking on a regular peer-to-peer Mac network, even if you don't have a predefined TCP/IP setup.

Here's the basic setup involved:

1. Go to the Apple menu, and choose TCP/IP from the Control Panels submenu.

 I just want to emphasize that this setup is designed as a simple way to share files via TCP/IP, not to replace your network's existing setting. If you have another networking system in effect, consult the person responsible for establishing that system for further information before changing anything.

2. Choose Configurations from the File menu.

3. Click on your Default setting, and choose Duplicate, which will create a second setup with the same information.

4. Click the Make Active button.

5. Click Rename and give a name to the configuration you're creating. Use a name that will clearly identify the setup, especially if you must switch to different setups for your local network and in order to access an ISP.

6. Choose Ethernet from the Connect Via pop-up menu in the TCP/IP Control Panel (as shown in Figure 17-11).

7. Choose Manually from the Configure pop-up menu. There will be fields where you need to enter your Mac's IP address and subnet mask.

8. If your Mac's IP number is displayed in the File Sharing Control Panel (as it would when you first set up Mac OS 9), enter it in the IP Address text box. If you don't have a number, try 192.168.6.1.

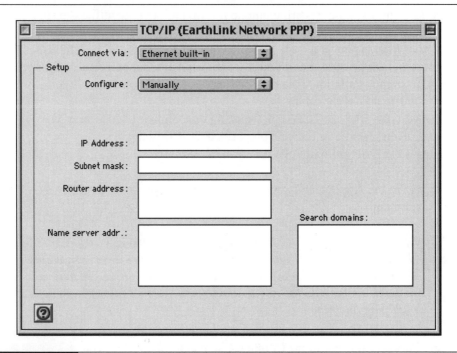

FIGURE 17-11   Make your settings for TCP/IP networking here

NOTE
I could write a whole chapter just on the methodology of IP numbering, the Subnet Mask, and so forth. Let's just say that the number entries I'm offering here are workable and will function in your setup if you follow these instructions.

9. Under Subnet Mask, enter 255.255.255.0. This information is used to identify the network to which your computer is connected.

10. Repeat these steps for each Mac on your network, changing the IP address for each computer. If the other Mac doesn't display an IP number, try 192.168.6.2 and so on. Only the number that follows the last period should be changed, each to reflect a specific Mac.

11. Click the close box on the TCP/IP Control Panel, and OK the option to save your setting.

12. From here on, you'll be able to share files simply by entering the other computer's IP address when choosing AppleShare via the Chooser.

CAUTION
If you intend to access the Internet, you'll have to remember to switch your TCP/IP setting before making your connection. A quick way to switch TCP/IP setups is to use a handy shareware Control Strip module, TCP CC. You can locate a copy at http://www.versiontracker.com.

Is It Faster?

Your mileage may vary. Apple won't officially say whether changing your network setup will provide any greater level of performance. Their technical information document on the subject fits in the "maybe yes, maybe no" category.

Network Browser and Mac OS 9

Beginning with Apple's Network Browser application, you had an alternate way to connect to a networked computer. Now that Apple lets you do that through the Internet too, however, it makes Network Browser less friendly. If you have an ISP set up in the TCP/IP Control Panel, whenever you open Network Browser, it'll log on for you. If your TCP/IP configuration accesses your local network, this won't be a problem. Otherwise, you'll want to stick with the Chooser for regular networking or create a special TCP/IP configuration for your local network, as explained earlier.

Networking via TCP/IP

How to Protect Your Files on a Network

Just as your access to the Internet requires a username and password, similar protections are available when you share files from your Mac. However, the concept of personal file sharing also means that security measures with some added controls are, at best, skimpy.

Here are a few suggestions for maximum security (within the limitations of the process):

- **Give yourself a hard-to-remember password.** The principles that apply to creating a password with your ISP apply here as well. Use a combination of letters and numbers, random if possible (write it down, of course). Don't use birth dates or your lucky number, or any other password someone is likely to guess.

- **Configure Mac OS 9's Multiple Users feature.** Set up the Multiple Users feature so someone else can't get to your Mac while you're away. Once Multiple Users is set up, be sure to go to the Finder's Special menu and use the Logout command to prevent others from gaining use of your Mac. Otherwise, someone can get to your Mac and delete or change the password in the File Sharing Control Panel and the Users & Groups privilege settings.

- **Use Mac OS 9's file encryption system.** This feature puts an Encrypt command at your beck and call. To protect your document, select it, choose Encrypt from the Finder's File menu, give it a password, and the file will be protected. To open the file, the recipient will have to enter the correct password at the prompt.

- **Get security software.** If you're not using Mac OS 9 (or if you want access options other than what Multiple Users offers under OS 9), consider a dedicated security product. Such programs as ASD Software's FileGuard and DiskGuard, and Power On's DiskLock and OnGuard, let you prevent unauthorized users from gaining control of any Mac system, from disk to file level (depending on the settings). That way, someone cannot simply go to the computer directly and mess with the file sharing configuration.

- **Set Users & Groups privileges.** Assuming you have your Mac under control, set up Users & Groups, as I explained in more detail in the section entitled "Setting Users & Groups Privileges."

■ **Consider a file server and server software.**   Apple's AppleShare
software and Mac OS X Server give you centralized control of user access
and privileges. A server computer puts needed files for the network in one
place, for convenient access by everyone and the maximum possible level
of protection. If you have one of the newer Mac models, desktop or
consumer, you can take advantage of Mac OS X Server's NetBoot feature.
It allows these Macs to actually boot and load their system software from
across the network. With Fast Ethernet, for example, there should be little
or no difference in the level of performance the computer achieves. Either
setup is probably best suited for the larger Mac networks, though I've seen
such programs used in installations with as few as 10 or 15 computers and
a handful of printers.

Setting Access Privileges on Dedicated File Servers

You want to know how your files can best be protected from tampering. With the
peer-to-peer file sharing setups described earlier, you can set a file for read and
write access, read access only, write access only, or no access at all. You can grant
these rights to the owner of the file—the person who creates the file—a group of
users, and everyone. In limiting the number of users and groups to which you can
apply permissions, the Macintosh OS significantly limits your ability to lock down
your files—that is unless you help it along.

There are other options that will provide that help. Two are direct from Apple:
one is called AppleShare IP, the other Mac OS X server (a UNIX-based system
based on the technology Apple acquired when it bought Steve Jobs's NeXT
company). Both are client-server programs that provide robust tools to administer
a network.

Another option requires that you explore that other computing platform, and
this option is especially applicable if you are in a mixed-platform environment.
It involves setting up a server using Windows NT or Windows 2000 Server. These
setups don't suffer from the limitations of personal file sharing if you set
privileges using the network administrative tools they provide.

With AppleShare IP, Mac OS X, Windows NT, or Windows 2000, you can set
the file permissions right from the server, so that one group of users has write access
to your files while another has read access only. These are especially valuable
options to consider if you need to assign large numbers of users various types of
file and networked volume access.

If you are using one of these solutions, you need to spend the time to set up
your file permissions so that they give you the maximum amount of flexibility in

how you access your files and still limit the ability of other users on the network to make changes. While the capability to secure your Mac workstations has improved somewhat with Mac OS 9, you may still want to consider looking at Apple's server solutions or those offered by other platforms if you want the maximum amount of network security.

Remember, however, that setting up a Windows NT, Windows 2000, or UNIX server is no cakewalk. It requires a lot of attention to detail, and lengthy procedures to configure each and every step of sharing your Macs and establishing access privileges. You'll find yourself wandering through many complicated dialogs and configuration setups. But if you do follow basic setup instructions carefully, you'll find it an alternative that is at least worth consideration, particularly on a large computer network.

From Networks to System Extensions

Networking on your Mac is usually just a matter of turning on file sharing, but as you see from this chapter, sometimes you need to do more to protect your files or ensure best possible performance.

A common cause of network problems and, in fact, many of the problems that afflict Mac is a system extension conflict. That and adding system-related utilities form the topic of the next chapter.

Chapter 18

How to Add System Utilities with Confidence

My first Macintosh froze up within two hours after I turned it on. For a second, I thought the message was kind of cute: a "bomb" icon within a white, rectangular screen.

But the result wasn't quite as cute. The keyboard froze, the mouse froze, and I was left without the ability to get any work done. I tried clicking on the convenient Restart button on the screen and it did absolutely nothing. So I had to force a restart (I cover this topic later in this chapter, in the section "Forcing a Restart").

It was my first encounter with the realities of personal computing. Computers are not appliances, no matter what the advertising copywriters tell you. They can and will crash at unexpected, inconvenient moments.

This chapter is designed to focus on a number of areas that can make your Mac look better and work better. That, in itself, will be useful. But some of these changes may, in the end, also give your Mac fits. We'll cover them subject by subject.

Appearance Control Panel Problems

Apple did wonders for the look and feel of your Mac desktop when they introduced the Appearance Control Panel, beginning with Mac OS 8. Many of the features for which you formerly had to use third-party system extensions are now comfortably handled with Apple's software.

That creates, of course, fewer possibilities of conflict, but it also gives you somewhat fewer opportunities to decorate your Mac's desktop.

Here are a few potential pitfalls you'll see with the Appearance Control Panel (I'm basing this on the version that shipped with Mac OS 9), as shown in Figure 18-1:

■ **Font anti-aliasing problems**   The theory goes that lettering on your screen will appear cleaner and easier to read if you choose the Smooth All Fonts On Screen option (see Figure 18-2). On the other hand, you may find that lettering has a "smeared" effect as a result. This is especially true with LCD screens, such as you find on an iBook or PowerBook. In addition, smoothing may cause display problems in some older programs. My suggestion is that you turn it off.

NOTE   *In some cases, particularly on desktop Macs, you may find that font smoothing looks good. If that's the case, don't be concerned about my feelings against it.*

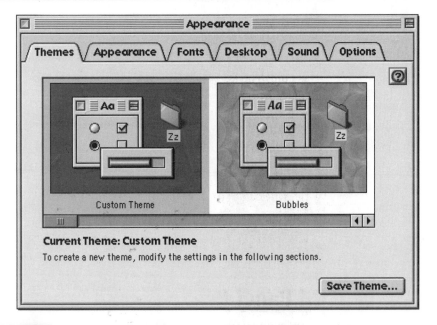

FIGURE 18-1   Apple's Appearance Control Panel can give your Mac a
desktop makeover

NOTE   *Even if you turn off font smoothing, you may find it turns on again when
you do a clean system software installation or switch themes. If it returns,
revisit the Fonts tab in the Appearance Control Panel and turn the feature
off again.*

■ **Blotchy, blurry desktop pictures**   If the pictures are very small, less
than 128x128 pixels, Apple's Appearance Manager will tile them—that is,
they'll put them side by side, with enough copies to fill your screen. If
the picture is larger, it'll be expanded to fill your entire screen. But if the
picture isn't big enough, it'll be scaled upward a lot, and that may reduce
quality to unacceptable levels. If you want to have a single desktop picture,
make sure it's large enough to fill your screen without enlarging (how large
depends on the size of the picture compared to the size of your desktop as
measured in pixels).

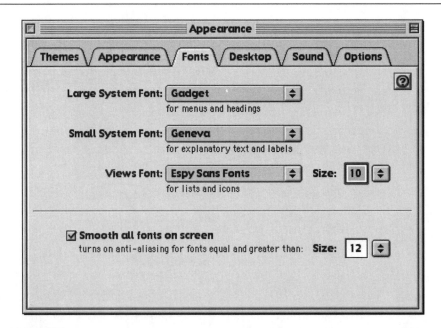

FIGURE 18-2   Font smoothing may make things look better or worse, depending on your setup. In this instance, with the feature applied, the lettering tends to look somewhat "smudged"

■ **Slow screen redraws**   Unless you have the fastest Power Macintosh G3 or G4, your Mac's video display circuitry may be working overtime to display a fancy image. That's especially true if you are in a situation where your Mac is running out of memory (system or video). If you run into this problem, consider going back to one of Apple's palette of desktop patterns.

Desktop Decoration Programs—Good or Bad?

There are limits to Apple's innovation in the Appearance Control Panel. If you find the decorative possibilities don't please you, you'll be tempted to look for third-party solutions.

One such program is Kaleidoscope, a shareware program that extends the ability of your Mac way beyond the constraints of the Appearance Control Panel (see Figure 18-3). It can even mimic the motif of non-Apple operating systems, such as the BeOS (an alternate operating system, designed by a company headed by a former Apple executive, which currently works on pre-G3 Macs and Intel CPUs). Figure 18-4 shows my iMac fitted with this setup.

The cautions I describe in the section entitled "A Guide to Using System Enhancements" apply to this product category too. As Apple updates its system software, you can expect desktop appearance enhancements to require updates. Fortunately, the authors of Kaleidoscope have kept their close ties with Apple and regularly update the program with new features, new desktop themes, and better compatibility.

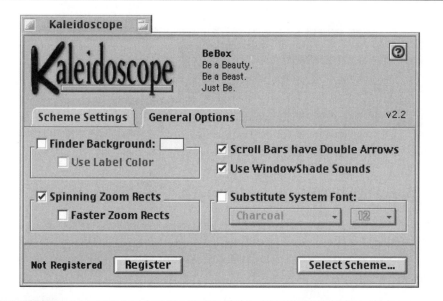

FIGURE 18-3   You can use Kaleidoscope to make your Mac's desktop go where it hasn't gone before

Desktop Decoration Programs—Good or Bad?

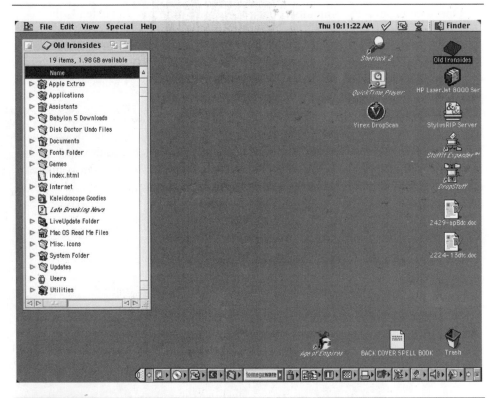

FIGURE 18-4   Kaleidoscope mimics the look of the Be Operating System, which was an attempt to replace the Mac OS with an industrial-strength system

Use System Enhancements with Few Problems

You don't like Apple's Open and Save dialog box? No problem, there are programs out there that will make it look different, wider, more robust, with extra added features. Consider ACTION Files (see Figure 18-5), Default Folder, or DialogView.

NOTE   *I am making no effort whatever to be complete in my list of system enhancements. There are thousands of such programs. One great Web resource to find them is http://www.versiontracker.com. You'll also find demonstration versions of several of Power On's ACTION Utilities programs on this book's CD.*

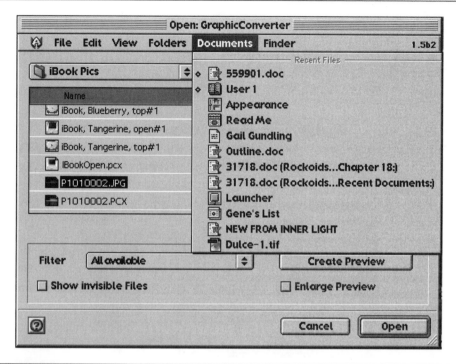

FIGURE 18-5 Power On Software's ACTION Files gives your Open and Save dialog boxes point of view

What about the font menus? Wouldn't it be nice if they showed you the font in WYSIWYG fashion, grouped fonts by families in submenus? And what about telling you what sort of font you have, PostScript or TrueType? Try ACTION WYSIWYG Menus, Adobe Type Reunion Deluxe, MenuFonts, or TypeTamer.

NOTE *Some programs, such as AppleWorks and Word 98, offer a WYSIWYG-style font menu as an option, but without the doo-dads offered by the third-party programs. An example is grouping fonts into family submenus, for easier access.*

Don't like Apple Menu Options (the program that puts up those submenus in the Apple menu)? Would you like similar submenus to appear anywhere on your Mac's desktop with a click here or there, or maybe by pressing one keyboard combination or another? More full-featured solutions include ACTION Menus, BeHierarchic, and MenuChoice.

Use System Enhancements with Few Problems

My reference to desktop submenus doesn't refer to the Contextual Menus feature that's part of Mac OS 8 or later and supported in some programs.

And then there's Apple's venerable Launcher, a place where all you have to do is click once on a button to open a program, a document file, a folder, a disk. Isn't there a better way to accomplish this magic? Wouldn't you like it to display just the names rather than the icons? Or be able to create extra launching docks in different parts of your screen? Try DragStrip (shown here and included on this book's CD), DragThing, OneClick, Power Launch, SmartLaunch, Square One, or the Tilery.

How about a more convenient way to capture screen images for your documentation? How do authors like me do it? Is just pressing COMMAND-SHIFT-3 or the extra variations (such as COMMAND-SHIFT-4) sufficient, or have you grown tired of seeing Picture 1, Picture 2, etc., on your drive? How about being able to save the picture to a different location on your drive, giving it a unique file name, changing the format, capturing the image of a game in motion? Well, there are such programs as Captivate and the one I used for this book, SnapZPro.

Almost anything you can imagine, some enterprising programmer has probably found a way to perform the task. And so these handy system utilities can pepper your System Folder and your Mac's desktop. The nice thing is that they can extend the capabilities of your Mac. The bad thing is that there's the tendency for things to go out of whack as Apple updates its system and makes more and more sweeping changes.

A Guide to Using System Enhancements

With thousands of possibilities for mischief here, I won't even try to list the conflicts of any particular program. More to the point, the authors of these programs are usually dedicated and responsible and responsive to handling problems when they occur.

If you take a few precautions, you'll find some wonderful ways to enhance your Mac computing experience:

- ■ **Don't install two or more enhancements that do the same thing.** Whether it's a dialog box enhancer or font menu modifier, pick only one. If you choose any two programs that have the same function, they will quite possibly prevent one another from working properly. At worse, they'll cause crashes. If you're not sure whether you like one program or another, try each separately (making sure the other has been disabled in Extensions Manager), then make your decision.

- ■ **Watch diligently for updates.**   Any time Apple updates its system software, the very same system tools that allow such enhancements to work may be changed. Programs that enhance Finder functions are especially vulnerable. It's not a bad idea to check such Web sites as VersionTracker to look for a new version. Some authors or publishers may even have mailing lists, and they'll let you know about a new version and what is fixed or changed.

- ■ **Be careful about using older system enhancements with new system versions.**   That program that may have worked perfectly fine on your Mac five or ten years ago may fail miserably with Mac OS 9. If you cannot find a newer version out there, consider removing it from your System Folder. Perhaps there's something newer that'll work just as well.

> NOTE   *A very unusual exception to this rule is ApplWindows, a free program that delivers pop-up menus of open programs and documents, and hides programs you're not using. It was last updated in 1993, yet is still mostly functional on my Macs with Mac OS 9. For a copy, check http://www.versiontracker.com.*

Use System Enhancements with Few Problems

■ **Pay your shareware fees.** Many of the best system enhancements are shareware. You don't pay for them in advance, but the authors expect you'll send them the small fees if you continue to use the program after a 15 or 30 day trial. If you want these programs to be updated and enhanced, so you can continue to use them as Apple upgrades its operating system, you'll want to make sure you reward them for their work.

NOTE *It's a sad, sad fact that only a small fraction of those using shareware programs ever pay for them. While some publishers, such as Ambrosia Software, manage to keep going under these conditions, others simply stop writing software or join commercial publishers and produce the same programs at much higher prices.*

Desktop Rebuilding for Fun and Profit

As I have explained in several parts of this book, the Mac OS Finder keeps tabs of file icons, documents, and the programs that launch them using desktop files. These files are marked by the Finder as "invisible," which means you cannot see evidence of their presence without a program that can view such files.

NOTE *If you use Microsoft Word, for example, you can use the All Files option in the Open dialog box to view the listings for the Desktop DB and Desktop DF files (although you won't be able to actually open them).*

Mac programs and documents are identified by a file type and creator. The first tells you what sort of file it is (text or otherwise), and the second identifies the program that created the document.

For example, the Word 98 files I used to write this book are identified with the file type of W8BN and the file creator as MSWD.

If the desktop file becomes corrupted for any reason (a system crash or hard drive directory damage, to name the usual causes), you may find the pretty icons change to white-colored documents. When you double-click on a document, you may get a notice that the application that created it can't be found, or the wrong application may be launched.

The solution is to rebuild the desktop file. The simplest way to do this is to restart your Mac, and when the last extension icon appears on the screen, hold down the COMMAND-OPTION keys. When you see the prompt asking if you want to rebuild the desktop, release the keys and click OK. If your Mac has more than one disk volume on it, you'll see the same prompt for each volume, which you'll OK until the process is done.

As the desktop rebuilds, you'll see a progress bar showing the process. It can take mere seconds for a small hard drive with very few files, up to several minutes or more for large volumes with thousands of files on them.

Apple's official recommendation for desktop rebuilding, however, is a bit more complex than that. They suggest you use Extensions Manager to turn off all system Extensions except for Mac OS Easy Open (or File Exchange for Mac OS 8.5 or later). Then rebuild the desktop following the preceding steps.

> NOTE *I'll cover use of Extensions Manager later in this chapter, in the section entitled "Using Extensions Manager to Test for Conflicts."*

Once you have rebuilt the desktop the Apple way, go back to Extensions Manager and restore your original settings, then restart.

I have not seen any real advantage in following this advice, other than the possibility that a non-Apple system extension will harm the desktop rebuild process (some versions of Adobe Type Manager prior to version 4 could do this). However, if you want to be as safe as possible, it doesn't hurt to spend a few moments setting this up this way.

If the desktop rebuilding process doesn't work, check Chapter 13, which covers use of such programs as Alsoft's DiskWarrior, MicroMat's TechTool Pro, and Symantec's Norton Utilities to fix disk directory damage. These programs can also fix problems with so-called "bundle bits," which can result in improper or missing file or folder icons.

Another solution to the desktop rebuild problem is to use the desktop rebuild feature of TechTool Pro or Conflict Catcher (described later), which ensures a better, more thorough rebuilding process. Rather than just rebuild or update the desktop files, these programs actually delete them first. After you restart, the Finder automatically rebuilds the desktop from scratch.

> NOTE *A free program from MicroMat, called simply TechTool, (included on this book's CD) can rebuild the desktop, zap the PRAM, and check the System file for damage. It doesn't handle any of the advanced disk and hardware diagnostics of the commercial version of the program, however.*

Use System Enhancements with Few Problems

How to Check for System Conflicts

When your Mac crashes, it can be a frustrating experience. It usually happens when you're in the midst of doing a complex job, which taxes your Mac's capabilities, and you're minutes away from having to deliver the document to someone in your office or a business contact.

With so many thousands of system and software and hardware combinations, it's inevitable that problems will arise from time to time. There is no possible way for me to list every conceivable possibility of a conflict. No book can be that large. Instead, I'll cover the ways you can isolate the cause. Once you do that, you can stop using the offending program or seek out help or updates from the publisher.

System Crashes: Finding the Cause

The most vexing sort of system problem is the one that isn't consistent. One day everything is fine, the next day, your Mac crashes at an unexpected moment, in a program that never gave you a lick of trouble before.

This sort of problem is part and parcel of the personal computing experience. Software has bugs, the operating system has bugs, and until computers are truly as elegant as your basic toaster oven, you can expect such happenings as a normal part of your computing experience.

About the closest remedy on the horizon (it may be out by the time you read this book) is the consumer version of Mac OS X, which is supposed to provide improved features to guard against system hang-ups. These include protected memory, which simply means that a program gets its own, custom segment of RAM. So if something happens to cause that program to freeze, you can go on and use another program without having to restart.

Well, that's part of a remedy, assuming you will have a Mac that can run the new system version. And that feature depends on a program being "Carbonized," Apple's jargon to identify programs that have been recompiled by the programmers to support its "Carbon" application programming library, which is required to take advantage of all the great features of Mac OS X.

NOTE   *As this book went to press, Apple would only commit to supporting the consumer version of Mac OS X on an Apple computer that originally shipped with a G3 CPU or faster. Older Macs or Mac clones with G3 upgrades were not considered compatible (though this situation could change by the time the new operating system ships).*

Regular programs should run on Mac OS X, in most cases, but they won't work any better than on Apple's older systems.

So what do you do if you have the regular version of the Mac OS and regular freezes? Well, that's a horse of a different color. There are tried and true methods that will help you isolate the cause of the problem.

Using Extensions Manager to Test for Conflicts

Apple gives you a free program to manage your system Extensions, Extensions Manager (see Figure 18-6). You can use it to turn individual Extensions off and on as necessary, with just a restart to change things around.

Extensions Manager isn't nearly as adept at handling these chores as a great utility from Casady & Greene, Conflict Catcher. But since it's free, I'll focus this section on using it. I'll get to Conflict Catcher later.

Here's a way to help isolate the cause of repeatable system problems. The ones that happen at random are much harder to deal with. For this section, I'll divide the diagnostics into two categories, with specific steps for each.

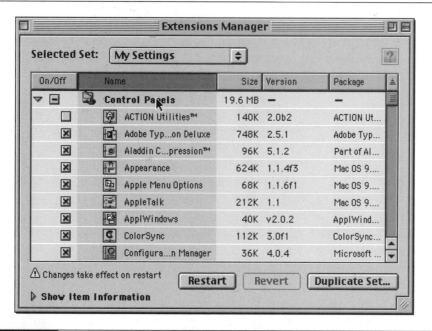

FIGURE 18-6   Apple's Extensions Manager is free, and it's a useful starting point to help you seek out possible system-related problems

How to Check for System Conflicts

FORCING A RESTART   If your Mac freezes up, there are several ways to get out of the situation and make it restart. Here are the common methods:

- **Force quit**   Press COMMAND-CONTROL-ESC. You should see a message asking if you want to force the program to quit. If this works, the program will quit gracefully, at which point you should restart your Mac in the normal way before proceeding any further.

- **The "Three Fingered Salute"**   This is a tried and true method to restart many (but not all) Macs. If your Mac hangs at the Force Quit attempt, or after the program quits, press COMMAND-CONTROL-POWER ON. If your Mac supports the feature, it'll restart. This command sequence won't work on the first generations of Macs using USB keyboards and mice, and on some PowerBooks and older Macs. So you have to resort to the next method.

- **Press the Reset switch**   Where is it? Depends on which model you have. On older Macs, there was actually a small switch with a little left-pointing triangle that you used to force the restart process. Even the newest generation of Blue & White Power Macintosh G3s and the G4s have this feature. But on some PowerBooks and the first generation iMac models, the actual reset switch is recessed, located below this little triangle. In order to access the switch, you have to straighten the end of a paper clip, then insert it gently into the hole, and press the button and release.

> **TIP**   *For first-generation iMacs there is a solution to the paper clip dilemma. It's called the iMacButton, and it costs $9.95 (last I checked) from this Web site: http://www.imacbutton.com. The product consists of a large button with adhesive backing that you install by inserting into the little hole located behind the removable door on the right side of the computer and hold tightly for a few seconds (until it sticks).*

MAKE A SYSTEM PROFILE FIRST   Before you proceed, you'll want to make a record of your Mac's System Folder configuration. That way you have something to check over as you proceed to isolate the cause of those crashes.

1. Go to the Apple menu, then select Apple System Profiler (it only comes with Mac OS 7.6 and later). The one provided with Mac OS 9 will bring up a screen similar to the one shown in Figure 18-7.

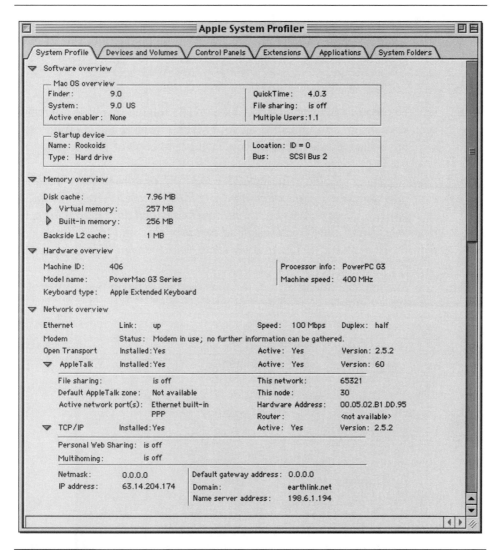

| FIGURE 18-7 | Apple's System Profiler program is a handy guide to isolating potential conflicts |

NOTE   *You can locate and download the latest version of Apple System Profiler from Apple's support Web site at http://asu.info.apple.com.*

2. Choose New Profile from the File menu (see Figure 18-8).

3. Check all items related to System Folder Controls (on the right side of the screen). Uncheck the ones on the left (you don't need them).

4. Click OK to generate your report.

5. Once the report is displayed (it may take up to a minute or a little longer if you have lots of stuff installed on your Mac), go ahead and choose Print One Copy from the File menu, so you have a hard copy of your report.

TIP

If you are using an older Mac with Mac OS 7.5.5 or earlier, there's still a way to generate a profile without paying for a system upgrade. Go on the Internet, visit http://www.versiontracker.com, and do a search for a program called TattleTech. Download that program, and follow its instructions to create and print a profile of your System Folder's contents.

Now you've completed the first step. It's time for you to begin the process of figuring out what's caused your computer to misbehave.

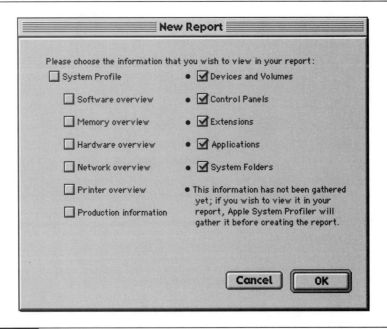

FIGURE 18-8   Select your Profile options from this screen

MAC CRASHES AT STARTUP   Before you go any further, take a look at the Mac's startup routine. If the crash occurs before all Extensions have loaded, look at the icons that appear just before it happens. Something that loads after those icons may be the culprit.

NOTE   *Most of the items in the Extensions folder load alphabetically, as do the contents of Control Panels folder. I say most, because some of the items in the Extensions folder, such as networking and USB drivers, will load ahead of the pack (usually they won't display an icon).*

Follow these steps:

NOTE   *Keep your printed System Profiler report handy as you continue through this process. You'll want to see what your starting point was.*

1. Restart your Mac (force a restart if necessary).

NOTE   *In order for you to follow these steps to their logical conclusion, take a pad and pencil out and be prepared to write down the steps you're taking. Or if you have another Mac, open a blank word processing document and create a log of your conflict isolation process.*

2. As soon as it starts, hold down the SPACEBAR, which will, within a few moments, bring Extensions Manager to the front.

3. Look over the list of Extensions and Control Panels and see if you can locate the ones that load after the particular icon you've seen. If you're not certain what the icon signifies (and you're using Mac OS 7.6 or later), look at the miniature icons in the Extensions Manager window. When you spot the one you saw, disable the next two or three extensions (assuming they're not Apple's), then continue the restart process (simply by closing the Extensions Manager window).

4. If your Mac starts normally now, look in the System Folder and locate the icons you disabled. Use the Finder's Get Info command to identify them, if their source or identity isn't obvious. Armed with that information, you can decide whether to quit using the file or contact the publisher about an update that may address your problem.

5. If the crashes continue to occur, follow steps 1 through 4 again. Not all of the things in your Extensions and Control Panels folder put up an icon, and

you may have to go hunting for something that loads a bit later on in the chain (remember, Extensions load alphabetically).

MAC CRASHES AFTER STARTUP   Whether your Mac crashes right away or it gives up the ghost when you perform a specific function, such as launching an application, you can follow these steps to find out what went wrong:

1. If you get regular crashes when doing a specific task, such as launching an application, or just starting your Mac, go to the Apple menu, choose Control Panels and select Extensions Manager from the submenu.

NOTE   *When you start with a Base extension set, your Mac will only be running with the very basic things it needs to operate. And that has severe limits. If you're using a program, such as one from Microsoft, that requires certain Extensions to work, this can be a problem; worse Microsoft's First Run installer will be launched if you're using one of their recent programs, and it'll try to restore the missing extensions. But if you successfully boot your Mac without trouble, this should be enough to go to the next step.*

2. If your system startup is successful, you can continue. If not, restart with Extensions off (SHIFT key held down at startup) and wait for the Extensions Disabled message on your Mac's screen. Then release the keys. If you start up successfully, you'll want to reinstall your system software. I cover that subject in Chapter 2. Otherwise, just continue.

NOTE   *If the startup process doesn't work even with Extensions off, you'll have no choice but to run right for your system CD and reinstall your system software.*

3. If the startup with a Base set continues without interruption, it's time to go to the next step. Open Extensions Manager, then choose Duplicate Set from the File menu, which brings up the screen shown here:

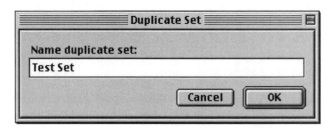

NOTE *When you uncheck an Extension with Extensions Manager, all that happens is that it's moved to a folder with the "Disabled" label on it; the action doesn't actually delete anything. Checking the Extension moves it back to the original position in the original folder.*

4. Give your duplicate set a name (for later reference) that helps you identify it for system diagnostics. Call it Test Set, if you want, or anything that seems appropriate to the occasion. The set will be identical to the Mac OS 9 Base set, but you'll be able to modify it as you want (you can't change the Base or All settings).

5. Look through your list of Extensions and Control Panels and activate half of the ones that are deactivated. Consult your System Profiler report for this information. And don't forget to log what you're doing, in case you have to continue this process through several restarts.

6. Restart.

7. Try to do whatever function causes a crash. If you need to launch a program that requires a specific system extension, go to Extensions Manager and activate just the ones you need, if you're able to determine that from the list. For Microsoft, it's easy. Anything labeled Microsoft or MSL is needed. Otherwise Office 98 and later Microsoft programs will just replace the missing Extensions (so you end up with active and inactive copies).

8. If the problem is gone, go ahead and open Extensions Manager, then activate half of the remaining system Extensions you had previously used and restart again.

9. Try again to reproduce the crash.

10. Continue activating half of the remaining system Extensions on each restart until the problem returns. When it does, follow the steps in the next section.

IF THE SYSTEM CRASH OCCURS AGAIN Now we're getting closer to the source of the problem. You know that one of the Extensions and Control Panels you turned on has caused your Mac to crash. Should this occur, follow these steps:

1. Restart your Mac.

2. As soon as it restarts, hold down the SPACEBAR and wait for the return of Extensions Manager.

How to Check for System Conflicts

3. When you see Extensions Manager, turn off half the Extensions and Control Panels you activated on the previous session, then continue the startup process.

4. Repeat the steps needed to reproduce the crash. If they continue, repeat steps 1 to 3, each time turning off half of the remaining Extensions (aside from the basic Apple stuff in Base Set, of course).

After you've located your culprit, try running your Mac without that Extension or control panel and see if the problem goes away. If it does, congratulations! You've solved what is most likely quite a vexing problem and now you can continue to use your Mac with comparative reliability.

If you need the program you disabled, you'll want to contact the publisher about an update, or look for another program that performs the same function.

The Conflict Catcher Alternative

Apple's Extensions Manager has the advantage of being free and available with your Mac OS. However, as you see in the preceding section, the process of isolating a system conflict can be a tedious process of trial and error, and you may be quite lucky to find the answer to your problem.

If you want to let the software do it for you, there's a better option. It's Jeffrey Robbin's Conflict Catcher, from Casady & Greene. Robbin once worked as a system software programmer for Apple and has worked diligently to keep his program up to date, while expanding the feature set to incorporate every single possibility for System Folder management.

NOTE   *I've included a limited-time demonstration version of Conflict Catcher on this book's CD.*

This is just a brief list of the features of the version current when this book was written (8.0.6):

■ **Conflict Test**   I'll cover this in the next section. The program uses its own internal "fuzzy logic" to turn the programs in your System Folder off and on to help you isolate the cause of a repeating crash.

■ **Merge System Folders**   When you do a clean system install (as I describe in Chapter 2), Conflict Catcher will guide you through the complex process of picking the stuff from your previous System Folder that you want to put in your newly installed System Folder. Then it does it all for you, in minutes.

- **Reference Library**   Want to know what that file in the System Folder is used for? Apple's Extensions Manager will tell you about Apple's software, but Conflict Catcher has a useful reference database covering thousands of third-party programs too. And there are Internet links to the publishers, so you can check for updates.

- **Check for corrupted system files**   As part of its Conflict Test, Conflict Catcher will check your System Folder for damaged files (as shown here), and that includes fonts and Preference files. Corrupted Preference files are quite a common cause of frequent system crashes. If a damaged file is found, Conflict Catcher will offer to try to fix the problem (don't get optimistic, it's not always successful at this).

- **Clean desktop rebuilds**   The normal process of rebuilding the desktop will just update the existing desktop files. But if the files are damaged, the problems of application launching and icon display won't be solved. Conflict Catcher rebuilds the desktop by deleting the existing files, forcing a replacement, rather than rebuild at the next restart. This is often the better way to go.

USING CONFLICT CATCHER TO TEST FOR CONFLICTS   If you have a repeatable conflict that's causing your Mac to crash, you can harness Conflict Catcher's Conflict Test to help find the cause.

NOTE   *Conflict Catcher doesn't do everything by itself; you have to work with the program to help it isolate the problem for you.*

I'll assume you've installed the latest version of Conflict Catcher before trying this. From there, just follow these steps to harness the power of this unique program:

1. Restart your Mac, then hold down the SPACEBAR to bring up the Conflict Catcher window (see Figure 18-9).

How to Check for System Conflicts

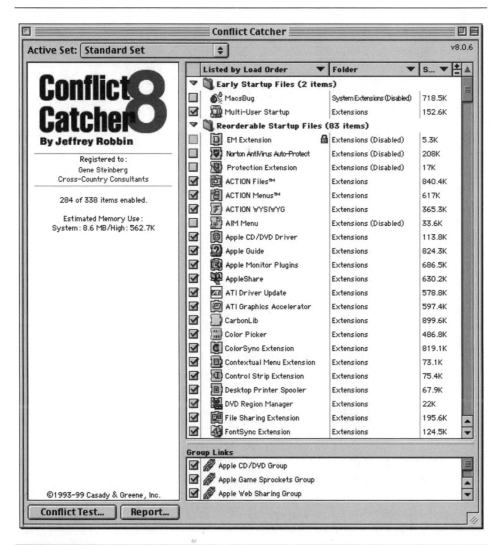

FIGURE 18-9 Conflict Catcher is ready to find why your Mac is crashing

2. When you see Conflict Catcher, click on the Conflict Test button, which brings up the screen shown here:

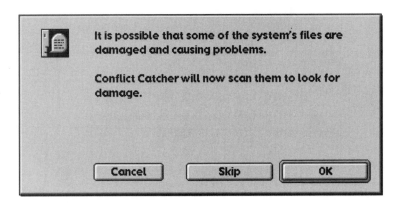

It is possible that some of the system's files are damaged and causing problems.

Conflict Catcher will now scan them to look for damage.

Cancel   Skip   OK

3. Prepare to work with the program to start the test. The first step is a startup-file scan, which will check your System Folder to be certain there are no damaged files.

NOTE   *You can easily skip these preliminary steps, but I suggest you follow them, to allow Conflict Catcher to do its stuff as efficiently and completely as possible.*

4. Once Conflict Catcher reports on the status of its System Folder run, click the OK button to move on to the next step.

5. On the next screen, Conflict Catcher will ask you if you are presently facing that system problem. Click Yes if you are (which is, I assume, what you'll be doing).

6. Now you'll be asked to write a short comment on the problem you're having (see Figure 18-10). This is done to help you track the original problem. Conflict Catcher doesn't use it for its own work. Click OK to continue.

How to Check for System Conflicts

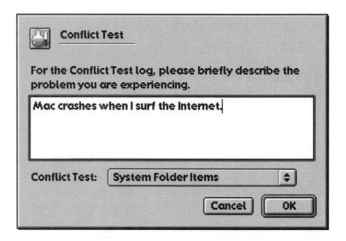

Type in a short description of your system-related problem

7. The next step is important: you'll be asked to click the Needed Files option, so you can select the system Extensions you need for your work, such as all those files with the word Microsoft in them for that company's software. When you make your selection, click OK to move on.

NOTE   *Certain Apple system Extensions are required for your Mac to run and they will, in fact, remain active even if you restart with Extensions off. Conflict Catcher will not disable those files nor allow you to do so.*

8. If you want to take a guess as to which System Folder item is causing your problem, click on the Intuition button, which brings up the screen shown in Figure 18-11, and then click on the name so Conflict Catcher will focus on it first. Click OK to move to the final step.

9. You're almost there now. Just click the Start Conflict Test button, and on the next screen click Restart to begin the actual test process.

The miracle of Conflict Catcher's Conflict Test is about to begin. Once your Mac has restarted, go ahead and duplicate the conditions that caused the crash, such as launching or working in an application or printing a document.

Once you've done that, restart (force a restart if your Mac crashes again).

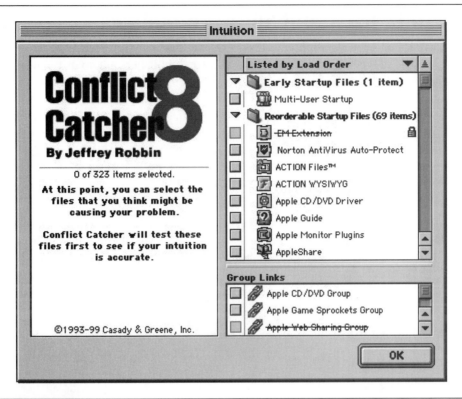

| FIGURE 18-11 | If you have a suspect, let Conflict Catcher know, to speed up the process |

After restart, Conflict Catcher will put up a dialog asking you to specify whether the problem is gone or still exists. Using that information, the program will continue to vary the System Folder lineup. It will probably take about 10 restarts for the program to specify a likely culprit.

Once Conflict Catcher has produced the suspect, you'll have the option to disable it and then to continue another test to see if any other programs are contributing to the problem.

I won't guarantee Conflict Catcher will always find the villain, but it has saved my life on many occasions, and it's definitely worth a try, since a three-day demo is freely available from the publisher's Web site (http://www.casadyg.com) and, of course, on this book's CD.

Where to Learn About Software Updates

How can it be? Apple Computer seems to release one software update or another every couple of weeks. And your regular software publishers are no different. Just keeping up with this confusion can be a challenge that no single person can overcome.

Fortunately, there are folks who have devoted a great part of their time to checking for software updates, and as I'll explain at the end of this chapter, Apple has a neat way of dealing with it. They check for updates from far-flung places, and they make the information available to you on the World Wide Web.

Here are some of these Internet-based resources with their addresses and some information on what additional material they offer:

- **MacCentral (http://www.maccentral.com)**   Stan Flack's MacCentral Web site has news and views and product update information. Since it's a part of the same publishing combine that produces *MacWeek Online* and *Macworld* magazine, you can expect a surprising range of information about your Mac and keeping it healthy and happy.

- **MacFixit (http://www.macfixit.com)**   Ted Landau, a *Macworld* contributing editor, heads up this site. The focus is on problems and their solutions, and it's usually updated five times a week. They also have active message boards, and a band of visiting experts who can provide answers and feedback on specific issues.

- **Macintouch (http://www.macintouch.com)**   Ric Ford, former *MacWeek* columnist, tracks the latest reports and rumors about doings in the Mac universe and offers new product listings. The site is updated daily and you will find a lot of exclusives. The focus, though, is on problems, and when bugs or complications arise with a new Mac or software, you may learn about it here.

- **Macsurfer's Headline News (http://www.macsurfers.com)**   This site is a digest listing containing links to Mac news from popular Web sites and the mainstream press. You'll be surprised at the scope of the coverage. I've seen reports here from Mac Web sites in Italy and online business sites in the United Kingdom.

- **Starship's Lair (http://www.starshiplair.com)**   Well, this is a little self-serving, perhaps, but I have set up my own Web site to be more than just a place to hawk my books. I have designed it from the ground up to be an information center, and I will be presenting regular tips and tricks for my readers there. (Notice I didn't list my site first.)

- **VersionTracker (http://www.versiontracker.com)**   The title says it all. The site keeps day-to-day tabs on just about all the hardware and software publishers known to produce Mac products. They offer you direct links to upgrades, updates, and new product information. The site is updated as often as once an hour. If you mark this one as a "favorite" in your Web browser (bookmark it), you'll become an expert on what updates are available and when.

And Now, Apple's Solution

For Mac OS 9, Apple has finally realized that it's not easy to keep track of system updates you might need. So they will do the walking for you, to paraphrase that old line used for Yellow Pages advertising.

One great feature of Mac OS 9 is the ability to receive software updates from Apple automatically. All you need to set this up is an Internet connection and maybe a minute of your time. The feature, called Software Update, can be set to automatically connect to Apple's Web site and retrieve the updates you need.

This is a brief description of how to set it up:

1. Go to the Apple menu, choose Control Panels, then scroll to and select the Software Update Control Panel (see Figure 18-12).

2. You have two ways to get your updates. One is on demand, by clicking Update Now. Once you activate that feature, your Internet service will be dialed and Apple's Web site will be checked for any updates that apply to your version of the Mac OS.

CAUTION   *If you're a member of AOL or CompuServe, and you use their regular dial-up access numbers, you need to connect to the service first before you can use the Software Updates feature.*

Where to Learn About Software Updates

FIGURE 18-12 Apple lets you retrieve your needed updates automatically

3. If Apple has updated software for you, you'll see an onscreen dialog listing the updates that are available. To retrieve them, simply check the box next to the item, then OK the download. After the download finishes, each software installer will run, in turn, until all updates are made. Then you'll just have to restart your Mac to put the new software into action.

4. The other way to use the Software Updates Control Panel is to schedule regular visits to Apple's Web site to search for such updates. To activate that feature, locate the Update Software Automatically check box and check it.

5. Click Set Schedule, and you'll see a scheduling screen where you will make your settings (see Figure 18-13).

6. All you have to do now is click on the check boxes representing the day or days of the week for the automatic update scans, and the time of day.

7. When you're done, click OK to store the settings.

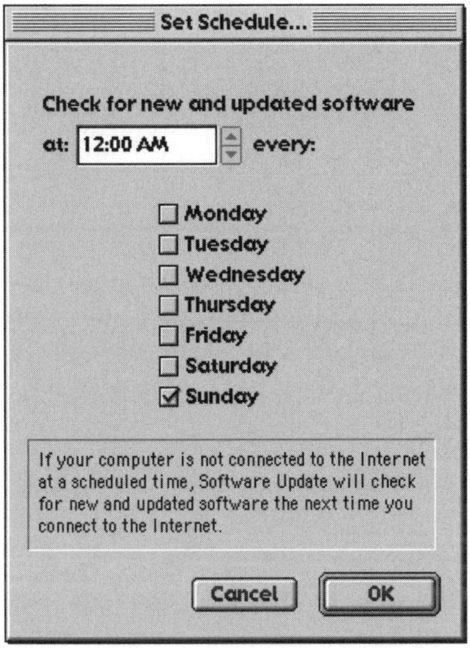

FIGURE 18-13   Pick a schedule to check for Apple system updates

After the Software Update schedule is activated, your Mac will attempt to connect to your Internet service at the appointed time and get your updates. Just remember, though, your Mac must be left on for this to happen; it won't just redial the next day if you miss a scheduled session.

To keep abreast of Apple software updates, you will probably want to schedule the sessions no more often than once every two to four weeks. Apple seldom produces its updates any more often than that!

Summing Up

In this chapter, you discovered the world of system enhancements and system headaches, and you learned some tried and true techniques to rescue your Mac from constant crashes.

In Chapter 19, we'll take a look at the wide world of desktop video editing.

Chapter 19

How to Make Video Capture Hardware Work

In the old days, when you wanted to edit a movie, you had to physically splice the film—cut it apart, move it to its new location, and put it back together. In the days of reel-to-reel tapes, you did pretty much the same thing with radio plays. You cut the tape apart physically, took out passages and moved scenes around, and then re-attached it with a special type of splicing tape.

I did this many times at home, creating my own little plays and variety shows, and I especially enjoyed taking out words and phrases, to fix a bad "take" as they say in show business. I finally exercised the skills for a paycheck when I became a radio broadcaster.

NOTE   *I suppose this dates me somewhat, but there was such a thing as television back then, too—there just weren't any low-cost VCRs to play around with.*

Another way to edit required having two decks. You used one to build your master tape, the other to pick segments. For video, you even had little editing computers that would, once you had marked your edits, do your work on automatic pilot. The editing computer would go back and shuttle the tapes to their marked locations and play them back as you continued to record the finished production.

Even though computers do most of the movie and video editing chores these days, the basic principles are the same. You create a project (your production) and piece it together with scenes from one source or another; then add titles, music, audio, and special effects; and now you have your number one movie or TV show—well, not quite, but you get the idea.

Are You Ready to Capture Video?

Apple Computer pioneered in delivering easy-to-use computers, and even though they remain the minority platform by a great margin, their influence is significant.

They also have dominance in the entertainment industry. The majority of computers you see on your movie or TV screen are Macs. Yes, it's product placement and Apple works hard to get it, but their models are also distinctive-looking enough to stand out from a great percentage of the computing pack.

Macs are also used behind the scenes for editing and special effects. In fact, it's not uncommon for a video production house to have a bank of Mac systems handling commercials, TV shows, and other productions.

The biggest development, though, was to bring this great technology down to the consumer level. Today, with an iMac DV, a digital camcorder, and Apple's iMovie software, you can easily create productions that, at least in terms of picture quality, rival professional productions.

A Brief Look at Video Editing Techniques

When you edit a video, you take the basic production, called raw footage, and you can add transitions (special effects, such as dissolves, that smooth the transfer from one scene to another), titles, narration, music—the limit is your imagination. Once you've done your editing, you transfer the finished product to the final master tape.

There are two different ways to edit videos: nonlinear and linear (the old-fashioned way).

Linear editing is still widely used today. It consists of taking video clips and adding them one at a time in order onto a final tape. However, this process can be very time-consuming and tedious, and it doesn't allow for much in the way of creativity.

On the other hand, nonlinear editing can give you the ability to take a collection of totally separate clips from different tapes, transitions, and sound tracks—whatever raw material you have—and add them in any sequence you wish. Once you're done, you "print" the project to tape in one, smooth sequence.

Putting Together Your Video System

Video editing can be a fun and exciting process. You can go wild making your own movies and transferring them onto tape to show to the whole family, or shoot weddings, birthdays, and special events.

Depending on the level of quality you wish to achieve, there's some very specific equipment you need to create your original videos, transfer them to your Mac's hard drive, and edit the final production.

If you're just setting up a system for family or friends or a small business, a regular Power Macintosh or iMac DV is probably sufficient. All you need to add is a digital camcorder (these can be had for prices beginning at less than $1,000 these days) and software (unless you're using an iMac DV, which comes with iMovie).

NOTE   *If you have a PCI Mac without a FireWire port, that's not a problem either. Orange Micro and other companies make low-cost FireWire interface cards for many of these models.*

If you have an analog camcorder, you're not left out. A lower-cost video capture board can work with most any Mac with a PCI slot. A video capture board is a device that will convert the analog video signal to digital when it's transferred to your Mac's hard drive, and, when edited, let you "print" it on your camcorder or

Are You Ready to Capture Video?

VCR after converting the signal back to analog. In addition, some Macs, beginning with the Quadra 840AV, have built-in video puts, but they aren't going to provide anything near state-of-the-art quality.

If you intend to deliver your videos to a commercial marketplace, prepare to spend thousands for a suitable system (the success of *The Blair Witch Project,* which essentially originated on home video equipment, notwithstanding).

Regardless of your budget, if you have the will and the imagination, there are incredible things you can do at the editing screen once you get involved in a project.

Selecting and Installing the Right Video System

To start making your mere video into a masterpiece, you need a variety of hardware and software. I'll cover some of those needs in more detail in this section.

The Camcorder

You'll need some sort of video recording device to film your movie. If you have an older computer and you don't need the best quality possible, an analog camcorder will do you just fine. If you have a camcorder with one of the so-called "high-band" video technologies, such as Hi8 and SVHS, you can create master tapes that will look simply superb on a regular VHS VCR when you make a regular copy of the finished project.

Of course, if you have the new iMac DV, a Power Mac G3 (Blue & White) or G4, or even an older computer with a FireWire card, you may want to opt for a new, low-cost digital camcorder, which will probably cost less than what you spent for an analog camcorder just a few years ago.

Just about all the major consumer electronics companies have gotten into the act. You can get digital camcorders from such companies as Canon, JVC, and Sony. Most of them have a FireWire port, though it's not always called FireWire. Sony calls their FireWire ports i.Link. Other companies identify the feature by its technical name, IEEE 1394.

When you connect your camcorder to an open FireWire port on your Mac, you can use a video editing program to transfer video directly from your camcorder to your computer, eliminating the need for sometimes expensive video capture boards and devices.

Can You Hook Up an Older Camcorder to a FireWire Port?

If you happen to have an analog camcorder with a regular composite audio/video port lying around the house and a computer outfitted with a speedy FireWire port, don't feel left out. You can probably buy an A/V-to-FireWire converter, so you can use the camcorder with your computer. Or just consider a regular video capture board. Check your local camcorder or electronics dealer to see what they have. If the dealer doesn't have what you want, check with the manufacturer's Web site or contact their customer service department to see if this is possible.

Video Capture Cards

If your computer is not equipped with FireWire, you may need some sort of video capture device to transfer the video from your camcorder to your computer.

NOTE   *I say "may" because, as I said earlier, some Macs do have video input and, possibly, video output capabilities. But they are strictly entry-level, and you shouldn't expect better than standard VHS quality from these options.*

There are video capture cards that can be placed in an available PCI slot in your computer. An exceptionally low-cost option is ATI's Xclaim VR 128, which costs a mere $239 (based on the most recent suggested retail price).

The card features ATI's Rage 128 graphic accelerator chip, similar to the one Apple uses on many of their models these days, so you can go ahead and use it with your regular display. In addition to providing accelerated 2-D and 3-D display, it doubles as a video capture board. The card has video inputs and a TV output, and claims to be able to perform real-time video capture at resolutions of up to 640x480, at 30 frames per second. This ought to be enough to look good on an SVHS VCR.

Farther up the line is the MiroMOTION DC-30plus, from Pinnacle Systems. Costing less than $700, this card can slide into the PCI slot of most Macs. It uses Motion-JPEG, an industry standard compression method, to reduce file size, yet maximize picture quality. In addition, a copy of Adobe Premiere is included, so you can begin to edit videos right out of the box. The DC-30plus has an onboard digital audio chip, so it doesn't have to use your Mac's onboard sound capability. This will help ensure synchronization of sound and video, especially on longer projects.

If you're looking for something that can produce near-professional caliber videos, consider the TARGA 1000 and the TARGA 2000 in the Pinnacle Line. Professionals also work with systems from such firms as Avid and Media 100.

If you want to explore any of these systems in more detail, please check the following Web sites:

ATI: http://www.atitech.ca
Avid: http://www.avid.com
Media 100: http://www.media100.com
Pinnacle Systems (MiroMOTION and TARGA): http://www.pinnacle.com

Can You Capture Video with USB?

If you have a regular iMac or iBook, you shouldn't feel completely left out when it comes to doing home video editing. A case in point is the Interview USB by XLR8, a division of Interex. Considering the limitations of USB speed (up to a maximum of 12Mbps), don't expect miracles.

However, the low-cost video capture device promises full motion video at 320 × 240 pixels, which is sufficient to deliver quality that should approximate that of a regular VHS tape deck. This sort of picture ought to work fine for home use, so don't sell it short. More information can be had at the company's Web site, http://www.xlr8.com.

Video Capture Software

All right, you've got yourself a video editing station in the making. There's a camcorder to capture the picture, and some way to transfer it to your Mac's hard drive, such as a FireWire port or video capture card. There's one more variable in the video editing equation, and that's the editing software, which brings to your screen the capability to capture the video scenes and make a finished project.

Many of the video capture boards are outfitted with Adobe Premiere, which can provide professional quality editing. The learning curve isn't so difficult (see Figure 19-1) that you will have to wait long to capture and edit your first production.

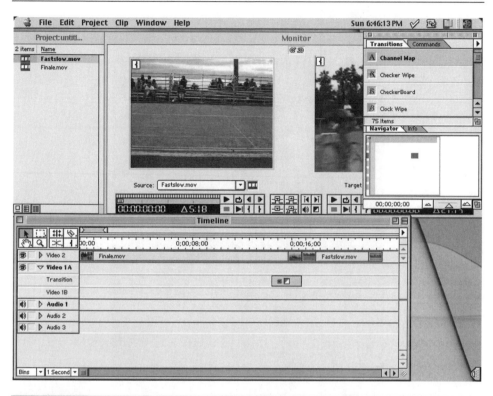

FIGURE 19-1   Adobe Premiere is a tool that both amateurs and pros can use with great success

However, having said that, it doesn't mean it's especially easy to do sophisticated work. You will want to take some time poring over the manual and Help screens to get the maximum possible performance from this program.

Apple's entry into the video editing business is Final Cut Pro (shown in Figure 19-2), which is priced and designed toward a professional audience. Its system requirements are prodigious. You need a Mac with a 266MHz G3 CPU or faster, 128MB of built-in RAM, a 6GB A/V capable hard drive, and Mac OS 8.5 or later.

NOTE   *As this book was written, the MiroMOTION DC-30plus was not compatible with Final Cut Pro or QuickTime 4.0. You may want to check for the promised driver update before you consider this product.*

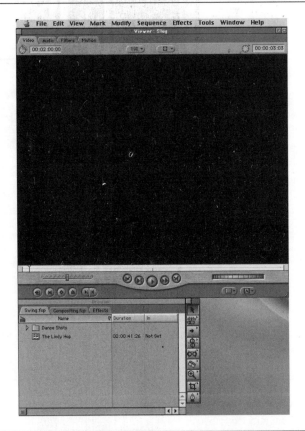

FIGURE 19-2   Feature-laden Final Cut Pro is geared to the professional video editor

The new iMac DVs and DV Special Editions come with their own video editing software called iMovie. In keeping with the iMac's consumer focus, iMovie is designed strictly for the casual user. Its clever interface is easy to master. All you have to do is hook up your DV camcorder to your iMac DV (shown in Figure 19-3), and you have a complete video editing workstation.

NOTE   *Although iMovie is tailor-made for any Mac with a FireWire port, it had not been released for separate sale as of the time this book was written.*

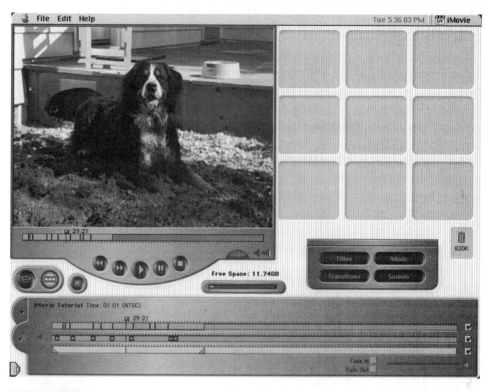

| FIGURE 19-3 | iMovie reduces complex video editing chores to the simplest level possible |

Where Do I Store It?

Before transferring your video to your computer, be prepared to have a huge amount of space available on your hard drive. A typical video can take up as little as 100 megabytes of space and up to two gigabytes or more. Changes in Apple's File Manager for Mac OS 9 make it possible to handle even larger video clips, but you'll want to make sure your video editing software can handle files that size.

You should also have a fast SCSI or FireWire drive and lots of RAM available (64MB or more). However, the high-speed IDE drives Apple uses in its current products are quite capable of handling video capture chores. If you have an older

Mac, make sure your hard drive is A/V capable, meaning it can sustain long file transfers without having to recalibrate, which will result in dropped frames as the drive briefly pauses while capturing or printing your video. The stock drives on older Macs aren't always capable of delivering this level of performance (and Apple's specs don't mention any such limitations). Fortunately, just about any of the large hard drives available from dealers these days will suit, but if you have concerns, check the drive maker's Web site for information as to whether the product is suitable for A/V projects.

NOTE *While it is possible to use such removable media as a Jaz 2 drive as your source drive, don't expect to capture videos of the highest possible quality. You'll need to slow down the capture rate, which will result in lower quality. More to the point, removable drives are not apt to be as reliable as fixed hard drives for prolonged use. Products of this sort are better suited for archival purposes.*

Consider RAID for Serious Video Work

A RAID (redundant array of inexpensive disks) installation uses two or more drives that can be accessed as a single drive. This can provide ultra-fast video transfer performance. You can also use RAID to mirror your drives, so that the same data is copied to two or more drives at the same time. This is insurance against the possibility that one drive may go down during an important editing session, resulting in loss of data. To deliver good performance with a RAID system, you also want to get a high-performance SCSI card.

NOTE *As of the time this book was written, FireWire RAID systems were coming to market. One supplier is VST Technologies (http://www.vsttech.com), who also supplies standalone FireWire devices.*

How to Handle Video Capture Problems

As easy as it is to edit your videos, it's nevertheless true that video editing on a Mac requires attention to proper setup, to avoid operating system quirks that'll cause lost frames and inferior quality.

In this section, I've collected a list of common setup issues and some application-specific problems that you might encounter, along with their solutions.

Preparing for Your Editing Session

Before you begin to capture and edit your project, you'll want to take some precautions to make your Mac into a reliable video editing workstation:

■ **Use a high quality video source.**   Old-fashioned VHS camcorders are cheap these days, but the quality level is not going to please you once you copy it back to the camcorder, then begin to make copies of your finished production. Each generation on an analog tape deck results in further loss of quality. The better the quality of your camcorder or tape deck, the better the finished movie. Even if you don't go for a DV camcorder, a Hi8 model, which can be had for several hundred dollars, is perfectly capable of near-broadcast quality.

■ **Capture your videos onto a speedy hard drive.**   This is a must! At the very least, you need a speedy drive, capable of sustained reading and writing of over 3.5 megabytes per second (the minimum capture rate for high quality video capture from a capture board). The rule of thumb is that the drive must be capable of handling at least twice that speed to sustain long transfers. Otherwise, you will lose frames or be forced to lower the capture rate, which will, in turn, provide inferior quality pictures.

■ **Prepare to optimize the drive regularly.**   In Chapter 13, I suggested that having to regularly optimize your hard drive wasn't all that essential. When it comes to video editing, ignore the statement. When you do this sort of work, you'll be transferring huge files on a regular basis, and the drive is bound to become fragmented quickly. You'll want to get hold of a copy of one of the hard drive optimizing programs, such as Alsoft's Plus Optimizer, MicroMat's TechTool Pro, or Symantec's Norton Utilities.

NOTE *Some video capture boards come with Alsoft's Disk Express Pro, which optimizes in the background, when your drive is idle. It's a brilliant piece of work from programmer Al Whipple and his clever crew, because you don't have to monitor your drive's fragmentation situation. However, as of the time this book went to press, the publisher was still working on a version that would support Mac OS 9 and Apple's HFS+ file system, so you may want to check this further before you attempt to use that program.*

■ **Disable nonessential system extensions.**   Anything that runs in the background, such as virus protection software, can slow you down. Best thing to do is create a so-called Mac OS Base set in Extensions Manager (or Conflict Catcher), then save it as a new set. Once you've done this, add whatever driver software the video card or software requires, plus, of course, Adobe Type Manager if you're doing titles with PostScript fonts.

■ **Deactivate AppleTalk.**   While this ought to be done automatically by your capture software, it's a good idea to double-check. Network activity may cause pauses in the capture process that will cost lost frames.

■ **Switch off virtual memory.**   While Apple's virtual memory feature works well, and the speed lost these days is minimal, it's a no-no for video capturing—the process of paging code to your hard drive will affect the capture process. Go to the Memory Control Panel, switch off virtual memory, and restart before you edit videos.

■ **Put media in removable drives.**   When you have a removable device, the driver software polls the port regularly, again affecting capture speed. You'll also want to put floppies and CDs in their respective drives.

Capturing Live Video from a Camera

Most of the time, you'll simply be copying an existing videotape to your Mac. But it is quite possible to capture a live event. Here's what to do:

1. Connect your camcorder to your Mac's video input or FireWire port.

2. Switch the camcorder to Camera mode and set the Lock/Standby switch on the camcorder to Standby.

NOTE   *Check your camcorder's documentation on how to use specific features and how the features are labeled on your particular unit.*

3. Remove any tape cassettes that are in the camcorder. If any tapes are left in there, the camcorder could time out and go into sleep mode. If you need to have a tape in the camcorder, make sure the write-protection tab is locked, so you don't accidentally copy the image to it.

4. Be sure the camcorder's demo mode is not active. Some camcorders will automatically switch to demo mode when left on standby without a tape inside. Check for any demo function in your camcorder's settings menu and disable it.

Common Video Editing Problems with iMovie

Apple's iMovie software is so easy to use, it's easy to forget that it is doing a tremendously complex set of tasks when you capture and edit your projects.

Here are some common problems and solutions when capturing and playing back video in iMovie:

- **Missing audio or audio dropouts in videos exported to tape** If there's no audio when you play back the production on your DV camcorder, open up your project file, then lower the volume level of the affected clip with the volume slider in the audio viewer. Once you've done this, export the movie again.

- **No video when in capture mode** If you can control your DV camcorder with iMovie, try this: disconnect the FireWire cable while the device is still on, then reconnect it and try again. This usually fixes the problem.

- **Device Too Slow Alert when using FireWire storage device** If you are capturing video to a FireWire drive, check the manufacturer's Web site for an updated version of their driver software. Once you retrieve the software, install it and restart. See if the problem is solved.

NOTE

If you have Mac OS 9 and USB devices attached to your iMac, disable any third-party USB drivers and see if they are recognized at the next startup with Apple's own USB Device Extension. You'll find that SuperDisk and Zip drives are. The presence of Imation's SuperDisk drivers, for example, will seriously impact FireWire drive performance.

Common Video Editing Problems with Final Cut Pro

Final Cut Pro is a serious, robust video editing tool that provides superb performance. But there are problems that will arise on occasion which you'll have to address.

Here are some of those common problems and some solutions:

- **Camcorder or video deck not recognized** First, check to be sure your device control or FireWire cable is properly connected, and also that your camcorder is set to VCR mode (check the product's manual if in doubt of the proper setting). Once you've made sure you have the proper configuration, quit Final Cut Pro. Then turn on the camcorder, and launch the program again. Make sure that the proper protocol for your camcorder is selected in the Device Control tab, located in the Preferences window.

How to Handle Video Capture Problems

■ **Video doesn't show up on external NTSC display** The first thing to check is the cables. Make sure they are properly connected, and that one hasn't slipped out. It is easy, for example, for S-video cables to just pop off. You'll also want to make sure that your camcorder is in VCR mode. Return to Final Cut Pro, look at your General Preferences tab, and make sure the proper hardware is chosen from the View External Video Using pop-up menu. You need to select Rendered Frames from this menu in order to display those frames before they are output to an NTSC video source. One more thing: you need to choose the External Video submenu from the program's View menu, and select All frames or Single frames.

■ **Dropped frames on NTSC display during DV playback from Timeline** In order to address this issue, try reducing the project's Canvas or Viewer display size to 50 percent. Go to the General Preferences tab and turn off Mirror On Desktop During Playback. Your next step is to disable the View As Sq. Pixel feature in the View pop-up menu. As a final step, try reducing the display's bit depth from millions of colors (24-bit) to thousands of colors (16-bit). You probably won't notice much, if any, difference.

■ **Video doesn't appear on display** First thing to do is make sure your cables are properly connected (you didn't disconnect one end when you moved things around, right?). You'll also want to consult Final Cut Pro's Capture preferences tab and make sure that your QuickTime video settings are correct.

■ **Poor quality playback or stuttering video** If you see these symptoms during your editing session, make sure you aren't using such keyframe compression options as Cinepak or Sorenson when working with your media.

■ **No sound from computer when playing footage from camcorder or deck** Once again, check your cables. Make sure the audio cables haven't come loose somehow. You'll also want to revisit the Capture preferences tab and make sure your QuickTime audio configuration is correct.

■ **No audio from camcorder speakers or headphones** First, check the Sound (or Monitor & Sound) Control Panel and make sure the proper audio inputs are selected. Then try the cables. Be sure they are properly seated. If you are scrubbing (scanning) audio using the program's Audio tab in the Viewers menu, increase the output volume.

■ **Some camcorder or desk functions don't work**   The first thing to check is the cables. Be sure the connections are good and tight. Also check the Device Control tab in the program's Preferences window and make sure the protocol needed to control that device is selected. If your video device uses FireWire, try switching from Apple FireWire to Apple FireWire Basic and see if it fixes the problem.

Common Video Editing Problems with Adobe Premiere

You'll find that many of the difficulties that afflict the other programs are there in equal form with Adobe Premiere, plus a few others specific to this program. There will be different solutions, but most come to the same result.

Here's a list of common problems and solutions:

■ **File doesn't appear in Import dialog box**   First thing to do is check to be sure the file format is supported by Premiere. If you have a Windows file, check to be sure it has the proper filename extension. You may also try opening that file in another program that recognizes the format. If the file can't be opened in a program that supports the file, it may be the file itself is damaged (in which case try to get another copy). If the file opens in another program but not in Premiere, it may be one of Premiere's plug-in modules is damaged. In this case, reinstall the program.

■ **Only first frame of still image series imported**   This is usually a configuration issue. Check to see that the first file in the sequence and the Numbered Stills option are selected in Premiere's Import dialog box.

■ **Low image quality during playback of previewed or exported image**   The typical symptom is a pixilated, blurred, or distorted picture. The usual cause is failure to specify a correct data rate when you are using Motion-JPEG as your codec. Check the setting of the Quality slider and enter a specific data rate (check your capture medium's instructions for the best settings).

■ **Audio and video not in sync during export or playback**   Go to Premiere's Project Settings dialog box, and set the timebase to 29.97 fps and the frame rate to 30 fps. If you set the timebase to 30 fps (which would seem a logical assumption), it'll throw the audio out of sync with the video, making your project look like a badly dubbed movie.

■ **Tracks not in sync**   Check your project window to see if there are red triangles displayed at the In locations of the audio and video clips that fail to sync. Click on each of these red triangles and select the timecode that appears on the screen. This action will resynchronize the audio and video.

■ **Export, playback, or preview operation seems slow**   The first thing you'll want to do is make sure the size of the frame is correctly set. Consult your Export Settings or Project Settings and make sure they match up closely. You may also want to check your audio and video filter selections. Look for the Keyframe or Rendering Options from the Export Settings or Project Settings dialog box. Choose Ignore Audio Filters and Ignore Video Filters and see if that helps.

■ **Flickering during playback**   Check your source clip and see if it flickers. If the flickering only turns up in an exported clip, select In. Then apply Premiere's Flicker Removal option. If these steps do not help solve your problem, consult your hardware and software setups to make sure they are correct.

■ **Can't drag an audio or video clip in the timeline**   You have to check to be certain the track you want to drag isn't next to another audio or video track. If this is the case, there will be no place to drag the clip. Also check to see if the track has been locked by mistake.

■ **Exported or previewed video runs too short or too long or is the wrong clip**   When you export video in Premiere, first check the Export Settings dialog box. Look for the Range option in the General Settings panel. Make sure that your project work area is properly specified. When you select Work Area under the Range option, Premiere will dutifully export the work area as part of your project.

Ready to Edit Video?

Some of the issues in running video editing software are complex and arcane, but most of the basic steps, such as dragging clips and extras into your project window, are very intuitive. If you pay attention to detail and setups, you'll do fine with your Mac video workstation, even if that workstation is an easy-to-use iMac DV with iMovie.

In the next chapter, we'll move from videos to the analog world of modems.

Chapter 20

Making the Modem Connection

There are few Mac users who don't surf the Internet at one time or another. Although so-called high-speed Internet connections are beginning to spread across the landscape, most of you are still using a regular analog modem to get connected to the Net.

In this chapter, I'll focus on the ways to set up your modem for best performance, and why you may not be getting the top quality connections you expect. Since the modem is just one leg of your Internet hookup, you'll want to read the next two chapters as well, which focus on Internet performance and what you can do to make your Web browser work faster for you.

Making 56K Work

At one time it was thought that the fastest regular modem would be V.34, with a top speed (if everything is all right, which is not always certain) of 33,600 bps. However, the modem manufacturers managed to find a clever way around that limitation, using digital technology.

Basically, Internet services use digital lines to connect to phone companies. They employ a digital-based technology to encode the information so they can pump it faster through the phone lines. The theoretical maximum speed is 56K. Forgetting for the moment that the FCC limits top speeds (explained in the next section), you will still have trouble realizing the potential, as you'll see shortly.

However, this marvelous technology only works downstream. That means you can receive data at these higher speeds, but sending data is limited to no more than 33,600 bps. That's because your connection to your local phone company is still analog.

For most purposes, this limit doesn't really matter. Graphic-heavy Web pages, streaming audio and video, and file downloads will get to you faster, and on average, you're not as apt to send as much content in the reverse direction. Well, at least that's how the theory goes.

The Cold, Hard Facts About Modem Connection Speeds

You've read the ads for all those new modems. 56,000 bps connection: sounds great, right? This is especially true if you're migrating from a much slower modem, say with 14,400 bps performance. The reality, however, is not always what it's cracked up to be. First off, no 56K modem can connect at 56,000 bps.

The FCC mandates a top limit of 53K. The technical reasons aren't important, but the fact of the matter is that your modem has that handicap from the get go.

The second problem: High-speed modems take phone lines to their technological limits. Unfortunately, phone lines are generally rated strictly for voice transmission, and your local phone company is not apt to guarantee that you'll ever be able to achieve high connection speeds.

In the real world, if you're right up close to the phone company's switching center and have brand new phone lines at your home or in your neighborhood, maybe you'll get speeds from 50K to the maximum 53K. For the rest of you, you should realistically expect actual connection speeds of 34,000 bps to 48,000 bps. I live in a relatively new neighborhood, and the latter is what I usually get, but some folks down the street don't do as well, so it's not altogether consistent.

If you are far from your phone switching center, and perhaps the lines in your neighborhood are old, you would be extremely lucky to see anything approaching 56K-class speeds. You'll be lucky to get 26,400 bps or 28,800 bps.

NOTE   *To make matters more confusing, before the V.90 56K standard was approved, modem manufacturers competed with two preliminary standards. One was K56flex, the other x2. If your modem hasn't been upgraded from the preliminary standard to V.90, you'll want to contact the manufacturer about getting a V.90 update. Usually the update files (which update the modem's firmware) can be downloaded direct from the company's Web site.*

The Right Way to Hook Up a Modem

You have just brought home your new modem (or your smiling delivery person brings it). All you do is plug it in and turn it on, right?

When it comes to setting up a modem, such simple processes aren't always successful. The modem lights are blinking nicely (of course the blinking lights only apply if you have an external modem), but you cannot connect to your online service. Or you connect all right, but you're disconnected unceremoniously within just a few seconds or minutes.

Is it you or the modem or your Mac? In this section, I'll cover some of the basics of modem installation. Then I'll get on to the business of helping you deal with common setup and connection problems.

The Right Way to Hook Up a Modem

Before You Install Your Modem

When you set up your modem, it's a good idea to consider first whether or not you intend to also use it for faxing. Every new modem you buy comes with fax software, and it would seem a great convenience to be able to prepare documents and fax them without having to resort to printing them first. In practice, this doesn't always work as well as you might hope. While fax software these days is flexible, here are a few of the reasons why you might prefer to stick with a separate fax machine:

- **Fax software is buggy.**   Every time Apple updates its system software, one class of products that may have problems is fax software. Fax software is heavily tied to various system functions to send and receive faxes immediately, at a preset time, and to notify you that the fax was received. If your Mac crashes regularly when trying to, for example, send a fax, check with the software publisher to see if they have a newer, better version. The one that comes with the modem may not be the latest, or it may be a "lite" version lacking some features that may be useful to you. In addition, some popular programs, such as Microsoft Word and QuarkXPress, have traditionally had conflicts with fax software. You may want to check with your application software publisher as well when troubles arise.

- **Fax software doesn't handle vector graphics.**   If you do desktop publishing and you work with EPS documents, fax software will have a problem, since such software doesn't support the PostScript page description language. When you fax such documents, your illustrations will be no better than bitmapped pictures on your screen. They'll be usable, but jagged, and grayscale shadings will lack distinction. You may wonder why nobody has come up with a fax-based PostScript feature to deal with this. Actually, a long-gone company once tried to offer a PostScript interpreter for fax software, but it never worked as advertised. I have also asked the publishers of the existing fax programs about this limitation. In general, they feel it would either be too expensive to develop, or the market wouldn't be sufficient for them to make a profit from the venture. So that's where it stands.

> NOTE   *Despite the inability to handle EPS files, fax software tends to be superior to a standalone fax machine in rendering regular photos and other graphic images.*

■ **Your Mac must be on all the time to receive faxes.** Well, let me amend that. Your Mac could be in Sleep mode, and awake when a fax is coming. But the unit is still on nonetheless. If your Mac is off, the fax can't be received. Consider this issue if you expect your business contacts to send you faxes after hours.

■ **You must scan printed documents.** If you have a printed document you want to fax, you must first scan it (which means you must buy a scanner if you don't already have one), save it as a file, then fax that file. This may be fine for an occasional printed piece, but if you intend to fax a lot of material this way, it can become a time-consuming process. You may end up needing a separate fax machine anyway.

NOTE *A clever alternative to the need for separate devices is the multifunction printer. Very few are available in Mac form (notable exceptions are some products from Canon and Epson). Since the basic image scanning engines are the same, these manufacturers build in scanning, faxing, copying, and printing features. But then again, you still end up with a standalone fax machine here.*

None of the preceding shortcomings should necessarily mean you should not use your modem's faxing feature, however. I know of one client who uses a fax modem for the convenience of sending letters and desktop publishing documents directly from his Mac. But the very same client keeps a regular fax machine on hand for faxing printed pieces or documents with EPS graphics. It gives you the best of both worlds.

Installing Your New External Modem

Before you install the modem, check the manual or setup brochure to see if you need to install any special software. If you intend to use the modem as a fax machine, you'll need to use an installation disk. If you just want to use the modem, it depends. Some installation disks will include modem scripts for Apple's Remote Access (Open Transport/PPP), or additional features that can only be accessed via software (such as Global Village's famous menu bar display).

From there, follow these basic steps:

1. For an external modem, make sure it's plugged in to the electrical outlet, your phone lines, and, of course, your Mac.

The Right Way to Hook Up a Modem

NOTE
Some modems are actually bus powered, meaning they draw their current right from a connection directly to your Mac. For an older Mac, it would be the ADB port (the one to which you connect keyboard and mouse), and for the newest generation of Macs, it may be the USB port. The modem's manual should explain all this.

2. Take the installation disk and CD and insert into your Mac's drives.

NOTE
If your modem comes with a floppy disk, and you have a Mac without a floppy drive, contact the manufacturer and see if they can send you a CD version. If you don't intend to use the fax feature, you may not need to install anything except, perhaps, a modem script for your Internet connections. The lone exception to this is a Global Village modem, since their software puts up a neat menu bar display showing modem activity.

3. Locate an installer icon and double-click on it. If there's no installer icon, check the manual or setup instructions for information. You may simply have to manually drag some files to the System Folder or elsewhere on your Mac's drive and restart.

4. As soon as your modem's software is installed, try logging on to your Internet or online service and test the fax capability, if it applies, to see if the modem is performing as you expect. If anything's wrong, read the next section for help.

NOTE
If you don't already have an Internet connection, you may find some possibilities in the box in which your new modem was shipped. Look for special offers from AOL, EarthLink, and other services. The great thing about these offers is the free trial period. If you don't like one service, you can switch to another without having to pay an extra fee.

Setting Up the Modem Control Panel to Recognize Your Modem

If your modem doesn't come with a special software installer, check the supplied disk or CD for a modem script (CCL file) for the Modem Control Panel. While Apple supplies modem scripts for a variety of models, the ones prepared by the manufacturer are often optimized for better connections.

An Overview of Internal Modems

It was once just the province of Apple's consumer products and laptops, but now all new Apple computers are fitted with internal modems (or come with provisions for them).

While this may not sit well with the folks who make Mac modems, it's a great convenience for you, because you don't have to fret over installing a new hardware device and finding the right connection scripts or software.

But as with other products, Apple hasn't made the internal modem equation as simple as it should be. Good examples are Apple's desktop line. If it comes standard equipment, fine. But if you wish to add an internal modem to any of Apple's desktop models beginning with the original beige G3, you'll find that each product generation requires a different modem. So you cannot, for example, transfer the modem you pull from the communications slot of a beige G3 into the Blue & White G3 or G4 and vice versa. And it's not that each of these products has a better internal modem than the previous generation either.

When you buy a Power Macintosh, try to get one with the modem included, or order one when you order your computer—and don't expect that it'll serve duty for anything but that specific model.

If you don't find a modem script with your new modem, check the manufacturer's Web site (that is, assuming you get online all right). Once you have downloaded the file, here's how to install it:

1. Take the modem script and drag it to the closed System Folder icon. This will produce an alert screen similar to this:

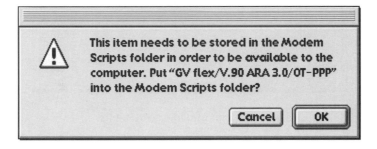

This item needs to be stored in the Modem Scripts folder in order to be available to the computer. Put "GV flex/V.90 ARA 3.0/OT-PPP" into the Modem Scripts folder?

Cancel   OK

The Right Way to Hook Up a Modem

2. OK the alert screen to install your modem script file in the appropriate location. The file will be placed in the Modem Scripts folder, which is located within the Extensions folder (in your System Folder).

NOTE

If you don't see a Finder prompt that your modem script is going to the correct place, you may have an older system version or there may be something in the file that isn't alerting the Finder where it should go. You probably don't have to worry over that. Just place it manually within the Modem Scripts folder and it should appear on your list of available modem drivers.

3. Go to the Apple menu, select Control Panels, and choose Modems from the scrolling list. This brings up the Control Panel screen shown in Figure 20-1.

4. Select your modem script from the list.

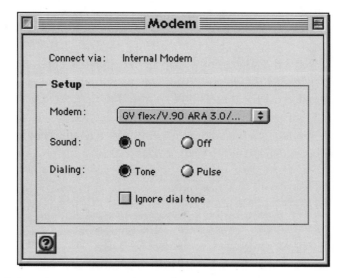

FIGURE 20-1   Choose a modem script from the scrolling list

5. Click on the Connect Via: pop-up menu to pick the port to which your modem is attached, if the correct one isn't listed. A regular Mac modem attaches to the Modem Port. Otherwise, choose Modern/Printer Port, Internal Modem, USB modem, or whatever port setup applies to your particular setup.

NOTE *If the exact make and model still isn't listed, recheck the name of the modem script you installed to see if it's there or not. You may need to close and reopen the Modem Control Panel for the list to update.*

6. Leave the Sound and Dialing radio buttons as they are unless you want to turn off the modem's dial-out sound or you're using a phone service without touch-tone capability.

7. Click the close box to retain the settings.

8. You will be asked whether you want to save your settings. Click the Save button to retain your new settings, Cancel to keep the ones that are already there.

NOTE *If you make your Modem Control Panel change while logged on to an Internet service, the settings won't be used until you've disconnected from your service, then logged on again.*

GLOBAL VILLAGE MODEM USERS: CAN'T FIND THE SCRIPT?   The regular installation of a Global Village modem will usually install the correct modem script in your Modem Scripts folder. If it doesn't (and this may apply to older versions of the software), you may find the file in another location on your hard drive.

Just open the folder that contains your Global Village software. Look for a folder labeled TelePort (or PowerPort) Accessories. You'll find modem scripts distributed through one or more folders, along with simple setup instructions. There will also be a Read Me that contains information on setting up such programs as AOL, CompuServe, and FreePPP to properly recognize the Global Village modem.

The Right Way to Hook Up a Modem

SETTING UP FreePPP TO USE YOUR MODEM   If you have an older version of the Mac OS, or just never got around to trying Apple's Internet Dialing facility, you might still be using a program such as FreePPP or MacPPP to make your connection. I don't want to throw cold water on your choice, though it's a fact that Apple's own software works just fine in most circumstances.

If you decide to continue to use FreePPP or MacPPP, however, the setup may not be quite as automatic. Here's how you'd configure FreePPP, for example, to work with your modem:

1. Double-click on the FreePPP Setup application to launch it.

2. Click on the triangle at the lower left of the setup screen, so it points downward. This will give you a visual display of the settings you make (so you can confirm your choices).

3. Click on the Modems tab.

4. Click the New button, which will bring up the FreePPP Modem Configuration screen.

5. Enter the name of your modem in the Modem config name text field.

6. If the port to which your modem is attached isn't shown, click on the Connected To pop-up menu and choose the correct port from the list. For regular Macs, it'll say Modem Port. For other types of Macs, it may say Modem/Printer Port, Internal Modem, or USB modem, whichever applies.

7. From the Port Speed pop-up menu, pick the highest setting, which is probably 115200 bps (unless your modem maker specifies another setting).

8. Choose CTS & RTS (DTR) from the Flow Control menu (unless your modem maker says otherwise).

9. Make sure the Dial Type is Tone unless your dialing system doesn't support it.

10. Now here's the biggie: FreePPP has an option called AutoDetect init string under Modem init string settings. The purpose of this feature is to allow FreePPP to pick a modem profile that supports your modem. Go ahead and select this one, unless your modem maker specifies a different setting.

NOTE

If you do not get a satisfactory modem connection using the AutoDetect option, click the Use button instead and enter either of these two settings: AT&F1W2 or AT&FW2. Your modem's manual will indicate whether AT&F or AT&F1 enables the default or factory setting (and that's the one you want to use). The W2 setting is designed so the actual connection speed is displayed when you connect to your Internet service.

11. Now click on the General tab, and choose Open TCP/IP for Apple's Open Transport, or Open MacTCP if you have an older Mac with MacTCP installed.

SETTING UP CONFIG PPP TO USE YOUR MODEM   The other connection choice, especially for older versions of the Mac OS, is MacPPP, which uses the Config PPP Control Panel. If you are using this option, just follow these steps to make it work with your new modem:

CAUTION

If you have a newer Mac, you are better off sticking with Apple's Remote Access or Open Transport/PPP for your Internet connection. The older MacPPP software may not be compatible with any of the new system and hardware versions.

1. Go to the Apple Menu, select Control Panels, and choose Config PPP from the submenu.

2. Select the port to which your modem is attached in the Port Name pop-up menu. For older Macs with a standard modem, you may choose Modem Port. Other Macs may list Modem/Printer Port, Internal Modem, USB, or something similar.

3. From the Echo Interval pop-up menu, leave the setting in the off position.

4. Click the Config button to set up a connection profile for your Internet provider. This will bring up a PPP Server dialog.

5. Enter the name of your PPP Server (or Service) in the text field. The name of your Internet provider ought to be sufficient.

6. Pick the highest setting from the Port Speed pop-up menu (it's probably 57600).

The Right Way to Hook Up a Modem

7. Choose CTS & RTS (DTR) from the Flow Control menu (unless your modem maker says otherwise).

8. In the Modem Init text field, enter a string for your modem. Consider AT&F1W2 or AT&FW2, depending on what your modem maker uses for its default or factory setting. The latter part, W2, is used so that Config PPP will report the correct connection speed.

The rest of your settings depend on your Internet service's requirements, so check their documentation or recommendations. I'll tell you how to get the best possible performance from your Internet connection in the next chapter.

It's True! Most Modems Are Basically the Same Inside

Despite the fancy advertising, variety of bundled software, and markedly different case designs, at heart many of the modems you buy are made from some of the very same stuff. The digital signal processing (DSP) chips these modems use are commonly made by Conexant or its predecessor in the modem chip market, Rockwell. There may be some variations in the way a modem manufacturer uses this core technology, but in the end, basic performance ought to be similar.

There are some exceptions to this rule, notably the U.S. Robotics division of 3Com, which uses modems incorporating chips from Texas Instruments.

Why It Won't Connect

You have followed my instructions or the manufacturer's to the letter. You have checked every single step, yet your modem just won't give you a reliable connection, or maybe it just won't connect at all. Is it time to toss it out and try another modem?

Let's explore some of the reasons why a modem doesn't work and some quick solutions.

Defective Modem

Even if the modem appears to dial out, and, with an external modem, the lights flash on and off in the appropriate fashion, the modem may be defective. If it's brand new, you should return it to your dealer; otherwise most manufacturers have product warranties of from five to seven years and should be able to handle your request for a replacement promptly. Some manufacturers may offer an overnight exchange, for which you have to give a credit card number as a deposit to guarantee return of the defective unit. Others require that you ship the defective product back first for repair or replacement.

Bad or Incorrect Cable

When higher speed modems came out, beginning with the 9,600 bps models, they used a special cable known as a "hardware handshake" cable. You can't immediately tell this cable from the older one, but the difference is glaring. The new cable will work just fine with high-speed modems; the older ones won't support the connections. New modems come with the right cable. If you plan on hooking up an older cable to a newer modem, my advice is don't! You can buy a brand new cable from your Mac dealer for $10-20 and you'll avoid the aggravation.

If you're sure the cable is correct (it came with your new modem, for example), it still could be defective. Try another cable if all the following connection solutions listed don't help you.

Missing Modem Port

If you've just hooked up a new external modem to an older desktop Mac that still has an internal modem installed, more than likely, you'll find that your Modem Port isn't available, so you cannot make it dial out to your Internet or online service.

This is a common problem on Apple's Performa modems, which shipped with low performance internal modems (often 14,400 bps) and no upgrade options. In order for you to make an external modem work, you need to remove the internal modem. That will free up your software.

If you're not sure how to remove the modem (and it's no more complicated than opening the case to install a memory upgrade), have your dealer handle the job for you. It should take them no more than 15 minutes to perform the task.

TIP

If you are using your internal modem on a Performa and the connection port for it doesn't appear in Remote Access (Open Transport/PPP), FreePPP, or MacPPP, you may just need to install the proper software. The System or Restore disk that came with your Performa should have a set of installer files labeled Apple Express Modem or Apple GeoPort Telecom. The correct software needs to be installed so your Internet software realizes there really is an internal modem there. If you're not sure which you need (and the manual isn't of any help), try installing both.

Why It Won't Connect

Slow Connection Speeds

First of all, you'll want to take a realistic view of what speeds you can achieve (see "The Cold, Hard Facts About Modem Connection Speeds" earlier in the chapter). But even if you're near a phone company switch and in a newly developed area, it's quite possible you'll encounter troubles getting good performance. Here are a few possible solutions for you to consider:

■ **Try another connection number.**   If you live in a city of reasonable size, you will probably find several access numbers for your online service. If you're an AOL member, you can use the Setup feature to locate another access number for a given area code or country. Other services will usually have a list of access numbers at their Web sites or you can telephone their technical support people for help. If there's no other access number in your area, try one in a nearby city as a test to be sure there's not another cause for this problem.

■ **Check the modem setup or modem string.**   Modem strings are little instructions that tell a modem how to handle certain functions (see the section "What's a Modem String and How Do I Use It?" for the specifics). If you enter the wrong string, the modem may not be able to use some of its features, or may not connect at all. If you're connecting via Apple's Remote Access (Open Transport/PPP) software, the easiest way to pick the right modem string is simply to select the modem script that most closely matches the make and model of your modem. When you reinstall system software, it's very likely you'll find the selection has changed and you need to select it again. Follow the steps described earlier in the section entitled "The Right Way to Hook Up a Modem" to make sure everything is set up properly.

NOTE   *If you're using AOL, try their software's auto detect feature. If the software picks the wrong modem, you'll have a chance to pick the right one from the scrolling list after the setup process is complete.*

■ **Modem needs firmware update.**   Nearly all current modems have Flash ROMs, which means the code that operates the modem (a modem's equivalent of an operating system) can be upgraded to fix bugs and improve performance. You can usually get the latest updates (called "firmware") from a manufacturer's Web site. A great source of information about new and updated software is the Mac VersionTracker Web site (http://www.versiontracker.com).

■ **Using an older Mac?**   Mac computers beginning with the Centris and Quadra series (these models came out before the first generation of Power Macs) introduced a special serial port called GeoPort, which was fast enough to comfortably handle the requirements of 28,800, 33,600 and 56,000 bps modems. Older Macs have slower serial ports, and they may not achieve good performance with such products. Your only choice here is, if possible, lower the Port Speed setting, from 57,600 to 28,800 bps or even lower and see if you get better performance. You'll be able to adjust these settings in such programs as AOL, CompuServe, FreePPP, and MacPPP.

■ **Remove other phone devices on your line.**   Each item you have on your phone line, from phones to fax machines to modems, uses a small amount of current from the line. If you have too many devices connected, it could impair performance. The best way to check for this problem is to remove everything except your modem, and make sure it is plugged directly to the wall jack (and not to just another phone device). If it seems as if another phone device is contributing to the problem, it'll be up to you to decide whether to keep the other device disconnected or have it checked for a possible hardware problem.

> TIP
>
> *If you need to have your modem working regularly throughout the day, without interruption, it's probably a good idea to give it its own dedicated phone line. That will free up your other line for regular phone calls.*

■ **Have the phone lines checked.**   If you hear static on the line (even light static), rest assured your modem's performance will be impaired. Contact your local phone company to deal with this problem. Bear in mind that their primary concern is voice quality, not modem quality. But since phone companies are now actively promoting business or small business use, you might actually find a sympathetic ear from a customer service representative.

■ **Try another modem.**   If all else fails, it could be your modem is defective. It may not matter that it dials out and makes a connection. Sometimes problems with a modem are more subtle than working or not working. If you have another modem or access to one, try it and see if performance is better. If it is, contact the manufacturer's technical support people for assistance.

Busy Signals

An Internet service's access number is basically just a network of modems, with a finite capacity. When that capacity is reached, you get a busy signal, same as when you call a regular private phone line that's being used.

The easiest solution is just to try again. Apple's Remote Access, Open Transport/PPP, and FreePPP can be set to automatically redial a number after a small delay. If you continue to get busy signals, try logging on at a different hour. Internet services tend to be busiest during the so-called primetime hours in the evenings or on weekends.

If you get persistent busy signals, try another telephone access number for your service, if available in your city. If you cannot get satisfactory performance from your Internet service, you may want to consider another provider. Check the ads in your newspaper or favorite computing magazine, or use one of those free online service offers you get in the mail.

TIP

When you install a new Mac or a new version of the Mac operating system, you may want to install the Internet Connection option. This will allow you to pick an Internet provider via Apple's Internet Setup Assistant.

Sudden Disconnects

Sometimes your modem will appear to connect just fine, but after a few minutes, you're logged off, apparently for no reason. First and foremost, check the earlier section entitled "Slow Connection Speeds." The same solutions may apply to either problem. Then check out these possible causes:

■ **Your online service logged you off.**   America Online and some Internet services will log you off if you're inactive for a period of time. For AOL, it's usually 45 or 46 minutes, and other services will usually specify in their instructions or online information how long they wait before disconnecting you. This problem is doubly difficult on AOL because you may be downloading a file using a separate Web browser, such as Internet Explorer or Netscape. AOL won't sense the modem activity because they only recognize it with their built-in browser, or at least that's how the theory goes. Otherwise, their idle-time feature seems to only function when you access features that are strictly on AOL. Even writing email or a message for a message board isn't counted as being active, because the modem isn't sending or receiving any information.

■ **Your Internet dialer disconnected you.**   Apple's Remote Access and Open Transport/PPP have a Connection check box under Options that specifies you'll be disconnected if you're idle for 10 minutes. You will find similar options in FreePPP. Since these features aren't turned on by default, you may want to double-check to see if they're on or not.

NOTE   *If you have a habit of forgetting to log off your Internet service when you finish your session, you may want to leave the automatic log-off option checked.*

■ **Call waiting interrupted your line.**   Call waiting is a great feature. It lets you literally have two phone lines in one and to switch between two calls (if you like juggling acts). Unfortunately, the little noise a call waiting announcement makes can also drop your Internet connection. If you have this feature, be sure to insert a *70, (including that comma) as part of the number that's being dialed. It will disable call waiting for that call. Apple's DialAssist control panel in recent Mac OS versions can be set up to add these numbers—or just enter it manually. AOL's software setup also includes a provision for inserting this number string.

How to Test Your Modem's Real Connection Potential

Here's a fast way to see how well your modem can handle a high-speed connection. It involves calling up 3Com's LineTest center. 3Com is the manufacturer of U.S. Robotics modems, but this test should work with any V.34 or V.90 model.

To run this test, you'll need a terminal program such as MacComCenter, Microphone, or Zterm. You can download the latter from http://www .versiontracker.com. In addition, AppleWorks (formerly ClarisWorks) has a communications module that'll do just fine (in fact it's probably the only thing you may ever use it for). Now just follow these steps:

1. Dial up 3Com's test number, using this command: **ATDT1-847-262-6000**. Your modem will go through its usual dialing connecting routine, and then you'll see a series of text prompts.

NOTE   *Don't be intimidated by a text-based interface. Just follow the instructions you see carefully, as they may change from time to time from the ones I list here.*

2. When you're asked if your terminal program handles graphics, press ENTER to continue.

3. You'll then be asked to enter your name. In response, type **line** and press ENTER.

4. Then you're asked to enter your list name. Reply by typing **test** and again press ENTER.

5. Over the next minute or so, 3Com's LineTest feature will run some diagnostics on the connection you've made. If your 56K modem is really connecting at a 56K speed, you'll see "This connection supports 56K technology!" From here, press the ENTER key twice to see the actual statistics on your connection, which include the most important piece of information—connection speed. Figure 20-2 has an example of a typical result from this test.

6. To end your LineTest session, type the letter **g**, then press ENTER. You'll be disconnected within a few seconds.

If your modem fails to connect at a 56K speed, you'll see this message: "56K is not currently possible on this connection, or is likely to be highly impaired." This is no problem if you don't have a 56K modem, but if you do, it may indicate other problems you'll need to address, some of which, as I explain in this chapter, may simply be beyond your ability to control.

NOTE   *This line test feature can, itself, be a little flaky. If you cannot make a connection to run the test, just try again at a later time.*

What's a Modem String and How Do I Use It?

As I said earlier in this chapter, modems are analog devices that convert your computer language to little beeps and squawks that your phone system can handle. But in order to talk with your modem and get good performance, the Mac has to give it a set of commands, called a modem initialization string. The string is designed to activate specific features of your modem, so you get the best possible performance.

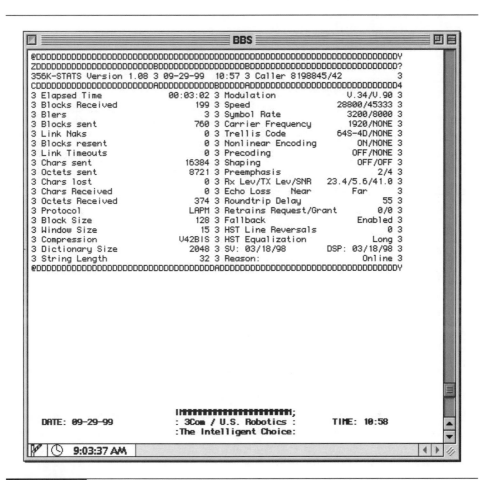

FIGURE 20-2   This LineTest session, done with Microphone, demonstrates a pretty decent connection speed for the author's modem

For the most part, you shouldn't have to bother with a modem string. When you set up your modem, and configure Apple's Remote Access and Open Transport/PPP, and your Internet software, including AOL and CompuServe, this all should be done behind the scenes simply by selecting the proper make and model of your modem.

Case History

The Case of the Modem That Wouldn't Reset

I installed a brand new Global Village 56K internal modem in my Blue & White Power Macintosh G3. Everything worked just great. Apple's clever industrial design team has done wonders to prevent headaches when putting things inside your Mac (although the first-generation iMac remains a distinct exception).

The modem worked just dandy until it locked up when connecting to the Internet. I tried to reset the modem, to no avail. Global Village has a control panel (called PowerPort, TelePort, or on mine, GlobalFax Controls) with a reset button. When I tried it, the control panel lost all information about the modem, reporting that no modem was detected.

The modem was still locked up. I tried connecting with my Internet software over and over again, and it wouldn't work. I restarted my Mac, and still the modem wasn't recognized. On a hunch, I shut down the Mac (through the normal procedure), waited a few seconds and restarted. The modem was recognized again by GlobalFax Controls, and it worked like a charm!

I telephoned Global Village's technical support folks and asked just what went wrong. The response was simple: with an external modem, if it locks up, you just turn the unit off and then on again. With an internal modem, your Mac is the on/off switch, powering all internal devices, so your Mac has to be shut down and restarted to accomplish the same result.

AOL, for example, even has an auto-detect feature (see Figure 20-3), which is used to check your modem's hardware and pick a profile optimized for best performance.

For other programs, such as FreePPP and MacPPP, you may have to enter the settings manually. Usually the modem maker will give you the proper setup information. Sometimes you'll have to make a good guess. I'll give you some of the basic commands in Table 20-1.

NOTE *U.S. Robotics modems usually have a separate volume control that handles sound functions, so the sound-related strings are not needed.*

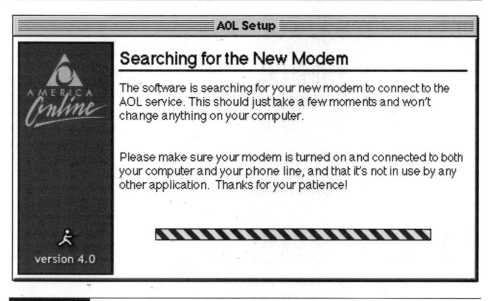

FIGURE 20-3 AOL probes your modem to pick the right profile

Modem String	Function
AT	The beginning command for the start of a string. Stands for "attention."
ATA	This command is used to answer an incoming call.
AT&F	On some modems, this command reverts to default or factory settings.
AT&F1	On some modems, you use this command for default or factory settings.
ATLX	This command is designed to control the volume of your modem's speaker. X may be used for 0, the lowest setting, or 3, the highest. The numbers in between, 1 and 2, provide intermediate settings.
ATMX	This command is designed to silence your modem. Use 0 to turn the speaker off, 1 to turn it on.
ATDT[+ phone number]	Use this command to manually dial out in a terminal program.
ATZ	This command will end your connection and revert the modem to its previous setting.
Lx (1, 2, 3)	Sets modem's speaker volume, 1 being the lowest, 3 being the highest. This feature doesn't work on internal modems.
M0	Turns off modem speaker. This feature doesn't work on all modems.
W2	Reports correct modem connection speed.

TABLE 20-1 Common Modem Strings and Their Functions

The Truth About 115,200 bps Connections

This happens occasionally: you connect to your Internet or online service and you see a connection speed reported at 115,200 bps. I have already explained in this chapter how a conventional analog modem's speed is limited by the FCC to 53,000 bps, and it's usually less. So how can your modem report higher speeds, such as 57,600 bps, or 115,200 bps? A miracle? Nope, an incorrect modem string.

In the section on setting up such programs as FreePPP and MacPPP, I mentioned entering the W2 string. The reason I recommend these two characters is because they will tell your modem to report the correct connection speed when you first connect.

You won't see 115,200 bps anymore, but you'll see the real speed.

NOTE
I have deliberately left out higher speed protocols, such as cable modems or DSL (Digital Subscriber Line) in this chapter. They involve new technologies that provide performance way beyond what a regular modem can handle. I'll cover these so-called "broadband" features in the next chapter.

Summing Up

The world of modems can sometimes seem daunting, especially since they don't always work as seamlessly or as predictably as you think they should. But usually with a little adjustment here and there, you'll find you get the level of Internet performance you expect.

In the next chapter we'll move the discussion to the Internet. You'll learn how to cope with Internet performance problems and how to make your surfing go more swiftly.

Chapter 21

Dealing with Internet Access Problems

The Internet has advanced from its humble origins at the government and university levels to encompass a multibillion dollar industry that affects most everyone who uses a computer. For example, an Apple Computer survey of new iMac users reported that fully 90 percent use their computers to surf the Internet.

You use the Internet to send and receive email, visit Web sites, download software, post messages, chat, join online communities, and buy lots and lots of merchandise, from books to cars, and a lot more in between.

Getting good Internet performance should be a given. New Macs have high-speed modems, and Internet and online services have spent untold amounts of money to improve their services. Alas, the reality is something else altogether.

As you saw in the previous chapter, there are ways to spruce up your modem's performance to get the best possible connection speed. But even after you have done all that to tune up your connections, you may find that getting reasonable speed from the Internet is a challenge. And that's what this chapter is all about.

Solving Internet Connection Problems

Many of the issues I discussed in the previous chapter can be responsible for the problems you may have in getting on the Net. Check that chapter for information on problems that may be caused by your modem rather than the service to which you're trying to connect.

Bad or Lost Internet Connections

If your modem is set up properly, here are some other causes of problems getting on the Internet:

- ■ **Improper TCP/IP settings** In order to connect to a regular Internet service provider (ISP), you need to specify the correct connection protocol and correct IP numbers in your TCP/IP Control Panel (see Figure 21-1). If you specify the wrong information in either category, you either won't connect at all, or you'll connect but be unable to access one or more of the service's features. Each ISP will have its own unique settings. In addition, if you use a cable modem or access the Internet at your company (which may have a special connection to the Internet, such as a secured firewall), other settings may be required. If your modem seems to be set up properly, you will need to verify your Internet settings using whatever information you received from the ISP or system administrator. If there's no documentation around as to what the settings are, contact your ISP directly for the details.

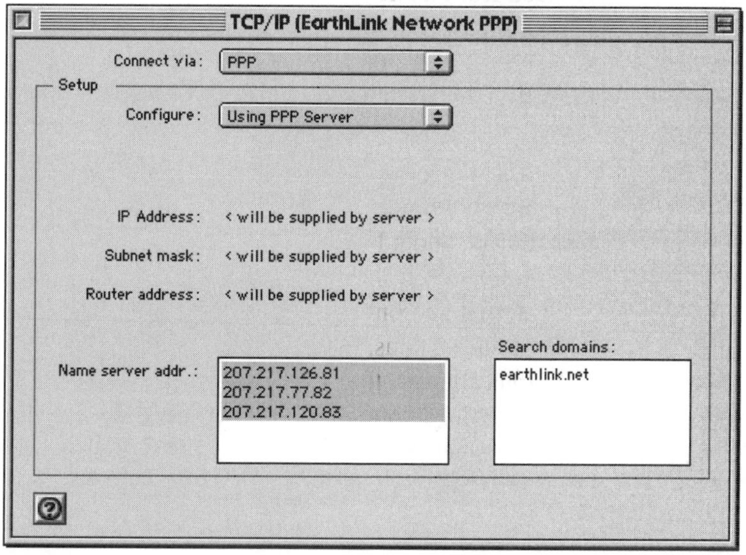

FIGURE 21-1   The TCP/IP Control Panel must be set up properly to access a specific ISP. The settings you see here applied to EarthLink as of the time this book was written. Your mileage will vary

NOTE   *Older versions of the Mac operating system used the MacTCP Control Panel for Internet configurations. While the interface looks different, the information you need to supply will be essentially the same.*

■ **Missing TCP/IP settings**   If you recently reinstalled your system software or you've set up a new Mac, you may have to reenter these settings (unless you use the following tip).

TIP   *Before you install a new Mac or do a "clean" system software installation, make copies of the files labeled Internet Preferences, TCP/IP Preferences, and Remote Access Connections (this one's in the Remote Access folder). These are all located in the Preferences folder, inside your Mac's System Folder. Having these settings files will greatly simplify your setup process, and it never hurts to have a backup in case your original settings are damaged due to a system crash.*

■ **Corrupted TCP/IP settings**   Hard drive directory damage or a system crash can destroy your Internet settings if it happens when you're trying to access your ISP. You should be ready to replace them when necessary with a backup.

NOTE

To make matters all the more confusing, I have seen situations where ISPs have sent out a set of installer disks that place the wrong setup information in your TCP/IP Control Panel. If you have entered everything correctly, and performance is still unsatisfactory, you may wish to contact the service's technical support people for assistance.

■ **User authentication failed**   When you set up your Internet access, you not only have to enter the proper phone numbers in the Remote Access (or Open Transport/PPP) Control Panel, but the proper username and password as well. If one or the other is missing or incorrect, you may connect, but you won't be able to log in. The same setups will apply if you're using AOL, Config PPP, or FreePPP to dial your Internet connection.

TIP

When you enter your password, be sure you're not confusing a zero with the letter "O". You need to enter the letters and/or numbers correctly, upper- and lowercase included.

NOTE

ISPs use something referred to as "authentication servers" to verify a member's username and password. If the system is not working for some reason, you may find that you cannot connect to your Internet service even if your Mac's settings are 100 percent correct. If you encounter this problem, try connecting again later. If that doesn't work, I suggest you contact your ISP about it.

The Magic and Mystery of Internet Config

Aside from your modem and TCP/IP settings, there's one more key player in the great drama of getting connected to the Internet, and that's the Internet Config application. For Mac OS 8.5 and later, this program was used as the basis of the Internet Control Panel.

Now, it would seem to be an easy matter to have all of your Internet settings in a convenient place, but in the real Mac world it doesn't quite work out that way.

Each Internet program that relies on Internet Config has its own way of storing its specific program settings. And in some cases, such as with AOL, Microsoft Internet Explorer, and Microsoft Outlook Express, you may not be able to see the results except in the programs themselves (or in the way they behave).

One key example of this is the location of the Web cache file for AOL and Internet Explorer. I'll cover more about how to deal with a Web cache in the next chapter, but for now, let me simply explain that, when you install and set up AOL 4.0, it uses the very same Web cache as Internet Explorer. Even if you change the location of Internet Explorer's Web cache, AOL will diligently insist on placing it right back where it was (in the America Online folder, within the Preferences folder in your Mac's System Folder) the very next time you bring up a Web site on AOL.

So rather than fight the inevitable, I'll cover the proper setup of Internet Config (or the Internet Control Panel). So even if a program chooses to mess with some of its more arcane aspects, you'll at least have done what you can to get things to work properly.

The Internet Config/Internet Control Panel by the Numbers

When you install and set up AOL, it does what it needs to do to your Internet configuration behind the scenes. And some ISPs, such as EarthLink, include their own custom software installers that'll do all the setups for you automatically as the installer is run.

That's convenient if you don't intend to switch services and you don't install a lot of extra Internet software. But if you do any of that, or simply reinstall your system software, you run the risk of changing your Internet Config settings in a way that you didn't expect, with unexpected results.

Following is a brief tutorial on the proper setup of Internet Config (using the Internet Control Panel from Mac OS 9). First, let's look at the Internet Config main screen, as shown in Figure 21-2. You see it when you launch the Internet Config application.

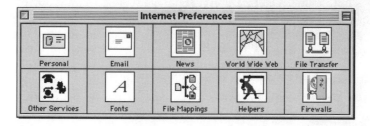

FIGURE 21-2   Internet Config puts up a screen with icons representing each setting you can make to your Internet setup

Solving Internet Connection Problems

NOTE *When you install Internet programs such as Netscape, you'll find a proliferation of copies of Internet Config, one for each installation. It's not much different from all those copies of SimpleText and its predecessor, TeachText, which used to turn up all over your hard drive. Best advice is to locate the latest version and trash the others. If you're using Mac OS 8.5 or later, you can safely toss out all copies of Internet Config without worrying about hurting your Internet settings.*

To change settings, just click on an icon that represents the change you want to make and enter the information in the text entry fields. Since Apple's Internet Control Panel replaces Internet Config, I'll use that as a guide to show you what settings you need to enter. The ones I'll be showing apply to either program.

A Fast Guide to Internet Control Panel Sets

If you use more than one ISP, you will want to take advantage of the ability to make multiple sets in the Internet Control Panel. Once you create a new set and save it, you can switch to and from that set via the Active Set pop-up menu on the Internet Control Panel screen.

Here's a brief list of the extra features you can explore should the need arise. They are all available from the File menu:

■ **New Set**   This setting creates a blank Internet set, and is not recommended, since you have to enter all the basic information from scratch.

■ **Duplicate Set**   This is also available as a button on the Internet Control Panel screen. Making a duplicate set is actually the best way to create a new set. You can take the basic setup information from another set and adapt it to a different service, and that's a lot easier than reentering the information.

■ **Rename Set**   Use this option to rename any set (active or not) as you prefer.

■ **Delete Set**   You can use this option to delete a set, so long as it isn't active.

NOTE
None of the settings I'm describing in this section will have any effect on AOL's software. Some of the settings, such as a default Web home page and the location for downloaded files, can be set by opening AOL's software and choosing Preferences from the My AOL toolbar's submenu.

1. Click on the Apple menu, select Control Panels, and choose Internet from the submenu. This brings up the screen shown in Figure 21-3.

TIP
If you don't like the default name for your Internet settings, click on the File menu, choose Rename, and rename your sets as you prefer. This is useful if you have several Internet accounts or multiple users, and need to set aside a different configuration for each.

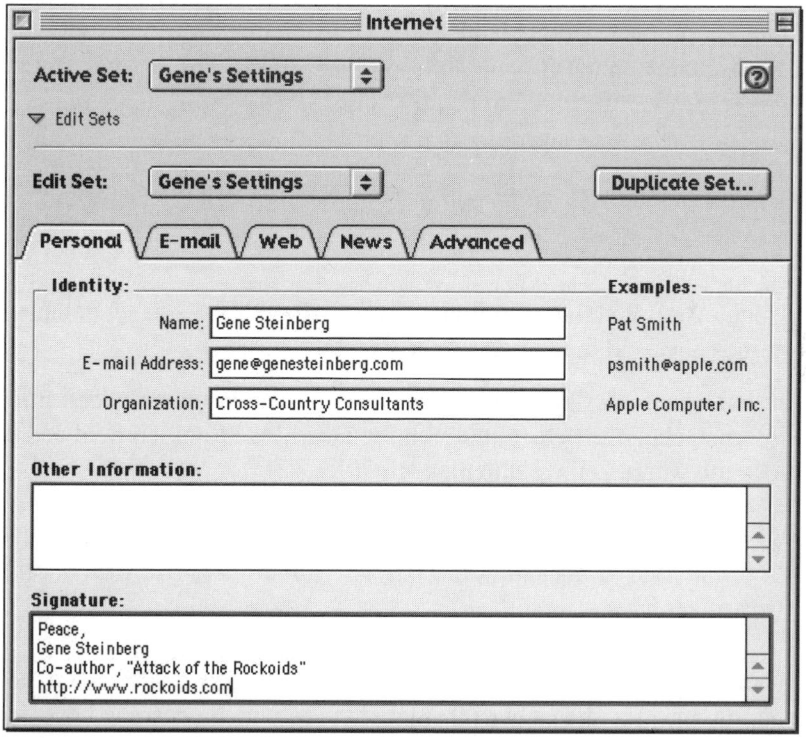

Solving Internet Connection Problems

FIGURE 21-3   These are the author's Personal settings in the Internet Control Panel

2. Enter the information you want to use to identify yourself in email and newsgroup postings in the Identity column. If you have additional information you want to post, place it in the Other Information field.

NOTE *If you see a narrow rectangular screen in your Internet Control Panel with none of the settings panels I'm describing, it may be that the screen view was collapsed at some point. Just click the little arrow to the right of the Edit Sets label to expand the view and to bring up the proper screens.*

3. If you want all of your email and newsgroup postings to have an automatic signature, insert it in the correct field. Some programs may require that you set a program-related preference for this feature (and, sad to say, AOL doesn't support it yet).

4. The foregoing settings, however, don't do anything as far as telling your Internet provider who you are when you sign on to retrieve your email. To do that, click on the E-mail tab (see Figure 21-4). The settings you put on this screen will be given to you by your ISP (the ones shown in the figure are for EarthLink only).

NOTE *Some ISPs refer to the Incoming Mail Server as a POP (point of presence) server.*

5. Click on the Web tab (see Figure 21-5), which is used to set default Web home pages and the search site you prefer.

6. If you want to designate a special place for all files downloaded from the Internet, click the Select button in the Download Files To field and pick the location where you want to place the files.

TIP *I recommend you pick the Desktop folder for your file downloads (same location as your drive icons). That way you are less likely to forget where you might have placed them.*

7. If the Default Web Browser setting isn't what you want, click on the pop-up menu to the right of that label to see which ones you have and select another one.

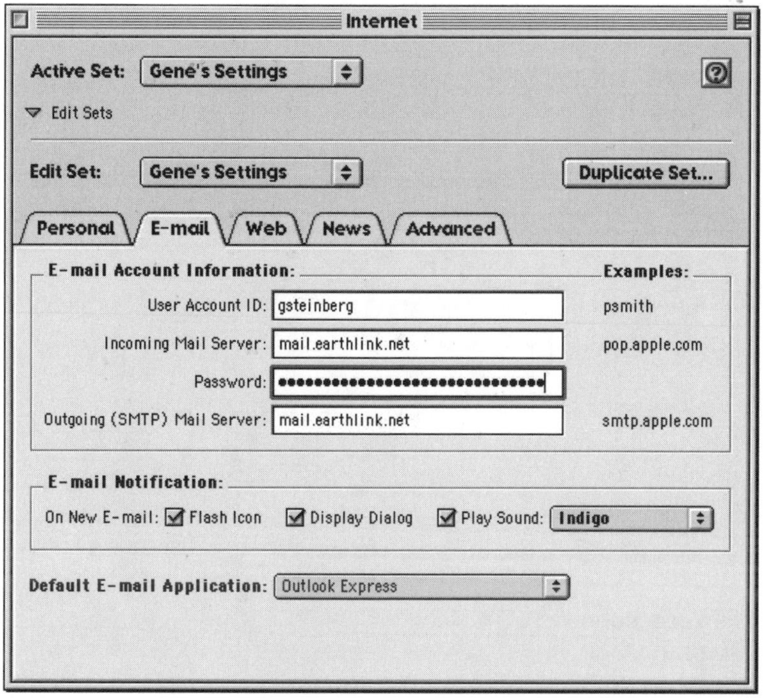

FIGURE 21-4   Place your Internet provider's email configuration information and your password in the text fields

8. Once your Web preferences are done, click the News tab to enter information about your ISP's newsgroup server settings. If you don't intend to access any newsgroups, you need not be concerned over this screen.

NOTE   *Some ISPs, such as EarthLink, insist that you set your newsgroup software to log into the service to retrieve messages. This is done as a backlash to problems with some unsavory folks forging newsgroup messages on another service's facilities to get away with posting spam announcements.*

9. The final setting is available when you click the Advanced tab (see Figure 21-6). I'm only showing it here for information. While most home or small office users won't need to touch these settings, there are situations where you may have to change them. Here's a brief look at some of these features:

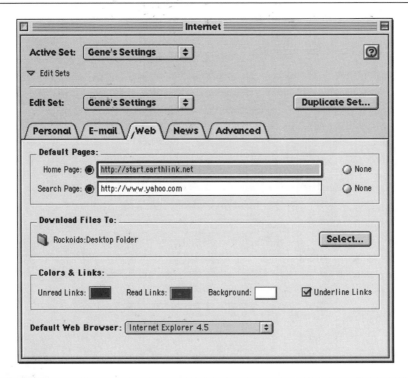

FIGURE 21-5   This screen includes such things as your preferred home page, and where you'd like to place downloaded files

- **File Transfer**   This setting establishes default FTP servers, useful if you travel outside the USA.

- **Helper Apps**   This setting allows other applications to work with your Internet software to provide extra features. For example, StuffIt Expander or StuffIt Deluxe are usually specified to open compressed files you download from the Internet.

- **Fonts**   Specify the fonts you want to use with your Internet software.

- **File Mapping**   This setting works with the File Exchange Control Panel to specify which Mac programs will be used to work with PC programs with specific file extensions (such as .doc for Microsoft Word).

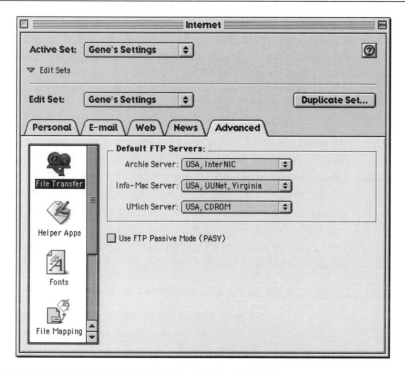

FIGURE 21-6   The Advanced tab is generally used for special settings, such as firewalls and helper applications that work with your Internet software

- ■ **Firewalls**   If you are in a corporate or university environment, firewalls are used to protect your network from outsiders. In order to access the Internet, your firewall settings would have to be specified.

- ■ **Messages**   Use this feature to enter a custom message for email or newsgroup messages.

- ■ **Hosts**   This is another special-purpose option, used when your network administrator requires specific settings for an office or university situation.

10. Once your settings are complete, click the close box of the Internet Control Panel. You'll see an alert asking if you want to save the changes. Click Save to confirm your settings, Don't Save if you want to restore the prior settings. Click Cancel if you prefer to return to the Internet Control Panel to make more adjustments.

Solving Internet Connection Problems

Internet Software Problems

Internet software has been implicated as the cause of a number of Macintosh ills—mysterious crashes while you're online or sudden bursts of memory usage (as indicated in the About This Computer window)—even when the crashes occur with software that isn't Internet related. Why, this is so is beyond the scope of this book.

It's quite possible that the fact that Internet software is usually free may mean that software publishers are not quite as inclined to test such products as thoroughly as retail products that earn a profit, but that's not necessarily a fair comment (and the publishers will deny it anyway). The climate for conflicts may just be the result of the fact that such programs are being asked to do a lot of complex tasks at the same time.

Whatever the cause, when you experience a crash on your Mac, you're probably more concerned with finding an answer than worrying how the program got that way. In Chapter 18, I describe easy techniques to help you diagnose system-related crashes. If none of the solutions I provide here or in the next two chapters help you solve your Internet software crashes, you'll want to read that chapter as well.

> **CAUTION** *Remember that whenever a program quits or your Mac freezes for any reason, be sure to restart the computer right away. A crash will make your computer less stable, and trying to run a crashed program again without a restart may only make matters worse.*

Here are some common causes of crashes and other problems while surfing the Net, and their solutions:

- **ObjectSupportLib**   This system extension (which goes in the Extensions folder) was required for AppleScript and other functions before the arrival of Mac OS 8 and later system versions. Apple thoughtfully merged the program into the System file to reduce System Folder clutter, but some older software installers (from AOL, Netscape, and others) dutifully placed it in the Extensions folder anyway. In theory, its presence isn't supposed to matter. The System file overrides the function. In practice, removing this file has made some mysterious system crashes disappear. So be on the lookout for it if you're using Mac OS 8 or later.

- **Corrupted Web cache**   Follow the instructions in Chapter 22 to delete your Web cache. Such steps are among the first things you should do when you experience a crash when running your browser.

■ **Corrupted preferences files**   This is a major cause of crashes when using a specific program. These files are in use all the time. Every single change you make to how a program runs will end up in that preferences file, and if it becomes corrupted, you may experience frequent, unexplained crashes when opening an application or just doing one function or another. Unfortunately, it's not always easy to find the preferences files, as each Internet program puts them in another location, not necessarily the Preferences folder inside the System Folder. My suggestion is that you use Apple's Find File or Sherlock program to locate all files with the name of your Internet program in it, then pay attention to the one with the word "preferences". That's the one you should remove and place on the desktop. Then start the program again and see if the problems still occur. You'll have to redo your program settings, of course, but this step could also stop the problems you're having.

CAUTION   *You should not attempt to remove a program's preferences files while the program is running. Quit the program first. Otherwise, the program may crash.*

NOTE   *If you launch an Internet program, such as Internet Explorer or Netscape, after removing the regular preferences file, you will probably have to endure a brief questionnaire or setup routine to restore your basic program settings.*

■ **Not enough memory**   If your Mac has the bare minimum of built-in RAM, and it probably does if you bought it without getting a RAM upgrade, you may find that your Internet software crashes frequently or you are getting messages about running out of memory. At the very least, it may just run slowly. The best solution is to add as much RAM as you can, because Internet programs use lots of it.

■ **RAM allocation**   If your Mac has enough RAM installed, you can often make an Internet program run better by allocating more to it. Web browsers, in particular, benefit a lot from added memory. Just use the Finder's Get Info command to change the Preferred memory setting. Increasing in blocks of 500K to 1000K is best. You should check the program after each change to see if things improve.

■ **Buggy Internet software**   Internet software gets frequent updates to fix one problem or another. You might want to check the publisher's Web site for information about problems and solutions. Another great source of information is the VersionTracker Web site at http://www.versiontracker.com.

- ■ **System extension conflicts** This is the usual bugaboo with any Mac. I suggest you read Chapter 18 for a no-frills strategy to isolate extension conflicts.

- ■ **Java** Java makes it possible for Web sites to embed fancy graphics and animation. Unfortunately, there are different versions of Java used for

Case History

Mysterious Extensions Appear in Your System Folder

When you install new software, sometimes you just cannot predict what files a program needs to run. In the old days, the application's folder contained everything. You tossed out that folder, and all elements of the application went with it.

As programs and system software become more and more complex, however, various and sundry files show up in different parts of the System Folder. There are extensions that contain various files, settings files in the Preferences folder, and perhaps a module or two for the Control Strip and Contextual Menus Items folder.

And that isn't all. If you install Netscape Communicator, you'll find a mysterious item appearing on your menu bar that accesses the Netscape branded version of AOL Instant Messenger (whether or not you even care about using that program).

Solution? Go to your Extensions folder and look for two extensions, AIM Menu and Idle Time. Remove them and restart. Presto! No more menu bar link to Instant Messenger.

Another AOL-related extension is OpenOT, which was designed to address an AppleTalk conflict with Macs using Apple's Open Transport networking software. If you're using Mac OS 8 or later, remove OpenOT from the Extensions folder. Apple fixed the problem in newer system versions, but this wayward extension has been implicated as the potential cause of some system crashes.

these sites and different versions used by Apple or with your Web browser. Sometimes your Mac may freeze when you access a Java-capable site. If this happens, there's not much you can try other than (after restarting of course) trying a different browser or looking for an update to your browser or to Apple's Java software. If you can get on the problem Web site at all, contact the webmaster or the company running the site and alert them as to your problem. In the meantime, you may just want to switch off the browser's Java feature (it'll be a program preference) till the problem is resolved.

How to Speed Downloads and Uploads

It would be nice to be able to tell you that once your Internet and modem settings are correct and you have given your Internet software extra doses of RAM, everything will run the way you want it to. But what if performance is still not what you expect? You try to retrieve a needed software update or send an important document file to a business colleague, and it seems to take a very long time for the process to end.

Here are a few tips to get the best possible download and upload performance:

- **Check for faster dial-up access numbers.**   Make sure the number you use to dial your ISP supports the fastest speed of which your modem is capable. While most services have upgraded their numbers for 56K access, some numbers still support slower speeds. You should double-check this, or just try another number when connection speeds aren't what you expect. Chapter 20 has more information on this subject.

- **Don't log on during evening primetime.**   It doesn't matter how many access numbers your ISP has in your city or how big their network is. When you log on during the hours when most other folks are trying to access the Internet as well, performance may suffer. You'll get the best possible performance from your Net connection during the early morning hours. This is important if you want to download a big file, which can tie up your Mac for quite a long time.

- **Use the latest Internet software.**   This is especially true for Web browsers, as the publishers try to find ways to make them run faster and retrieve Web pages and files more efficiently. I'll cover this subject in more detail in the next chapter.

How to Speed Downloads
and Uploads

■ **Check disk cache setting.**   The disk cache is used by your Mac to speed up frequently accessed data, and it can give your computer a little performance boost. The fastest way to set it properly (for Mac OS 7.5 and later) is to click on the Apple menu, select Control Panels, and choose the Memory Control Panel from the submenu. Click the Default button to access Apple's recommended settings. Then restart.

> NOTE
>
> *The Default button will usually turn virtual memory on, even if you're not using it. So you'll want to double-check this setting, and turn off this feature if you don't intend to use it.*

Getting Top Performance from Your Internet Connection

The Internet is getting more and more graphic heavy every day. Attractive artwork, animation, sound, and video help bring people to a Web site. But they also make it take a lot longer for you to access a site.

Consider these possibilities if you want top-flight Internet performance:

■ **Get a faster modem.**   At the time this book went to press, a 56K modem went for roughly $100, give or take a few dollars and the manufacturer's rebate of the week. Read Chapter 20 for information on optimizing modem performance.

■ **Upgrade to a "broadband" Internet service protocol.**   Both cable modems and DSL are touted as the next great thing for high-speed Internet access. I'll cover these subjects in more detail at the very end of this chapter.

■ **Get a RAM upgrade.**   Internet software works best with a healthy dose of RAM (especially a Web browser). If you've got too little, you may run out of memory when trying to run more than one program, or be forced to use virtual memory, which, with a small amount of real RAM available, may not give you satisfactory performance. Chapter 4 covers the topic of RAM upgrades.

■ **Get a faster Mac or an accelerator card.**   Almost every Power Macintosh model, even the first ones in the block that came out in 1994, can use a G3 upgrade. Before you spend a few hundred dollars on such an upgrade path, though, you'll want to check pricing on an all-new or more recent Mac. You may be able to get a newer, faster Mac for a similar amount of money (assuming you can get a reasonable sum for selling your old Mac). This subject is covered in more detail in Chapter 3.

The Low-down on Broadband Access

How times have changed! It wasn't so long ago when a 28,800 bps or 56,000 bps modem seemed to speed along at a blazing rate. Web pages appeared much faster, and it didn't take quite as long to retrieve software from an FTP or Web site.

But as files get bigger and the Web offers more and more multimedia content (including streaming audio and video), performance seems to drag. And ongoing network problems in the evening hours contribute to this mess.

Fortunately, there are ways afoot to speed up your Internet access to do the same things Apple's G3 microprocessor did to speed up your Mac computing experience. But it means the days for the conventional analog modem are probably numbered.

Here's a fast look at the newest methods out there to speed up delivery of Internet content to your Mac.

Cable Modems

If you have cable TV, it's quite possible your cable provider is offering Internet service too. A cable modem attaches direct to your Mac's Ethernet port or your hub, using settings you make with your TCP/IP Control Panel. The result? Ultra-fast Internet access, using the cable provider's own high-speed network. Depending on a firm's promotional literature, they are advertising speeds of over 1,000,000 bits per second. Awesome! In addition, pricing may not be all that high, especially when the service is first offered and the cable provider wants to build a customer network fast.

The reality is something else altogether, however:

- **Speed depends on traffic load.**   You are sharing your cable with others, and if there's a lot of traffic on the network (especially during the primetime evening hours), your speed will suffer, so take promises of any particular performance level with a grain of salt. But even at their worst, cable modems perform a whole lot faster than your 56K modem.

- **Upload speed may be limited.**   To limit excess traffic on their network, cable services may throttle back the potential speed for uploading. This may not be very important to you, unless you intend to send large files via email or FTP to an Internet site on a regular basis.

■ **You may have to change your email address.**   When you hook up to a cable modem, you may have to sign up with the cable provider's own Internet service, not the one you have now. This may be an inconvenience if you're used to a specific ISP, or perhaps have lots of online contacts you'd have to notify if you go to another company. If this represents a problem, see if your ISP is offering or plans to offer DSL access (which is described in the next section).

■ **Availability may be limited.**   This is the real kicker. You just may not be able to get a cable modem, period. Your cable provider not only has to have the facilities to offer this service, they need to wire your area for digital service. That can take a while, a long while (figure months or even years).

■ **There may be security issues.**   When you are using a cable modem, you are, in effect, part of a large Ethernet network. If you plan to use file sharing, be sure to turn off guest access in the Users & Groups panel. You may want to turn off file sharing altogether, except during the actual file exchange process. And don't be surprised if you see someone else's LaserWriter in your Chooser. If you have concerns about network security, contact your cable provider and see what protection they offer.

DSL

Another fast-rising high-speed Internet feature is DSL, short for Digital Subscriber Line. DSL takes your existing copper phone lines and uses digital technology to pump data through at a much higher rate.

Speeds depend on the sort of DSL service that's available in your city, from 256K to 1500K! A similar service, ADSL (Asymmetric DSL), offers top speed on file and Web downloads, but limits uplink speed (how much depends on the service). ADSL has been approved by the International Telecommunications Union (ITU), the agency that handles such standards, and it was designed with the hope of delivering high-speed access to a greater number of users at lower cost.

Unfortunately, not everyone can get this service, be it regular DSL or ADSL. For one thing, you have to be within three miles of your phone company's switching center. In addition, your phone company may need to install new switching equipment to accommodate this feature.

However, if you live in a large metropolitan area or a newly developed neighborhood, it is quite likely that you do meet these basic requirements. Contact your local phone company or Internet service for specifics about availability.

If you are able to receive DSL service, you will still have to pay for a special modem (or routing device), costing as much as $300 or more, and pay an extra installation charge. When you factor in monthly rates of $30 to $60 plus the cost of your Internet service, it begins to add up. However, as the service is deployed in more areas, competition heats up, and the costs per installation go down, you may expect prices to fall to more respectable levels.

NOTE
As with analog modems, so-called DSL modems will become more inexpensive as time goes on. Some services may even offer to rent a unit to you in exchange for ordering their service.

As with cable modems, DSL is always on, and uses your Ethernet network and your Mac's TCP/IP Control Panel for access, so setup isn't terribly difficult.

It remains to be seen which broadband access protocol, cable or DSL, emerges triumphant. But if 56K is getting you down, and you'd like to harness the real power of the Internet, these technologies are definitely worth more than a second look.

Getting Top Performance from Your Internet Connection

Chapter 22

Making Your
Web Browser Browse

Your Internet access experience is largely focused on one piece of software, the Web browser. The browser is the easiest Internet software to use and without doubt the most aggravating.

When you connect to your Internet service, your Web browser is putting a face on your Internet access (well, except for such services as AOL, which has their own unique interface and considers the browser just one part of the service).

What to Do When You Cannot Access a Site

There's not much you can do to get better browser performance if you cannot first access the sites you want. I cover connection problems in Chapters 20 and 21. But once you tackle those issues, there's more you can do if a site still won't show up.

You may have accessed the very same site just an hour earlier. Now you try again and get a message that it's not available, or your Web browser just chugs along and nothing happens. Here are some common causes and solutions:

- **Sorry, wrong address.**   If you even mess up one letter in the URL, you'll get either the wrong site or a message (see Figure 22-1) that the server can't be found. All you can do is recheck the address and make sure it's entered correctly.

- **DNS server can't be found.**   This is another typical message you'll get if you try to access a site that, for some reason, isn't available (it's Netscape's version). Check and maybe reenter the URL. You should also verify that you haven't been disconnected from your Internet service.

- **Computer cannot establish a network socket connection.**   You see this message if you try to access a site via Netscape, but you didn't make a proper connection to your Internet service. If you see it, verify that you really logged on, and if not, try logging on again (you may have to actually use the Disconnect feature of your Remote Access or PPP dialer to do this).

- **Site is down for maintenance.**   This can happen early in the morning, when Web hosting servers and Internet services schedule maintenance on their equipment. Your best solution is to try at a later hour and see if the problem is still there.

| FIGURE 22-1 | You get this message from Internet Explorer if a site cannot be accessed |

■ **Site has closed.**   It happens. A business goes under, or they choose to cancel a Web site for one reason or another. Or maybe they changed the name. Usually, at least for a while, a big site will set up a way to redirect the user from the old name to the new one, but after a period of time, the older address may no longer point to the new one. Your best solution here is to try to contact the business directly.

■ **Your Internet provider has a problem.**   Whether it's AOL or a regular Internet service provider (ISP), they will have scheduled maintenance from time to time. If you succeed in logging on, check the service's site for system status. On AOL, you use the keyword **AOL Update** to access this information feature. EarthLink subscribers can check the System Status page at their Web site (http://www.earthlink.net/assistance/status/status.html).

■ **User identification failed (a dilemma for AOL users).**   This has nothing whatever to do with the user identification and password you use when you access your ISP. It's an error message that shows up on occasion with AOL's browser. You can try logging off and logging on again, or even deleting the Web cache of your AOL browser (see "Removing Web Caches"). Sometimes one of these solutions will work. But just as often it's an AOL problem, and till they fix it at their end, you're out of luck.

■ **Attempt to load failed.**   If you cannot access a site, make sure you're really logged on. It's possible you're disconnected. If you don't have some visual indication that you are online (a modem light or a light on your regular phone, for example), just close your Internet connection and log on again. If you still experience this problem, try the same site or another Web site to be certain that the problem isn't just a one-time thing.

■ **Attempt to load problem for AOL 3.0 and 4.0 users.**   If you're an AOL user, and you get a message that your attempt to access a site has failed, try this: Open the Preferences (from the My AOL toolbar icon's menu in version 4.0). Then scroll to the AOL Link option, and make sure the option to use AOL Link when connecting with your modem is checked. Click the Configure button on this screen and restart. This is a common AOL problem. If it's not cured that way, reinstall your AOL software, and use their Update feature to retrieve your account from your previous copy.

■ **128-bit browser needed.**   There are two types of security with Web browsers today. The standard 40-bit is secure enough for most purposes, but experienced computer hackers can usually break through given enough time. The second option is 128-bit, which, the theory goes, would take years and years and years to overcome. The browser you get on your Mac or via an online service is usually 40-bit. But such places as banks and brokerage houses will not let you access your accounts from their Web sites without 128-bit. If you get this sort of message, you can visit Microsoft's Web site at http://www.microsoft.com or Netscape at http://www.netscape.com, and check their Downloads areas for the 128-bit secure version. You will have to certify you're a USA or Canadian resident before you can retrieve that version.

NOTE   *When you download AOL's software direct from the service, you have the option of choosing a version with a 128-bit browser (if you access the download area from one of their dial-up numbers in the USA or Canada). But even if you install that version, some sites won't recognize the browser as having the proper level of security. If you run into this dilemma, you should contact both the site's customer service people and AOL for assistance (so they can, perhaps, work together to resolve it).*

Making Your Browser Run Faster

Even if you've followed the suggestions I made in Chapters 20 and 21 to make sure your modem and Internet connection are running at top efficiency, it's possible your browser isn't quite delivering the performance you expect. Fortunately, there are still more things you can do to get things up to speed.

Tips on Speeding Up a Web Browser Cache

There are caches and there are caches. It seems that Macs are filled with caches of one sort or another. You have a disk cache, which is a Memory Control Panel setting that's used to speed up disk access, especially when you reopen a folder window or relaunch an application. Your hard drive has a cache used to make it work a bit faster.

Your Web browser uses a cache, too. But it's not a piece of RAM. It's a set of files (or one file if you're using the latest versions of Internet Explorer and AOL's bundled browser) that contain the Web files you've retrieved.

Every time you access a Web site, your browser consults the cached files to see if the artwork is already there, and if not, retrieves it directly from the Web site. Of course, the process is not quite that simple. The browser is using its own internal logic to locate cached files and purge the older, less used ones.

When you set up your browser, a fixed size for the cache is established. As you'll see from the following problems and solutions, you can change that size, or purge the cache and start over for improved performance.

Removing Web Caches

As the cache gets filled with older artwork, sometimes the browser doesn't work as efficiently, and the benefits of having the files on your Mac are lost. The best thing to do is just start over. Here's how to do it with the AOL and other popular Web browsers:

Netscape Navigator (or Communicator)

1. Choose Preferences from the Edit menu.

2. Look for the Advanced category, and click on the arrow to expand the view (if the view isn't already expanded).

3. Click on the item labeled Cache (see Figure 22-2).

4. Click on the button labeled Clear Disk Cache Now.

5. OK the confirmation message you see next. Now you just have to be patient. If you have a big cache, it'll take a few seconds for the purging process to complete.

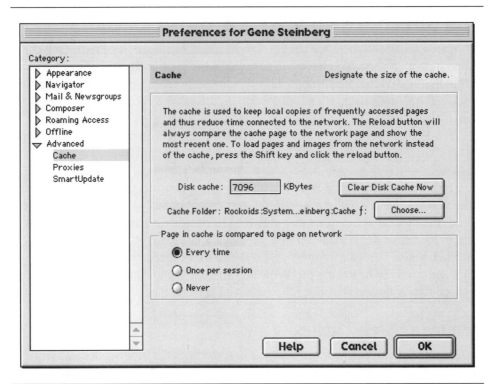

Category:

▷ Appearance
▷ Navigator
▷ Mail & Newsgroups
▷ Composer
▷ Roaming Access
▷ Offline
▽ Advanced
   Cache
   Proxies
   SmartUpdate

Cache   Designate the size of the cache.

The cache is used to keep local copies of frequently accessed pages and thus reduce time connected to the network. The Reload button will always compare the cache page to the network page and show the most recent one. To load pages and images from the network instead of the cache, press the Shift key and click the reload button.

Disk cache: [7096] KBytes   [Clear Disk Cache Now]

Cache Folder: Rockoids:System...einberg:Cache ƒ: [Choose...]

┌─ Page in cache is compared to page on network ─┐
│ ● Every time   │
│ ○ Once per session   │
│ ○ Never   │
└──┘

[Help]   [Cancel]   [OK]

FIGURE 22-2   Purge and adjust your Netscape browser cache settings from this screen

Microsoft Internet Explorer

1. Choose Preferences from the Edit menu.

2. Click on the arrow to the left of the Browser category to expand the view (if it's not already done).

3. Then click on the Advanced category, which brings up the screen shown in Figure 22-3.

4. Click the Empty Now button to clear the cache. The purging process is done in the blink of an eye.

NOTE   *Beginning with Microsoft Internet Explorer 4.0.1, the cached artwork is placed in a single file, called cache.waf. This is done to speed access of the artwork. When you empty the cache, the cache.waf file isn't actually deleted, just the cached information inside the file.*

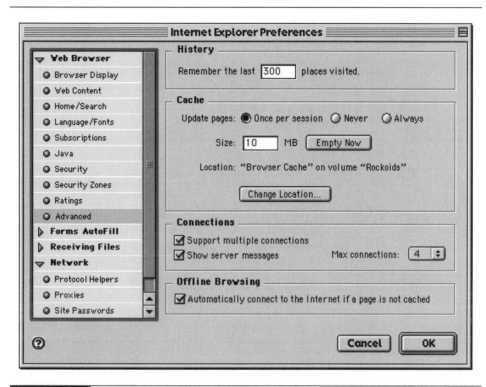

FIGURE 22-3   Here's Internet Explorer's cache management screen

AOL 4.0

1. Choose Preferences from the My AOL toolbar icon's menu.

2. Scroll to the WWW option.

3. On the screen that appears (see Figure 22-4), click the Empty Cache Now button. AOL shares the cache file allocated to Internet Explorer once it's set up, and purging its contents is nearly instantaneous.

4. Click OK to close the Preferences window.

Deleting Cache Files

If emptying a browser cache doesn't solve your problem, you may just want to trash the actual files. First quit your browser, so you can actually empty the Trash can.

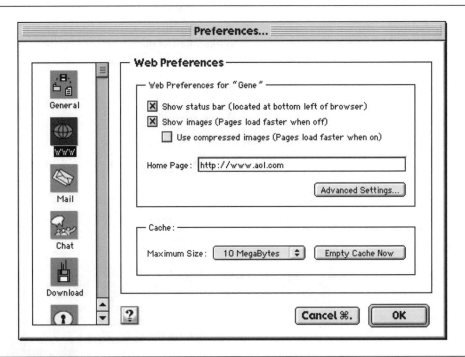

FIGURE 22-4   AOL's browser cache is shared with Internet Explorer

For Internet Explorer, do a Sherlock (or Find File) search for the cache.waf file (depending on whether or not you use AOL it may be in different locations), drag it to the Trash, then empty the trash.

Netscape's Cache folder is generally located in a folder labeled Cache ƒ, usually in a folder with your Netscape username on it, inside the Netscape Users folder (it was called Netscape ƒ with older versions of the program), which is placed in your System Folder's Preferences folder (complex, but that's how it goes). When you find it, take the whole Cache ƒ folder, drag to the Trash, then empty the trash.

 Don't delete the Netscape Users folder itself, because it contains other files you need, such as your email address book, stored email, and bookmarks (used to display your favorite Web sites).

Boosting Web Cache Size

If you do a lot of Web surfing, the Web cache you set may fill it much too quickly, so the browser has to return to the site for updated artwork. This can slow down performance. By default, most browsers are set with a Web cache of 5MB. If you are unhappy with this setting, use the instructions in the following sections to locate and change your cache settings. You can change the Web cache to 10MB, or maybe somewhat higher.

CAUTION *Too high a Web cache may be as harmful as too small. If you go much above 10MB, your browser may end up spending too much time checking the cache before retrieving an updated version of the site, which can slow things down. It's a balancing act, but I've had good luck with a 10MB setting for AOL, Internet Explorer, and Netscape.*

As they say in the automobile business, your mileage may vary, so don't hesitate to do a little experimentation. If you reduce your cache size, first delete the existing cache, so you can start with a clean slate.

Netscape Navigator (or Communicator)

1. Choose Preferences from the Edit menu.

2. Look for the Advanced category, and click on the arrow to expand the view (if the view isn't already expanded).

3. Click on the item labeled Cache, which brings up the screen that was shown in Figure 22-2.

4. Enter the cache figure in kilobytes.

5. Click the OK button to store your settings.

Microsoft Internet Explorer

1. Choose Preferences from the Edit menu.

2. Click on the arrow to the left of the Browser category to expand the view (if it's not already done).

3. Then click on the Advanced category, which brings up the screen shown in Figure 22-3.

4. Enter your Web cache setting in the Size text box, using MB.

5. Click OK to save your settings.

Tips on Speeding Up
a Web Browser Cache

AOL 4.0

1. Choose Preferences from the My AOL toolbar icon's menu.

2. Scroll to the WWW option.

3. On the screen that appears (see Figure 22-4), go to the Cache column at the bottom and choose a Web cache size from the pop-up menu.

4. Click OK to close the Preferences window and store your settings.

NOTE   *As mentioned earlier, AOL 4.0 and Internet Explorer share cache settings, so the change you make to one will, ultimately, affect the other.*

Using a RAM Disk to Speed Web Performance

One of the limitations of Web caching performance is the speed of your hard drive. Although it won't work in all situations, you can give a RAM disk a try and see if it makes your browsing experience run faster.

A RAM disk is used to set aside a portion of your Mac's built-in memory to mimic a hard drive. You can actually copy files and even a System Folder to it, and use that as a startup disk. Unfortunately, with application folder sizes going up by leaps and bounds and System Folder sizes exceeding 200 and 300MB, the utility of a RAM disk is much more limited. You'd actually have to be able to give up that amount of memory to the task. Even a bare bones System Folder (containing just the very basic Apple system extensions), a Finder, and a System File and other files your Mac may need to boot, may be too large for use on a RAM disk.

These cautions aside, though, you might want to give it a try for your Web cache to see if it helps (you don't have to worry about fitting a System Folder in there). Here's what to do:

1. Click on the Apple menu, choose Control Panels and select Memory from the submenu, which brings up the screen shown in Figure 22-5.

2. Look at the RAM Disk column at the bottom of the screen, and click the On button.

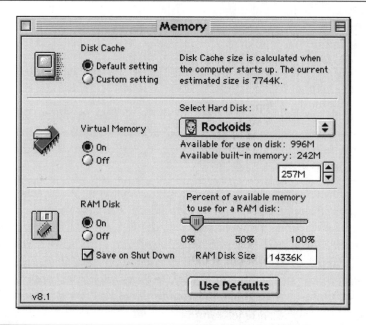

FIGURE 22-5   Use the Memory Control Panel to create a RAM disk

3. Turn the slider to set aside a percentage of your Mac's built-in RAM for use as a disk cache. You may also manually enter a figure for your RAM disk in kilobytes in the text field.

4. Click the Save on Shut Down option, if offered, so your RAM disk can be saved to disk when you close down your Mac for the day. That way its contents will still be there next time you reboot.

> **NOTE**   *If your Memory Control Panel doesn't have a Save on Shut Down option, rather than wonder why (most likely you just need a system software upgrade), you would be better off not trying this feature.*

5. Close the window and restart your Mac. After your Mac has completed the restart process, you'll see a RAM disk icon on your Mac's desktop below the icon for your hard drive.

6. Open your Web browser's Preference panels and bring up the Cache settings screen.

7. Both Internet Explorer and Netscape have options to change the location for your Web cache (see Figures 22-3 and 22-4 again). Click on the appropriate button, then, in the dialog box, select your RAM disk as the location for the Web cache.

8. Click OK to store your settings. From then on, your Web cache will be accessed from the RAM disk as long your RAM disk mounts at startup.

CAUTION *If you're using AOL (or AOL and Internet Explorer, even if separately), you will not be able to put your Web cache in a RAM disk, unless it also contains your active System Folder. AOL just doesn't support the option to put specific settings files in another place. You could try making an alias of the America Online folder and put them in your Preferences folder, in the System Folder, but there are no guarantees that the effort will succeed.*

9. If you find that using a RAM disk for your Web cache doesn't work, just revisit the Memory Control Panel, turn off the RAM disk and restart to dispose of the disk and its contents.

Connectix Surf Express Deluxe Promises "Intelligent" Caching

Connectix, the publisher of a number of performance enhancement utilities for the Mac, has a program that's designed to speed up Web performance by using an enhanced cache management scheme.

Surf Express Deluxe works as a proxy Web server, creating its own custom cache that is designed to accelerate Web performance. The program uses an internal algorithm to gauge the sites you access most often, then makes the cache artwork for those sites available at an accelerated rate. It'll also access updated content from the sites you visit most often at the same time you're working on other applications (as long as you're logged on to your Internet service, of course).

They promise a performance improvement rate of from 4 to 36 times your previous speed. Since your mileage may vary, I'll only tell you that the program does seem to make Web pages load faster, as long as you revisit them on a regular basis. The first time you visit a Web site, it works no faster than the regular way. You can check out a demonstration version of the program from the publisher's Web site: http://www.connectix.com.

Case History

Hundreds of Thousands of Macs Ship with Beta Online Software

It is becoming more and more common for software publishers to post preview or beta versions of new software. There's an undeniable marketing advantage to such practices. It helps introduce potential customers to the new product, maybe even get them hooked on using it before the actual release.

Sometimes there's an advantage from the programming standpoint as well. The publisher is able to deliver the software to a wide range of potential users and get some feedback about potential problems or shortcomings that can be addressed before the software is released in its final form.

There's no shortage on the number of such products that have come out. Apple, AOL, Microsoft, Netscape, Symantec, and other companies have put out these public betas or previews from time to time. What makes it confusing, however, is when the preview shows up already installed on your new Mac or on your new system software disks. A case in point is the preview version of AOL 4.0.

The final version of AOL 4.0 wasn't finished in time for the arrival of the iMac, or for Mac OS Systems 8.1 through 8.5.1. So Apple included the preview edition instead. This version didn't even have the same Web browser as the final release.

On the other hand, users of Windows 98 didn't fare any better. The version of AOL software that came with the original Windows 98 installation was also a preview.

Tips on Speeding Up a Web Browser Cache

Coping with Web Slowdowns

A corrupted or clogged cache file isn't the only cause for slow Web performance, though it's a common one. If clearing the cache (or dumping the files) doesn't do the trick, here are some additional things you may want to consider:

- **Problems at the Web site**   Some Web sites are actually run by a single computer, possibly a regular Mac or PC desktop computer. When capacity is filled, everyone's access slows down. Even larger sites have a finite capacity. All you can do is try again at a different hour.

- **Heavy Web traffic**   Whenever a popular Web site has a huge amount of activity, such as when a new movie trailer (such as the one for *Star Wars: The Phantom Menace)* is posted, or a new software update is offered, things may slow to a crawl. Your best bet is just to try again at a later time (early in the morning is best; set your alarm clock).

- **Heavy traffic at your Internet service**   Whether you use AOL, CompuServe, or a regular ISP, there are times when the service's network will be clogged. Evening hours, equivalent to a prime time on a TV network, will tax their servers. If you intend to do heavy duty Web surfing, you may want to avoid those hours.

Internet Software Crashes

Internet software has been implicated as the cause of a number of Macintosh ills—mysterious crashes while you're online or sudden bursts of memory usage (as indicated in the About This Computer window)—even when the crashes occur with software that isn't Internet related. This is beyond the scope of this book and a matter that would probably be more interesting to a computer programmer. In addition, it's not important whether the problems are caused by the fact that Internet programs are usually free, hence a publisher may not be as inclined to test them thoroughly. There doesn't seem to be a lot of evidence for that theory. The most important thing here is the solution to the problem.

Chapter 21 covers a number of problems with Web software and solutions. In addition, you'll want to read Chapter 18, which covers fast techniques to find the cause of a system extension conflict. Along with those suggestions, I have two more problems and their solutions to offer here:

- **Corrupted Web cache**   In addition to slowing down your Web access, the cache files may contribute to other problems. For example, you access a site, your browser calls up the cache file, and your Mac crashes. It's hardly likely you'll be able to pick exactly which cache file has caused the problem (doubly so with AOL and Internet Explorer, which use a single cache file). One fast way out of this dilemma is simply to follow the steps I outlined earlier in the section called "Removing Web Caches."

- **AOL 4.0 swells system memory**   If you're using AOL 4.0, you'll find that system RAM needs jump up by a number of megabytes when AOL software is running. That's because it uses many additional system resources to access all of the many components that are part of the program. You can reduce the system memory expansion considerably if you use your Mac with virtual memory (which you activate with the Memory Control Panel). For Mac OS 8.0 and later (especially Mac OS 9), you'll find that the traditional slowdowns with virtual memory are no longer as obvious (and sometimes applications even launch faster when it's active). That's one reason why Apple puts virtual memory on by default.

> NOTE   *Although Apple has improved virtual memory performance for its recent system versions, older browser versions may have problems with it. It never hurts to turn off virtual memory (in the Memory Control Panel) as a test, to see if problems vanish as a result.*

How to Make Online Graphics Look Sharper

First and foremost, your Web experience is governed by the graphical display. There's almost no limit to what a Web site may provide, ranging from a simple picture to a full-blown video.

Naturally you have no control over how the folks who created the Web site set up their graphics. Some will opt for high quality at the expense of it taking longer for you to receive the artwork. Others value speed above everything, since it's been shown that Web sites that deliver their artwork faster may get a greater number of visitors.

How to Make Online
Graphics Look Sharper

Case History

Shimmering Pool of Water Causes Crash

As an audio and home theater buff, I enjoy visiting Web sites devoted to these subjects. One of those sites, which belongs to a popular American audio component manufacturer, has a fancy home page, in which the faceplate for one of their top-selling products is reflected in a shimmering pool of water. At least that's how it is supposed to work, but every time I'd access the site from Internet Explorer, my Mac would crash.

I went through the usual routine of trashing the Web cache, isolating questionable system extensions—the whole nine yards.

Everything worked just fine with Netscape.

The webmaster for the site had no solution. The site looked fine to them and it worked fine, he said. They didn't seem upset that a potential visitor to the site had to endure such grief.

Finally, I decided to switch Internet Explorer's Java option to the Microsoft Virtual Machine. The site no longer crashed. On the other hand, I never saw the shimmering pool of water either, but at least I could examine the site safely for other treasures.

For AOL Users Only

AOL has a feature in its Web browser that compresses Web artwork into a special format (called .ART if you want to be technical). The advantage is that you see the pages faster, but quality may suffer (a lot in some cases). And if you try to save the artwork to your hard drive, it will be in a format you can only read with AOL's software. Since the speedup really isn't all that much, here's how to rid yourself of this feature with AOL 4.0 (it's a little different with AOL 3, but the basic steps are close enough):

1. Launch AOL (don't bother signing on).

2. Choose Preferences from the My AOL toolbar's drop down menu.

3. Scroll to the WWW option.

4. On the screen that appears (refer back to Figure 22-4), uncheck the Use Compressed Images option.

5. Click OK to store your settings.

Breathe a sigh of relief that your artwork will look better and you won't have to endure headaches trying to open any of the artwork in another program.

Web Artwork Advice for All Users

Whether you're on AOL or not, there are ways to make Web-based artwork look nicer. Try these suggestions:

- **Delete the Web cache to fix poor quality artwork.**   If artwork previously retrieved by your browser gets damaged, it may crash your Mac, or the artwork will just not display properly. Consider deleting the Web cache if the quality of artwork deteriorates.

- **Refresh the page.**   For whatever reason, maybe heavy network traffic, there's a problem in delivering the Web artwork to your Mac. The pages look grainy, or parts are missing. When you click the Refresh or Reload button on your browser, the page is retrieved from scratch from the Web site and often this fixes the problem (but not always).

NOTE

Netscape has a Super Refresh feature, where you hold down the OPTION key when you choose Reload from the View menu. It's supposed to provide a more efficient retrieval of the Web page. I've not seen any difference, but it doesn't hurt to try.

- **Try another browser.**   Not all browsers interpret the same artwork in the same fashion. Your Mac comes with both Internet Explorer and Netscape installed (if it's a recent model). As long as you don't use up too much of your Mac's RAM, there's no problem in running both browsers at the same time during your Internet connection. In addition, you'll want to check the publisher's Web sites for updates that might address a specific problem or improve performance. And, by the way, you can even run these two programs if you're an AOL member as part of your AOL connection (if you have enough memory to run all the programs at once).

How to Make Online
Graphics Look Sharper

■ **Check your monitor settings.**   Web artwork is usually optimized to look good on both Mac and Windows computers, which means there's a compromise. But if you set up your Mac at the highest possible color depth (millions of colors if possible), you'll benefit from being able to see all the color your Mac is capable of delivering. You can also calibrate your monitor with ColorSync (see Chapter 10 for the specifics) to get the best possible color balance on your Mac.

Summing Up

If you follow through on the information in this chapter, you'll be able to resolve many of the problems you might encounter surfing the Web, and you'll be able to get better performance.

In the next and final chapter, I'll cover another aspect of your Internet experience, email.

Chapter 23

Making Email Work for You

Email has come to dominate our lives. Whether it's in the office or on the Internet, you just open your email program, write a message, and send it. Next to cell phones, it's *the* way to communicate.

In theory, email ought to be one of the simplest things you can do on your Mac. In practice, there are complexities. Sometimes the mail doesn't get through; sometimes your email program can't manage more than a few sessions without a crash. And then there are all those side issues, such as how to handle email attachments and the threat of virus infections that make the process even more involved.

   This chapter focuses on how to harness the power of email without having to put up with the nasty side effects.

When Email Doesn't Reach Its Destination

More often than not, email doesn't get to the right place because you made a simple mistake. You left out a letter, a number, or an underscore, or entered the domain (service) name incorrectly. Usually you'll get some kind of message explaining what happened and why. Then all you do is send the message again.

   But getting a notice isn't a given. Some services won't "bounce" email with any sort of notice, so you may want to consider these possible solutions.

- **Send it again.**   Sometimes the message just, well, gets lost. Internet traffic is a gigantic relay race. Data is passed from computer to computer, from service to service. That it works most of the time is a miracle, and sometimes it doesn't.

- **Recheck the address.**   Yes, even a single incorrect character in the username or domain name (the name of the service) can make the email go astray. You may not even get a message indicating it went to the wrong place, especially if the incorrect address is real (just not the person you wanted to contact).

- **Try a different address.**   If your recipient has another email address, use it. See if it works.

- **Remove file attachments.**   As I will explain later, services often impose restrictions on the size of email attachments, so if the email isn't getting there, try it without the attachment and see if it works any better.

■ **Try another email program.**   If you're not on AOL, you have a choice of some really terrific programs, and the two major ones are free. If, for example, Outlook Express isn't working for you, try Netscape Communicator (or vice versa). If you want a different range of features, consider such commercial options as Eudora Pro from Qualcomm or Mailsmith from Bare Bones Software.

NOTE   *When it comes to Internet email there is no guarantee it'll get there right away. Sometimes it seems to arrive in an instant, at other times it takes hours. You may just have to be patient.*

Case History

There is Only One Gene

Having a single-name screen name (email address) on AOL is supposed to be a sign of distinction (or at least it means you've been there a long time). But sometimes it can be a curse.

A case in point: On AOL, I'm known simply as Gene (it's gene@aol.com for non-members). It's not that I got there first; in fact, there was another Gene on AOL, but that fellow left the service, and I was able to create the screen name before anyone else got there.

Unfortunately, it creates the climate for mistakes.

As I have said in this chapter, there is no room for an incorrect email address, just as there is no room for an incorrect phone number. One wrong letter, an incorrect domain, and you get the "wrong number."

Hardly a day passes when I don't receive email or an instant message on AOL from someone thinking I am somebody else. Folks mistake me for their long-lost brother, father, or schoolmate. I have received emails congratulating me on my birthday, my recovery from an illness, plus personal documents that include financial statements and tax returns.

Naturally, I correct these folks about their mistakes, and no, I don't look into their private files to see what's what. Most folks are glad I caught them in a serious mistake; some get, shall we say, huffy that I'd dare tell them they made a mistake.

But the upshot is that you should be absolutely, completely sure that you have your recipient's email address correctly entered before you send your messages.

When Email Doesn't Reach Its Destination

How to Handle Email Attachments

You have just finished a project on your Mac, and your client needs the files right away. So you open your email software, click the Attach button, and speed it on its way. Two hours later, your client calls, frantically worrying over the fact that the email never arrived. You assure your client the files were sent and to just be patient.

But another hour passes, and your email is bounced back to you, with some arcane message or other that doesn't make any sense, since you know the email address is correct. What went wrong?

Here are some things you might want to consider when sending attachments with your email messages:

■ **Avoid large attachments.** An Internet or online service may have limitations as to how big a file attachment can be, and that information isn't always readily available. With the exception of messages from one AOL member to another (see also the section entitled "AOL Email Quirks and Solutions"), I'd recommend you try to restrict your email attachments to 2MB in size. You can use StuffIt to compress your files to the smallest possible size. If the file ends up larger than 2MB, you may want to break up the file into segments and send it as separate pieces or consider another way to transfer the file. Some Internet providers give you free FTP or Web space (it's 2MB on AOL, 6MB on EarthLink). You can use that space to contain files. Or you may just want to place the files on a disk and send it in the traditional fashion to your recipient.

> **TIP**   *If you plan on handling large file attachments, you might want to contact a Web hosting service and see if they can set you up with some FTP space for file transfers. The price is often cheaper than what it would cost to store a regular Web site (for example, pair Networks, at http://www.pair.com, charges a mere $5.95 a month for FTP-only service).*

■ **Try again.** Maybe you didn't address the email properly or there was a network-related problem that prevented the message from going to its proper destination. If the file is mission critical, it doesn't hurt to try a second time to be sure. If your recipient has more than one email address, try sending to another address, or just send the email to all the addresses at once (if the recipient doesn't mind getting multiple copies, of course).

Is There a Danger from Email Viruses?

You read the email warnings. Don't open this, that, or the other email or your files will be destroyed, your hard drive wrecked, your life made miserable. Is there any reason to worry?

Absolutely not (but with just one condition).

First and foremost, the only way a virus can be activated or transferred is for you to download and launch an infected file. While email programs (other than AOL) do download the file as part of the process of retrieving the messages, you'd still have to launch an infected file for it to do some damage. Just reading an email message is not going to cause your Mac to go haywire because of a virus.

But that doesn't stop folks from sending bogus warnings about such things. A big example dates back to 1994. Tens of thousands of folks received email warnings about something called the Good Times virus. This is the myth, and many of you no doubt got email about it way back then if you were active on the Internet:

"The FCC has discovered a virus which infects your computer if you read a message with 'Good Times' or some other evil phrase in the subject line. Simply reading the message with your eyeballs will destroy your computer's processor by setting it into an 'nth complexity infinite binary loop.'"

An "nth complexity infinite binary loop" sounds like something even a science fiction writer like me, used to technobabble, would worry about.

The fact of the matter is that there never was such a virus, and the statement that just opening email can infect you happens to be false. If you receive a warning of this sort, don't pass it on. Just delete it, or let the sender know it's a fake (probably they were taken in as well).

A Real Email-driven Virus

Even though opening a message won't pass a virus on to your Mac, it doesn't mean that a virus-infected file can't be attached to your email. That is where the real threat may exist.

In March 1999, there was a real virus threat and it caught even experienced system administrators unaware. Fortunately, users of the other platform were most vulnerable to this problem (Mac users would only suffer a side effect if they used Microsoft Word 98 for the Mac).

One day, email by the ton reached recipients around the world with the words "Important message from…" in the subject line, and giving the name of someone these recipients knew. The body of the message included such lines as "Here is that document you asked for…" and sure enough a Microsoft Word document was included.

As I said, this particular virus was most destructive if you used Windows or worked in a cross-platform installation that used Microsoft Office for Windows (and most do). If a Windows user actually downloaded and launched that document it would invoke a macro virus, called Melissa, which would replicate itself and send the very same message on to the first 50 email addresses in your address book. Worse, Melissa would disable the virus alerts that Word puts up to warn about macro viruses.

Since Microsoft Word macros work on both Macs and PCs, the threat was everywhere. While the damage to Mac users was basically to the Normal template under Word 98, that in itself would be enough to cause trouble when you tried to create and edit documents. For Windows users, the virus was potentially a complete and devastating way to mess up your email system.

Fortunately, the publishers of virus software worked overtime to produce updates that would detect and eradicate Melissa (and the new strains of a similar nature that emerged shortly thereafter).

But even with Melissa, the plain truth is the same: Your Mac cannot get infected by a virus sent via email unless you actually launch an infected file; the normal process of downloading isn't enough to trigger the virus.

The moral of the story is this: When you get a file attachment you're not expecting, even if you know who sent it, it never hurts to write back and verify the recipient really sent it to you. If you're sending a file, include a message in the body of your email explaining specifically what the file is and what it is to be used for, so the recipient knows it's nothing suspicious.

How to Avoid Email Problems

Even if you address your email correctly, put in a proper subject line, and prepare your message, there are no guarantees that the message will get to the recipient in the same form—or at all. Some of the problems are due to factors you can't control, such as your software or the service you and the recipient are using.

But there are precautions you can take to make sure that your email comes through reasonably untarnished, especially if there are attachments added.

AOL Email Quirks and Solutions

With more than 18 million members around the world, a great percentage of the Internet's email traffic goes to and from members of the world's largest online service.

But because of the inconsistent way in which AOL handles email, problems may arise if you don't observe a few simple precautions:

■ **Don't send multiple attachments from the Internet to AOL members.** AOL doesn't support the MIME (Multipurpose Internet Mail Extension) protocol. What that means is that you cannot attach more than a single item to AOL's email without it using its built-in compression software to make an archive. The archive will be StuffIt on the Mac, and WinZip on the Windows platform. When you receive a file with multiple attachments from the Internet, it'll come as a single attachment, which you must then run through a decoding program. Fortunately, the latest versions of StuffIt Expander and such shareware programs as Decoder can extract the contents of the MIME file, but sometimes it just won't work as advertised. If you must send more than a single file via your Internet service to an AOL member, use StuffIt first to compress them all into a single archive.

■ **Avoid large files outside of AOL.**   As of the time this book was published, AOL's limit was approximately 2MB for files sent to and from the Internet. For email from one AOL member to another, it's a more practical 16MB. If you must send large files regularly to anyone on AOL, having a membership there may be a good idea.

NOTE   *If you use an Internet service provider to log on to AOL (rather than their dial-up network), you'll benefit by paying a much lower monthly fee for the service (less than half the regular monthly rate).*

■ **Be careful addressing email from AOL to the Internet.**   AOL doesn't handle email addresses quite the same as the rest of the world. For one thing, their variation of an email address, a screen name, allows for a space between words, something that's a no-no in most of the rest of the online world. If you're on the Internet and want to send email to someone with a

How to Avoid Email Problems

space in his or her name (such as "bear bear@aol.com"), don't forget to put an underscore between the words: bear_bear@aol.com. Otherwise, the space will likely be ignored and someone with the name of bear@aol.com will mistakenly get your email.

■ **AOL mailbox sizes are limited.** AOL only allows you to have 550 messages in a member's incoming mailbox at any one time. The older ones are purged automatically, seven days for received email, 30 days for sent email. But if you get a lot of email in a short time, the sender may just get a "mailbox is full" message. If you're on AOL, you'd best be advised to read your email promptly, and use the service's Personal Filing Cabinet feature to store email you want to save beyond the time limit.

■ **Don't be alarmed about messages from MAILER-DAEMON@aol.com.** Such messages are not viruses or anything threatening. They are just notices that your email couldn't be delivered, and the body of the message will contain information as to why.

■ **Don't use special formatting for email sent to non-AOL members.** AOL has a number of formatting features, such as typeface, style, size, and color. In general, these formatting features don't pass through to the Internet, or if they do, formatting may not be completely retained. So the best thing to do is just to leave the standard text formatting if your email is being sent to folks outside the service.

■ **Don't embed a photo in your AOL message to the Internet.** This feature, which was introduced in AOL 4.0, is not something that will translate to Internet email. If you want to send a photo to someone outside the service, make it an email attachment instead.

A Cause of Possible AOL Software Crashes

AOL offers a Personal Filing Cabinet as a way to store your received email, so you have it after their email servers delete the message. Unfortunately, this feature is prone to occasional file corruption and may even crash your Mac if it gets too large.

There are a couple of ways to help reduce this problem. One method is to compact the Personal Filing Cabinet every so often. This action is a way of rebuilding the file's database, to remove deleted material and make it work more efficiently. In theory, the program should be set up to do that automatically when you quit the AOL software, but in practice it doesn't always happen.

Here's how to compact the Personal Filing Cabinet (this applies to AOL 4.0):

1. Launch your AOL software. It's not necessary to sign on.

2. Choose Preferences from the My AOL toolbar icon's menu.

3. Scroll to the Filing Cabinet option, which brings up the screen shown in Figure 23-1.

4. Click the button labeled Compact Personal Filing Cabinet Now.

5. Click OK to close the Preferences window.

Another means of protection is simply to back up your Personal Filing Cabinet file (there's one for each screen name on your account). That way you have a copy in case the original is damaged.

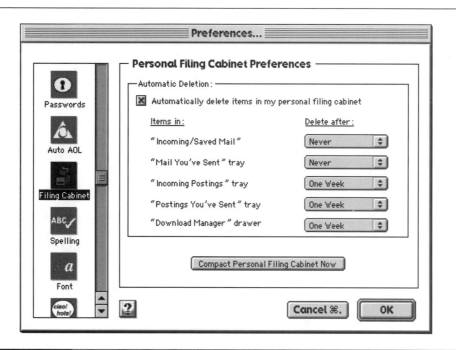

FIGURE 23-1   You can clean up your AOL Personal Filing Cabinet from this screen

You'll find it in the System Folder's Preferences folder, in a folder labeled America Online. Look inside that folder for another folder labeled Data. Inside that folder will be a file with your screen name and the words "Filing Cabinet" after it, such as mine, "Gene's Filing Cabinet." Use the Finder's Duplication function to make a copy, or just drag the file to another location on your Mac, holding down the OPTION key (so it duplicates rather than moves the file).

Internet Email Quirks and Solutions

AOL isn't the only source of email quirks. Some of the very same problems and solutions apply when you use a regular Internet service provider. I'll cover them here:

- **Crashes when you open Netscape Messenger email**   Netscape's Messenger module has a feature that lets you compact a message folder. This removes deleted data and optimizes the file. To use it, just select the email folder you want to compact, and choose Compact This Folder from Netscape's File menu (it's only there if you have the Messenger module open). You'll probably also want to use the Empty Trash Folder function every so often, as a lot of trashed email will just bloat your email files.

- **Mysterious, unexplained program quits**   Internet software tends to be memory intensive. If you have enough built-in memory on your Mac, and you have bulging files of received email, use the Finder's Get Info command to give the software a memory boost. Try increasing memory allotment in 1MB increments (and don't forget to quit the program before you change the preferred setting).

CAUTION   *If you're using Mac OS 8 or later, watch out for the dreaded ObjectSupportLib file, which sometimes turns up in the Extensions folder. Older software installers may put the extension in there. ObjectSupportLib is not needed, because the functions are now in the System file, and it may cause crashes if the file is present. If you find this file, trash it right away and restart.*

- **Mailbox full messages**   AOL isn't the only service that puts restrictions on the size of an email box. If your recipient has an interoffice email system and has gone on vacation, or has not checked the email in a while, the mailbox may really be filled. The only solutions are to wait and try sending the email again at a later time, see if the recipient has another email address, or try a telephone call.

Try an Email Forwarding Service

It's not uncommon to have several email accounts or even to switch from one service to another, as you experiment to see which provides the best performance and service. You may work as a contractor and switch from one office to another, hence changing email addresses more than you like. Or you might travel and use one service at home or the office, and another for the road.

Whatever the case, you may want to consider an email forwarding service. Such firms will give you a single, convenient email address, and you can designate where email will be automatically sent at any point in time.

Three well-known firms that provide this service are Pobox (http://www.pobox.com), Bigfoot (http://www.bigfoot.com) and iFORWARD (http://www.iforward.com). If you're using a Web-based email service, you may already have automatic forwarding.

Getting a Handle on Email Spam

On the Internet, spam is not a form of lunchmeat of mixed content. It's downright annoying, sometimes worse than the mail you get in a physical mailbox, because you can't just rip it up (though you can delete such messages if the titles are obvious, and that's not always the case). It fills your emailbox and you are forced to wade through annoying announcements about pornography or one questionable promotion or another.

NOTE   *As enticing as some junk email might seem, I have never seen any evidence that any of the work-at-home or pyramid promotion schemes advertised actually work. The reason junk email is so widely sent is because it's very cheap to do, costing just a fraction of what it would cost to mount a regular direct mail campaign to one's physical mailbox.*

Fortunately, email programs do deliver ways to help you filter out this junk, though, for the most part (except for Outlook Express 5 from Microsoft), it has to be done on a case-by-case basis. As you receive email, you simply create filters that apply to the specific domains or that have a keyword in the subject line that is common.

Here's how you do it with some of the popular email programs:

America Online

The unfortunate side effect of being the number one online service on Earth is that AOL is a target for junk mail, far beyond that of other services. AOL's legal eagles, however, have gone to court to fight junk emailers and have won a few legal victories, so the problem is not as bad as it used to be.

In addition, AOL has in place a Mail Controls feature that you can use to filter out the most offensive email you receive (and even block mail from folks you don't want to hear from for any reason). Here's how it works:

1. Log on to AOL, using your master account name (this is the one you used when you joined AOL, which appears first on your list of screen names).

NOTE   *As an option, you can give "master" status to your other AOL screen names. This feature lets you set Mail and Parental Controls while using those names.*

2. Type the AOL keyword **Mail Controls**. This will bring up a screen similar to the one shown in Figure 23-2.

3. Click on the Set Up Mail Controls button, which will bring up the screen shown in Figure 23-3.

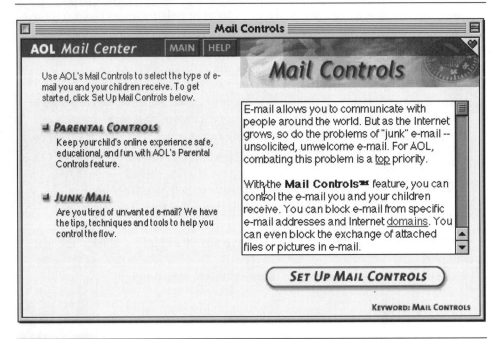

FIGURE 23-2   AOL's Mail Controls feature is used to block email from other services, or from specific individuals and domains

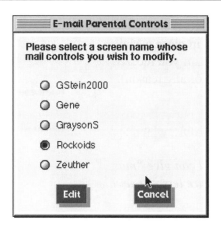

FIGURE 23-3   Pick an AOL screen name from the list

4. Choose the screen name to which you want to apply Mail Controls, then click the Edit button. This will bring up the actual editing screen, shown in Figure 23-4.

5. Enter the email address or domain from which you want to block email in the text entry field, and click Add to include them, or choose a setting to apply to all email.

TIP   *If you only wish to receive AOL email from a small number of recipients, use the fourth option shown in Figure 23-4, to block all email except from specified recipients. Then enter the email addresses of your recipients, one by one, in the text field.*

6. Once your Mail Controls are set, click the OK button to store your settings.

7. Repeat your settings for each screen name on your AOL account.

NOTE   *The filtering features I'm describing in the next few sections can be used not just to remove junk email, but also to sort email into different categories, forward the messages to another account, automatically download attachments and so on. With a little practice, you can apply a host of powerful filters to your favorite email program.*

How to Avoid Email Problems

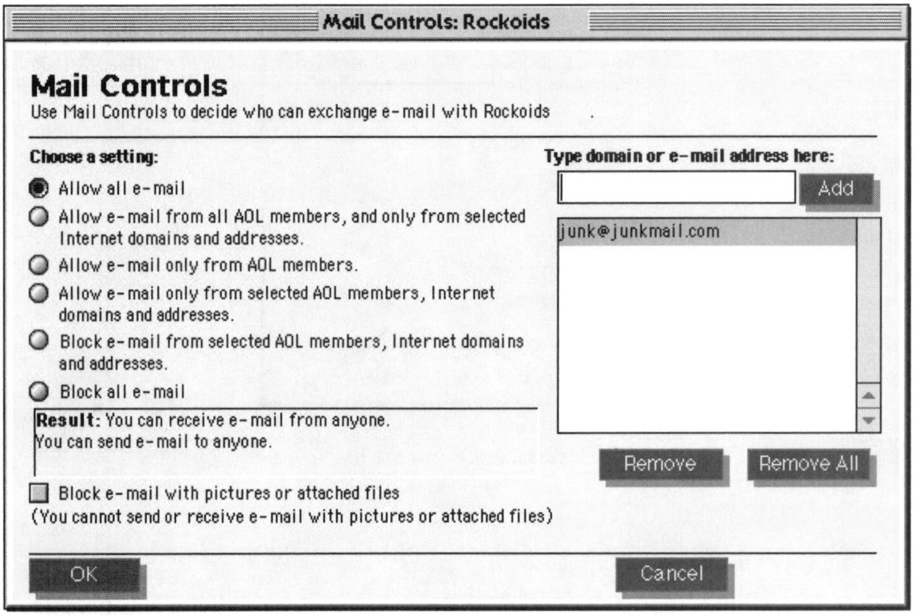

```
                    Mail Controls: Rockoids

  Mail Controls
  Use Mail Controls to decide who can exchange e-mail with Rockoids  .

  Choose a setting:                              Type domain or e-mail address here:
  ● Allow all e-mail                             [                    ]  [ Add ]
  ○ Allow e-mail from all AOL members, and only from selected
    Internet domains and addresses.             junk@junkmail.com
  ○ Allow e-mail only from AOL members.
  ○ Allow e-mail only from selected AOL members, Internet
    domains and addresses.
  ○ Block e-mail from selected AOL members, Internet domains
    and addresses.
  ○ Block all e-mail
  Result: You can receive e-mail from anyone.
  You can send e-mail to anyone.
                                                 [ Remove ]  [ Remove All ]
  □ Block e-mail with pictures or attached files
  (You cannot send or receive e-mail with pictures or attached files)

  [ OK ]                                        [ Cancel ]
```

FIGURE 23-4   AOL gives you a wide range of email blocking features as part of their Mail Controls

Claris Emailer

Even though Apple is no longer updating this excellent email program, it has some great features that are still useful. And it's the only non-AOL program (other than AOL NetMail) that you can use to retrieve your AOL email.

> **NOTE**   *I still love Claris Emailer and will continue to use the program as long as it remains compatible with Apple's fast-changing system software. To quote our fearless technical editor, John Rizzo, "Emailer rules!"*

Here's how to set up an email filter with Emailer:

1. Choose Mail Actions from the Setup menu, which brings up the screen shown in Figure 23-5.

2. Click the New button, which brings up the screen shown in Figure 23-6.

3. Enter a name for your mail action. Junk mail is perfectly fine.

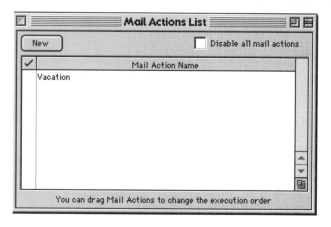

FIGURE 23-5 Create an Emailer action from this screen

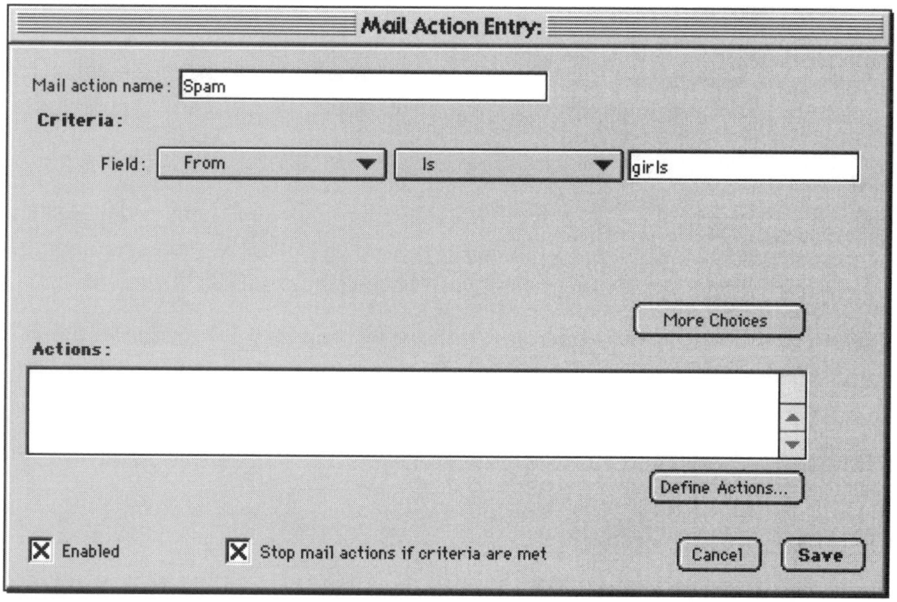

FIGURE 23-6 Set up your Mail Action script from this window

4. Enter the Criteria in the appropriate field. It's best to include one or more keywords that appear in a typical piece of email.

5. Under actions, click the Define Actions button.

6. On the next screen, select an option to apply to messages that meet your Criteria. The option I suggest is to place it in the Deleted Mail folder (which means, of course, that the email will be removed automatically).

Eudora Pro

Despite the fact that there are great free email programs, Qualcomm's Eudora Pro remains popular because of its powerful mail handling features. And as with the other programs, it has a flexible Filters feature that lets you block email from selected sources.

NOTE *The description I'm providing here is based on Eudora Pro 4.2.1. The filtering function is substantially changed from earlier versions of the program.*

1. Launch Eudora Pro.

2. Choose Filters from the Window menu, which will bring up a setup screen similar to the one shown in Figure 23-7 (which I've already completed).

3. Under Match, click the email category to which your filter applies.

4. Choose the words that will trigger the filter and enter them under Header. Click on the pop-up menu adjacent to the keyword and pick a category. I chose "contains" for this example in both Header fields.

5. Under actions, pick a function from the pop-up menu. I picked Redirect To and then entered Trash in the text field, which is where I want all my junk email to go.

6. Click the close box to store your settings.

Netscape Communicator

Netscape Communicator is no slouch when it comes to providing powerful email filter capability. By setting up a reasonable set of email actions you should be able to block a reasonable amount of junk email.

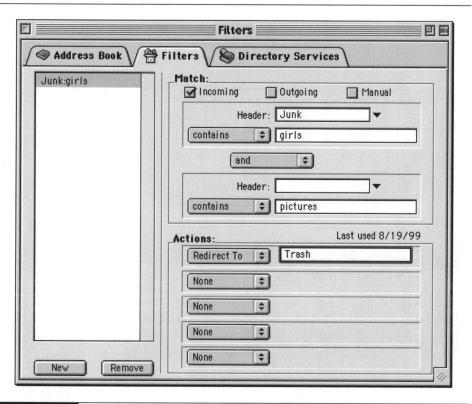

FIGURE 23-7 Eudora Pro puts all of its filters in a single tabbed window

Here's how to use the Message Filters feature of Netscape's Messenger email module:

1. Launch Netscape.

2. Choose Message Filters from the Edit menu, which brings up a screen similar to the one shown in Figure 23-8 (this one has my Junk Mail filter already applied).

3. At the top of the screen, select the location where your rules will apply from the pop-up menu. I chose Inbox, which is where your newly received email will show up.

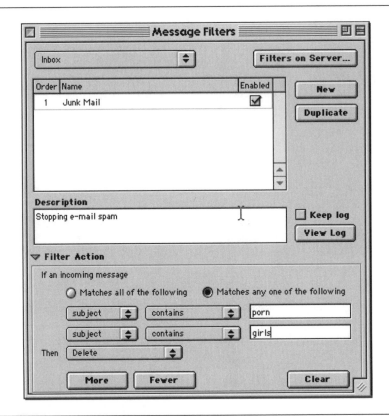

Use Netscape Messenger's Message Filters feature to block or redirect your email

4. Give the rule a name in the text field, then click the Enabled check box to activate it.

5. Under Description, type a short description of the purpose of the filter.

6. Click the arrow at the left of the Filter Action label (if it's collapsed).

7. Choose the various matching categories from the pop-up menus.

8. Under Then, choose an action from the pop-up menu. I picked Delete for this example.

9. Click the close box to activate your settings.

Outlook Express

Microsoft's Outlook Express has the great benefit of not only being free, but containing just about every useful email feature you might need.

Chief among them is a Junk Mail Filter, which is part of version 5 of the program. This feature uses the program's internal logic to figure out whether the email you're getting fits into the junk category. One of those criteria is a forged email address, a common occurrence in junk mail.

> **NOTE** *If you have an older version of Outlook Express, I suggest you update. The newest version of the program is always available from Microsoft's Web site at http://www.microsoft.com.*

Here's how to use the feature:

1. Launch Outlook Express 5.

2. Choose Junk Mail filter from the Tools menu, which brings up the screen shown in Figure 23-9.

3. Click the Enable Junk Mail Filter check box to activate the feature.

4. Drag the Sensitivity slider to control how carefully the program checks email for evidence that it fits into the junk category. If you subscribe to Internet mailing lists, you'll probably want to try a setting between Low and Average so legitimate email isn't flagged as junk by mistake. Otherwise, you can experiment with a higher setting.

5. If you want to make sure the filter isn't applied to email from a specific domain, enter that domain in the text field at the bottom of the Junk Mail Filter setup screen.

6. Choose the actions to be applied to your junk mail from the bottom of the screen.

7. Click OK to store your settings.

If you find your Junk Mail Filter settings aren't strong enough, or are too strong, it's easy to go back and change the settings.

How to Avoid Email Problems

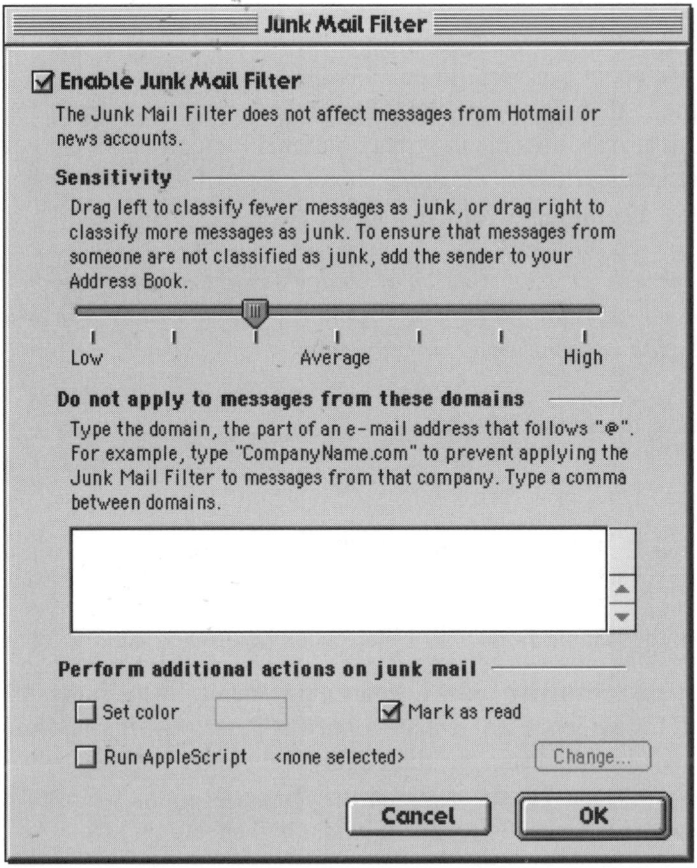

FIGURE 23-9 The Outlook Express Junk Mail Filter is designed to clean up your email box

You can also apply powerful filters to specific types of email from Outlook Express 5. Here's how:

1. Launch Outlook Express.

2. Choose Rules from the Tools menu, which brings up the screen shown in Figure 23-10.

3. Click the tab that applies to the Rule you want to apply. For regular Internet email accounts, for example, you'd probably choose Mail (POP). The other email categories will depend on the sort of service you have (the

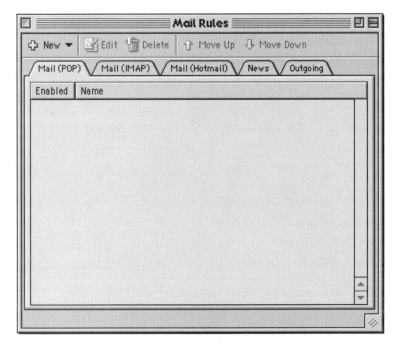

FIGURE 23-10   Outlook Express's Rules feature can be used to block email from various addresses or move to a different folder in the software

program also supports office email systems). This will bring up the screen shown in Figure 23-11 (which has already been filled out).

4. Enter a Rule name in the text field at the top.

5. From the If category (which applies to the conditions under which a filter is applied), choose the criterion from the pop-up menu, which includes a number of categories, including From and Subject lines.

6. Enter the keyword or words you want to use in the text field.

7. Under the Then category (which covers what will be done if the conditions are met), pick the action from the pop-up menu. I chose the Delete message option, but there are other choices, such as automatically moving a message to a specific folder.

8. Click the Enabled check box to be sure the rule is active.

9. Click OK to store your settings.

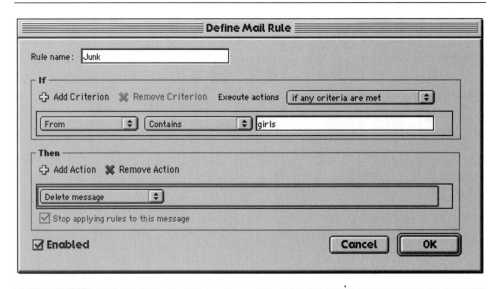

FIGURE 23-11   Set up your Outlook Express Rules from this screen

How to Complain About Junk Email

If filters of one sort or another don't stop the flood of junk mail, there's another possible remedy: complain to the Internet provider from whom the email seems to have originated. I say "seems" because quite often the address you see in the "From" line is a forgery, someone hiding their tracks and blaming someone else for their annoying behavior. But if you use the option in your email software to show Internet headers (that's automatic with AOL), the folks who investigate may likely be able to track it down to the real offender.

Just use your email program's Forward feature to send the actual email message, along with your comment or complaint, to either of these addresses: abuse@<domainname> or postmaster@<domainname>. Insert the actual domain from which the junk email seems to originate in the space for the domain name, such as aol.com, earthlink.net, and so on.

Most of the major Internet and online services have tough rules against members sending such material, and they will definitely investigate the problem.

CAUTION

It really doesn't help to send an email complaint to the source from which the junk mail originated. Even if the address is real and not a forgery (in other words, an innocent party may get your complaint), when you send your email to the sender of such material, you're just confirming that your address is correct. And all that does is make you eligible to get more junk email.

Summing Up

Are we there already? Yes, this is the final chapter of this book.

I hope you enjoyed our little trip into the world of Mac troubleshooting and upgrading. If you have questions or suggestions for future editions, feel free to write me: gene@starshiplair.com. I look forward to hearing from you.

How to Avoid Email Problems

Appendix A

About the CD-ROM

When I first considered whether to include a CD-ROM with this book, I was unsure. For one thing, most of the CDs I've seen are filled with so much useless material to fill 650MB storage space that it's hard to find the material you really want. So, rather than select a large quantity of files just to look impressive, I have focused this CD very tightly on the sort of material that suits our subject matter. First and foremost, I looked for information you will want if you intend to upgrade your Mac and troubleshoot for system-related problems.

I also looked for a few items that would provide useful system enhancements, such as managing your font library, improving display of font menus and dialog boxes, and other system features.

I hope you find these files useful, and I would love to hear from you with suggestions for CDs for future editions. Write me at gene@starshiplair.com. Or visit either of my Web sites: http://www.starshiplair.com or http://www.rockoids.com.

What Kind of Software Is This?

I have labeled each product carefully so you'll know what you are getting before you click on the installer icon.

- **Freeware**   This means you can use it as long as you want and you don't have to pay the publishers or authors anything.

- **Demoware**   These are fully or mostly functional limited-time demos. You get to use the software for the period of time mentioned in the installation screen or documentation. If you like the software, you can generally go right to the software company's Web site and place your order to receive the full version or a special key to unlock the version you have.

- **Shareware**   You are strictly on the honor system with these products. If you like what you see, just pay the requested fee to the author of the shareware or the software company who owns the shareware. If you want to see the program supported and developed in the future, do pay the modest price listed in the program's documentation.

How to Install the Software

When I chose this software, I deliberately selected items that were easy to install and set up. All you have to do is the following:

1. Open the folder in which the software comes.

2. Double-click on the installer icon.

3. Follow the prompts to continue the installation process. You'll probably have to agree to a software license and select a location for your installation.

4. When you're done, you can either quit the installer or, in the case of some of these products, you'll have to restart your computer.

Once installed, the software will be ready to run without a lot of complex configuration. Most of it comes with easy online documentation. If you have questions, check the Help menu or the electronic documentation.

The Bill of Fare

Here's a capsule description of the contents of the CD:

Adobe Systems Inc.

■ **Adobe Acrobat Reader (freeware)**   Just about every set of online documentation you get with a program these days is in Adobe's Portable Document Format (PDF). You can view these documents on your computer's display and see the original with all the special formatting intact. What's more, you can print the document on any printer, whether PostScript or not, and get the best quality your printer can deliver.

Aladdin Systems

■ **StuffIt Expander (freeware)**   This is the standard of compression software for the Macintosh. StuffIt Expander lets you expand files created

What Kind of Software Is This?

in StuffIt, Compact Pro, Zip, and several other formats. Despite the sophistication of the program, there is no need to read complex instructions. Once installed, just drag the icon for the file you want to expand and drop it on the StuffIt Expander icon, and the program will do the rest for you.

- **DropStuff (shareware)**   This is a shareware program that lets you easily compress your documents in the popular StuffIt format via drag and drop. If you like the program, just pay the small fee directly to the publisher. You can also get a special discount if you want to upgrade to the full-featured version of StuffIt Deluxe.

> **NOTE**   *If you have one of the newest Apple models, such as the iBook, iMac, Power Mac G4, or PowerBook G3, you'll find that the latest versions of Aladdin's compression utilities are already installed. Just check the Aladdin folder, located inside the Internet Utilities folder, within the Internet folder.*

- **DragStrip (shareware)**   Is your Mac's desktop getting just a little, shall we say, untidy? Well, DragStrip (see Figure A-1) puts up neat little icon docks on your screen. You can drag applications, files, folders, and disks to these icon docks, for fast one-click access to your work. DragStrip can also store information about recently used files. This is another shareware program. If you like it, just pay the modest fee to the publisher to get a user license.

- **MacTicker (shareware)**   Do you invest in the stock market, or do you just want to keep tabs on stocks for possible future investments? Aladdin's MacTicker will probe the Internet and dig up information from the major financial sites. The information appears right on your Mac's desktop, in the form of a regularly updating stock ticker. You can set MacTicker to track the stocks that interest you and deliver a fully detailed report on the companies you specify.

Casady & Greene

- **Conflict Catcher 8 (demoware)**   This is a program that has garnered top reviews from just about every Mac publication and online Mac news service (see Figure A-2). Not only does it manage the stuff in your System

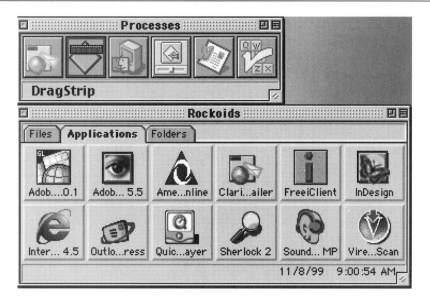

FIGURE A-1   DragStrip offers you numerous convenient ways to organize your
Mac's desktop

Folder, but Conflict Catcher's exclusive Conflict Test can be used to help
you find the source of system-related conflicts. If you want to learn what
one of those strangely named system-related files does, Conflict Catcher's
huge database will give you the information, as well as links to that
company's Web site if you want to know more about the program.
You'll also appreciate its ability to merge System Folders if you do a
clean system reinstallation.

■ **Spell Catcher 8 (demoware)**   Wouldn't it be nice if someone could
watch over you and tell you when you've made a spelling mistake, without
you having to run a special spell check when you're done? That's just one
of the great features of Spell Catcher, and it works in virtually any
program, even those that do not have their own spell checking feature. I
have a secret for you—I run this program all the time, and it's the reason
my publisher doesn't complain to me about spelling mistakes. Another
feature, GhostWriter, records your keystrokes, so you can recover what
you type in the event a crash wipes out your file before you can save it.

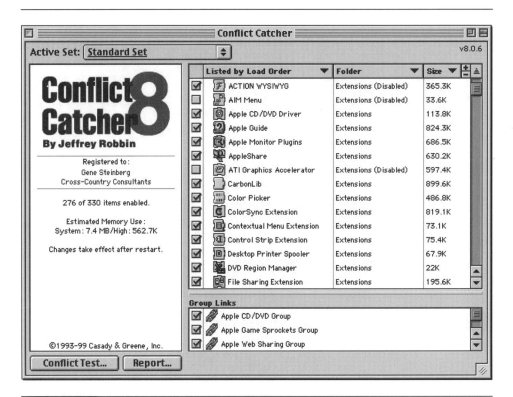

FIGURE A-2   Conflict Catcher offers the ultimate in System Folder management

DiamondSoft

■ **Font Reserve 2.5 (demoware)**   As you read in Chapter 6, fonts can be complex and troublesome. DiamondSoft's Font Reserve helps you easily organize your font library. It works behind the scenes to sort your fonts the way you like, and it offers special tools to allow some programs to actually open a font automatically if you open a document that needs those fonts. This is a "lite" version, which is designed to support up to 100 fonts. If you like the program, you'll want to buy a copy. This version also includes a special version of Power On's ACTION WYSIWYG, a convenient font menu organizer (see extended description later in this section).

Extensis

■ **Suitcase 8.1 (demoware)**   One of the earliest font managers was Suitcase, created in the late 1980s. Extensis Suitcase is the direct descendant of that program, filled with special features to help you get the most out of your font library. If you like this limited-time demo, you can upgrade directly from the publisher. It also includes a special version of DublClick's MenuFonts, for organizing your font menus.

MicroMat

■ **TechTool v1.1.9 (freeware)**   This is a free "lite" version of MicroMat's popular diagnostic program. It lets you rebuild the desktop, zap the PRAM, and check your System file for signs of possible damage. If you like the program, the publisher invites you to order TechTool Pro, which adds a wealth of features, including the ability to check, repair, and optimize your hard drive, and test your Mac hardware.

NewerRAM

■ **GURU (freeware)**   How much RAM can you install on your Apple product? Do you need special RAM? What about upgrading the video memory? NewerRAM's GURU is a convenient database that lets you check for definitive information on the memory upgrades available for your Mac.

PowerOn Software

■ **ACTION Files (demoware)**   This program is a highly regarded successor to SuperBoomerang (part of Now Utilities), a program that enhanced the Open and Save dialog boxes. ACTION Files (see Figure A-3) adds a menu bar to every Open and Save dialog box, offering extra features such as the ability to rename a file and search for the files on your Mac or any networked drive. There's also a "rebound" feature that jumps right back to the last document you opened with a particular program.

■ **ACTION GoMac (demoware)**   While a Mac OS user may not lust for much from the Windows platform, except perhaps for more applications, there's one convenient feature that may be useful to you. That's the Start menu, and that's ACTION GoMac's core feature. It puts up a Start menu and a taskbar, so you can quickly switch from one application to another. There's more to this program than that, such as the ability to customize the Start menu and remember recently opened applications and documents.

The Bill of Fare

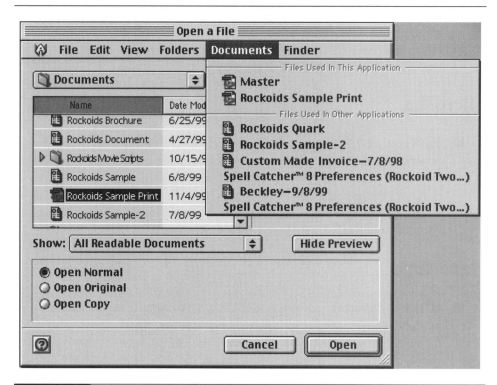

FIGURE A-3   ACTION Files extends your Open and Save dialog boxes

■ **ACTION Menus (demoware)**   Reminiscent of NowMenus, another part of the Now Utilities suite, ACTION Menus matches Apple Menu Options in giving you submenus in your Apple menu. What's more, it provides fast-access menus on your menu bar for recently opened disks, files, folders, and programs. Every one of the features can be customized in many ways. You can even add custom command shortcuts to menu bar commands.

■ **ACTION Space Doctor (demoware)**   This has nothing to do with the characters you see on such TV shows as *Star Trek*. ACTION Space Doctor is a program that helps you get more space on your hard drive, by making it easy to convert to Apple's HFS+ disk format (which was first introduced with Mac OS 8.1). The feature reduces the minimum file size on larger drives, so you get more efficient use of the drive. Normally, you have to initialize a drive in HFS+ (Mac OS Extended) to convert. But this program does it "in place," without needing to wipe out your files.

■ **ACTION WYSIWYG (demoware)**   This is a new slant on font menu
organizing. Not only does it show you the font in its actual style, but it
groups the fonts into convenient family submenus for fast access. And to
keep your font menus ultra-short, ACTION WYSIWYG also splits your
font menu into multiple panes, so you can work with a large font library
without having to pore through a lengthy menu every time you want to
select another typeface (see Figure A-4).

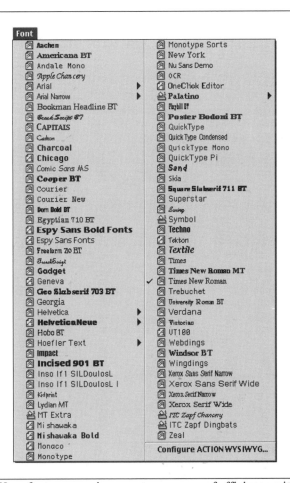

FIGURE A-4   Your font menu gains an extra measure of efficiency with this program

Glossary

10BaseT   The standard form of Ethernet networking, using twisted-pair wires that resemble regular telephone wires. Ethernet capability has been offered in all Apple computers for several years. *See also* **Fast Ethernet.**

A

ADB (Apple Desktop Bus)   Apple's original implementation of a bus standard for input devices, such as a keyboard, a mouse, or a trackball. *See also* **USB.**

access privileges   Used for file sharing, the act of allowing other users different levels of access to your shared drive.

active application   The application you are currently using, the one you are working in.

active matrix screen   Typically used on a laptop computer, a form of LCD display, using a separate circuit for each pixel. By activating each pixel separately, it provides clearer, faster display than the other type of LCD display, passive matrix. All current PowerBooks and the iBook have active matrix displays. *See also* **passive matrix display**.

AirPort   Apple's wireless networking product line, which provides networking services at approximately 10BaseT Ethernet speeds among devices for distances of up to 150 feet.

alias   A Mac OS feature, which creates a file that links or points to the original file, folder, or disk. You can activate an alias by double-clicking it; the original item is opened. You can use an alias to help organize your Mac desktop, by keeping the original items in their original folders.

Altavec   The original name for the Velocity Engine, used in the G4 CPU to provide noticeably speedier performance for programs designed to support the feature.

Anonymous FTP   A method to access files from an FTP resource by logging in as a guest. *See also* **FTP.**

AOL (America Online)   The world's largest online service with, as of the time this book went to press, almost 20 million members around the world. AOL owns a number of other companies, including Netscape and the former number one online service, CompuServe.

AppleScript A scripting language that is a part of the Macintosh operating system. It allows a user to automate repetitive functions by writing little scripts that function as mini-applications.

AppleShare The server and client software that comes standard with the Mac operating system. You use AppleShare to exchange files with other networked Macs.

AppleTalk The network standard protocol Apple Computer uses. There are two types of AppleTalk. The original protocol, AppleTalk Phase 1, was introduced with the first Mac in 1984. A later version, AppleTalk Phase 2, is designed to address the networking limitations of the original version. All Macs (including the iMac and the iBook) use AppleTalk.

application Software that provides a specific productivity function, such as a word processor, an illustration program, or a Web browser. Examples of applications include Adobe PhotoDeluxe, AppleWorks, Microsoft Word, and QuarkXPress.

arrow keys The keys used for navigation on a computer. The arrow keys are designed to move the cursor in all four directions.

ASCII (American Standard Code for Information Interchange) The ASCII character set includes the basic 128 characters, including letters, numbers, and basic symbols.

ASCII text file A file that includes ASCII characters, without the special formatting that identifies paragraph and text formats.

archive When you compress a file to make it smaller, the file you create is called an archive. An archive may contain one or more compressed files.

attach A feature of email, in which you connect or link one or more files to your message. When you send your message, the file or files you attach go with it.

B

Backup The process of making extra copies of your files, in the event the originals are corrupted or destroyed. Backups may be made of individual files, folders, or an entire disk.

BBS (bulletin board system) Essentially, the original online service. A BBS consists of one or more computers that store information, such as files, messages, news, and email. Online services, providing a nationwide network of local access phone numbers, grew out of the concept of a BBS.

beta   The common word for prerelease software. Beta software usually contains all or most of the features of the finished product, but will have bugs that may cause performance anomalies or system crashes. *See also* **preview software.**

BinHex   A file format commonly used for encoding Mac binary files. The process converts the files to text format, usually bearing the file suffix ".hqx." It's designed to allow for transfer of files among multiple computer operating systems, yet retain the two elements of the Mac file format, the resource fork and the data fork.

bit   The smallest unit of computer data. Eight or more bits make a byte. *See also* **byte.**

bitmap   A standard for storing and generating computer-based images, which are made up of single dots (or pixels).

bitmap fonts   A font designed for display in a single point size. Compare with scalable fonts, in PostScript and TrueType formats. Bitmap fonts designed to be used with scalable fonts are called screen fonts.

bits per second (bps)   Typically the speed at which a modem transfers data. Normal speeds range from 28,000 bps to 56,000 bps. Higher speeds can be achieved via so-called "broadband" connection methods. *See also* **cable modem, DSL.**

boot   Refers to the process of starting your computer (it comes from the word "bootstrap").

browser   A program designed to download Web pages, and reproduce the text, images, animations, and sound that comprise the original page.

byte   A byte represents a single piece of computer data. It contains 8 or more bits, which are represented by the binary numbers 1 and 0. *See also* **bit.**

C

cable modem   A technology that lets you access the Internet through your regular cable TV connection. The cable modem is close in function to a router, which directs the signal to your Mac using its Ethernet port. Cable modem service may require rewiring by your cable provider, and it's not available in all areas.

cache   A portion of memory or storage space set aside to hold frequently used data. By using a cache, performance is boosted.

card   For personal computers, a printed circuit board installed inside a computer's case. It provides expanded capabilities, such as the ability to add an extra display, high-speed networking and high-speed disk access.

CCD (charge-coupled display)   CCDs are typically used in camcorders and scanners to deliver high-quality images.

CD-ROM (compact disc read-only memory)   A standard based on the audio CD, it lets you store computer data on a CD, and is commonly used today for games and as a carrier for software installers and backed-up files.

character set   The content of a font. It contains letters, numbers, and special symbols, such as a copyright symbol or a number sign. *See also* **ASCII.**

check box   A feature of the Mac operating system and other graphical computer interfaces. It consists of a small square box in a dialog box. It's used to turn certain program features on or off. You click on a check box and a check appears inside, which activates a specific program feature. When you click again on the check box, the checkmark is removed, and the feature is turned off.

Chooser   A Mac program used to selected AppleTalk network and printer connections.

click   The process of pressing and releasing the button on a mouse or other pointing device.

client   A computer that receives services from another computer, which is known as a server. Internet software, for example, is considered client software, since it receives content from the Internet.

clip art   Boilerplate or canned images used for enhancing a document one creates. Some firms and Web sites provide clip art collections for you to install or download.

Clipboard   In the Mac operating system, a temporary location in which an item is stored, so you can transfer it to another place in the document you are working on or in another document.

close box   A feature of the Mac operating system, in which you click on a small square in the upper-left side of a title bar to close that window.

collapse box   A box at the extreme right side of a window (in Mac OS 8 or later), which you click to reduce a window to just its title bar, and click again to restore to the previous size. A previous version of this feature was known as WindowShade.

Command key   The main keyboard modifier key found on a Macintosh. It's used, along with one or more keystrokes, to activate a specific function. It is identified on a keyboard by an apple or cloverleaf symbol (usually both).

command line   An older style computer interface, in which you type in commands rather than click on an object to perform a specific function. The most popular command line interface is the MS-DOS operating system.

commands   A set of instructions you give to your computer to tell it to carry out a specific function or set of functions.

compression   A technique used to make a file smaller, by providing pointers to or removing redundant data. Compression protocols such as StuffIt and Zip are said to be *lossless*, because the compressed files can be restored to their original form. Another compression type is *lossy*, which actually removes portions of a file that may not be audible or visible. The popular image formats GIF and JPEG are lossy in nature, as is the compression protocol used to pack a complete motion picture onto a 5.25-inch DVD.

CompuServe   Before AOL gained ascendancy as the world's largest online service, CompuServe was there first. Today, CompuServe is an affiliate of AOL, and offers services to a more professional audience, with a rich resource of business information. *See also* **AOL**.

configuration   The term used to describe the settings you make to such things as your Internet and network setup.

control panel   A program used to direct system-related functions or the functions offered by a system extension. Examples of control panels include Mouse, which adjusts the speed and double-clicking performance of a pointing device, and Monitors, which sets up your display.

coprocessor   An extra computer chip that is generally used to handle extra chores, such as enhanced graphics or math performance. In current Mac CPUs, the functions of the math coprocessor are integrated into the CPU.

CPU (central processing unit)   The brain of a computer. It refers either to the principal microchip the computer is built around (such as the Pentium or PowerPC chip) or the box that houses the main components of the computer.

CRT (cathode ray tube)   The picture tube that is the main component of most computer displays and regular TVs. *See also* **active matrix, LCD, passive matrix**.

D

daisy chain   The way many computer devices are connected when using such topologies as ADB, LocalTalk, SCSI, and USB. You hook up one device, attach a second device to the first, and so on.

database   On a computer, a file that contains structured data that can be accessed and manipulated in a variety of ways. Databases are used for business records, address books, and so on.

DAVE   A program from Thursby Software Systems, Inc., that you use to network Macs and Windows computers. It is especially useful in smaller networks, because you don't have to go through the fuss and bother of working with the complexities of setting up a Windows NT or Windows 2000 network server.

debugger   A program or a component of a program used to locate and help fix programming errors. One example of a debugger is MacsBug, a program provided by Apple Computer to help programmers test software and identify potential problems.

default button   You will find a default button in many dialog boxes. It is the one surrounded by a bold border, which you activate automatically with the ENTER or RETURN key.

desktop   Also known as the Finder Desktop, the graphical background of the Mac operating system in which disk, file, and folder icons are displayed against a background pattern of one sort or another.

desktop publishing   A program designed to create and design completely formatted documents useful for printing or display. Word processing programs can be used for desktop publishing, but for professional-caliber work, such programs as Adobe InDesign, Adobe PageMaker, or QuarkXPress are used.

device   A component that is part of a computer system. It may consist of a disk drive, keyboard, mouse, modem, printer, removable drive, or scanner.

device driver   The software that allows your Mac to communicate with a device, such as a printer or scanner. Examples of a device driver include the LaserWriter driver that comes with all Mac OS computers.

DHCP (Dynamic Host Configuration Protocol)   This network protocol is used to automatically assign an IP address to a networked computer. The IP addresses are considered "leased," because they can be reused if they are not accessed for a period of time (usually specified by the network administrator).

dialog box   A window in which you must OK an alert, check a box, or enter information in order to provide a result, such as naming and saving a file, or starting or canceling an operation.

DIMM (dual inline memory module)   A type of RAM module, typically used on many recent Macs. Compared to a SIMM (single inline memory module), a DIMM has a wider data path, which allows for speedier memory access.

dimmed   *See* **grayed out.**

DIP (dual inline package) switch   The small on or off switches you find on a hard drive, modem, or other device. They are used to configure the product to support specific features or, in the case of a drive, to set SCSI ID or termination.

directory   A list of files or folders found on your Mac.

disk   The common storage medium for computer files. Such storage mediums come in the form of floppy disks for a floppy drive or media (such as Jaz or Zip disks) used for removable drives. A hard drive consists of one or more disks in an airtight enclosure.

disk cache   This sort of cache allocates part of RAM to store frequently used information from a disk. The end result is faster retrieval, which speeds up performance.

disk drive   A device that contains one or more disks used to store computer data.

display   A device used to display the visual representation of a computer's output. Displays can use either CRT tubes or LCDs.

display adapter   Typically, a plug used to convert the signals from your Mac or graphic card so they can be seen on your display.

document   A file you create with an application. Documents may contain words, images, or animated matter. They are stored on a disk for later viewing, editing, or printing.

document window   A window that appears within an application in which a document you created in that application is displayed.

domain   A portion of an Internet address that identifies the name of the organization, network being accessed, or the designated address of a computer server—for example, apple.com, which is Apple Computer's domain, or rockoids.com, which is the author's site devoted to a science fiction adventure series. In email, the information after the "@" symbol represents the domain, such as earthlink.net or aol.com.

double-click   The act of clicking a mouse button twice in fairly rapid succession. It is done to open an icon (which will, in turn, open a file, launch a program, or bring up a directory).

double-click speed   An adjustment you make, in the Mouse Control Panel, that determines how fast you must click the mouse button to activate a function, such as opening an icon.

download   The act of transferring a file from one computer to another. When you download something, you receive it. In contrast, you upload something to send it to another computer.

downloadable font   A scalable font sent to a printer to allow a document containing that font to be printed. Two downloadable font formats are PostScript fonts and TrueType fonts.

DPI (dots per inch)   Measures the sharpness of a display or printer output.

drag   An action done with a mouse or other pointing device. It is done by clicking the mouse button, then dragging the cursor (and whatever it selects) to another portion of the screen, then releasing the button.

drag-and-drop   The process of selecting an item and moving it to another location.

DSL (digital subscriber line)   A technology that uses your regular telephone line to offer very fast Internet service, with speeds typically ranging from 256Kbps to 1.5Mbps. The ability to hook up to DSL depends on whether you are close to a phone company switch (usually three miles or less) and whether your ISP offers the service.

DVD-ROM (digital versatile disc read-only memory)   Based on the popular DVD format used for video movies, DVD-ROM stores computer data, up to 5.2GB worth. A variation of the format, DVD-RAM, can be used to store data.

The latter medium is suitable for backup purposes, but as of the time this book was written, a final standard hadn't been set.

E

Email   The abbreviation for electronic mail. It's the method used to transfer messages from one computer or network to another.

emulation   The method used to imitate another computer CPU or operating system. When Apple switched to PowerPC CPUs, they used an emulator to work with older software that supported the 680x0 CPU family. The programs that let you create a Windows environment on a Mac, such as Connectix Virtual PC and FWB's SoftWindows, are emulators.

Erase Disk   Available from the Mac OS Special menu, used to format a selected floppy drive or hard drive.

Ethernet   The standard for high-speed networking. It's available on all currently produced Apple computers. The standard version offers performance of up to 10Mbps. The high-speed version, called Fast Ethernet, transfers speeds at up to 100Mbps. The newest Ethernet variation, Gigabit Ethernet, is capable of speeds of up to one billion bps.

EtherTalk   Apple's method of supporting its AppleTalk networking protocol over Ethernet (though it's not been used since Apple introduced Open Transport).

extension   This word has two definitions. For Macs, it is a special program that adds or extends functions of the operating system. Such programs are placed in the Extensions folder within the System Folder. The second use of an extension is file naming. DOS and Windows files, for example, have three-letter extensions that identify a specific type of file, such as .doc for Microsoft Word files.

F

Fast Ethernet   This variation of the Ethernet network standard offers speeds that are up to 10 times faster than regular Ethernet, up to 100Mbps.

FAT   A term with two definitions. For Macs, it is a program compiled with computer code that supports both 680x0 and PowerPC Macs. For DOS and Windows users, it stands for File Allocation Table, and it's the disk file system.

Fax/data modem   The kind of modem that has taken over the market since the early 1990s. It functions as a modem to transmit and receive data, and can also support sending and receiving faxes, when used with software that supports the feature.

file   In the computer world, an item (such as a document or a program) stored on a disk or opened, using a computer's memory.

file extensions   The DOS and Windows operating systems identify a file's type via a three-letter extension or suffix. A typical example is using .jpg for a JPEG file, or .doc for a Microsoft Word file.

file server   A computer that serves as a repository for files shared across a network (including the Internet). File servers may be dedicated, performing just file handling tasks, or non-dedicated, in which the computer may also function as a regular workstation.

file sharing   A feature of the Mac operating system in which users may share files across a network.

File Sharing Control Panel   A control panel used to configure and activate the file sharing feature.

file system   The technology used on a storage medium that handles files stored on a disk.

Finder   The application that provides the unique look and feel of the Mac operating system. It is used to provide both a desktop display and file handling features.

FireWire   Also known as IEEE 1394 or (by Sony) i.LINK, a high-speed peripheral standard that's capable of speeds of up to 400Mbps. It allows you to daisy-chain up to 63 devices, including digital camcorders, hard drives, removable devices, and scanners, without having to set special ID numbers or termination.

firmware   Software stored in a ROM chip, used by computer hardware to provide specific operating functions.

fixed disk   *See* **hard disk.**

fixed-width font   More often called a "monospaced" font, a font in which all characters have equal width spacing. Examples include Courier and Monaco. Fonts in which width values vary are called proportional fonts. *See also* **proportional font.**

floppy disk   Although it's been phased out of new Apple computer products, the floppy disk is one of the earliest storage mediums. The word "floppy" refers to the flexible material inside the disks, used to store the data. *See also* **hard disk.**

flow control   The phrase generally applies to modems or networking functions. It's a method where one device communicates with another, indicating when information can be transferred. It's also known as a "handshake."

folder   A directory on Mac and Windows computers (and other graphical operating systems). A folder is a container that may contain files or other folders.

font   A collection of letters, numbers, punctuation, and symbols all fitting a specific design or size. Fonts that are of fixed size are typically bitmap fonts. Outline font formats, such as PostScript and TrueType fonts, are scalable fonts, meaning they can be specified in any size supported by the program in which they're used. *See also* **PostScript fonts, TrueType fonts.**

font family   A label for a group of fonts of similar style, such as the various forms of Helvetica or Times. It also refers to a class of fonts, such as serif or sans serif.

format   (1) Preparing a disk to receive files by clearing out all existing data and setting it up to support a specific computer operating system. A related process, initializing, wipes out a drive's directory. (2) The way in which the text in a document is set up, such as the type style, the size, paragraph indents, and so on. (3) The file type, such as an Adobe Photoshop document, or a Microsoft Word document.

FPU (floating point unit)   This is a coprocessor that supports mathematical calculations. The original 680x0 Mac CPUs required separate FPU chips. The PowerPC chips have integrated FPU functions and don't require separate chips.

fragmented   Usually a description of a condition in which the pieces of a file are spread around widely separated parts of a disk. Memory can also be fragmented, when you quit and relaunch multiple programs on your Mac.

freeware   Software offered without charge, but the author or publisher retains rights to the product. Contrast this with the term shareware.

FTP (File Transfer Protocol)   The Internet protocol for file transfers among Macintosh, Windows, and UNIX. *See also* **Anonymous FTP.**

full backup   The process of making a complete copy of the disk you wish to back up.

G

G3   The popular label for the PowerPC 750 CPU, developed by IBM and Motorola and used in a number of Apple Computers.

G4   The newest family of PowerPC CPUs, also known by its design name, 7400.

GB (gigabyte)   The equivalent of 1,000,024 megabytes.

GIF (Graphic Interchange Format)   A popular file format for compressed graphic images, developed by CompuServe. GIF files are commonly exchanged on the Internet, and are used for images on Web sites, because of their ability to provide animation and other effects.

Gopher   A method of searching information on the Internet. A Gopher program typically locates text documents, but some of these programs can also deliver information about images and sounds.

grayed out   A phrase used to indicate that a specific command is not available or accessible or has been disabled.

grow box   *See* **zoom box.**

H

Handshake   *See* **flow control.**

hard disk   A type of disk drive that contains one or more rigid platters used for data storage, sealed in an airtight enclosure. Hard drives can typically support as little as 10MB (obviously these are just the very old hard drives) to capacities exceeding 73GB (based on capacities available as of the time this book was written).

hardware   Various components of a computer system, which include the core component, consisting of CPU and disk drives, as well as displays, printers, and scanners. Contrast with software.

hardware handshaking   A special type of modem cable that supports automatic handshaking or flow control. All external high-speed modems require a hardware handshaking cable.

hierarchical menu   Also known as a submenu, identifies an extra menu that appears when you drag and hold the mouse cursor over an item.

highlighted   When you select an object or text, it is shaded in a dark color or reverse video to indicate it has been chosen.

home page   On a Web site, the opening page, typically used to offer a description or introduction of a site and provide links to other content on the site and elsewhere.

HTML (Hypertext Markup Language)   The language of the Web, consisting of text documents with tags or formatting keys that describe how the text will look in a Web browser. A Web site contains one or more HTML documents.

HTTP (Hypertext Transfer Protocol)   The protocol used for the transfer of HTML and similar files, generally from sites on the World Wide Web.

hub   A device that serves as a central connection point for connecting network or serial devices. Hubs are used for such things as Ethernet networking and to expand FireWire and USB ports.

hyperlink   A text or graphic that, when you click on it, takes you to another page in a document or a Web site.

I

icon   A picture that provides a graphical representation of an item on a Mac or Windows computer (or a UNIX computer with graphical interface). Icons can represent such things as an application, a file, a folder, or disk drive.

IDE (Integrated Drive Electronics)   A type of hard drive used on both Macs and PCs. Compare with FireWire and SCSI.

IEEE 1394   *See* **FireWire.**

i.LINK   *See* **FireWire.**

incremental backup   A backup that consists strictly of the files that have been added or changed since your last full backup.

infrared port   A feature on some Macs and other computers that allows for wireless networking. It has since been replaced by Apple's AirPort wireless networking products.

initialization files   Also known as INITs, the original designation for system startup programs that are now known as extensions or system extensions.

initialize   Usually, the process of resetting a hardware device or recreating a disk directory. *See also* **format.**

insertion point   The flickering vertical bar you see in a text area, indicating where text is to be entered.

Intel   The world's largest manufacturer of CPUs, maker of the 80x86 and Pentium chips used in DOS and Windows-based computers.

interface   (1) The process of communicating with another component in a computer system. (2) The face that a program puts forth to the user. Also known as user interface.

Internet   The worldwide collection of computer networks that provides a variety of services, such as email, FTP, and the World Wide Web.

intranet   A system of networking using Internet technologies within a single organization.

ISP (Internet service provider)   A company that offers a connection to the Internet. Such services include large national operations, including AT&T WorldNet and EarthLink, and smaller companies that offer connections in one or two cities. These include FastQ, which is affiliated with the Arizona Macintosh User Group, and Teleport.com. *See also* **AOL, CompuServe.**

J

Java   Developed by Sun Microsystems, a platform-independent programming language often used to display special visual effects on the World Wide Web. When you access a Web site using Java, a small program, called an applet, is downloaded to your browser (if it supports Java, and all recent browsers do) and run to display the appropriate content.

JPEG (Joint Photographic Experts Group)   A format for compressed images, which makes files that are typically smaller than a GIF. It's best for handling images rather than text, and is capable of extremely high quality, sometimes indistinguishable from the original.

K

kilobyte Equivalent to 1024 bytes. It is usually abbreviated as K, and is used to describe such things as file size, memory, and hard drive storage. *See also* **megabyte.**

L

L2 cache A special type of cache memory that resides between the CPU and the main memory or on the processor chip and is used to store frequently used instruction data, allowing the CPU to process those instructions faster. The primary memory cache, on the CPU chip, is called the L1 cache.

LAN (Local Area Network) The common type of network that includes computers and printers, and is used to share data, programs, and messages.

laptop A small personal computer, equipped with one or more batteries for power, designed for convenient transportation.

laser printer A printer that works in a fashion similar to a copy machine, using a laser beam to generate high-quality output.

LCD (liquid crystal display) LCD is the display technology used in laptop computers and some high-priced computer displays. The most common types of LCD displays are active matrix and passive matrix.

LED (light-emitting diode) LEDs are employed for display purposes in some electronic products.

link *See* **hyperlink.**

list box Typically found in a dialog box, offers a listing of items, such as files and folders, that you can select.

LocalTalk The network hardware that, until recently, was built into all Macintosh computers. It uses the AppleTalk protocol to offer network services. Current Apple computers only support Ethernet as a network standard.

M

MacBinary The file format used for transferring Macintosh files between different computer platforms. It places the data and resource folks of a Mac file in the datafork, so it can be easily transferred over the Internet and to other computing platforms. MacBinary files are usually saved in BinHex format.

Macintosh HD   The common name of a Mac's hard drive when it leaves the factory.

Mac OS   The popular abbreviation and Apple's official trademark for the Macintosh operating system, for example, Mac OS 9. Contrast to the former use of the word System to identify operating system version, such as System 7.

macro   An automated sequence of functions designed for simple repetition of complex tasks. The Microsoft Office program suite offers macro functions, as do other programs. Some programs, such as Adobe Photoshop, refer to macros as "actions."

math coprocessor   *See* **FPU.**

maximize   When you click on a window's grow box to its largest size, you've maximized it.

Mb   *See* **megabyte.**

Mbps (megabits per second)   1,048,576 bits per second. Speed at which data is transferred. Hopefully, as modems and serial transmissions become faster, Mbps will be used to discuss their speed.

media   Typically, the name for items that carry data, such as floppy disks, hard drives, CD-ROMs, hard disks, removable drives, and tape drives. It can also refer to items that carry data for network transfer, such as cables and wireless technology.

megabyte   1,024 kilobytes of computer data.

MegaFLOPS   Short for a Million Floating Point Operations Per Second, representing computer power.

memory   The temporary storage area for computer data. Memory products include RAM and ROM. Sometimes hard drives and other storage mediums are referred to incorrectly as memory.

memory protection   The ability of a computer operating system to allocate a dedicated portion of memory to a program, which is designed to enhance stability. Mac OS X, for example, is designed to offer protected memory.

M

menu   In a graphical operating system, such as the Mac OS, a small screen in which a series of commands are available for the user to select.

menu bar   A single-line horizontal bar, which appears at the top of the screen on a Mac, containing menus.

MHz (megahertz)   Each hertz being one cycle, the speed at which a computer's CPU runs. Since many factors govern CPU performance, the MHz rating isn't the only factor to use in comparing speeds of different CPU families.

MIDI (Musical Instrument Digital Interface)   A protocol that allows for communication between musical instruments and computers.

MIME (Multipurpose Internet Mail Extension)   A method in which binary files (such as images, sound, and word processing documents) can be transferred via email.

MIPS (millions of instructions per second)   The speed at which a computer handles data. Supercomputers are said to handle billions of instructions per second, which is why the G4 CPU was promoted by Apple Computer as a "supercomputer on a chip," because if its capability of achieving such levels of performance.

modem   A device used to convert a computer's digital language to analog signals to allow for data to be exchanged, typically over a telephone line.

monitor   *See* **display.**

monochrome   A type of computer display (no longer being made) that is capable of displaying just a single color.

motherboard   Also known as a logic board, the printed circuit board that stores the main components of a computer.

mouse   Invented in the 1960s, a small pointing device with a ball on the bottom, and one or more switches at the top. As you move the mouse, the cursor on a computer's screen moves as well. A so-called upside-down mouse, with the ball at the top, is known as a trackball.

MPEG (Moving Pictures Experts Group)   The standard for compressed audio and video. It is "lossy," meaning that data is lost as part of the compression process, but it is designed so the lost data has minimal impact on what you see and hear.

MS-DOS (Microsoft Disk Operating System)   A text-based computer operating system, also known as DOS.

multimedia   A combination of various components of a computer experience, such as animation, audio, graphics, text, and video.

multiprocessor   A computer that has more than one CPU running at the same time for faster processing speeds.

multisync   A type of display that can run at different scan rates, providing a selection of different resolutions. All current displays are multisync.

multitasking   A technique that allows a computer to perform more than one task at a time. On a Mac, multitasking is cooperative, meaning the programs themselves do the task management, as opposed to preemptive, a part of Mac OS X, in which the operating system does the task management.

multithreading   The capability of a program to perform more than a single function at the same time. Compare to multitasking.

N

Netscape   The company who made the original commercial Web browser for the Macintosh, Windows, and UNIX operating systems, now part of AOL. Although the program is known by the name of the company, its full name is either Netscape Navigator or Netscape Communicator.

network   The process of linking two or more computers and other devices, such as printers, so they can exchange data.

newsgroup   An Internet-based discussion group, also known as Usenet.

notebook   *See* **laptop.**

O

object-oriented graphics   Graphic objects that are represented by mathematical shapes rather than pixels. This allows for the objects to be scaled to any size without loss of quality.

open   An operation in which you display the contents of a file, folder, or disk, or launch an application.

Open Transport   Apple's networking technology, used for local networking and Internet networking.

Open Transport/PPP   Apple's software for dialing up an ISP, now known simply as Remote Access.

operating system   The software that provides the core functionality of a computer, also known as system software. Operating systems include the Mac OS, MS-DOS, Windows in its variations, UNIX, and others.

P

passive matrix display   A type of LCD display used on laptop computers. The display is accomplished with parallel wires running horizontally and vertically across the screen, which power the screen pixels. Current products do not use this type of display. Compare to active matrix.

password   A combination of letters, numbers, or both used to control access to a computer, the contents of a computer's drive, or a network or Internet service.

PC (personal computer)   Although the name usually applies to small IBM and compatible desktop and portable computers, Apple's computers are also, strictly speaking, personal computers.

PC100   A high-speed RAM module that's used on a number of new Apple computers. It supports 100MHz logic board speeds.

PCI (peripheral component interconnect)   An expansion bus standard used on both Macs and PCs. It allows for installation of printed circuit boards (cards) that provide enhanced graphic display, faster networking, faster SCSI, video capture, and other capabilities.

PCMCIA (Personal Computer Memory Card International Association)
A standard for hardware expansion cards, about the size of credit cards, used mostly on laptop computers. Commonly known as a PC card.

PDF (portable document format)   A standard for creating and viewing electronic documents, created by Adobe Systems.

peripheral   A device, added to a computer, that provides enhanced functions, such as a display, printer, or removable drive.

pixel   A single dot, the smallest graphic unit of display.

plug-and-play   Various hardware standards designed to allow you to easily hook up a device without having to go through special configuration steps. The ideal method of plug-and-play allows you to hook up a device without needing to turn off the device or the computer to which it's connected or having to do a special configuration to recognize the device (other than, perhaps, installation of a software driver). Both FireWire and USB are plug-and-play standards. Also known as PnP.

plug-in   An add-on program that will enhance an application's capabilities. For a Web browser, plug-ins are typically added to provide multimedia features (such as QuickTime and RealAudio). Some program plug-ins are also referred to as XTensions (for QuarkXPress add-ons) and XTras (used in some Macromedia products).

point   The act of placing the mouse cursor over a specific object on your screen.

pointing device   The name of an input device used to point to objects on a screen. A mouse and trackball are both common pointing devices.

POP (Post Office Protocol)   The standard that allows a user to receive email from a mail server. It's used by most ISPs.

pop-up window   A window that will pop up on your screen when selected.

port   A jack into which you plug a cable from a device to make it work with your Mac.

post   The act of placing a message on a message board, either a newsgroup or a message board on an online service.

PostScript   Developed by Adobe Systems, a page description language that uses mathematics to describe the contents of a page. It is device-independent, meaning that output devices, such as laser printers, can reproduce the page at their maximum possible resolution.

PostScript fonts   A scalable font technology based on PostScript, which allows a font to be used in all available sizes with maximum quality. PostScript fonts are considered industry standards in the publishing and printing industries. Compare with TrueType, another scalable font format.

PowerPC   The generic name of a family of CPU chips designed by Apple, IBM, and Motorola. The current crop of PowerPC chips are the G3 and G4.

P

PPD (PostScript printer description)   Usually consists of a text file that provides information to a printer about the device's unique features, such as extra paper trays or special paper size handling capabilities.

PPP (Point to Point Protocol)   A TCP/IP standard that allows a modem to access the Internet or an online service.

PRAM (parameter RAM)   A small amount of RAM on a Macintosh used to store basic system settings, such as display, networking, serial port, and startup disk. Zapping the PRAM is the act of clearing this portion of RAM to eliminate erratic system problems.

preview software   A version of software designed to promote interest in a new product. The software is usually in beta form, meaning it probably has bugs that may cause performance anomalies or system crashes.

printer driver   A program that works with a computer and printer, allowing the two devices to communicate with each other.

printer fonts   Sometimes called outline fonts, the PostScript fonts that are downloaded to a printer and used to output your actual text. Sometimes also known as soft fonts. Compare with bitmap fonts.

print queue   A list of files sent to the printer that are waiting to be printed.

print server   A device, computer, or software designed to host and manage a print queue.

program   *See* **application.**

proportional font   A font in which each character has a different space or width value, with a letter such as "i" having a narrow width and the letter "m" having a much wider width. Contrast with fixed-width or monospaced font.

pull-down menu   When you click on a menu bar, the pull-down menu provides the list of available commands. On the Windows platform, it's referred to as a drop-down menu.

Q

queue   A list of files destined for printing or processing of some sort.

QuickDraw 3D   Apple's technology for creation and display of three-dimensional objects.

QuickTime   A multimedia technology from Apple Computer that provides support for dozens of audio and video standards. QuickTime technology is used for video editing, and to create online audio and video presentations. The software is available in both Mac and Windows versions.

QuickTime TV   A standard from Apple Computer designed to compete with RealAudio and RealVideo. It lets you view streaming audio and video productions on the Internet. Apple has entered the competition with big guns, by making the source code freely available and not charging a license fee for use of its server software (the software that sends the streaming productions).

R

radio button   A small circular button that appears in a dialog box. Clicking on it will activate a specific function.

RAM (random access memory)   The memory used as a temporary storage location for computer data.

RAM disk   A portion of RAM set aside to emulate the functions of a hard disk.

read-only file   The name for a file that you can read but cannot change, either because it's password protected or it's on a storage medium you cannot write to (such as a CD-ROM).

RealAudio   The most popular protocol for streaming audio and video productions. RealAudio and its companion program, RealVideo, are available free, but users of the streaming software pay a license fee for its use.

reset switch   A button on a Mac that forces the computer to restart, used to get the Mac working again when it crashes.

resolution   A measurement of the number of pixels in a document or display screen.

RISC (reduced instruction set computer)   A type of CPU, such as the PowerPC chip, which uses a smaller set of instructions to perform. The speed with which the instructions are processed accounts for the high performance of RISC-based CPUs.

ROM (read-only memory)   A computer chip onto which data is written that cannot be changed and does not disappear when the computer is switched off. A special type of ROM, called Flash ROM, allows for the data to be changed with a special software program. Compare with RAM.

router   Software or a hardware device that directs data to different segments of a computer network.

S

scalable font   A font designed to work in all sizes available to an application. Scalable fonts usually are provided in PostScript and TrueType formats.

screen fonts   *See* **bitmap fonts.**

screen saver   A program that darkens the screen or provides a moving picture when your computer is idle for a specified period of time. With CRT-based monitors, it is designed to prevent a so-called "burn-in" effect, in which areas displayed for long periods of time are permanently etched onto the display. The jury is out about whether screen savers really work or not with modern computer displays, and they do nothing for an LCD display.

scroll   The act of moving through a display or document window.

scroll arrow   The arrow located at each end of a scrollbar that's used to navigate through the contents of a window or list box.

scrollbar   The little bar that appears at the right and bottom of a window or list box when it's too small to show all of its contents.

SCSI (Small Computer Systems Interface)   A standard used for storage devices. SCSI capability has been removed from Apple computers, in favor of FireWire and USB.

SDRAM   A type of memory used on first-generation iMacs and some Apple laptop computers.

select   The act of marking or choosing an item so you can perform an action on it. With a mouse or other pointing device, you select the item by clicking on it.

serial port   A port provided on older Macs for use by modems and non-network printers. *See also* **USB.**

shareware   Software that is freely distributed, for which the author or publisher requests payment if you like using it after a brief trial.

SIMM (single inline memory module)   A type of computer memory module, mostly used on older model Macs and other personal computers.

SMTP (Simple Mail Transfer Protocol) A counterpart to POP, used for sending email. SMTP transfers email to server computers across the Internet, using TCP/IP.

software A file that contains instructions that tell a computer how to perform specific tasks. These include the Mac OS, the applications you run, device drivers, and so forth.

source code A text file that contains the information from which a computer program is compiled. Apple has released source code for some elements of Mac OS X and its QuickTime streaming software.

spool The act of transferring data to a device, usually a printer. A spool file is a file that contains the instructions needed to perform an action, such as printing a document. *See also* **print queue.**

spring-loaded folders A feature of the Mac OS (beginning with Mac OS 8) in which a folder expands to reveal its contents when you click and drag your input device over the folder.

startup disk The disk used to start your Mac, containing a usable System Folder. Startup disk settings can be made with the Startup Disk Control Panel.

StuffIt The industry-standard compression program for the Mac. StuffIt uses a special algorithm to make files smaller by using pointers to redundant data. StuffIt archives (a file containing files compressed with StuffIt) are routinely transferred via disk, networks, or the Internet. This is the Mac counterpart of the Zip format, which dominates the DOS and Windows computing platforms. *See also* **compression, Zip.**

submenu A secondary menu that displays when you click a pointing device and hold it over the main menu's name. Also known as a hierarchical menu.

SuperDisk A removable disk standard that supports 1.4MB floppies and a special floppy-like high-capacity format. It's become popular since Apple removed floppy drives as standard issue on their computers. SuperDisk media can hold up to 120MB of data.

SuperDrive A floppy disk drive installed on many older Macintosh computers, which supports 400K, 800K, and 1.4MB floppies. With proper translation software, such as File Exchange, a SuperDrive can also read MS-DOS floppies.

surf The act of exploring the Internet, typically the World Wide Web.

surge suppressor   A device designed to provide protection of electronics from power surges from a power line or due to a lightning strike. Surge suppressors typically have several outputs for connection of computer equipment and other electronic components (such as a TV or VCR).

swap file   Used with virtual memory, a portion of your hard disk set aside to handle data that doesn't fit within the available amount of RAM.

system   The basic file that provides core functionality of the Mac OS, also known as a system file. It can also refer to the operating system itself, such as System 7, an older generation of the Mac OS.

system disk   *See* **startup disk.**

system software   *See* **operating system.**

T

TCP/IP (Transmission Control Protocol/Internet Protocol)   The networking standard used for Internet networking and connections.

text box   An enclosure on a document, icon, or dialog box window in which you insert text.

title bar   The top area of a window in which its name is displayed.

toolbar   A row of buttons in an application that you click on to activate a specific function.

trackball   A pointing device that resembles an upside-down mouse, in which you move the ball rather than the device itself to point to objects on your computer's screen.

tracking speed   An adjustment in the Mouse or Trackpad Control Panel that sets how fast a mouse pointer moves across the screen.

trackpad   Used on laptop computers, a pointing device consisting of a little square or rectangular pad on which you use your finger to move the cursor across the screen.

TrueType fonts   A scalable technology first released in 1990 by Apple Computer, in part as a way to avoid paying the then-high licensing fees for PostScript fonts. Beginning with Mac OS System 7, built-in support was provided for display of TrueType fonts. Both Mac and Windows computers come with a small selection of TrueType fonts.

twisted-pair cable   The type of wiring used for both telephone and network connections. Twisted-pair cable is made up of two pairs of wires. One pair is used for receiving data, the other for transmitting.

type style   An attribute of a type face, such as regular (or normal), bold, italic, shadow, strikeout, or underline.

typeface   A collection of characters, numbers, and symbols in a distinct form or design.

U

UNIX   A popular operating system first developed by AT&T in 1972. It provides all the features considered critical to a modern operating system, such as preemptive multitasking and protected memory. There are many UNIX-based systems, including Linux and Mac OS X.

UPS (uninterruptible power supply)   A device that provides backup power in the event of a power failure. UPS devices available for personal computers commonly have a large battery that's used to provide power for a brief period to give the user time to shut down the computer safely without risk to the files or disk drives.

URL (uniform resource locator)   The address of a specific site on the Internet.

USB (universal serial bus)   A high-speed serial port standard used on current Apple computers, beginning with the iMac. It is used for input devices, digital cameras, storage devices, and other products.

Usenet   *See* **newsgroup**.

user interface   *See* **interface.**

utility   A program designed to help a computer function better. A utility may include a hard disk diagnostic program or something that enhances computer performance, such as Adobe Type Manager, which offers clear rendering of PostScript fonts.

V

virtual memory   A method of extending available memory on a computer by setting aside a portion of the hard drive to store and swap data that exceeds the size of available RAM.

W

Web   *See* **World Wide Web.**

Web browser   *See* **browser.**

window   The rectangular screen in which the contents of a disk, folder, or document are displayed.

Windows 95 and 98   The consumer versions of Microsoft's 32-bit graphical operating system, which offers preemptive multitasking, so long as the application is also 32-bit.

Windows NT and 2000   The so-called high-end versions of Windows, used for content creation and for networked servers.

word processor   A program that allows you to create, edit, and format text. Examples of word processors include one of the components of AppleWorks and Microsoft Word. Such programs also offer graphic editing capabilities of one sort or another.

World Wide Web (WWW)   A collection of Internet sites that offer a variety of content, ranging from text to pictures to animation and sound. You view a Web site with a browser, software designed to interpret Web documents, which are coded in HTML. *See also* **browser, HTML.**

WYSIWYG (What You See Is What You Get)   Pronounced "wizzywig," describes the ability to display a close representation of the look and feel of a document on your Mac's display.

Z

Zip   The DOS, Windows, and Unix counterpart to StuffIt. It's a protocol that uses a special algorithm to reduce file size by using pointers for redundant data. Files compressed with Zip (which are said to be "zipped") are commonly used for file transfers. There are also Mac versions of Zip, used to provide cross-platform compatibility, and all current versions of StuffIt also can expand Zip files. *See also* **compression, StuffIt.**

Zip drive   A storage device developed by Iomega Corporation, using a small disk, resembling a thick floppy. Zip drives store either 100MB or 250MB of data.

zoom box   A box at the right of a window that is used to expand or reduce the window's size.

Index

WARNING: BEFORE OPENING THE DISC PACKAGE, CAREFULLY READ THE TERMS AND CONDITIONS OF THE FOLLOWING COPYRIGHT STATEMENT AND LIMITED CD-ROM WARRANTY.

Copyright Statement

This software is protected by both United States copyright law and international copyright treaty provision. Except as noted in the contents of the CD-ROM, you must treat this software just like a book. However, you may copy it into a computer to be used and you may make archival copies of the software for the sole purpose of backing up the software and protecting your investment from loss. By saying, "just like a book," The McGraw-Hill Companies, Inc. ("Osborne/McGraw-Hill") means, for example, that this software may be used by any number of people and may be freely moved from one computer location to another, so long as there is no possibility of its being used at one location or on one computer while it is being used at another. Just as a book cannot be read by two different people in two different places at the same time, neither can the software be used by two different people in two different places at the same time.

Limited Warranty

Osborne/McGraw-Hill warrants the physical compact disc enclosed herein to be free of defects in materials and workmanship for a period of sixty days from the purchase date. If the CD included in your book has defects in materials or workmanship, please call McGraw-Hill at 1-800-217-0059, 9am to 5pm, Monday through Friday, Eastern Standard Time, and McGraw-Hill will replace the defective disc.

The entire and exclusive liability and remedy for breach of this Limited Warranty shall be limited to replacement of the defective disc, and shall not include or extend to any claim for or right to cover any other damages, including but not limited to, loss of profit, data, or use of the software, or special incidental, or consequential damages or other similar claims, even if Osborne/McGraw-Hill has been specifically advised of the possibility of such damages. In no event will Osborne/McGraw-Hill's liability for any damages to you or any other person ever exceed the lower of the suggested list price or actual price paid for the license to use the software, regardless of any form of the claim.

OSBORNE/McGRAW-HILL SPECIFICALLY DISCLAIMS ALL OTHER WARRANTIES, EXPRESS OR IMPLIED, INCLUDING BUT NOT LIMITED TO, ANY IMPLIED WARRANTY OF MERCHANTABILITY OR FITNESS FOR A PARTICULAR PURPOSE. Specifically, Osborne/McGraw-Hill makes no representation or warranty that the software is fit for any particular purpose, and any implied warranty of merchantability is limited to the sixty-day duration of the Limited Warranty covering the physical disc only (and not the software), and is otherwise expressly and specifically disclaimed.

This limited warranty gives you specific legal rights; you may have others which may vary from state to state. Some states do not allow the exclusion of incidental or consequential damages, or the limitation on how long an implied warranty lasts, so some of the above may not apply to you.

This agreement constitutes the entire agreement between the parties relating to use of the Product. The terms of any purchase order shall have no effect on the terms of this Agreement. Failure of Osborne/McGraw-Hill to insist at any time on strict compliance with this Agreement shall not constitute a waiver of any rights under this Agreement. This Agreement shall be construed and governed in accordance with the laws of New York. If any provision of this Agreement is held to be contrary to law, that provision will be enforced to the maximum extent permissible, and the remaining provisions will remain in force and effect.

NO TECHNICAL SUPPORT IS PROVIDED WITH THIS CD-ROM.